## PUBLISHER COMMENTARY

Field Manual (FM) 3-13, Information Operations, serves as the foundational doctrine for Army, Navy, Marines and Air Force information operations. The purpose of this book is to bring together all five manuals in one document to better align with joint doctrine, while recognizing the unique requirements of information operations in support of the land, sea and air force. This manual provides overarching guidance to effectively integrate information operations into the operations process in order to create decisive effects in the information environment.

This book contains:

DoD Directive 3600.01 Information Operations (IO)

Army Field Manual (FM) 3-13, Information Operations

Air Force Doctrine ANNEX 3-13, Information Operations

Navy NWP 3-13, Navy Information Operations

Marine Corps MCWP 3-40, Marine Air-Ground Task Force Information Operations

Joint Publication JP 3-13, Information Operations

This subject is growing in importance as other nations' armed forces are increasingly adopting the significant benefits of information warfare in creating an asymmetric warfare. Make no mistake, countries like China and Russia view the U.S. as vulnerable simply because we have developed high-tech weaponry that is increasingly networked. If they can render U.S. weapons useless with coordinated cyber-attack and electronic warfare, then they think they have a chance to turn the table and force the U.S. to negotiating a settlement of hostilities. The books we publish cover a wide range of topics that are carefully designed to work together to produce a holistic approach to acquisition and procurement primarily for government agencies and constitute the best practices. This holistic strategy to acquisition covers the gamut of subjects from development of procurement strategy to conducting audits of the supply chain.

**Why buy a book you can download for free? We print this so you don't have to.**

Some documents are only distributed in electronic media. Some online docs are missing some pages or the graphics are barely legible. When a new standard is released, an acquisition professional prints it out, punches holes and puts it in a 3-ring binder. While this is not a big deal for a 5 or 10-page document, many acquisition and financial management documents are over 1,000 pages and printing a large document is a time-consuming effort. So, an acquisition professional that's paid $50 an hour is spending hours simply printing out the tools needed to do the job. That's time that could be better spent doing procurement functions. We publish these documents so acquisition professionals can focus on what they were hired to do – acquisition of needed goods and services.

Here are two other books you may be interested in since they are now translated to English.

They are both available on Amazon.com

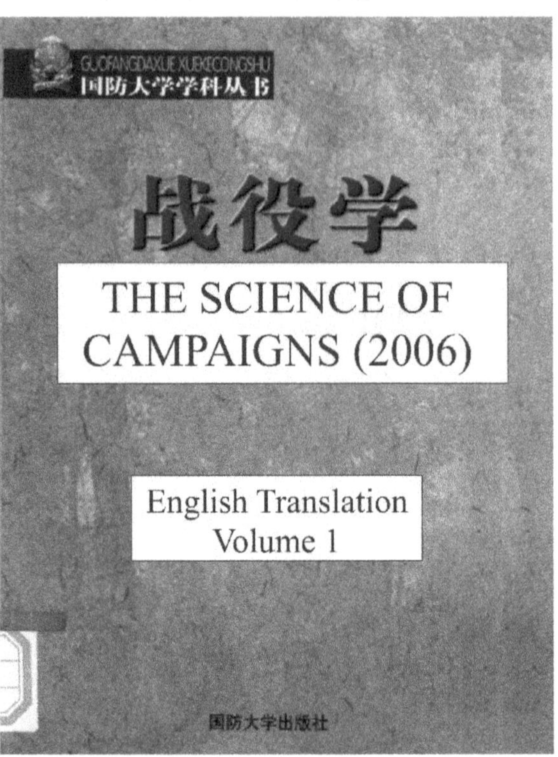


Following is a quote about the Chinese language versions of these books from a team of authors from RAND Corporation who worked on a 2015 report:

**"To the best of our knowledge, these are the most authoritative publicly available sources on Chinese military thinking about the campaign level of warfare."**

# Department of Defense
# DIRECTIVE

**NUMBER** 3600.01
May 2, 2013

USD(P)

SUBJECT: Information Operations (IO)

References: See Enclosure 1

1. PURPOSE. This directive:

a. Reissues DoD Directive 3600.01 (Reference (a)) in accordance with the authority in DoD Directive 5111.1 (Reference (b)) and, pursuant to the authority and guidance in Secretary of Defense Memorandum (Reference (c)), updates established policy and assigned responsibilities for IO.

b. Updates IO definitions.

c. Directs the establishment of the Information Operations Executive Steering Group (IO ESG).

2. APPLICABILITY. This directive applies to OSD, the Military Departments, the Office of the Chairman of the Joint Chiefs of Staff (CJCS) and the Joint Staff, the Combatant Commands (CCMDs), the Office of the Inspector General of the Department of Defense, the Defense Agencies, the DoD Field Activities, and all other organizational entities within the DoD (hereinafter referred to collectively as the "DoD Components").

3. POLICY. It is DoD policy that:

a. IO will be the principal mechanism used during military operations to integrate, synchronize, employ, and assess a wide variety of information-related capabilities (IRCs) in concert with other lines of operations to effect adversaries' or potential adversaries' decision-making while protecting our own.

b. IRCs constitute tools, techniques, or activities employed within a dimension of the information environment (IE) that can be used to achieve a specific end at a specific time and place. IRCs can include, but are not be limited to, a variety of technical and non-technical activities that intersect the traditional areas of electronic warfare, cyberspace operations, military information support operations (MISO), military deception (MILDEC), influence activities, operations security (OPSEC), and intelligence.

c. The development and management of individual IRCs will be the responsibility of various DoD Components and will be brought together at a specific time and in a coherent and integrated fashion for use against adversaries and potential adversaries in support of military operations.

d. DoD IO will be synchronized with information and influence activities of other U.S. Government (USG) organizations to ensure consistency across USG activities in the IE.

e. DoD IO will be coordinated and, as practicable, integrated with related activities conducted by allied nations and coalition partners.

f. Consistent with existing statutory requirements and manpower polices, Service and joint IO forces must be an appropriate and cost effective total force mix of active and reserve military personnel, government civilian personnel, and contracted support.

g. IO will be included across Active and Reserve Components, and government civilian professional education curriculums to foster an understanding of IO and IRCs across all ranks and positions within DoD.

h. IO tactics, techniques, and procedures (TTPs); technologies; and lessons learned will be shared among DoD Components and, as practicable, with allied nations and coalition partners to fully facilitate the synchronization, integration, and effectiveness of IO while reducing redundancies in capabilities across the DoD.

i. IO will be integrated into joint exercises and joint training, security cooperation guidance for theater planning, communication strategy, and deliberate and contingency planning.

j. DoD IO programs and activities will incorporate an explicit means of assessing the results of operations in relation to expectations.

k. DoD IO activities will not be directed at or intended to manipulate audiences, public actions, or opinions in the United States and will be conducted in accordance with all applicable U.S. statutes, codes, and laws.

l. DoD IO information gathering programs and activities will be coordinated and deconflicted with DoD intelligence activities as set forth in DoD Directive S-5200.37 (Reference (d)) and DoD 5240.1-R (Reference (e)). Human-derived information gathering activities in support of IO will remain separate from authorized HUMINT and related intelligence activities.

m. All DoD IO activities will be conducted in accordance with CJCS Instruction 3121.01B (Reference (f)).

n. The IO ESG will serve as the primary coordination forum within DoD to inform, coordinate, and resolve IO issues among the DoD Components and, as appropriate, deconflict IO issues as they are represented in established DoD policy and programmatic decision forums. The IO ESG's organization, membership, policies, and procedures will be established in a separate DoD Instruction.

4. RESPONSIBILITIES. See Enclosure 2.

5. RELEASABILITY. **Unlimited**. This directive is approved for public release and is available on the Internet from the DoD Issuances Website at http://www.dtic.mil/whs/directives.

6. EFFECTIVE DATE. This directive:

a. Is effective May 2, 2013.

b. Must be reissued, cancelled, or certified current within 5 years of its publication in accordance with DoD Instruction 5025.01 (Reference (g)). If not, it will expire May 2, 2023 and be removed from the DoD Issuances Website.

Ashton B. Carter
Deputy Secretary of Defense

Enclosures
1. References
2. Responsibilities
Glossary

ENCLOSURE 1

REFERENCES

(a) DoD Directive 3600.01, "Information Operations (IO)," August 14, 2006, as amended (hereby cancelled)
(b) DoD Directive 5111.1, "Under Secretary of Defense for Policy (USD(P))," December 8, 1999
(c) Secretary of Defense Memorandum, "Strategic Communication and Information Operations in the DoD (U)," January 25, 2011
(d) DoD Directive S-5200.37, "Management and Execution of Defense Human Intelligence (HUMINT) (U)," February 9, 2009, as amended
(e) DoD 5240.1-R, "Procedures Governing the Activities of DoD Intelligence Components That Affect United States Persons," December 7, 1982
(f) Chairman of the Joint Chiefs of Staff Instruction 3121.01B, "Standing Rules of Engagement /Standing Rules for the Use of Force for US Forces, and the Law of Armed Conflict (LOAC)," June 13, 2005
(g) DoD Instruction 5025.01, "DoD Directives Program," September 26, 2012
(h) Secretary of Defense Memorandum, "Changing the Term Psychological Operations (PSYOP) to Military Support information Operations (MISO) (U)," December 3, 2010
(i) "Trilateral Memorandum of Agreement signed by the Department of Defense, the Department of Justice and the Intelligence Community Regarding Computer Network Attack and Exploitation Activities," May 9, 2007
(j) Joint Publication 1-02, "Department of Defense Dictionary of Military and Associated Terms," current edition

ENCLOSURE 2

RESPONSIBILITIES

1. UNDER SECRETARY OF DEFENSE FOR POLICY (USD(P)). The USD(P):

a. Serves as the Principal Staff Advisor (PSA) to the Secretary of Defense for oversight of IO in the DoD. In this capacity, the USD(P):

(1) Is the primary coordination point of contact for DoD Components and other USG organizations for issues related to IO.

(2) Is the single point of fiscal and program accountability for IO.

(3) Links OSD, Joint, and Service IO policies, capabilities, and programs.

(4) Fully integrates IO with national and DoD strategy and planning functions.

b. Provides policy oversight, guidance, and advice for DoD IO to include providing policy guidance on IO force development and employment.

c. Coordinates within OSD, the Joint Staff, and the Military Services to address the Combatant Commanders' IO requirements, which includes the development of IRCs, ensuring adequate test and evaluation resources, and ensuring IRC integration across the CCMDs.

d. In coordination with the DoD Components responsible for the individual IRCs:

(1) Oversees, coordinates, and assesses the efforts of DoD Components to plan, program, and develop IRCs for use in the IE.

(2) Assesses the effectiveness of the IRCs as part of IO in operational applications.

e. Provides IO policy guidance for all phases of operations planning, including security cooperation.

f. Establishes DoD policy on MISO matters in accordance with Secretary of Defense Memorandum (Reference (h)), and reviews and approves all CCMD MISO programs to be conducted during peacetime or in contingencies short of declared war.

g. Establishes and oversees DoD policy regarding the coordination of IO conducted by DoD Components with other USG organizations in support of U.S. national security strategy and policy in accordance with Reference (h), so specific information objectives, target audiences, themes, and actions are synchronized. This specifically includes coordinating MISO policy, plans, and programs with other USG departments, agencies, and activities.

h. Establishes and oversees DoD policy regarding the coordination and, where practicable, the integration of IO efforts with allied and coalition partners.

i. Coordinates with the Under Secretary of Defense for Personnel and Readiness (USD(P&R)) on policies for the establishment and maintenance of professionally trained and educated Service and joint IO forces. These forces will consist of a total force mix as described in paragraph 3f above the signature of this directive.

j. Develops standardized fiscal methodologies for IRCs in accordance with Reference (c) and in coordination with the Under Secretary of Defense for Intelligence (USD(I)), the Under Secretary of Defense (Comptroller)/Chief Financial Officer, Department of Defense (USD(C)/CFO), and the Director, Cost Assessment and Program Evaluation (DCAPE). As part of this responsibility, the USD(P) will maintain procedures to ensure fiscal accountability for IO as well as the individual IRCs.

k. Conducts programmatic assessments of DoD IO in coordination with DCAPE.

l. As one of the co-chairs of the IO ESG, establishes and maintains the IO ESG.

m. Assists in the development of Joint Electromagnetic Spectrum Operations (JEMSO) policy and coordinates with the Under Secretary of Defense for Acquisition, Technology, and Logistics (USD(AT&L)) and Commander, United States Strategic Command (USSTRATCOM) regarding the development, acquisition, and employment of JEMSO capabilities used to support IO.

n. Coordinates with the Assistant to the Secretary of Defense for Public Affairs to ensure that DoD IO is consistent with the policy established in this directive and that DoD IO is not directed at or intended to manipulate U.S. audiences, public actions, or opinions and is conducted in accordance with all applicable U.S. statutes, codes, and laws.

o. In coordination with the USD(I):

(1) Provides policy oversight for OPSEC; MILDEC; deconfliction of DoD IO and intelligence activities; and the development, acquisition, and integration of MILDEC capabilities used to support IO.

(2) Provides input to the DoD OPSEC program as required.

(3) Coordinates on intelligence related matters that support the integration of IRCs used during military operations.

(4) Assists in the development and maintenance of a DoD instruction on policy for intelligence support to IO, information gathering activities, and IE characterization.

2. <u>USD(I)</u>. The USD(I):

a. Facilitates coordination of IO activities within the Intelligence Community consistent with Memorandum of Agreement (Reference (i)).

b. Serves as the OSD program management lead for the DoD OPSEC and MILDEC programs.

c. In coordination with the USD(P):

(1) Develops and oversees the implementation of policy for intelligence support to IO, information gathering activities, and IE characterization.

(2) Establishes and oversees the implementation of policies and procedures for the conduct of DoD OPSEC and MILDEC as warfighting enablers and military competencies, and the coordination and deconfliction of DoD IO and intelligence activities.

(3) Coordinates on intelligence related matters that support the integration of IRCs used during military operations.

(4) Develops, approves, and maintains DoD instruction on policy for intelligence support to IO, information gathering activities, and IE characterization.

3. USD(AT&L). In partnership with the Secretaries of the Military Departments, the USD(AT&L) researches IRCs affecting IO and coordinates these activities with the USD(P).

4. USD(P&R). The USD(P&R):

a. Develops policies for the establishment and maintenance of professionally trained and educated Military Service and joint IO forces in coordination with the USD(P) and the Secretaries of the Military Departments. These forces will consist of a total force mix.

b. Develops and distributes polices for the establishment and maintenance of professionally trained and educated Military Service and joint IO forces in collaboration with USD(P).

5. USD(C)/CFO. The USD(C)/CFO:

a. In coordination with the USD(P) and DCAPE, develops standardized fiscal methodologies for IRCs when applied to support IO. Included in this activity is the maintenance of procedures to ensure fiscal accountability for IO as well as the individual IRCs when they are employed in support of IO.

b. Requires all organizations conducting MISO to capture costs for MISO as a separate and distinct entity from other IO-related costs.

6. DCAPE. The DCAPE:

a. As appropriate, reviews IO programs, costs, and effectiveness.

b. In coordination with the USD(P) and USD(C)/CFO, develops standardized fiscal methodologies for IRCs and IO activities.

7. DOD COMPONENT HEADS. The DoD Component heads:

a. Assign responsibilities and establish procedures within their respective DoD Components to implement this directive.

b. Support IO planning, coordination, operations, and deconfliction within DoD Components and other USG organizations.

8. SECRETARIES OF THE MILITARY DEPARTMENTS. The Secretaries of the Military Departments:

a. In coordination with the USD(P) and CJCS, implement joint IO policy and doctrine and develop, plan, and program IO into the full spectrum of military operations.

b. Develop and implement Service component IO policy, doctrine, and TTPs that are compatible with DoD and joint IO policy and doctrine.

c. Provide education and training to meet IO military and civilian force development goals to meet joint IO requirements.

d. Provide intelligence oversight training to IO staffs and units in accordance with Reference (e).

e. Share IO TTPs and technologies with DoD Components and, when release of such information and technologies is permitted, allied and coalition partners.

f. Establish and oversee policies that provide for IO reporting and assessment as well as the integration of individual IRCs to meet Combatant Commanders' needs and objectives.

g. In accordance with Reference (c) and in coordination with the USD(P), USD(C)/CFO, and DCAPE, annually provide comprehensive Service inputs required to ensure fiscal accountability for IO as well as individual IRCs.

9. CJCS. The CJCS:

a. Serves as the joint IO proponent. Functions as the oversight authority for IO policy execution within the CCMDs and joint task forces.

b. Develops procedures for a professionally trained and educated joint IO force in coordination with the USD(P&R) and USD(P).

c. Emphasizes the importance of including IO as an instrumental part of military operations through the development and validation of joint IO doctrine.

d. Validates IO needs through the Joint Capabilities Integration and Development System.

e. Incorporates IO into all military planning efforts, including joint exercises and training.

f. Serves as the joint proponent for MILDEC and OPSEC.

g. Ensures all joint education, training, plans, and operations are consistent with joint IO policy, strategy, and doctrine.

h. Evaluates the joint IO education and training system and conducts assessments of IO to ensure the requirements of the Combatant Commanders are met.

i. Consistent with Reference (c), oversees the Joint IO Warfare Center as a Chairman's Controlled Activity.

j. As one of the co-chairs of the IO ESG, establishes and maintains Joint Staff participation in the IO ESG.

k. Ensures coordination and deconfliction of joint IO and intelligence activities in all operational planning and execution.

l. Establishes a framework for sharing TTPs as well as lessons learned among DoD Components and allied and coalition partners.

10. COMBATANT COMMANDERS. The Combatant Commanders:

a. Utilize IO as the principal mechanism to integrate, synchronize, employ, and adapt all IRCs in the IE to accomplish operational objectives against adversaries and potential adversaries.

b. Develop, plan, program and assess IO as well as IRC execution in support of IO during all phases of military engagement and at all levels of war.

c. In coordination with the USD(P) and CJCS, identify in advance and seek, as appropriate, the delegated authorities required for employing IRCs in support of IO across the full range of military operations.

d. Identify and prioritize IO needs on their respective integrated priority lists.

e. Integrate IO into joint exercises and training, security cooperation guidance for theater planning, and deliberate and contingency planning.

f. Develop and share IO lessons learned through written and oral assessments communicated to other DoD Components and allied and coalition partners as appropriate.

g. Ensure that joint IO staffs and units under CCMD command and control have received intelligence oversight training in accordance with Reference (e).

h. Ensure coordination and deconfliction of CCMD IO and intelligence activities in all operational planning and execution.

11. COMMANDER, USSTRATCOM. The Commander, USSTRATCOM, is the joint proponent for JEMSO and computer network operations. In addition to the responsibilities outlined in section 10 of this enclosure and in coordination with the USD(P) and through the CJCS, the Commander, USSTRATCOM, coordinates JEMSO, space operations, and cyberspace operations in support of IO.

12. COMMANDER, U.S. SPECIAL OPERATIONS COMMAND (USSOCOM). The Commander, USSOCOM, is the joint proponent for MISO. In addition to the responsibilities outlined in sections 8 and 10 of this enclosure and in coordination with the USD(P) and through the CJCS, the Commander, USSOCOM, coordinates joint force MISO in support of IO.

13. DIRECTORS OF THE DEFENSE AGENCIES. The Directors of the Defense Agencies:

a. Integrate IO into joint exercises, training, and deliberate and contingency planning.

b. Develop and share IO lessons learned through written and oral assessments communicated to other DoD Components and, as applicable, allied and coalition partners.

## GLOSSARY

## PART I. ABBREVIATIONS AND ACRONYMS

| | |
|---|---|
| CAPE | Cost Assessment and Program Evaluation |
| CCMD | Combatant Command |
| CJCS | Chairman of the Joint Chiefs of Staff |
| | |
| DCAPE | Director, Cost Assessment and Program Evaluation |
| | |
| IE | information environment |
| IO | information operations |
| IO ESG | Information Operations Executive Steering Group |
| IRC | information related capability |
| | |
| JEMSO | Joint Electromagnetic Spectrum Operations |
| | |
| MILDEC | military deception |
| MISO | military information support operations |
| | |
| OPSEC | operations security |
| | |
| PSA | Principal Staff Advisor |
| PSYOP | psychological operations |
| | |
| TTP | tactics, techniques, and procedures |
| | |
| USD(AT&L) | Under Secretary of Defense for Acquisition, Technology, and Logistics |
| USD(C)/CFO | Under Secretary of Defense (Comptroller)/Chief Financial Officer, Department of Defense |
| USD(I) | Under Secretary of Defense for Intelligence |
| USD(P) | Under Secretary of Defense for Policy |
| USD(P&R) | Under Secretary of Defense for Personnel and Readiness |
| USG | United States Government |
| USSOCOM | United States Special Operations Command |
| USSTRATCOM | United States Strategic Command |

## PART II. DEFINITIONS

These terms and their definitions are proposed for inclusion in the next edition of Joint Publication 1-02 (Reference (j)).

IE. An environment that is an aggregate of individuals, organizations, and systems that collect, process, disseminate, or act on information.

IO. The integrated employment, during military operations, of information-related capabilities in concert with other lines of operations to influence, disrupt, corrupt, or usurp the decision making of adversaries and potential adversaries while protecting our own.

IO force. A force consisting of units, staff elements, and individual military professionals in the Active and Reserve Components, and DoD civilian employees who conduct or directly support the integration of IRCs against adversaries and potential adversaries during military operations as well as those who train these professionals.

IRC. A capability that is a tool, technique, or activity employed within a dimension(s) of the information environment that can be used to achieve a specific end(s).

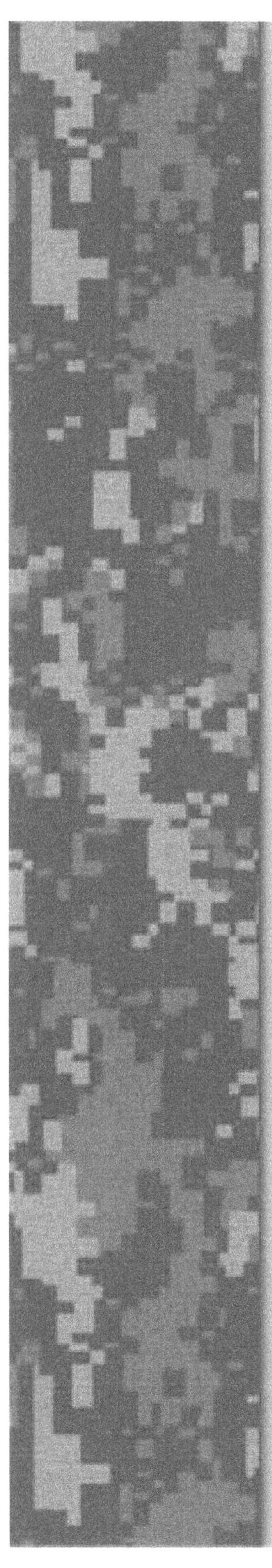

# FM 3-13

# INFORMATION OPERATIONS

**DECEMBER 2016**

**DISTRIBUTION RESTRICTION:**

Approved for public release; distribution is unlimited

**HEADQUARTERS, DEPARTMENT OF THE ARMY**

SUPERCESSION STATEMENT: This publication supersedes FM 3-13, 25 Jan 2013.

Field Manual
No. 3-13

Headquarters
Department of the Army
Washington, DC, 6 December 2016

# Information Operations

## Contents



**Distribution Restriction:** Approved for public release; distribution is unlimited.

***This publication supersedes FM 3-13, 25 January 2013.**

# Figures



# Tables

# Preface

Field Manual (FM) 3-13, *Information Operations*, serves as the Army's foundational doctrine for information operations. The purpose of this edition is to better align Army doctrine with joint doctrine, while recognizing the unique requirements of information operations in support of the land force. FM 3-13 discusses the conduct of information operations in today's complex global security environment, which requires a dynamic range of capabilities and skills: from technological capabilities, such as cyberspace operations; to individual capabilities, such as speaking a foreign language; from technical skills, such as those required to defend computer networks; to interpersonal skills, such as those required to conduct Soldier and leader engagements. This manual provides overarching guidance to effectively integrate information operations into the operations process in order to create decisive effects in the information environment.

The principal audience for FM 3-13 is all members of the Profession of Arms. Commanders and staffs of Army headquarters serving as joint task force or multinational headquarters should also refer to applicable joint or multinational doctrine concerning the range of military operations and joint or multinational forces. Trainers and educators throughout the Army will also use this manual.

Commanders, staffs, and subordinates ensure their decisions and actions comply with applicable United States, international, and, in some cases, host-nation laws and regulations. Commanders at all levels ensure their Soldiers operate in accordance with the law of war and the rules of engagement. (See Field Manual 27-10.)

FM 3-13 uses joint terms where applicable. Selected joint and Army terms and definitions appear in both the glossary and the text. Terms for which FM 3-13 is the proponent publication (the authority) are italicized in the text and are marked with an asterisk (*) in the glossary. Terms and definitions for which FM 3-13 is the proponent publication are boldfaced in the text. For other definitions shown in the text, the term is italicized and the number of the proponent publication follows the definition.

This manual seeks to minimize the use of acronyms but will use two acronyms routinely: IO for information operations and IRC for information-related capability. If other acronyms are employed, their use will be limited to the paragraph or section in which they appear, or a legend will be available.

FM 3-13 applies to the Active Army, Army National Guard (ARNG)/Army National Guard of the United States (ARNGUS), and the United States Army Reserve (USAR) unless otherwise stated.

The proponent for this publication is the U.S. Combined Arms Center, Information Operations Proponent Office. The preparing agency is the Combined Arms Doctrine Directorate, United States Army Combined Arms Center. Send written comments and recommendations on a Department of the Army (DA) Form 2028 (Recommended Changes to Publications and Blank Forms) directly to Commander, United States Army Combined Arms Center and Fort Leavenworth, ATTN: ATZL-MCK-D (FM 3-13), 300 McPherson Avenue, Fort Leavenworth, KS 66027-2337; by e-mail to: usarmy.leavenworth.mccoe.mbx.cadd-org-mailbox@mail.mil; or submit an electronic DA Form 2028.

## ACKNOWLEDGMENTS

*Assessing and Evaluating Department of Defense Efforts to Inform, Influence, and Persuade: Desk Reference*. Copyright © 2015. Christopher Paul, Jessica Yeats, Colin P. Clarke, & Miriam Matthews. RAND National Defense Research Institute.

*Assessing and Evaluating Department of Defense Efforts to Inform, Influence, and Persuade: Handbook for Practitioners*. Copyright © 2015. Christopher Paul, Jessica Yeats, Colin P. Clarke, & Miriam Matthews. RAND National Defense Research Institute.

*Assessing and Evaluating Department of Defense Efforts to Inform, Influence, and Persuade: An Annotated Reading List*. Copyright © 2015. Christopher Paul, Jessica Yeats, Colin P. Clarke, & Miriam Matthews. RAND National Defense Research Institute.

*Dominating Duffer's Domain: Lessons for the 21st-Century Information Operations Practitioner* (Report written for the Marine Corps Information Operations Center) Copyright © 2015. Christopher Paul and William Marcellino. RAND National Defense Research Institute.

# Introduction

Over the past two decades, Army information operations (IO) has gone through a number of doctrinal evolutions, explained, in part, by the rapidly changing nature of information, its flow, processing, dissemination, impact and, in particular, its military employment. At the same time, a decade and a half of persistent conflict and global engagement have taught us a lot about the nature of the information environment, especially that in any given area of operations, this environment runs the gamut from the most technologically-advanced to the least. Army units employ IO to create effects in and through the information environment that provide commanders a decisive advantage over adversaries, threats, and enemies in order to defeat the opponent's will. Simultaneously, Army units engage with and influence other relevant foreign audiences to gain their support for friendly objectives. Commanders' IO contributes directly to tactical and operational success and supports objectives at the strategic level.

This latest version of FM 3-13 returns to the joint definition of IO, although it clarifies that land forces must do more than affect threat decision making if they are to accomplish their mission. They must also protect their own decision making and the information that feeds it; align their actions, messages and images; and engage and influence relevant targets and audiences in the area of operations. While the term *inform and influence activities* has been rescinded, many of the principles espoused in the last version of FM 3-13 carry forward, especially the synchronization of information-related capabilities (IRCs).

IRCs are those capabilities that generate effects in and through the information environment, but these effects are almost always accomplished in combination with other information-related capabilities. Only through their effective synchronization can commanders gain a decisive advantage over adversaries, threats, and enemies in the information environment. While capabilities such as military information support operations, combat camera, military deception, operations security and cyberspace operations are readily considered information-related, commanders consider any capability an IRC that is employed to create effects and operationally-desirable conditions within a dimension of the information environment.

FM 3-13 contains nine chapters:

**Chapter 1** provides an overview of information operations. This overview includes an understanding of the operational and information environments; the definition of IO and the definition's component parts; IO's purpose; and how IO contributes to combat power.

**Chapter 2** discusses how IO supports decisive action through three weighted efforts: attack, defend, and stabilize. It also discusses three enabling activities that units must perform to ensure IO supports decisive action effectively.

**Chapter 3** overviews the roles, responsibilities, relationships, and organizations that lead, plan, support, and conduct IO. It involves the commander down to the individual Soldier.

**Chapters 4-7** examine IO's integration into the operations process. Chapter 4 discusses Planning; Chapter 5, Preparation; Chapter 6, Execution; and Chapter 7, Targeting Integration.

**Chapter 8** examines the assessment of IO. While IO does not employ a separate assessment methodology, it does have unique considerations for which units must account.

**Chapter 9** discusses IO at brigade and below. It provides insights for units to consider when planning, preparing, executing, and assessing IO at these levels.

# Chapter 1
# Information Operations Overview

1-1. Conflict is fundamentally a contest of wills. Winning this contest requires commanders to employ combat power to execute decisive action across the range of military operations. *Combat power* is the total means of destructive, constructive, and information capabilities that a military unit or formation can apply at a given time (ADRP 3-0). Combat power is comprised of eight elements, the last six of which are warfighting functions: leadership, information, mission command, movement and maneuver, intelligence, fires, sustainment, and protection.

1-2. Information operations (IO) creates effects in and through the information environment. IO optimizes the information element of combat power and supports and enhances all other elements in order to gain an operational advantage over an enemy or adversary. These effects are intended to influence, disrupt, corrupt or usurp enemy or adversary decision making and everything that enables it, while enabling and protecting friendly decision making. Because IO's central focus is affecting decision making and, by extension, the will to fight, commanders personally ensure IO is integrated into operations from the start.

## SECTION I –OPERATIONAL AND INFORMATION ENVIRONMENTS

1-3. An *operational environment* is a composite of the conditions, circumstances, and influences that affect the employment of capabilities and bear on the decisions of the commander (JP 3-0). It encompasses physical areas and factors of the air, land, maritime, space, and cyberspace domains, and the information environment, which includes cyberspace. The *information environment* is the aggregate of individuals, organizations, and systems that collect, process, disseminate, or act on information (JP 3-13). Although an operational environment and information environment are defined separately, they are interdependent and integral to the other.

## OPERATIONAL ENVIRONMENT

1-4. Several characteristics of the operational environment have a significant impact on land force operations. Each of these characteristics has a significant information aspect. They are:

- Speed and diffusion of information.
- Information asymmetry.
- Proliferation of cyberspace and space capabilities.
- Operations among populations.

1-5. Across the globe, information is increasingly available in near-real time. The ability to access this information, from anywhere, at any time, broadens and accelerates human interaction, across multiple levels (person to person, person to organization, person to government, government to government). Social media, in particular, enables the swift mobilization of people and resources around ideas and causes, even before they are fully understood. Disinformation and propaganda create malign narratives that can propagate quickly and instill an array of emotions and behaviors from anarchy to focused violence. From a military standpoint, information enables decision making, leadership, and combat power; it is also critical to seizing, gaining and retaining the initiative, and consolidating gains in the operational environment.

1-6. Threats, large and small, increasingly operate in an indeterminate zone between peace and war. They seek to avoid U.S. strengths and, instead take advantage of U.S. laws and policies regarding the use of information and cyber capabilities. Coupled with the nation's initial reluctance to engage in major combat operations, they achieve incremental gains that advance their agenda and narrative. They use a range of techniques including non-attribution, innuendo, propaganda, disinformation, and misinformation to sway global opinion favorable to their aims.

1-7. States and non-states are rapidly expanding their investment in cyberspace and space capabilities and forces. They recognize the leveling effect these domains, especially cyberspace, offer in terms of achieving parity or overmatch at minimum relative cost. A significant portion of the threat's information asymmetry comes from its growing capacity in space and cyberspace.

1-8. Threats operate among populations with whom they often share cultural or ethnic identity, making it difficult to distinguish threat from non-threat. This fact requires U.S. forces to interact and communicate, in nuanced fashion, with a wide range of audiences and actors in order to separate those willing to support U.S. intentions from those who are not. The ability of the threat to operate among populations and harness commonalities provides the threat yet another asymmetric advantage.

## INFORMATION ENVIRONMENT

1-9. The information environment is not separate or distinct from the operational environment but inextricably part of it. In fact, any activity that occurs in the information environment simultaneously occurs in and affects one or more of the operational environment domains.

1-10. The information environment is comprised of three dimensions: physical, informational, and cognitive. Within the physical dimension of the information environment is the connective infrastructure that supports the transmission, reception, and storage of information. Also within this dimension are tangible actions or events that transmit a message in and of themselves, such as patrols, aerial reconnaissance, and civil affairs projects. Within the informational dimension is the content or data itself. The informational dimension refers to content and flow of information, such as text or images, or data that staffs can collect, process, store, disseminate, and display. The informational dimension provides the necessary link between the physical and cognitive dimensions. Within the cognitive dimension are the minds of those who are affected by and act upon information. These minds range from friendly commanders and leaders, to foreign audiences affecting or being affected by operations, to enemy, threat or adversarial decision makers. This dimension focuses on the societal, cultural, religious, and historical contexts that influence the perceptions of those producing the information and of the targets and audiences receiving the information. In this dimension, decision makers and target audiences are most prone to influence and perception management.

1-11. The information environment has increased in complexity. Due to the widespread availability of the Internet, wireless communications and information, the information environment has become an even more important consideration to military planning and operations, because the military increasingly relies on these technologies. Activities occurring in and through the information environment have a consequential effect on the operational environment and can impact military operations and outcomes. Therefore, commanders and their staffs must understand the information environment, in all its complexity, and the potential impacts it will have on current and planned military operations.

# SECTION II – INFORMATION OPERATIONS DEFINED AND DESCRIBED

1-12. *Information Operations* (IO) is the integrated employment, during military operations, of information-related capabilities in concert with other lines of operation to influence, disrupt, corrupt, or usurp the decision-making of adversaries and potential adversaries while protecting our own (JP 3-13). This manual uses the term IO comprehensively to capture all activity employed to affect the information environment and contribute to operations in and through the information environment. IO includes:

- Integration and synchronization of information-related capabilities.
- Planning, preparing, execution, and assessment.
- The capability and capacity that ensures the accomplishment of IO, to include the units and personnel responsible for its conduct.

Breaking down the definition into constituent parts helps to understand its meaning and implications for land forces.

## Integrated Employment of Information-Related Capabilities (IRCs)

1-13. IO brings together IRCs at a specific time and in a coherent fashion to create effects in and through the information environment that advance the ability to deliver operational advantage to the commander. While IRCs create individual effects, IO stresses aggregate and synchronized effects as essential to achieving operational objectives.

1-14. An *information-related capability* (IRC) is a tool, technique, or activity employed within a dimension of the information environment that can be used to create effects and operationally desirable conditions (JP 1-02). The formal definition of IRCs encourages commanders and staffs to employ all available resources when seeking to affect the information environment to operational advantage. For example, if artillery fires are employed to destroy communications infrastructure that enables enemy decision making, then artillery is an IRC in this instance. In daily practice, however, the term IRC tends to refer to those tools, techniques, or activities that are inherently information-based or primarily focused on affecting the information environment. These include—

- Military deception.
- Military information support operations (MISO).
- Soldier and leader engagement (SLE), to include police engagement.
- Civil affairs operations.
- Combat camera.
- Operations security (OPSEC).
- Public affairs.
- Cyberspace electromagnetic activities.
- Electronic warfare.
- Cyberspace operations.
- Space operations.
- Special technical operations.

1-15. All unit operations, activities, and actions affect the information environment. Even if they primarily affect the physical dimension, they nonetheless also affect the informational and cognitive dimensions. For this reason, whether or not they are routinely considered an IRC, a wide variety of unit functions and activities can be adapted for the purposes of conducting information operations or serve as enablers to its planning, execution, and assessment. Some of these include, but are not limited to:

- Commander's communications strategy or communication synchronization.
- Presence, profile, and posture.
- Foreign disclosure.
- Physical security.
- Physical maneuver.
- Special access programs.
- Civil military operations.
- Intelligence.
- Destruction and lethal actions.

## During Military Operations

1-16. Army forces, as part of a joint force, conduct operations across the conflict continuum and range of military operations. Whether participating in security cooperation efforts or conducting major combat operations, IO is essential during all phases (0 through V) of a military operation. (See JP 5-0 for a detailed discussion of the joint phasing model).

## In Concert with Other Lines of Operation

1-17. Commanders use lines of operations and lines of effort to visualize and describe operations. A *line of operations* is a line that defines the directional orientation of a force in time and space in relation to the enemy and that links the force with its base of operations and objectives (ADRP 3-0). Lines of operations connect a series of decisive points that lead to control of a geographic or force-oriented objective. A *line of effort* is a line that links multiple tasks using the logic of purpose rather than geographical reference to focus efforts toward establishing operational and strategic conditions (ADRP 3-0). Lines of effort are essential to long-term planning when positional references to an enemy or adversary have little relevance. Commanders may describe an operation along lines of operations, lines of effort, or a combination of both. Commanders, supported by their staff, ensure information operations are integrated into the concept of operation to support each line of operation and effort. Based on the situation, commanders may designate IO as a line of effort to synchronize actions and focus the force on creating desired effects in the information environment. Depending on the type of operation or the phase, commanders may designate an IO-focused line of effort as decisive.

### To Influence, Disrupt, Corrupt, or Usurp

1-18. IO seeks to create specific effects at a specific time and place. Predominantly, these effects occur in and through the information environment. Immediate effects (disrupt, corrupt, usurp) are possible in the information environment's physical and informational dimensions through the denial, degradation, or destruction of adversarial or enemy information-related capabilities. However, effects in the cognitive dimension (influence) take longer to manifest. It is these cognitive effects—as witnessed through changed behavior—that matter most to achieving decisive outcomes.

### The Decision Making of Enemies and Adversaries

1-19. While there are differences among the terms adversaries, threats, and enemies, all three refer to those individuals, organizations, or entities that oppose U.S. efforts. They therefore must be influenced in some fashion to acquiesce or surrender to or otherwise support U.S. national objectives by aligning their actions in concert with commanders' intent. [The joint phrasing "adversaries and potential adversaries" is revised to "enemies and adversaries" to better align with Army terminology.]

1-20. Affecting enemy and adversary decision making necessitates affecting all contributing factors that enable it. These factors include, but are not limited to:

- Command and control systems, as well as other systems that facilitate decision making.
- Communications systems.
- Information content (words, images, symbols).
- Staffs, advisors, counselors, and confidants.
- Human networks and constituencies that influence the decision maker and to whom the decision maker seeks to influence; in other words, all relevant audiences in the areas of operations and interest.

### While Protecting Our Own

1-21. Friendly commanders, like enemy and adversary leaders, depend on an array of systems, capabilities, information, networks, and decision aids to assist in their decision making. Gaining operational advantage in the information environment is equally about exploiting and protecting the systems, information, and people that speed and enhance friendly decision making, as it is about denying the same to the threat.

## THE PURPOSE OF INFORMATION OPERATIONS

1-22. The purpose of IO is to create effects in and through the information environment that provide commanders decisive advantage over enemies and adversaries. Commanders achieve this advantage in several ways: preserve and facilitate decision making and the impact of decision making, while influencing, disrupting or degrading enemy or adversary decision making; get required information faster and with greater accuracy and clarity than the enemy or adversary; or influence the attitudes and behaviors of relevant audiences in the area of operations having an impact on operations and decision making.

1-23. To support achievement of these various ways, IO employs and synchronizes IRCs to affect the will, awareness, understanding, and capability of these audiences, while protecting our own. Will, awareness, understanding, and capability all contribute to and sustain decision making and, if compromised, can impair that decision making. In terms of will, awareness, understanding, and capability, advantage is achieved when commanders preserve their will to fight, as well as their situational understanding and their full capacity and ability to prosecute operations. Further, commanders achieve advantage when they preserve their freedom of action in the information environment while degrading enemy or adversary freedom of action.

## THREE INTERRELATED EFFORTS

1-24. IO is comprised of three inter-related efforts: a commander-led staff planning and synchronization effort; a preparation and execution effort carried out by IRC units, IO units, or staff entities in concert with the IO working group; and an assessment effort carried out by all involved. These three efforts work in tandem and overlap each other.

1-25. The planning and synchronization effort includes planning and synchronizing IRC employment to create effects in and through the information environment that result in advantage over the threat. Preparation and execution involves positioning and employing IRC assets in accordance with the IO working group synchronization plan to create desired effects at the right place and time. Assessment involves determining whether planned effects were achieved and recommending adjustments, as necessary.

1-26. The IO officer, IO working group, and the assistant chief of staff, intelligence (G-2/S-2), especially, contribute to the assessment. The IO officer prepares the IO portion of the assessment plan. The IO working group monitors execution of the assessment plan and compares desired results with actual results. The G-2 (S-2), in coordination with the assistant chief of staff, operations (G-3/S-3), contributes by ensuring collection assets are available and tasked to gather information needed to validate measure of effectiveness.

## ARMY-JOINT RELATIONSHIPS

1-27. IO, by its nature, is joint. Based on the theater campaign plan, each service component contributes to an integrated whole synchronized by the joint force headquarters. Army IO supports joint force missions two ways. The first is when Army or land component command IRCs are specifically tasked to support a joint force mission. The second is when the Army or land component command, in its support of the joint force, develops its own IO plan, specific to its mission and area of operations. In both instances, IRCs are synchronized across the joint force to create desired effects in and through the information environment, as well as prevent the diminishment or negation of one IRC's effects by another. In multinational operations, the U.S. joint force commander is responsible for coordinating the integration of U.S. IO with multinational information activities.

1-28. The IO officer at joint force headquarters (J-39) synchronizes joint IO efforts. All component commands participate in a synchronization process to maximize effects in the information environment. The process is informed by an IO working group, cell, or virtual center that delivers its recommendations to various decision-making boards. Examples include the Joint Targeting Coordination Board and Joint Intelligence Collection Board. The J-39 provides a staff capability that synchronizes all service-specific IRCs to achieve unity of effort in support of the joint force. Army forces submit requests for IRC or IO unit support and deconfliction measures through multiple channels to higher echelons. For example, requests may go through the J-6 for spectrum management, through liaison at the Air Operations Center for electronic warfare support, through a supporting cyberspace operations center for an effects request, or through the targeting cell for targeting vetting and validation. The J-39 and joint IO cell are kept informed in order to publish plans and orders depicting, maximizing, and assessing mutual support mechanisms for the joint force commander.

## INFORMATION OPERATIONS ACROSS THE RANGE OF MILITARY OPERATIONS

1-29. Army forces conduct IO within joint force parameters. From peace to war, and across the range of military operations, commanders integrate and synchronize IO to focus combat power and gain advantage in the information environment. In all situations, Army forces do not act in isolation. Army forces conduct operations in support of a larger joint or multinational plan. Figure 1-1, on page 1-6, depicts the three main categories of military operations within the range of military operations construct:

- Military engagement, security cooperation, and deterrence.
- Crisis response and limited contingency operations.
- Major operations and campaigns.

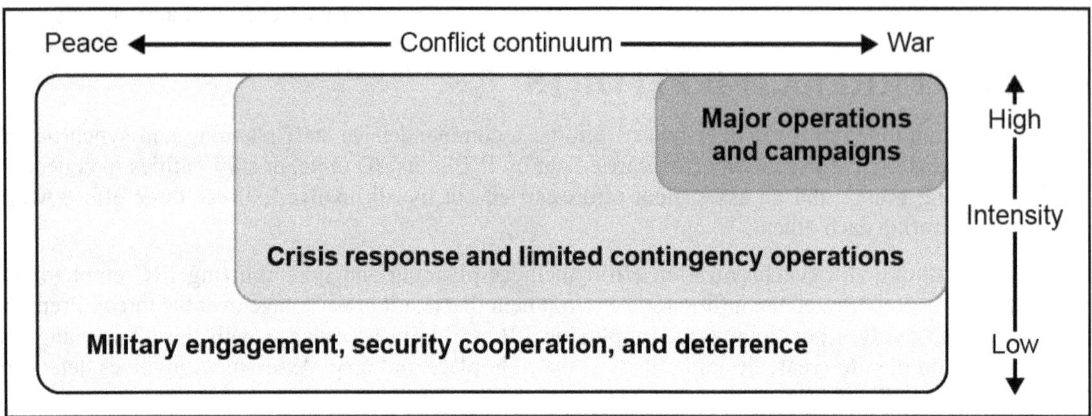


**Figure 1-1. The range of military operations across the conflict continuum**

## Military Engagement, Security Cooperation, and Deterrence

1-30. Military engagement, security cooperation, and deterrence operations are ongoing and recurring military activities that establish, shape, maintain, and refine relations with other nations and domestic civil authorities. The general objective is to protect U.S. interests at home and abroad. IO contributes significantly to military engagement, security cooperation, and deterrence. Military engagement and security cooperation depend heavily on influencing partners and potential partners to align with U.S. interests and, thereby, prevent threats from achieving objectives in or through these same partners and the countries and regions they inhabit. Military engagement and security cooperation are themselves forms of deterrence, but other forms are possible. Deterrence is not only the actual capacity to harm another state or non-state entity who fails to comply with or accommodate U.S. demands, but also the perception of that entity that the U.S. has the ability to do harm, if provoked. IO provides essential support to the shaping and maintaining of this perception through, among other things, the protection of friendly information (OPSEC).

1-31. Complementing IO support to military engagement, security cooperation, and deterrence, as well as crisis response, contingency operations and major operations and campaigns is the Attack the Network framework. This framework consists of activities that employ lethal and nonlethal means to support friendly networks, influence neutral networks, and neutralize threat networks. Since the aim of this framework and the purpose of IO are highly similar, commanders ensure their close coordination. (See ATP 3-90.37 for more information).

## Crisis and Limited Contingency Operations

1-32. Contingencies and crisis response operations may be single small-scale, limited-duration operations or a significant part of a major operation of extended duration involving combat. General objectives are to protect U.S. interests and prevent surprise attack or further conflict. These operations typically occur during periods of slightly increased U.S. military readiness, and the use or threat of force may be more probable. Many of these operations involve a combination of military forces in close cooperation with other organizations. Examples include counter-terrorism operations; counter-proliferation; sanctions enforcement; noncombatant evacuation operations; peacekeeping and peace enforcement operations; show of force; strikes and raids; and support to counterinsurgency.

1-33. Army forces conduct IO in accordance with existing contingency or crisis action plans (see JP 5-0). A potential or actual contingency requires commanders at all echelons to gather additional information and refine their contingency plans based on a specific area of operations or target set. Geographic combatant commanders may use the relationships and conditions in the information environment created during peace to influence threat decision makers to act in ways that will resolve the crisis peacefully. Other IO efforts may attempt to influence actors within a target group's political, economic, military, and social structures. Operational and tactical commanders prepare for IO as part of their deployment preparations. They coordinate preparations with the joint force commander to ensure unity of effort and prevent ***information fratricide*, which is defined as adverse effects on the information environment resulting from a failure to effectively synchronize the employment of multiple information-related capabilities which may impede the conduct of friendly operations or adversely affect friendly forces.**

1-34. The objectives during crisis are to halt escalation and move the level of conflict back towards peace. Therefore, commanders conduct IO to develop the situation and refine their situational understanding. Through the deliberate selection and effective synchronization of IRCs, commanders increase the potential that adversaries or other relevant decision makers will choose alternatives other than conflict or war.

### Major Operations and Campaigns

1-35. Major operations and campaigns are large-scale, sustained combat operations to achieve national objectives and protect national interests. Such operations may place the United States in a wartime state and are normally conducted against a capable enemy with the will to employ that capability in opposition to or in a manner threatening national security. Major operations may be part of a joint campaign comprised of multiple phases. The goal is to achieve national objectives and conclude hostilities with conditions favorable to the United States and its multinational partners, generally as quickly, with as few casualties as possible, and in a manner that conveys continuing strategic advantage for the United States and its partners.

1-36. During major operations and campaigns, commanders conduct IO to achieve decisive effects in and through the information environment against enemy forces. Well-synchronized IO planning and operational integration supports offense, defense, and stability tasks by weighting IO efforts appropriate to each task. For example, during offense, units conduct IO attack, defend, and stabilize actions, in appropriate combination, to help defeat and destroy enemy forces and capabilities, especially those that are information-related. Units also conduct IO to deny aspects of the information environment (physical, informational, and cognitive) that facilitate threat decision making, while preserving critical information infrastructure, content, and networks essential to friendly decision making.

## SECTION III – INFORMATION OPERATIONS AND COMBAT POWER

1-37. The information element of combat power is integral to optimizing combat power, particularly given the increasing relevance of operations in and through the information environment to achieve decisive outcomes. IO and the information element of combat power are related but not the same.

1-38. Information is a resource. As a resource, it must be obtained, developed, refined, distributed, and protected. IO, along with knowledge management and information management, are the ways that units harness this resource and ensure its availability, as well as operationalize and optimize it.

1-39. IO, a component of the mission command warfighting function, supports all other warfighting functions and makes each one more potent. The effects that IO achieves in the information environment amplify the effects of movement and maneuver, intelligence, fires, sustainment and protection, both constructive and destructive.

## MISSION COMMAND

1-40. The mission command warfighting function enables commanders to balance the art of command and the science of control in order to integrate the other warfighting functions. It also enables a shared understanding of an operational environment and the commander's intent. IO's focus on protecting information, information systems, and decision making, enhances commanders' ability to integrate the other warfighting functions and create necessary shared understanding. At the same time, it seeks to degrade the enemy's decision-making ability.

1-41. IO supports the accomplishment of several mission command warfighting tasks, including inform and influence audiences inside and outside an organization, conduct knowledge management and information management, synchronize IRCs, and conduct cyberspace electromagnetic activities. Informing and influencing are effects that occur in the cognitive dimension of the information environment. By effectively synchronizing IRCs and, when appropriate, conducting cyberspace electromagnetic activities, commanders tailor their influence and manner of informing to the situation and audience at hand. Information and knowledge management support the commander and staff's ability to access information quickly and completely, as well as segment and protect information, thereby enhancing their decision making and gaining advantage over adversaries and enemies.

## MOVEMENT AND MANEUVER

1-42. The movement and maneuver warfighting function moves and employs forces to achieve a position of relative advantage over the enemy through direct fire and close combat. IO seeks to influence or affect enemy decision making so that relative advantage is achieved even before close combat becomes necessary or diminishes the potency of threat actions so that they ultimately fail. Movement and maneuver, along with fires, always produce effects in the information environment, whether intentional or not, and these effects must be considered when planning operations (not just IO). At the same time, movement and maneuver can itself serve as an IRC when its chief objective is to send a message and influence behavior, such as when it is tied to a deception effort.

## INTELLIGENCE

1-43. Intelligence facilitates understanding the threat, terrain, and civil considerations. IO enhances and sharpens focus on the aspects of the information environment that influence or are influenced by the threat, such as the threat's IRCs. IO also enhances understanding of the ways that messages are received, transmitted and processed by relevant audiences in the area of operations. In turn, intelligence supports IO by collecting information essential to defining the information environment, understanding the threat's information capabilities, and assessing and adjusting information-related effects.

## FIRES

1-44. Fires provides collective and coordinated use of Army indirect fires, air and missile defense, and joint fires through the targeting process. IO effects are typically indirect rather than direct and like indirect fire, greatly benefit from deliberate selection, development and delivery. This fact is why IO targets, like offensive cyberspace operations and space targets, are a part of the targeting process and get nominated to the targeting board for approval.

## SUSTAINMENT

1-45. Sustainment provides support and services to ensure freedom of action, extend operational reach, and prolong endurance. IO, through the synchronization of IRCs, seeks to ensure freedom of action in the information environment which, in turn, contributes to enhanced mental and emotional endurance, not just of U.S. forces and their partners, but also of the indigenous populations affected by operations. While morale is a leadership function, it is facilitated through the preservation and sustainment of information, information systems, content, and flow and the ability of leaders to create shared understanding and purpose. Sustainment support and services, such as air dropping supplies to displaced persons or providing health service support, often contribute to effects in the information environment, making coordination between the IO officer and the assistant chief of staff, logistics or G-4 (S-4) essential.

## PROTECTION

1-46. The protection warfighting function preserves the force so that commanders can apply maximum combat power to accomplish the mission. IO is focused on the preservation of decision making and ensuring decision-oriented information is available at the right time and place. This means more than simply blunting or preventing the effectiveness of the threat's access to information; it means securing and defending our own.

## Chapter 2

# Information Operations and Decisive Action

2-1. Unified land operations applies land power as part of unified action to defeat the threat on land and establish conditions that achieve the joint force commander's end state. Combat power is the primary means by which Army forces apply land power. IO synchronization supports combat power by harnessing the information element to optimize the warfighting functions and leadership. In turn, this optimization enables commanders to seize the initiative through decisive action.

2-2. *Decisive action* is the continuous, simultaneous combination of offensive, defensive, and stability or defense support of civil authorities tasks (ADRP 3-0). IO contributes to decisive action through the continuous and simultaneous combination and synchronization of IRCs in support of offense, defense, and stability tasks. IO itself is not offensive, defensive, or stabilizing, but contributes to all of these simultaneously by weighting its efforts in such a way that it achieves requisite effects in and through the information environment in support of the commander's intent.

2-3. To support decisive action effectively, the commander and staff undertake three enabling activities—analyze and depict the information environment, determine IRCs and IO organizations available, and optimize IRC effects. These activities start with understanding and visualizing the information environment in all its complexity. They progress to determining the array of IRCs and IO organizations available to affect the information environment. They culminate with optimizing IRC effects through effective planning, preparation, execution and assessment (see paragraphs 2-12 to 2-22 for a detailed discussion of these enabling activities).

## WEIGHTED EFFORTS

2-4. IO weighted efforts are broad orientations used to focus the integration and synchronization of IRCs to create effects that seize, retain, and exploit the initiative in the information environment. Commanders, supported by their staffs, visualize and describe how IO will support the concept of operations by aligning and balancing the efforts of defend, attack, and stabilize with corresponding decisive action tasks as shown in figure 2-1 on page 2-2.

### IO Weighted Effort: Defend

2-5. When the IO effort necessitates a defend orientation, it seeks to create effects in the information environment that accomplish any one or combination of the following (not all inclusive):

- Physical dimension.
  - Locking or otherwise physically securing documents, equipment and infrastructure that facilitate decision making.
  - Protecting documents, equipment, and structures from destruction or degradation.
  - Protecting key personnel from attack or exploitation.
  - Using obscurants to mask movements.
- Informational dimension.
  - Encrypting communications.
  - Preserving the free-flow of information and access to data and information sources.
  - Employing knowledge management principles.
  - Proactively identifying instances of social engineering or malware and keeping virus and other protections current.
  - Using forensics to determine sources of attack.

- Countering enemy or adversary information efforts.
- Cognitive dimension.
  - Making decentralized decisions.
  - Checking facts and assumptions.
  - Using precedents or best practices.
  - Using red teaming.

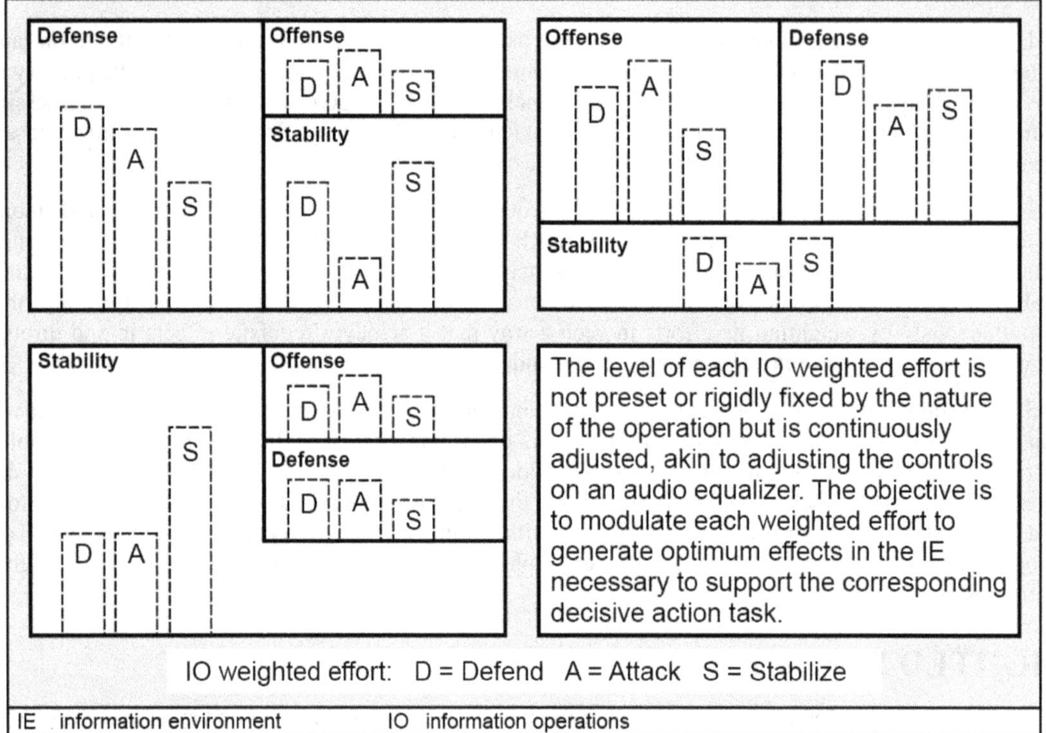


**Figure 2-1. IO weighted efforts**

2-6. IRCs that are most often synchronized to achieve a defend orientation in the information environment include, but are not limited to:

- Cyberspace operations.
- Electronic warfare.
- Military deception.
- MISO.
- Operations security (OPSEC).
- Physical security.
- Destruction and lethal actions.
- Special technical operations.

## IO Weighted Effort: Attack

2-7. When the IO effort necessitates an attack orientation, it seeks to create effects in the information environment that accomplish any one or combination of the following (not all inclusive):

- Physical dimension.
  - Destroying or degrading threat command and control (C2) systems.
  - Degrading or destroying threat leadership.
  - Destroying or impairing threat networks and critical nodes (human or infrastructure).

  - Using feints, ruses, demonstrations, and displays.
- Informational dimension.
  - Jamming communication and signals.
  - Corrupting data and information.
  - Employing denial of service attacks.
  - Intercepting or misdirecting data or content.
  - Manipulating information provided to adversary leaders.
  - Attacking the enemy's or adversary's narrative(s).
  - Using social engineering or spoofing.
- Cognitive dimension.
  - Creating ambiguity or confusion.
  - Causing an incorrect understanding of friendly intent.
  - Creating hesitancy or procrastination.
  - Enabling overconfidence in false signals and signs; under confidence or uncertainty in the true ones.
  - Degrading support for the threat.
  - Degrading legitimacy of threat narrative(s).

2-8. IRCs that are most often synchronized to achieve an attack orientation in the information environment include, but are not limited to:

- Cyberspace operations.
- Electronic warfare.
- Military deception.
- MISO.
- Destruction and lethal actions.
- Special technical operations.
- Space operations.
- Soldier and leader engagement (SLE).

## IO WEIGHTED EFFORT: STABILIZE

2-9. When the IO effort necessitates a stabilize orientation, it seeks to create effects in the information environment that accomplish any one or combination of the following (not all inclusive):

- Physical dimension.
  - Meeting with key leaders, decision makers, or people who can influence the behaviors of others.
  - Visibly demonstrating mutual commitment or support.
  - Establishing, supporting and utilizing new infrastructure or media that increases or enhances quantity and quality of communication between U.S.-led forces and relevant audiences.
  - Identifying and cultivating traditional or indigenous communicators.
  - Aligning Soldier and unit actions with their words and images.
- Informational dimension.
  - Employing audience- and culturally-attuned messages.
  - Countering threat or adversary information efforts and narratives through coordinated actions.
  - Aligning images and words with unit and individual Soldier actions.
  - Using messages crafted by native speakers and communicators.
  - Nesting messages with higher headquarters themes and messages and strategic communication guidance.
- Cognitive dimension.
  - Creating support for rule of law, local security forces, and legitimate authority.

- Enhancing understanding of U.S. operations and desired outcomes.
- Changing perceptions, attitudes, and, ultimately, behaviors.

2-10. The IRCs that are most often synchronized to achieve a stabilize orientation in the information environment include, but are not limited to:

- Combat camera.
- MISO.
- Presence, posture and profile.
- Public affairs.
- Civil affairs operations and civil military operations.
- SLE, including police engagement.
- OPSEC.
- Foreign disclosure.

### IO and Defense Support of Civil Authorities

2-11. IO does not participate in defense support of civil authorities. However, if requested by civil authorities and approved by the Secretary of Defense, select IRCs may support civil authorities in the conduct of their operations.

## IO ENABLING ACTIVITIES

2-12. To support decisive action, as well as accomplish IO's purpose, commanders, staffs, and in particular, the IO officer or representative, undertake and accomplish three enabling activities:

- Analyze and depict the information environment in all its complexity.
- Determine the array of IRCs and IO organizations (such as Theater IO Groups) available to affect the information environment and the advantages each offers.
- Optimize the effects of IRCs through effective planning, preparation, execution, and assessment.

### Analyze and Depict the Information Environment

2-13. To achieve advantage in the information environment, commanders, with specialized advice and support from the IO officer, ensure that IO planning is fully integrated into the operations process. This begins with analysis to understand, visualize, and describe the information environment.

2-14. A significant part of what makes the operational environment complex is the information environment because it includes such components as cyberspace, the electromagnetic spectrum, data flow, encryption and decryption, the media, biases, perceptions, decisions, key leaders and decision makers, among many others. What occurs in the physical dimension of the information environment and, more broadly, the operational environment, always has second- and third-order effects in the informational and cognitive dimensions of the information environment. Thus, there must be holistic and nuanced understanding of how these various components and dimensions interrelate and the whole operates.

2-15. This understanding is depicted through a series of information overlays and comprehensive combined information overlays, which vary depending on commanders' priorities, the nature of the operation, and the type of analysis being conducted. Modeling or mapping social or human networks also enhances this understanding. While complex, the information environment still needs to be captured in a way that the commander can visualize and understand it, draw necessary insights and conclusions, and make informed decisions. The IO officer should not be locked into any specific method for analyzing and depicting the information environment but develop a process and overlays that best serve the commander and, as appropriate, follow unit standard operating procedures. As new technologies and interactive capabilities emerge, they should be incorporated as tools to facilitate the visualization and understanding processes.

## Determine IRCs and IO Organizations Available

2-16. The IO officer is the staff focal point for information environment analysis and expertise, as well as IRC synchronization. The two are inextricably linked: effective IRC synchronization can only occur when the information environment is understood fully. Additionally, effective IRC synchronization can also only occur when a single entity can look across all IRCs and articulate their contribution to the fight and how they can mutually support each other. The IO officer, located in the assistant chief of staff, operations (G-3/S-3) staff section, in concert with the IO working group, is this synchronization entity. Three key responsibilities of the IO officer, therefore, are to build rapport with IRC units, determine ways to optimize each IRC's contribution through synchronization, and facilitate IRC operations and activities by coordinating support for them, while minimizing impediments.

2-17. In addition to building rapport with IRC units, the IO officer must build similar rapport with and knowledge of IO organizations available and the ways they augment and enhance the function's effectiveness. These units include the 1st IO Command (Land) and the reserve component regionally-aligned Theater IO Groups.

2-18. The IO officer also continually assesses whether the necessary assets and capabilities are available to achieve the commander's intent and concept of operations. If it is determined that augmentation—by specific IRCs or by IO units—is necessary, the IO officer or appropriate IRC representative requests augmentation or determines alternative courses of action to fulfill its scheme of IO and meet mission objectives.

2-19. Information-related organizations and entities also exist within the interagency and among Unified Action partners. IO officers not only must know these organizations and entities, they must invite their participation whenever feasible, particularly through their ad hoc or habitual membership in the IO working group, which coordinates, synchronizes, and deconflicts the information-related efforts of these partner organizations with its own efforts.

## Optimize IRC Effects

2-20. Optimizing IRC effects begins in earnest with receipt of mission and continues throughout the operations process. With information environment analysis and understanding already accounted for, other IO officer tasks necessary to ensure effective IRC synchronization and the optimization of their effects are:

- Participate in the military decisionmaking process (MDMP) and develop the scheme of IO.
- Convene and chair the IO working group.
- Work closely with IRC units and IO units to ensure capabilities are positioned, employed, and supported to fulfill the synchronization plan.
- Integrate targets within the information environment into the targeting process and develop, maintain and update IRC synchronization matrix.
- Coordinate and deconflict IRC synchronization with public affairs efforts to ensure unity of effort and compliance with legal and policy limitations and exclusions.
- Assess IO and IRC effectiveness in achieving planned effects and adjust as necessary.

This page intentionally left blank.

# Chapter 3

# Roles, Responsibilities, Relationships, and Organizations

3-1. Every member of a unit—from the commander, to the staff, to the IO officer or representative, to individual Soldiers and Army civilians—contributes to IO. Also essential to mission success are the IRCs supporting the unit's IO efforts, as well as any augmenting IO units. Each has a specific role and important responsibilities to fulfill or undertake, as well as vital relationships to forge and sustain, in order to achieve advantage in and through the information environment.

## THE COMMANDER

3-2. Commanders, at all levels, are responsible for knowing what threats their units face and how to exploit or defeat them. They are their unit's chief influencers and engage relevant audiences and actors, as necessary, to shape the information environment to their advantage. Commanders rely on their staff and IO officer, in particular, to assist in planning, preparing, executing, and assessing IO. They also personally direct and review analysis of the information environment, issue guidance on the employment and synchronization of IRCs, and direct adjustments based on assessment results.

3-3. Cognizant of the pervasive impact of the information environment on operations and the need to affect this environment to their advantage, commanders are mindful of the following:

- Every operation has, to some degree, an effect on the information environment.
- IO planning is integral to operations from the start.
- Effects in and through the information environment, if essential to success, are part of the commander's intent.
- Combat power cannot be optimized without IO.
- The warfighting functions (particularly movement and maneuver and fires) produce effects in the information environment, whether intentional or not.
- IO is essential to operational success at all levels, whether or not the unit has an assigned IO officer.
- All communication can quickly become global and have strategic consequences.
- IRCs can have lengthy lead times to coordinate and employ, as well as lengthy lag times before their effects are realized.
- The alignment of words, deeds, and images is essential to building trust and confidence with relevant audiences in the area of operations.
- IO requires prioritized intelligence support.
- Effects in the information environment are not always caused as expected; assessment is difficult and benefits from commanders' interest, prioritization and support.
- U,S. IO can be constrained by policy and law, while the threat is often unconstrained in its use of information.

## THE STAFF

3-4. Each staff section collaborates routinely, but to varying degrees, with the IO officer to plan, synchronize, support, and assess IO. Representatives from the G-2 (S-2), G-3 (S-3), assistant chief of staff, plans G-5 (S-5), assistant chief of staff, signal G-6 (S-6) and assistant chief of staff, civil affairs operations (G-9/S-9), in particular, serve as core members of the IO working group.

## Assistant Chief of Staff, G-1 (S-1), Personnel

3-5. The G-1 (S-1) is the principal staff officer for personnel functions. The G-1 (S-1) processes requirements for individual, team and unit augmentation or attachment. It coordinates reception of these individuals, teams, or units and validates their requirements. It also builds manning documents, as required. Additional IO-related responsibilities include, but are not limited to:

- Designating a representative to the IO working group.
- Providing IO-focused instructions in the personnel appendix of the sustainment annex.
- Reviewing the IO mission and mission, enemy, terrain and weather, troops and support available, time available, and civil considerations from a personnel support perspective.

## Assistant Chief of Staff, G-2 (S-2), Intelligence

3-6. The G-2 (S-2) is the principal staff officer for all matters concerning military intelligence, security operations, and military intelligence training. The G-2 (S-2) produces the intelligence used by the IO officer, element, working group and IRCs. IO-related responsibilities of the G-2 (S-2) include, but are not limited to:

- Participating as a core member of the IO working group and providing intelligence briefings or updates.
- Providing IO-focused instructions in the intelligence annex.
- Including requests for information from the IO officer in intelligence reach.
- Answering information requirements (IRs) submitted by the IO officer.
- Coordinating with counterintelligence; law enforcement; and information system developers, providers, administrators, and users to ensure timely sharing of relevant information.
- Preparing a threat assessment of enemy command and control systems, including:
  - Political, economic, social, and cultural influences.
  - Targets and methods for offensive operations.
  - Enemy decision-making processes.
  - Biographical backgrounds of key threat leaders, decision makers, and communicators, and their advisors. Including motivating factors and leadership styles.
  - A comprehensive comparison of enemy offensive information capabilities against friendly IO vulnerabilities.
- Collecting data to establish an electronic warfare database and command and control target list.
- Providing intelligence support to military deception operations; specifically:
  - Helping the G-6 (S-6) plan use of friendly information systems as deception means.
  - Establishing counterintelligence measures to protect the military deception operation from detection.

## Assistant Chief of Staff, G-3 (S-3), Operations

3-7. The G-3 (S-3) is the principal staff officer for all matters concerning training and leader development, operations and plans, and force development modernization. IO-related responsibilities include, but are not limited to:

- Exercising primary responsibility for IO staff functions and overseeing the IO officer, who is part of the movement and maneuver cell.
- With assistance from the IO officer, integrating IO planning into the military decisionmaking process.
- Validating or approving, as necessary, IO officer inputs, actions and outputs. Among the inputs and outputs, the mission statement, scheme of IO, and IO objectives require G-3 (S-3) review, refinement, and emphasis.
- If additional IRCs or IO units are required, prioritizing and facilitating the augmentation request or request for forces.
- Tasking units and assets necessary to achieve IO objectives.

- Providing plans and current operations briefings to IO working group meetings.
- Integrating information collection into operations, supported by the G-2 (S-2).
- Ensuring effective coordination and synchronization among the IO officer and IRC staff representatives and other members of the IO working group.

## Assistant Chief of Staff, G-4 (S-4), Logistics

3-8. The G-4 (S-4) is the principal staff officer for all matters concerning sustainment operations. IO-related responsibilities of the G-4 (S-4) include, but are not limited to:

- Ensuring required resources are included on the baseline resources item list and the commander's track item list.
- Coordinating sustainment per priorities and requirements.
- Tracking the operational readiness of IO units and equipment.
- Providing sustainment capability or vulnerability input to the IO estimate and course of action analyses.
- Advising the deception and IO working groups on how military operations will affect logistics personnel and equipment.
- Designating a representative to the IO working group.
- Providing IO-focused instruction in the sustainment annex.

## Assistant Chief of Staff, G-5 (S-5), Plans

3-9. The G-5 (S-5) is responsible for incorporating future plans into ongoing operations. The IO officer works closely with the G-5 (S-5) to ensure its efforts to affect the information environment support future plans and provide the commander necessary freedom of action to sustain the initiative and achieve decisive results. When required, the G-5 (S-5) and IO officer work closely to plan and implement deception efforts and ensure objectives are incorporated effectively into plans and operations orders.

## Assistant Chief of Staff, G-6 (S-6), Signal

3-10. The G-6 (S-6) is the principal staff officer for all matters concerning Department of Defense information network operations (also called DODIN operations), applicable portions of defensive cyberspace operations, network transport, information services, and spectrum management operations within the unit's area of operations. IO-related responsibilities of the G-6 (S-6) include but are not limited to:

- Coordinating information management with and providing information management data to the G-3 (S-3).
- Providing a representative to the IO working group.
- Providing IO-related instructions in relevant annexes and appendices.
- Directing the actions of subordinate DODIN operations and information management staff elements.
- Coordinating DODIN operations and information management support of information collection with the G-2 (S-2).
- Coordinating with the Army Cyber Operations and Integration Center for antivirus software and threat analysis and advisories, after receiving notification of its support from the G-3 (S-3).
- Coordinating with the regional cyber center for network intrusion devices, information, approved systems, and software, after receiving notification of its support from the G-3 (S-3).

## Assistant Chief of Staff, G-9 (S-9), Civil Affairs Operations

3-11. The G-9 (S-9) is the principal staff officer for all matters concerning civil affairs and civil military operations. The G-9 (S-9) evaluates civil considerations within missions and identifies centers of gravity that are civil in nature. IO-related responsibilities of the G-9 (S-9) include, but are not limited to:

- Providing a G-9 (S-9) representative to the IO working group.
- Providing IO-focused instructions in the civil affairs operations annex.

- Interfacing with IO officer on the use of civil military operations in support of the scheme of IO.
- Identifying and procuring civilian resources to support the scheme of IO.
- Advising the military deception officer of implications of military deception operations on civil affairs operations.
- Coordinating with the IO and psychological operations officers on trends in public sentiments.
- Coordinating with the IO officer, public affairs officer, and psychological operations officer to ensure messages are not contradictory.

# THE IO OFFICER

3-12. The IO officer (who heads the IO element at division and higher) or representative (at brigade and below) is the staff focal point for IO. The IO officer is responsible for the following specific tasks, among others:

- Analyzing the information environment to discern impacts it will have on unit operations and to exploit opportunities to gain an advantage over threat forces.
- Identifying the most effective IRCs to achieve objectives.
- Synchronizing IRCs to achieve objectives in the information environment.
- Assessing the risk, typically described as risk to mission and risk to force, associated with the employment of any capability, product, program or message.
- Providing input to the synchronization matrix for the use of available IRCs in support of unit operations.
- Identifying IRC gaps not resolvable at the unit level.
- Coordinating with other Army, Service, or joint forces to use IRCs to augment existing unit capability shortfalls.
- Providing information as required in support of operations security (OPSEC) at the unit level.
- Providing information as required in support of military deception at the unit level.
- Leading the IO working group.
- Assessing the effectiveness of employed IRCs.

3-13. The IO officer contributes to the overall intelligence preparation of the battlefield (IPB) by assisting the G-2 (S-2) in identifying and evaluating threat information capabilities, as well as the means to influence the population. Additionally, the IO officer submits to the G-2 (S-2) any IRs regarding intelligence shortfalls about the information environment and coordinates with the G-2 (S-2) in developing templates, databases, and other relevant products, including but not limited to:

- Religion, language, and culture of key groups and decision makers.
- Agendas of nongovernmental organizations.
- Size and location of threat IO or information warfare forces and assets.
- Military and civilian communication infrastructures and connectivity.
- Population demographics, linkages, and related information.
- Audio, video, and print media outlets and centers and the populations they service.
- Location and types of electromagnetic systems and emitters.
- Network vulnerabilities of friendly, neutral, and threat forces.

3-14. Additional tasks for which the IO officer is responsible include, but are not limited to:

- Participating in the military decisionmaking process.
- Developing IRs.
- Producing information and combined information overlays.
- Developing the scheme of IO.
- Through commander's communication synchronization, contribute to development of the commander's narrative.
- Integrating IO into the unit's targeting process.
- Deconflicting the employment of IRCs.

- Ensuring IO-related information is updated in the common operational picture.
- Integrating external augmentation.

3-15. Not all units are authorized an IO officer or element. Commanders may, therefore, adapt their staff structure to ensure IO objectives and IRC tasks are accomplished and appoint an officer or non-commissioned officer to perform the duties of the IO officer, outlined in this manual. Task organizing for IO is situation-, mission- and commander-dependent.

3-16. A key responsibility of the IO officer is to understand the command relationship with IRC units and build rapport accordingly. Building rapport typically begins with a visit to the IRC site location, an orientation on the IRC's potential contributions and limitations, and a collaborative determination of ways to optimize the IRC's effects with other IRCs through synchronization. This rapport-building is ongoing and primarily channeled through the IO working group, although one-on-one conversations will also occur.

3-17. When necessary, the IO officer must be ready to lead the planning and employment of select IRCs not clearly managed by a capability owner or proponent. Examples include, but are not limited to: military deception; OPSEC; and Presence, Posture, and Profile. The IO officer is also ready to coordinate for and integrate IRCs that are only found at higher echelons, such as cyberspace operations.

# INFORMATION-RELATED CAPABILITIES

3-18. IO seeks to optimize the combined effects of selected IRCs through effective planning, synchronization, and assessment. While a single IRC can affect the information environment to friendly advantage, synchronized IRC activities and operations can amplify and unify each other's effects and produce more efficacious and durable results. For example, variation and repetition of actions and messages tends to increase their overall effect, if not their acceptance. Using different IRCs, in combination, to execute actions and deliver messages, provides this requisite variation.

3-19. IRCs are diverse. In some cases, they are part of the force structure, such as military information support operations (MISO) units, civil affairs units, or combat camera units. Coordination of these IRCs will be with the IRC unit commander, G-3 (S-3), or designed representative. In other cases, IRCs are tasks or activities managed by a staff section, such as military deception, OPSEC, or special technical operations. Coordination of these IRCs will occur with the staff element's director or a specified action officer.

3-20. All IRCs units work collaboratively with the IO officer, as well as with other IRCs, to facilitate their synchronization into the IO portion of the concept of operations, also called the scheme of IO. They do this primarily through the IO working group but utilize any venue or engagement to advance their capability's contribution to the total effort. Most importantly, they articulate their capability's strengths, limitations, and risks to the commander and staff to facilitate decision making about their employment and synchronization.

# INFORMATION OPERATIONS SUPPORT UNITS

3-21. The G-3 (S-3), with the assistance of the IO officer, and in concert with organic IRCs, serves as the entry point for external IRCs (excluding public affairs) and IO support units, assets and resources and ensures their integration into overall planning, preparation, execution, and assessment. Among the support organizations that the IO officer helps the G-3 (S-3) to integrate are the 1st Information Operations Command (Land) (1st IO Command) and the reserve component theater information operations groups, which provide a range of IO subject-matter expertise, skills augmentation, and reachback.

## 1ST INFORMATION OPERATIONS COMMAND (LAND)

3-22. The 1st IO Command, a major subordinate command of the U.S. Army Intelligence and Security Command, is a brigade-sized, multi-compo unit. Under the operational control and tasking authority of the U.S. Army Cyber Command, it provides uniquely tailored IO and cyberspace operations (CO) planning, synchronization, assessment, and reachback support to the Army and other military forces. Consisting of a Headquarters and Headquarters Detachment and two battalions, it augments military forces with tailored IO and cyberspace operations support provided through deployable teams, opposing forces support, reachback planning and analysis, and specialized training to assist units in garrison, during exercises, and during contingency operations.

3-23. 1st IO Command also supports the Army by working to optimize IO interoperability with joint forces, other military forces, inter-agencies, and allies. It provides expeditionary cyberspace operations support to help units identify network vulnerabilities and enable IO.

## Deployable Modular IO Teams

3-24. Deploys a variety of mission-tailored IO and cyberspace operations teams. The configuration of each deploying team varies to meet operational requirements.

### *Field Support Team*

3-25. Provides IO subject-matter expertise to supported commands to assist with the planning, execution and assessment of IO during crisis, contingency, and exercise operations. Field support team members are trained in the operational integration of military deception, electronic warfare, MISO, OPSEC, cyberspace operations, and other activities impacting the information environment.

### *Vulnerability Assessment Team*

3-26. Assists supported commands in identifying and resolving IO and cyberspace vulnerabilities in order to improve the command's defensive posture. The vulnerability assessment teams deploy to provide either: Train and Assist (Blue Team) or Emulation of an Adversarial Attack (Red Team) support. Both are capable of assessing the supported command's OPSEC, physical security, and electronic security training and policies to identify vulnerabilities. Both vulnerability assessment teams also assist the supported command in identifying IO and cyberspace vulnerabilities tied to issues associated with unit procedures, equipment, and other resources, and in finding means to resolve or mitigate identified issues. In addition, the vulnerability assessment teams augment the U.S. Army Forces Command mission command assessment teams in conducting pre-deployment home station cybersecurity training, as well as execute the Command Cyber Readiness Inspections for Army Cyber Command in coordination with the Defense Information Systems Agency.

### *OPSEC Support Team*

3-27. The OPSEC support team is part of the 1st IO Command organizational structure, and augments vulnerability assessment teams and executes independent OPSEC support team missions. OPSEC support teams provide supported commands with OPSEC training, assist with developing OPSEC programs, and assess unit OPSEC programs.

### *World Class Cyber Opposing Force*

3-28. Provides cyber and information warfare opposing force support to designated commands during operational training events, such as major exercises and combat training center rotations. This force serves as a non-cooperative, multiple tier (criminal, hybrid, nation state) cyberspace threat opponent that challenges, trains, and develops leaders to successfully operate within a hostile information environment. The World Class Cyber Opposing Force executes its opposing force mission as the exercise dictates, and will operate either as an independent force or as a member of a larger opposing force.

## Reachback and Training Support

3-29. Provides IO planning support, intelligence analysis, and technical assistance to deployed 1st IO Command support teams, and to other commands requesting reachback support. Reachback tailors its analytical and intelligence efforts and products to support the current and future operations of the supported commands. Lastly, the reachback provides technical support for the execution of vulnerability assessments and World Class Cyber Opposing Force missions.

3-30. The 1st IO Command conducts training instruction throughout the year on the planning, integration and execution of IRCs in both a resident (at Fort Belvoir) and mobile training team format. The 1st IO

Command deploys mobile training teams to requesting commands and installations to provide IO and cyberspace training. Deployed mobile training teams have the ability to tailor instruction to meet the specific requirements of the requesting command. A list of the 1st IO Command training courses can be found in the Army Training Requirements and Resources System.

## THEATER INFORMATION OPERATIONS GROUPS

3-31. The Army relies upon Theater Information Operations Groups to provide enhanced information operations planning, synchronization, and assessment support to Army echelons at theater and army service component command down to brigade level. There are two Theater IO Groups, the 56th and 71st Theater IO Groups, in the U.S. Army National Guard and two Theater IO Groups in the U.S. Army Reserve, the 151st and 152nd Theater IO Groups. Each Theater IO Group consists of a group headquarters, a headquarters and headquarters company, and two IO battalions which mirror each other in their capabilities.

3-32. The mission of the Theater IO Groups is to provide IO subject-matter expertise to a supported command in the form of deployable modular IO teams and a reach back, as well as home station support capability. The Theater IO Groups and its battalion elements do not usually deploy as commands but instead form and deploy purpose-built IO teams designed to provide the necessary IO support required by the requesting command. To enhance the capabilities of the IO teams and reduce preparation time, the Theater IO Groups maintain regional focuses. This focus helps provide the supported command additional regional expertise and capability to plan, synchronize, and assess IRC activities in the conduct of IO within the area of operations. Having a regional focus, however, does not preclude a Theater IO Groups from deploying IO teams and providing IO support to organizations and commands outside of its regional focus area.

### Deployable Modular IO Teams

3-33. The Theater IO Groups task organize and deploy mission-focused, modular IO teams created from the various capabilities resident within the Theater IO Groups. In the field, the modular IO teams provide the supported command with IO planning, synchronization, assessment, and analysis of the information environment. These teams have the capability to plan, synchronize, and assess OPSEC and military deception in the supported command. When dictated by mission requirements, the Theater IO Groups S-2 can attach intelligence specialists to a deployed modular IO team. If a modular IO team is not required, Theater IO Groups can deploy individual elements to meet requested mission support focused on planning, synchronization, and assessment of IRCs. In the creation of the modular IO teams, the Theater IO Groups draw upon the expertise resident in the following Theater IO Groups elements.

#### *Army Service Component Command Support Detachment*

3-34. Provides the regionally-aligned Army Service Component Command with a culturally-aware, regionally-focused IO planning, synchronization, and assessment capability that can synchronize and assess IO. This detachment provides the supported Army Service Component Command with the expertise to integrate IRCs in concert with other activities into theater security cooperation plans, war plans, and contingency planning. The detachment augments the supported unit's organic IO element or acts as the supported command's IO element. It also serves as the base Theater IO Group element for task organization with other Theater IO Groups capabilities to create a theater, Army Service Component Command-level modular team.

#### *Field Support Detachment*

3-35. Provides a culturally-aware, regionally-focused IO planning, synchronization, and assessment capability that can synchronize and assess IO. This detachment provides the supported command with the expertise to integrate IRCs in concert with other activities into operations plans, operations orders, and contingency planning. It can either augment the supported command's G-3 (S-3) IO element or serve as that element. It also serves as the base Theater IO Group element for task organization with other Theater IO Groups capabilities to create a Corps and below modular IO team.

### *Military Deception Support Detachment*

3-36. Equips the supported command with a regionally-aligned military deception-focused planning, coordination, implementation, and assessment capability. Military deception support detachments are trained to identify deception opportunities, deception conduits and means, and develop plans focused on exploiting those opportunities and means. As part of its support functions, the military deception support detachment develops and maintains social-cultural threat databases to include methods and means of communication (conduits) for input to the targeting process. It can either augment or act as the supported command's deception cell.

### *Assessment Detachments*

3-37. Provide multi-disciplined IO effects assessments. They assess the information environment and integrate IO-related collection and assessment into initial planning. They develop criteria in the form of measures of effectiveness and measures of performance and establish indicators for evaluation. Each indicator represents an IR that should identify a set of sources and staff members who collect the information in the assessment plan. Measures of performance and effectiveness are simply criteria—they require relevant information in the form of indicators for evaluation.

### *OPSEC Support Detachments*

3-38. OPSEC support detachments provide planning, synchronization, implementation, and assessment of OPSEC programs to identify friendly critical capabilities, critical vulnerabilities, and critical information in military plans, operations, and supporting activities and prevent exposure to enemy intelligence systems. They determine and advise supported commanders on indicators that threat intelligence systems might obtain that could be interpreted or pieced together to derive critical information in time to be useful to enemies. In concert with other IRCs, they nominate and employ OPSEC measures that eliminate or reduce to an acceptable level, the vulnerabilities of friendly actions to enemy exploitation.

### *Web OPSEC Support Detachment*

3-39. Administers planning, synchronization, implementation and assessment of web-based OPSEC programs to identify friendly critical capabilities, critical vulnerabilities and critical information in military plans, operations, and supporting activities and prevent exposure to enemy intelligence systems. Recommends and advises on OPSEC implications to cyberspace operations.

### *Reachback and Home Station Support*

3-40. The Theater IO Groups maintain an intelligence support capability designed to produce detailed IO-centric analysis of the operational environment and potential threats (infrastructure; key leaders; information systems; IRCs; composition; vulnerabilities; and friendly, neutral, and threat indigenous networks and their relation to each other) in support of deployed teams. The Theater IO Groups also maintain a habitual relationship with intelligence organizations to provide IO-centric support and products. Deployed teams coordinate with the Theater IO Group's S-2 and Intelligence Integration Element for information which is used in the development of courses of action, target analysis, and creation of a combined information overlay.

### *The Intelligence Integration Element and Other Support*

3-41. Contains intelligence specialists who provide multidiscipline intelligence analysis in support of individual Theater IO Groups elements and deployable modular IO teams. Trained on IO in order to provide tailored intelligence support, these specialists can support from home station, deploy to augment command's resident IO element, or as members of an IO team. When deployed, these specialists can serve as the focal point for coordination with other intelligence elements.

3-42. In addition to intelligence reachback support, the Theater IO Groups can also provide technical support from home station through the Army Service Component Command support detachments and the web OPSEC support detachment. The Army Service Component Command support detachments are capable of providing theater support planning from either home station or on site at the supported theater Army Service Component Command headquarters. The web OPSEC support detachment is capable of deploying as part of a modular IO team but more often it provides support from home station where it has assured access to the internet and web based mission command systems.

---

*Note*: Commanders can request Theater IO Group's IO team augmentation, reach back support, and home station support by submitting a Request for Forces through their chain of command to their respective Army Service Component Command, where the request for forces will be forwarded to U.S. Army Forces Command for approval. After approval by Forces Command, the request for forces is passed to the National Guard Bureau or the United States Army Reserve for servicing. The employment will consist of mission-tailored and scaled IO teams provided, as needed, to either a single or multiple commands and echelons, or the dedication of the entire IO group to support an Army Service Component Command. In the latter case, the IO group will provide IO support to the Army Service Component Command and its subordinate command structures down to brigade.

56th Theater IO Group: Assigned to the Washington Army National Guard with one battalion located in the Maryland Army National Guard. Regional focus areas are U.S. Pacific Command, U.S. Central Command, and U. S. Northern Command.

71st Theater IO Group: Assigned to the Texas Army National Guard. Regional focus areas are U.S. Southern Command, U.S. Northern Command and U.S. Africa Command.

151st Theater IO Group: Assigned to the U.S. Army Reserve. Regional focus areas are U.S. Africa Command, U.S. European Command, and U.S. Central Command.

152nd Theater IO Group: Assigned to the U.S. Army Reserve. Regional focus areas are U.S. Central Command, U.S. Pacific Command, and U.S. European Command. (To be inactivated FY 2017)

---

# INDIVIDUAL SOLDIERS AND ARMY CIVILIANS

3-43. IO seeks to influence adversaries or enemies, as well as foreign audiences to acquiesce to or support our demands or align their actions in concert with the friendly commander's intent and objectives. One of the most potent and readily-available IRCs to influence these audiences is Soldier and leader engagement. ***Soldier and leader engagements*** **are interpersonal Service-member interactions with audiences in an area of operations**. When Soldiers and leaders, inclusive of Army civilians and contractors, align their words, images, and actions in support of the commander's communications strategy, they contribute to mission accomplishment in a forceful and enduring way. Additional actions necessary to conduct Soldier and leader engagements include, but are not limited to:

- Knowing and understanding the commander's intent.
- Studying local culture, habits, and ways of communicating.
- Memorizing approved talking points.
- Being alert to non-verbal cues or signals on both sides of any conversation or engagement.
- Following through on commitments.

This page intentionally left blank.

# Chapter 4
# Planning

4-1. *Planning* is the art and science of understanding a situation, envisioning a desired future, and laying out effective ways of bringing that future about (ADP 5-0). Planning helps commanders create and communicate a common vision between commanders, their staffs, subordinate commanders, and unified action partners. Planning results in a plan and orders that synchronize the action of forces in time, space, and purpose to achieve objectives and accomplish missions.

4-2. Commanders, supported by their staffs, ensure IO is fully integrated into the plan, starting with Army design methodology (ADM) and progressing through the military decisionmaking process (MDMP). The focal point for IO planning is the IO officer (or designated representative for IO). However, the entire staff contributes to planning products that describe and depict how IO supports the commander's intent and concept of operations. The staff also contributes to IO planning during IO working group meetings to include assessing the effectiveness of IO and refining the plan.

## PLANNING OVERVIEW

4-3. Planning activities occupy a continuum ranging from conceptual to detailed. Conceptual planning involves understanding operational environments and problems, determining the operation's end state, and visualizing an operational approach to attain that end state. Detailed planning translates the commander's operational approach into a complete and practical plan. Generally, detailed planning is associated with the science of control including synchronizing forces in time, space, and purpose to accomplish missions.

4-4. ADM helps commanders and staffs with the conceptual aspects of planning. These aspects include understanding, visualizing, and describing operations to include framing the problem and identifying an operational approach to solve the problem. The MDMP helps commanders and staffs translate the commander's vision into an operations plan or operations order that synchronizes the actions of the force in time, space, and purpose to accomplish missions. Both the problem the commander needs to solve and the specific operation to advance towards its solution have significant information-related aspects.

### IO AND ARMY DESIGN METHODOLOGY

4-5. ADM is a methodology for applying critical and creative thinking to understand, visualize, and describe unfamiliar problems and approaches to solving them (ADP 5-0). By first framing an operational environment and associated problems, ADM enables commanders and staffs to think about the situation in depth. From this understanding, commanders and staffs develop a more informed approach to solve or manage identified problems. During operations, ADM supports organizational learning through reframing—a maturing of understanding that leads to a new perspective on problems or their resolution.

4-6. Problems typically facing Army forces and unified action partners, within a given area of operations, are human-centered. Human problems are driven by human decision making, which can be affected directly or indirectly through the use of IRCs, including effects produced by movement and maneuver. Therefore, the most essential part of ADM from an IO perspective is framing the current state of the information environment to determine key decision makers and the ways by which their decision process can be altered. This analysis identifies and creates understanding of decision makers' beliefs, motivations, grievances, biases, and preferred ways of communicating and obtaining information.

4-7. Framing the current state and desired future state of the information environment are key aspects of framing an operational environment and developing an operational approach. The operational approach provides a guide for more detailed IO planning, to include determining the effects necessary to bring about the desired end state in the information environment and the required combinations of IRCs needed to produce these effects.

4-8. Commanders typically employ a combination of direct and indirect approaches to defeating the enemy. A direct approach attacks the threat's center of gravity or principal strength by applying combat power against it. An indirect approach attacks the enemy's center of gravity by applying combat power against a series of decisive points that iteratively lead to the defeat of the center of gravity while avoiding the enemy's strengths. IO contributes to both approaches, especially when the threat's center of gravity or principal strength is information-related. (See ATP 5-0.1, *Army Design Methodology* for a comprehensive discussion of various techniques used in framing the operational environment, framing the problem, developing an operational approach, and reframing).

## IO AND THE MILITARY DECISIONMAKING PROCESS

4-9. Commanders use the MDMP to understand the situation and mission confronting them and make informed decisions resulting in an operations plan or order for execution. (See FM 6-0 for a detailed description of the MDMP.) Their personal interest and involvement is essential to ensuring that IO planning is integrated into MDMP from the beginning and effectively supports mission accomplishment. IO planning is integral to several other processes, to include intelligence preparation of the battlefield (IPB) and targeting. (See ATP 2-01.3 for further information on IPB and Chapter 7 of this manual and ATP 3-60 for further information on targeting.) The G-2 (S-2) and fire support representatives participate in the IO working group and coordinate with the IO officer to integrate IO with their activities and the overall operation. Commanders use their mission statement for the overall operation, the IO mission statement, scheme of IO, IO objectives, and IRC tasks to describe and direct IO, as seen in figure 4-1.

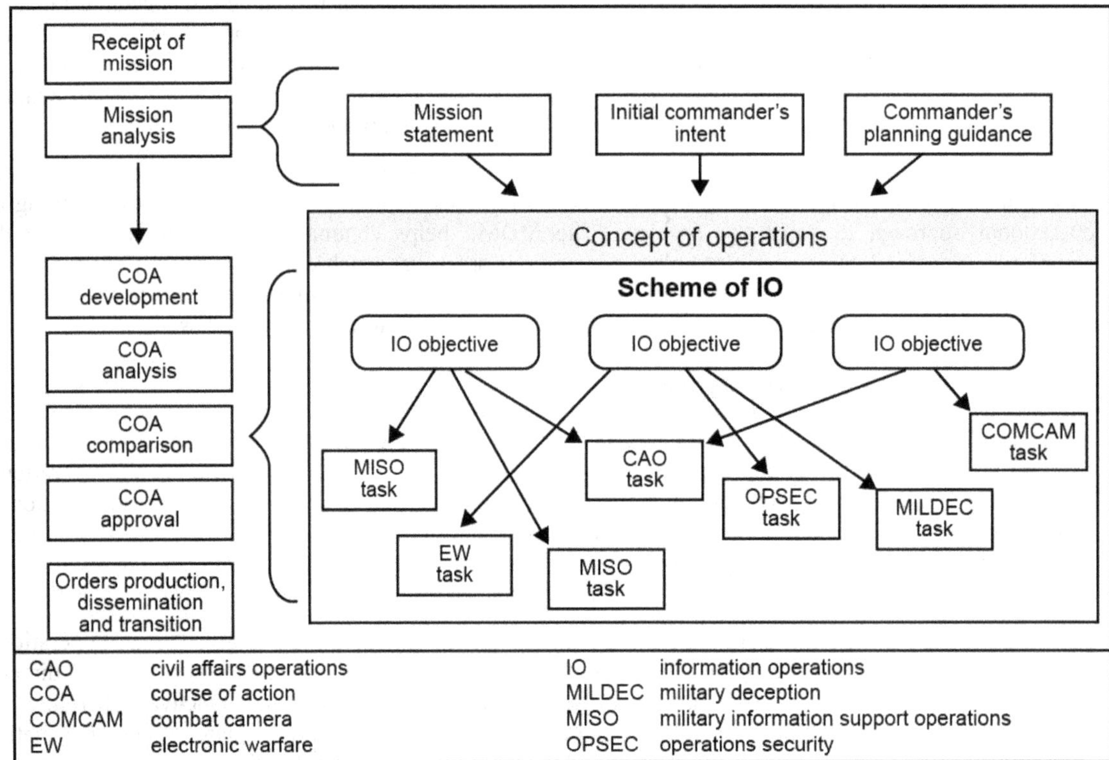


**Figure 4-1. Relationship among the scheme of IO, IO objectives, and IRC tasks.**

### Scheme of IO

4-10. The scheme of IO is a clear, concise statement of where, when, and how the commander intends to employ and synchronize IRCs, to create effects in and through the information environment to support overall operations and achieve the mission. Based on the commander's planning guidance, to include IO weighted efforts, the IO officer develops a separate scheme of IO for each course of action (COA) the staff develops. IO schemes of support are written in terms of IO objectives—and their associated weighted efforts—and IRC tasks required to achieve these objectives. For example, the overall scheme may be oriented primarily on defending friendly information but also include attack and stabilize objectives.

### IO Objectives

4-11. IO objectives express specific and obtainable outcomes or effects that commanders intend to achieve in and through the information environment. In addition to be being specific, these objectives are measurable, achievable, relevant, and time-bounded (or SMART), which facilitates their attainment and assessment (see chapter 8). IO objectives serve a function similar to that of terrain or force-oriented objectives in maneuver operations. They focus the IO effort on achieving synchronized IRC effects, at the right time and place, to accomplish the unit's mission and support the commanders' intent and concept of the operation.

4-12. Accurate situational understanding is key to establishing IO objectives. Operational- and tactical-level IO objectives must nest with strategic theater objectives. Joint and component staffs develop IO objectives to help integrate and synchronize their campaigns and major operations.

4-13. The IO officer develops objectives as part of developing the scheme of IO during COA development. These objectives help the staff determine tasks to subordinate units during COA development and analysis.

### Tasks

4-14. Tasks are developed to support accomplishment of one or more IO objectives. These tasks are developed specifically for a given IRC. In concert with IRC representatives, the IO officer develops tasks during COA development and finalizes them during COA analysis. During COA development and COA analysis, tasks are discussed in general terms but not assigned to a subordinate unit. During orders production, these tasks are assigned to IRC units.

### Flexibility and Lead Times

4-15. IO planning requires innovation and flexibility. Some IRCs, such as military information support operations (MISO), operations security (OPSEC), and military deception, require a long lead time for planning and preparation. Synchronizing IRCs into multiple lines of operation or effort requires extensive coordination. Achieving certain IO objectives may require senior-leader review and approval and more up-to-date intelligence. For some IRCs, there is a significant lag between execution and assessment of their effects. Planning requires a concentrated information collection effort during preparation and execution to obtain and analyze information for assessing effectiveness. These factors increase the challenges facing planners and decrease the time available to prepare. Nevertheless, early execution of select tasks can enhance efforts to shape the information environment in the area of operations.

## RECEIPT OF MISSION

4-16. Upon receipt of a mission, the commander and staff perform an initial assessment. Based on this assessment, the commander issues initial guidance and the staff prepares and issues a warning order (WARNORD). Between receiving the commander's initial guidance and issuing the WARNORD, the staff performs receipt of mission actions. During receipt of mission, the IO officer—

- Reviews and updates the running estimate.
- Participates in the initial assessment.
- Provides input to the commander's initial guidance.
- Provides input to the warning order.
- Prepares for subsequent planning.

## REVIEW AND UPDATE THE RUNNING ESTIMATE

4-17. Running estimates are integral to IO planning. A *running estimate* is the continuous assessment of the current situation, and is used to determine if the current operation is proceeding according to the commander's intent and if planned future operations are supportable (ADP 5-0). Running estimates help the IO officer record and track pertinent information about the information environment leading to a basis for recommendations to the commander.

4-18. The IO officer uses the running estimate to assist with completion of each step of the MDMP. An effective running estimate is as comprehensive as possible within the time available but also organized so that the information is easily communicated and processed. Normally, the running estimate provides enough information to draft the applicable IO sections of WARNORDs as required during planning and ultimately to draft applicable IO sections of the operation order (OPORD) or operation plan (OPLAN).

4-19. Variations on the standard, narrative format, such as the example provided in figure 4-2, enable the IO officer to spotlight facts and assumptions, critical planning factors, and available forces. The latter of these requires input from assigned or available IRCs. The graphical format also offers a clear, concise mechanism for the IO officer to articulate recommended high-payoff targets, commander's critical information requirements, and requests for forces. Maintaining both formats simultaneously provides certain benefits: the narrative format enables the IO officer to cut-and-paste sections directly into applicable sections of orders; the graphical format enables the element to brief the commander and staff with a single slide.

4-20. Running estimate development never stops. The IO officer continuously maintains and updates the running estimate as pertinent information is received. While at home station, the IO officer maintains a running estimate on friendly capabilities. If regionally aligned, the unit prepares its estimate based on research and analysis of the information environment within its region and anticipated mission sets.

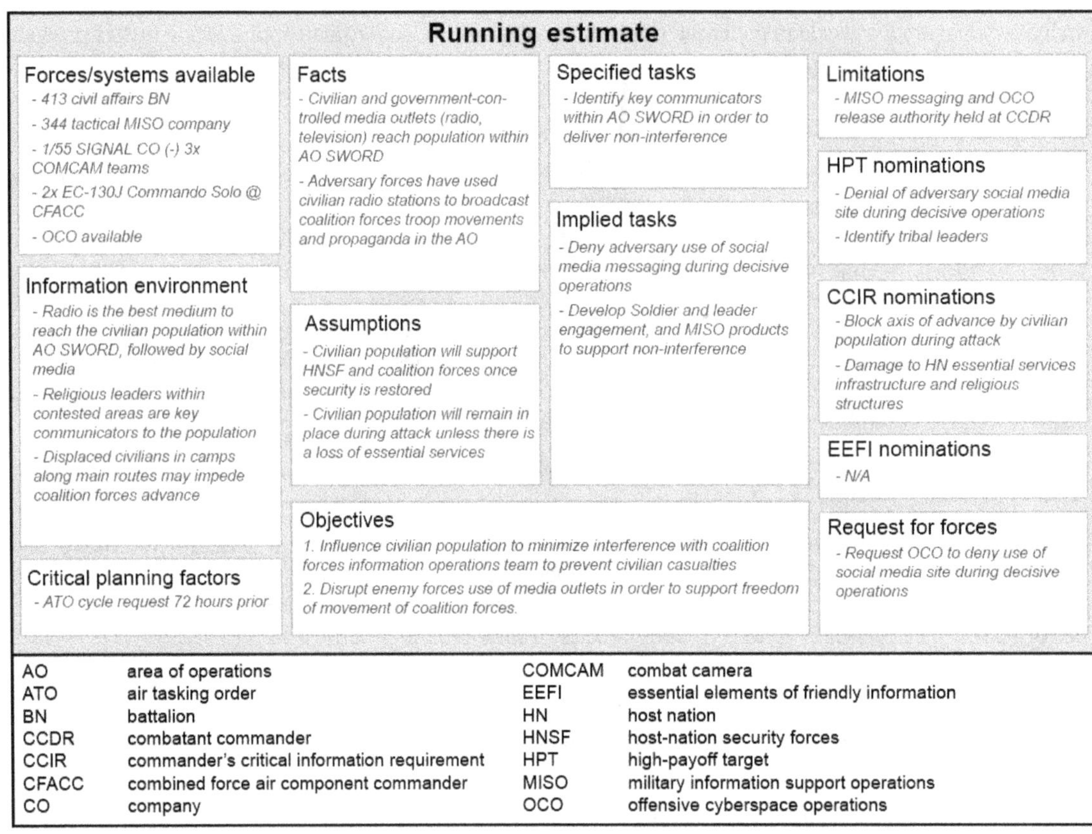


**Figure 4-2. Example graphical IO running estimate**

## Participate in Commander's Initial Assessment

4-21. Initial assessment primarily focuses on time and resources available to plan, prepare and begin execution of an operation. The IO officer assesses readiness to participate in ADM and MDMP, as well as what external support might be necessary to ensure effective IO planning.

4-22. During the initial assessment, the IO officer establishes a battle rhythm, including locations, times, preparation requirements, and the anticipated schedule. Upon receiving a new mission, the IO officer begins gathering planning tools, including a copy of the higher command OPLAN or OPORD, maps of the area of operations, appropriate references, and the running estimate. During initial assessment, the IO officer also coordinates with organic, assigned, and available IRCs and subordinate units to gauge their planning readiness.

4-23. Initial time allocation is important to IO because some operations and activities require significant time to produce effects or for assessment. The time available may be a limiting factor for some IRCs. The IO officer identifies activities for which this is the case and includes these limitations in estimates and recommendations.

4-24. The commander determines when to execute time-constrained MDMP. Under time-constrained conditions, the IO officer relies on existing tools and products, either his or her own or those of higher headquarters. The lack of time to conduct reconnaissance requires planners to rely more heavily on assumptions and increases the importance of routing combat information and intelligence to the people who need it. A current running estimate is essential to planning in time-constrained conditions.

## Provide Input to the Commander's Initial Guidance

4-25. Commanders include IO-specific guidance in their initial guidance, as required. Examples include authorized movements of IRCs, initiation of information collection necessary to support IO, and delineation of IRs.

## Provide Input to the Initial Warning Order

4-26. A WARNORD is issued after the commander and staff have completed their initial assessment and before mission analysis begins. It includes, at a minimum, the type and general location of the operation, initial timeline, and any movements or reconnaissance that need to be initiated. When they receive the initial WARNORD, subordinate units begin parallel planning.

4-27. Parallel planning and collaborative planning are routine MDMP techniques. The time needed to achieve and assess effects in the information environment makes it especially important to successful IO. Effective parallel or collaborative planning requires all echelons to share information fully as soon as it is available. Information sharing includes providing higher headquarters plans, orders, and guidance to subordinate IO officers or representatives.

4-28. Because some IRCs require a long time to plan or must begin execution early in an operation, follow-on WARNORDs may include detailed IO information. Although the MDMP includes three points at which commanders issue WARNORDs, the number of WARNORDs is not fixed. WARNORDs serve a purpose in planning similar to that of a fragmentary order (FRAGORD) during execution. Commanders issue both, as the situation requires. Possible IO officer input to the initial WARNORD includes:

- Tasks to subordinate units and IRCs for early initiation of approved IO actions, particularly for military deception operations and MISO.
- Essential elements of friendly information (EEFIs) to facilitate defend weighted efforts and begin the OPSEC process.
- Known hazards and risk guidance.
- Military deception guidance and priorities.

# MISSION ANALYSIS

4-29. Commanders and their staff conduct mission analysis to better understand the situation and problem, and to identify the purpose of the operation. It is the most important step in MDMP and consists of 18 sub-steps, many of which are performed concurrently. (See FM 6-0, Chapter 9) The IO officer ensures each output or product from this step includes relevant factors or tie-ins. The IO officer also participates in other staff processes (such as IPB and targeting) to ensure IO is properly integrated. For the IO officer, mission analysis focuses on developing information and products that will be used during the rest of the operations process.

## ANALYZE HIGHER HEADQUARTERS' PLAN OR ORDER

4-30. Mission analysis begins with a thorough examination of the higher headquarters OPLAN/OPORD in terms of the commander's initial guidance. By examining higher echelon plans, commanders and staffs learn how higher headquarters plan to conduct IO and which resources and higher headquarters assets are available. The IO officer researches these plans and orders to understand the—

- Higher commander's intent and concept of operations.
- Higher headquarters area of operations and interest, mission and task constraints, acceptable risk, and available assets.
- Higher headquarters schedule for conducting the operation.
- Missions of adjacent units.

4-31. Planning to conduct IO without considering these factors may result in an uncoordinated operation, which will hamper overall mission effectiveness. A thorough analysis also helps to determine if additional, external IO support is necessary.

## PERFORM INITIAL INTELLIGENCE PREPARATION OF THE BATTLEFIELD

4-32. During mission analysis, the G-2 (S-2) prepares IPB products or updates existing products and the initial IPB is performed upon receipt of the mission. The G-2 (S-2), with assistance and input from other staff elements, uses IPB to define the area of operations/interest, describe its effects, evaluate the threat, and determine threat courses of action. Figure 4-3, on page 4-8, lists possible IO-related factors to consider during each IPB step. During IPB, the IO officer works with the G-2 (S-2) to determine threat capabilities and vulnerabilities in the information environment regarding both the threat and other relevant targets and audiences in the area of operations.

### Define the Information Environment

4-33. The information environment has always affected military operations. IO officers, working with the G-2 (S-2), use available intelligence to analyze the information environment and the threat's use of information. This information is submitted to the G-2 (S-2) to answer intelligence gaps that address how information environment factors affect operations. The G-2 (S-2) obtains the information from strategic and national-level databases, country studies, collection assets and, when necessary, other intelligence agencies.

4-34. As part of defining the battlefield environment, the G-2 (S-2) establishes the limits of the area of interest. The area of interest includes areas outside the area of operations that are occupied by threat or other forces/groups that can affect mission accomplishment. This fact is particularly true from an information environment perspective. The ability to obtain and pass information has vastly expanded the capacity of actors to affect areas of operations from anywhere. The IO officer ensures that the G-2 (S-2) considers this factor of the information environment in defining the area of interest for IPB.

4-35. As stated in Chapter 2, one of the enabling activities of IO is analyzing and understanding the information environment in all its complexity. Using the IPB process to accomplish this task, the IO officer develops a series of information overlays, as well as combined information overlays, to depict the information aspects of the operational environment.

4-36. The IO officer provides input to help the G-2 (S-2) develop IPB templates, databases, social network diagrams, and other products that portray information about threats and other key groups or audiences in the areas of operation and interest. These products contain information about each group's leaders and decision makers. Information relevant to conducting IO includes, but is not limited to:

- Religion, language, culture, and internet activities of key groups and decision makers.
- Agendas of non-governmental organizations.
- Military and civilian communication infrastructures and connectivity.
- Population demographics, linkages, and related information.
- Location and types of radars, jammers, and other non-communication information systems.
- Audio, video, and print media outlets and centers; the populations they serve; and their dissemination characteristics, such as frequency, range, language, etc.
- Command and control or mission command vulnerabilities of friendly, adversary, and other forces or groups.
- Conduit analysis describing how threat decision makers receive information.

4-37. Threat templates portray how adversaries use forces and assets unopposed by friendly forces and capabilities. Threat templates are often developed before deployment. The G-2 (S-2) and IO officer may add factors from the information environment to a maneuver-based threat template, or they may prepare a separate IO threat template. The situation, available information, and type of threat affect the approach taken. IO-related portions of IPB products become part of paragraph 1b of the running estimate.

4-38. The G-2 (S-2) uses IPB to determine possible threat courses of action and arrange them in probable order of adoption. These courses of action, depicted as situation templates, include threat IRCs. A comprehensive IPB addresses threat offensive and defensive capabilities and vulnerabilities, and it is efficacious to friendly mission analysis to develop situation templates depicting how threats and others may employ these capabilities to achieve advantage.

### IPB Support of Targeting

4-39. IPB identifies high-value targets (HVTs) and shows where and when they may be anticipated. Some of these HVTs are IO-focused or related, such as a specific population group within an area of operation. The G-2 (S-2) works with the IO officer to develop IO-related HVTs into high-payoff targets (HPTs) for the commander's approval. The IO officer determines which HPTs are related to one or more objectives and develops tasks to engage those targets during COA development and analysis.

### Other IPB Products

4-40. IPB identifies facts and assumptions concerning threats and the operational environment that the IO officer considers during planning. These are incorporated into paragraph 2 of the running estimate. The IO officer submits IRs to update facts and verify assumptions. Working with the G-2 (S-2) and other staff sections, the IO officer ensures IRs are clearly identified and requests for information (RFIs) are submitted to the appropriate agency when necessary. IPB may create priority intelligence requirements (PIRs) pertinent to IO planning. The IO officer may nominate these as commander's critical information requirements (CCIRs) and also identify OPSEC vulnerabilities. The IO officer analyzes these to determine appropriate OPSEC measures.

| Define the Operational Environment | Describe the Environmental Effects on Operations | Evaluate the Threat | Determine Threat COAs |
|---|---|---|---|
| Portions or aspects of the information environment that can effect friendly operations.<br><br>Features/activities that can influence information and threat command and control (C2) or friendly mission command systems.<br><br>Political and governmental structures and population demographics.<br><br>Major cultures, languages, religions, and ethnic groups.<br><br>Civilian communication and power infrastructures (both physical and informational).<br><br>Non-state actors, non-governmental organizations and significant non-threat groups.<br><br>Types of and public access to media or press outlets. | IE effects on decisionmakers, C2 or mission command systems, and decision-making processes.<br><br>How the IE relates to the area of operations.<br><br>IE effects on friendly, threat, and other operations.<br><br>Combined effects of friendly, threat, and other information, and C2 or mission command systems on the information environment.<br><br>Effects of terrain, weather, and other characteristics of the area of operations on friendly and enemy information and C2 or mission command systems.<br><br>Effect of public media or press on friendly and threat operations. | Adversary and other group C2 systems, including functions, assets, capabilities, and vulnerabilities (both offensive and defensive).<br><br>Assets and functions (such as decisionmakers, C2 systems, and decision-making processes) that adversaries and others require to operate effectively.<br><br>Adversary capabilities to attack friendly information systems and defend their own.<br><br>Models of threat and other group C2 systems.<br><br>IO or information-related strength, vulnerabilities, and susceptibilities of adversaries and other groups. | How threats and other groups pursue operational or decisive advantage in the IE.<br><br>How, when, where, and why (to what purpose) threats and other groups will use information-related capabilities to achieve their likely objectives. |
| C2<br>command and control | COA<br>Course of Action | IE<br>Information environment | IO<br>Information operations |

**Figure 4-3. IO-related factors to consider during IPB**

## Determine Specified, Implied, and Essential Tasks

4-41. While the staff determines specified, implied, and essential tasks the unit must perform, the IO officer identifies specified IO tasks in the higher headquarters OPLAN or OPORD. The IO officer also develops IO-related implied tasks that support accomplishing identified specified tasks. These identified tasks are the basis of the initial scheme of IO developed during COA development.

IO officers look for specified tasks that may involve IO in the higher headquarters OPLAN or OPORD, paying particular attention to:

- Paragraph 1, Situation.
- Paragraph 2, Mission.
- Paragraph 3, Execution, especially subparagraphs on IO, tasks to subordinate units, and CCIRs.
- Annexes and appendices that address intelligence, operations, fire support, rules of engagement, IO, IRCs, information collection, assessment, and interagency coordination.

4-42. Some IO specified tasks, such as support to the higher headquarters deception plan, become unit objectives. Others, particularly those that address only one IRC, are incorporated under IO objectives as tasks. As the staff identifies specified tasks for the overall operation, the IO officer deduces the steps that are necessary to accomplish these specified tasks. These tasks become IO implied tasks. Once the IO officer identifies specified and implied tasks and understands each task's requirements and purpose, essential tasks are identified. An essential task is a specified or implied task that must be executed to accomplish the mission. If the command must accomplish an IO task to accomplish its mission, that task is an essential task for the command and is included in the recommended mission statement.

## Review Available Assets and Identify Resource Shortfalls

4-43. During this sub-step, the commander and staff determine if they have the assets required to perform the specified, implied, and essential tasks. The IO officer performs this analysis to determine if the requisite capabilities are on hand or available through coordination with higher echelons to achieve the effects in the information environment necessary to support the mission. At echelons below division, units have few organic IRCs other than movement and maneuver; Soldier and leader engagement; and presence, posture, and profile. If additional IRCs are required, the IO officer works with the operations officer to request these capabilities and ensure appropriate authorities exist. (See chapter 9 for further discussion of IO at brigade and below).

4-44. The IO officer compares available IRCs with the tasks that need to be accomplished to identify capability shortfalls and additional resources required. The IO officer considers how the following will affect attainment of IO objectives and whether additional capacity is required—

- Changes in task organization.
- Limitations of available units and IRCs.
- Nature of effects that need to be achieved in the information environment and the tasks to accomplish them.
- The need for redundancy or repetition to achieve desired effects.
- The level, quantity, and quality of expertise on hand.

## DETERMINE CONSTRAINTS

4-45. A constraint is a restriction placed on the command by a higher command. A constraint dictates an action or inaction, thus restricting the freedom of action of a subordinate commander (FM 6-0). IO constraints include legal, moral, social, operational, and political factors. They also include limitations imposed by various authorities, such as the Secretary of Defense or U.S. ambassador. Constraints may be listed in the following paragraphs, annexes or appendices of the higher OPLAN/OPORD—

- Commander's intent and guidance.
- Tasks to subordinate units.
- Rules of engagement (no strike list, restricted target list)
- Civil affairs operations.
- MISO
- Fire support.

4-46. Constraints establish limits within which the commander can conduct IO. Constraints may also limit the use of military deception and some OPSEC measures. One output of this sub-step is a list of the constraints that the IO officer believes will affect the scheme of IO.

## IDENTIFY CRITICAL FACTS AND DEVELOP ASSUMPTIONS

4-47. Sources of facts and assumptions include existing plans, initial guidance, observations, and reports. Some facts concerning friendly forces are determined during the review of the available assets. During IPB, the G-2 (S-2), with assistance from the IO officer and other staff elements, develops facts and assumptions about threats and others, the area of operations, and the information environment. The following categories of information are important to the IO officer—

- Intelligence on threat commanders and other key leaders.
- Threat morale.
- Media and/or press coverage of threat and other relevant audiences in the area of operations.
- The weather.
- Dispositions of adversary, friendly, and other key groups.
- Available troops, unit strengths, and materiel readiness.
- Friendly force IO vulnerabilities.
- Threat and other key group IO vulnerabilities.

4-48. The primary output of this sub-step is a list of facts and assumptions that concern IO. These are placed in paragraph 1c of the running estimate. The IO officer prepares and submits to appropriate agencies IO IRs for information that would confirm or disprove facts and assumptions. The IO officer reviews facts and assumptions as information is received and revises facts or converts assumptions into facts.

## Begin Risk Management

4-49. Commanders and staffs assess risk when they identify hazards, regardless of type. The IO officer assesses IO-associated risk throughout the operations process. The G-3 (S-3) incorporates the IO risk assessment into the command's overall risk assessment.

4-50. IO-related hazards fall into three categories:

- OPSEC vulnerabilities, including hazards associated with compromise of essential elements of friendly information.
- Mission command vulnerabilities, including those associated with the loss of critical assets or identified during the vulnerability assessment.
- Hazards associated with executing IO tasks.

4-51. During mission analysis, the IO officer assesses primarily OPSEC- and mission command-related hazards, as well as hazards associated with IO-related specified and implied tasks identified up to this point in mission analysis. The list of task-associated hazards is refined during COA development, after articulating IRC tasks that support IO objectives. The IO element uses experience in previous operations as a means of identifying known or expected hazards, and IRC representatives often best articulate hazards associated with their tasks.

4-52. As with all operations, IO entails risk. Resource constraints, combined with threat reactions and initiatives, reduce the degree and scope of advantage possible in the information environment. Risk assessment is one means commanders use to allocate resources. Staffs identify which hazards pose the greatest threat to mission accomplishment. They then determine the resources required to control them and estimate the benefits gained. This estimate of residual risk gives commanders a tool to help decide how to allocate resources and where to accept risk. (For detailed information on the integration of the risk management process, see ATP 5-19).

## Develop Commander's Critical Information Requirements and Essential Elements of Friendly Information

4-53. A *commander's critical information requirement* (CCIR) is an information requirement identified by the commander as being critical to facilitating timely decision making (JP 3-0). CCIRs include priority intelligence requirements (PIRs) and friendly forces information requirements (FFIRs). Staff sections, including the IO officer, recommend CCIRs to the G-3 (S-3). In a time-constrained environment, the staff may collectively compile this information. The G-3 (S-3) presents a consolidated list of CCIRs to the commander for approval. The commander determines the final CCIRs.

4-54. Establishing CCIRs is one means commanders use to focus assessment efforts. CCIRs change throughout the operations process because the information that affects decision making changes as an operation progresses.

4-55. During planning, staff sections establish IRs to obtain the information they need to develop the plan. Commanders produce CCIRs to support decisions they must make regarding the form the plan takes.

4-56. During preparation, the focus of IRs and CCIRs shifts to decisions required to refine the plan. During execution, commanders establish CCIRs that identify the information they need to make execution and adjustment decisions.

4-57. During mission analysis, the IO officer derives the information needed by the commander to determine how to employ IO during the upcoming operation. The IO officer recommends the IO IRs to be included in the CCIRs. This sub-step produces no IO-specific product unless the IO officer recommends one or more IO IRs as CCIRs. However, at this point, the IO officer should have assembled a list of IO IRs and submitted friendly-force-related IRs to the G-3 (S-3) and threat-related IRs to the G-2 (S-2).

4-58. The following is an example of CCIRs for a stability operation in which an information operation is the decisive operation:

- Who are the municipality's key players in ethnic violence?
- What are the interests of the political parties?

- Who are the formal and informal leaders within the political parties?
- How can friendly forces exploit political party interests to garner support?
- Which party represents the majority of the people, but also actively support progress within the municipality?
- What is the status of IRCs within the area of operations?

4-59. In addition to nominating CCIRs to the commander, the staff also identifies and nominates essential elements of friendly information, or EEFIs. EEFIs are elements of information to protect rather than to collect, and identify those elements of friendly force information that, if compromised, would jeopardize mission success. Although EEFIs are not CCIRs, they have the same priority as CCIRs and require approval by the commander. Like CCIRs, EEFIs change as an operation progresses (FM 6-0).

4-60. Submission of IO-focused requirements for potential inclusion as CCIRs, along with other CCIRs, enable the staff to develop the initial information collection plan. Approval of EEFIs enable the staff to plan and implement friendly force information protection measures, such as provided by military deception and OPSEC.

## Develop the Initial Information Collection Plan

4-61. The staff identifies information gaps, especially those needed to answer IRs. The IO officer identifies gaps in information needed to support IO planning, execution and assessment. These are submitted to the G-2 (S-2) as IO IRs. The initial information collection plan sets the priorities for information collection in order to answer CCIRs. The G-3 (S-3) issues the information collection plan as part of a WARNORD, a FRAGORD or an OPORD. Within these orders, the information collection plan is found in Annex L.

## Update Plan for the Use of Available Time

4-62. At this point, the G-3 (S-3) refines the initial time plan developed during receipt of mission. The IO officer provides input specifying the long lead-time items associated with certain IRC tasks (such as military deception and MISO). Upon receiving the revised timeline, the IO officer compares the time available to accomplish IRC tasks with the command's and threat's time lines, and revises the IO time allocation plan accordingly. The IO product for this sub-step is a revised time plan.

## Develop Initial Themes and Messages

4-63. Gaining and maintaining the trust of relevant audiences and actors is an important aspect of operations. Faced with a diverse array of individuals, organizations, and publics who affect or are affected by their unit's operations, commanders identify and engage entities vital to operational success. The behaviors of these entities can aid or complicate the friendly forces' challenges as commanders strive to accomplish missions.

4-64. The IO officer does not develop themes and messages. This is done by the public affairs officer and MISO element. The public affairs officer adjusts and refines themes and messages received from higher headquarters for use by the command. These themes and messages are designed to inform specific domestic and foreign audiences about current or planned military operations. The Office of the Secretary of Defense, Department of State, or geographic combatant commander (depending on the operation) provides applicable themes to MISO forces, which then develop actions and messages. The highest level MISO element in theater adjusts or refines the themes depending on the situation. It employs themes and messages as part of planned activities designed to influence specific foreign targets and audiences for various purposes that support current or planned operations.

4-65. The commander and the chief of staff approve all themes and messages used to support operations in their area of responsibility. Although the IO officer does not develop themes and messages, they do assist the G-3 (S-3) and the commander to de-conflict and synchronize IRCs used specifically to execute actions for psychological effect and deliver messages during operations.

## Develop a Proposed Problem Statement

4-66. Problem statements are typically developed during design. If this did not occur prior to mission analysis, it is accomplished during this step of the MDMP. If done during design, the commander and staff revise the problem statement based on their enhanced understanding of the situation. The key is identifying the right problem to solve, because it leads to the formulation of specific solution-sets. In identifying the problem, the commander and staff compare the current situation to the desired end state and list issues that impede the unit from achieving this end state.

4-67. Given the increasing impact of the information environment, the prevailing problem or impeding issues are likely to be information-related. Also, information-related problems can be more complex and multi-dimensional than geographical or technological problems or impediments. Therefore, it is essential to spend the time necessary to articulate the problem and impediments as carefully and clearly as possible.

## Develop a Proposed Mission Statement

4-68. The G-3 (S-3) or executive officer develops the proposed restated mission based on the force's essential tasks, which the commander approves or modifies. The IO officer provides input based on the current IO running estimate. The mission statement includes any identified IO essential tasks.

4-69. Mission statements should use tactical mission tasks, which are specific activities performed by units while executing a form of tactical operation or form of maneuver (See ATP 3-90.1). IO tasks do not always neatly fit into this framework, as they are rarely terrain- or combined arms-based. However, if they are framed in terms of friendly force actions (for example, influence the population in a certain area) or effects on threat forces (deceive the threat's reserve forces commander), and if they support the commander's intent and planning guidance, then they can be integrated effectively into the restated mission.

4-70. The IO officer also develops an IO mission statement that guides IO execution and ensures IO objectives are accomplished. The IO mission statement is explicitly stated in Appendix 15 (Information Operations) to Annex C (Operations) of the base order. (See FM 6-0, Appendix C, for additional details on functional area mission statements.)

## Present the Mission Analysis Briefing

4-71. The staff briefs the commander on the results of its mission analysis. The mission analysis briefing is an essential means for the commander, staff, subordinates and other partners to develop a shared understanding of the upcoming operation and the interrelationships among the mission variables and elements of combat power. IO input is based on its running estimate, analysis in the foregoing steps, and how IO impacts or is impacted by other areas and functions. Time permitting, the staff employs the outline provided in figure 4-4.

## Develop and Issue Initial Commander’s Intent

4-72. The *commander's intent* is a clear and concise expression of the purpose of the operation and the desired military end state that supports mission command, provides focus to the staff, and helps subordinate and supporting commanders act to achieve the commander's desired results without further orders, even when the operation does not unfold as planned (JP 3-0). The IO officer develops recommended input to the commander's intent and submits it to the G-3 (S-3) for the commander's consideration. When developing recommended input to the commander's intent, the IO officer assists the commander in visualizing and understanding the information environment, ways it will affect operations, and ways that IO can affect the information environment to the commander’s advantage.

## Develop and Issue Initial Planning Guidance

4-73. After approving the restated mission and issuing the intent, commanders provide additional guidance to focus staff planning activities. As appropriate, the commander includes their visualization of IO in this guidance. Commanders consider the following when developing their IO planning guidance:

- Aspects of higher headquarters IO policies or guidance that the commander wants to emphasize.

- Aspects of the mission for which IO is most likely to increase the chance of success or which may be IO-dominant.
- Risks they are willing to take with respect to IO.
- IO decisions for which they want to retain or delegate authority.

| Outline | Information Operations Input |
|---|---|
| Mission and commander's intent of headquarters two echelons up. | IO specified and implied tasks |
| Mission commander's intent, concept of operations of headquarters one echelon up. | IO specified and implied tasks |
| Proposed problem statement | Information-related problems within the IE. |
| Proposed mission statement | IO essential tasks |
| Review of commander's initial guidance | • Guidance concerning IO<br>• EEFI and CCIR<br>• Essential narrative elements |
| Initial IPB products | Information overlays |
| Specified, implied, and essential tasks | Specified, implied, and essential tasks for IO |
| Constraints | Any constraints placed on the command affecting IO |
| Initial risk assessment | • Recommended OPSEC planning guidance<br>• Recommended controls to protect information-related vulnerabilities and critical assets.<br>• Recommended controls for risk associated with IO tasks |
| Proposed themes and messages | Possible overlaps or conflicts among IRCs used to disseminate approved themes and messages. |
| Proposed timeline | • Time required to accomplish IO<br>• Analysis of time needed versus time available |

| CCIR | EEFI | IO | IPB |
|---|---|---|---|
| Commander's Critical Information Requirements | Essential element of friendly information | Information Operations | Intelligence preparation of the battlefield |

**Figure 4-4. Information operations input to mission analysis briefing**

4-74. Planning guidance focuses on the command's essential tasks. Commanders may give guidance for IO separately or as part of their overall guidance. This guidance includes any identified or contemplated IO objectives, stated in finite and measurable terms. It may also include OPSEC planning guidance, military deception guidance, and targeting guidance.

4-75. Factors that the IO officer considers when recommending input to initial planning guidance include:

- The extent that the command is vulnerable to hostile information-based warfare.
- Specific IO actions required for the operation.
- The command's capability to execute specific actions or weighted efforts.
- Additional information needed to conduct IO.

## DEVELOP COURSE OF ACTION EVALUATION CRITERIA

4-76. Course of action (COA) evaluation criteria are used during course of action analysis and comparison to measure the relative effectiveness and efficiency of COAs to another. They are developed during this sub-step to enhance objectivity and lessen the chances of bias. Typically, the chief of staff will develop the criterion and associated weight. The IO officer will propose possible refinement to ensure consideration of IO factors affecting success or failure and then employ approved criteria to score each COA.

## ISSUE WARNING ORDER

4-77. As the mission and operation dictate, the WARNORD will include essential IO tasks within the mission statement. It will note changes to task organization involving IRC or IO units and address IO factors in other relevant paragraphs, sections, or annexes, as appropriate.

4-78. Table 4-1 provides a summary of the inputs, actions and outputs required of the IO officer. Only those sub-steps within mission analysis with significant IO activity are listed.

**Table 4-1. Mission Analysis**

| *MDMP Sub-Step* | *Inputs* | *IO Officer Actions* | *IO Officer Outputs* |
|---|---|---|---|
| *Conduct IPB* | • Higher HQ IPB<br>• Higher HQ running estimates<br>• Higher HQ OPLAN or OPORD<br>• Higher HQ combined information overlay | • Develop IPB products<br>• Analyze and describe the information environment in the unit's area of operations and its effect on friendly, neutral, adversary, and enemy information efforts<br>• Identify threat information capabilities and vulnerabilities<br>• Identify gaps in current intelligence on threat information efforts<br>• Identify IO-related high-value targets<br>• Determine probable threat information-related COAs<br>• Assess the potential effects of IO on friendly, neutral, adversary, and enemy operations<br>• Determine threat's ability to collect on friendly critical information<br>• Determine additional EEFIs (OPSEC) | • Input to IPB products<br>• IRs to G-2 (S-2), as well as the foreign disclosure officer<br>• Refined EEFIs (OPSEC) |

**Table 4.1. Mission Analysis (continued)**

| *MDMP Sub-Step* | *Inputs* | *IO Officer Actions* | *IO Officer Outputs* |
|---|---|---|---|
| *Determine Specified, Implied, and Essential Tasks* | • Specified tasks from higher HQ OPLAN or OPORD<br>• IPB and combined information overlay products | • Identify specified tasks in the higher HQ OPLAN or OPORD<br>• Develop implied tasks<br>• Determine if there are any essential tasks<br>• Develop input to the command targeting guidance<br>• Assemble critical and defended asset lists, especially low density delivery systems<br>• Determine additional EEFIs (OPSEC) | • Specified, implied and essential tasks<br>• List of IRCs to G-3 (S-3)<br>• Input to command targeting guidance<br>• Refined EEFIs (OPSEC) |
| *Review Available Assets* | • Current task organization for information related capabilities<br>• Higher HQ task organization for information related capabilities<br>• Status reports<br>• Unit standard operating procedure | • Identify friendly IRCs (include capabilities that are joint, interorganizational, and multinational)<br>• Analyze IRC command and support relationships<br>• Determine if available IRCs can perform tasks necessary to support lines of operation or effort<br>• Identify additional resources (such as air assets) needed to execute or support IO | • List of available IRCs [IO running estimate paragraph 1b(4)]<br>• Request for additional IRCs, if required |
| *Determine Constraints* | • Commander's initial guidance<br>• Higher HQ OPLAN or OPORD | • Identify IO-related constraints | • List of constraints (IO appendix to Annex C; scheme of IO or coordinating instructions) |
| *Identify Critical Facts and Develop Assumptions* | • Higher HQ OPLAN or OPORD<br>• Commander's initial guidance<br>• Observations and reports | • Identify facts and assumptions affecting IRCs<br>• Submit IRs that will confirm or disprove assumptions<br>• Identify facts and assumptions regarding OPSEC indicators that identify vulnerabilities | • List of facts and assumptions (IO running estimate paragraph 1c.)<br>• IRs that will confirm or disprove facts and assumptions |

**Table 4.1. Mission Analysis (continued)**

| MDMP Sub-Step | Inputs | IO Officer Actions | IO Officer Outputs |
|---|---|---|---|
| Begin Risk Management | • Higher HQ OPLAN or OPORD<br>• IPB<br>• Commander's initial guidance | • Identify and assess hazards associated with IO<br>• Propose controls<br>• Identify OPSEC indicators<br>• Assess risk associated with OPSEC indicators to determine vulnerabilities<br>• Establish OPSEC measures | • List of assessed hazards<br>• Input to risk assessment<br>• Develop risk briefing matrix<br>• List of provisional OPSEC measures |
| Develop Initial CCIRs and EEFIs | • IO IRs | • Determine information the commander needs in order to make critical decisions concerning IO efforts<br>• Identify IRs to recommend as commander's critical information requirements | • Submit IRs |
| Determine Initial Information Collection Plan | • Initial IPB<br>• PIRs or IO IRs | • Identify gaps in information needed to support planning, execution, and assessment of early initiation actions<br>• Confirm that the initial information collection plan includes IRs concerning enemy capability to collect EEFIs | |
| Update Plan for the Use of Available Time | • Revised G-5 (S-5)/G-3 (S-3) plans timeline | • Determine time to accomplish IO planning requirements<br>• Assess viability of planning timeline vis-à-vis higher HQ timeline and threat timeline as determined during IPB<br>• Refine initial time allocation plan | • Timeline (provided to G-5 (S-5), with emphasis on the effect(s) of long-lead time events |
| Develop Initial Themes and Messages | • Public affairs themes and messages adjusted and refined from higher HQ<br>• MISO actions and messages adjusted and refined from higher HQ | • Assess impact of initial themes and messages on the information environment<br>• Assess whether planned IO effects will reinforce themes and messages<br>• Contribute to development of talking points aimed at influencing perceptions and behaviors | • PA themes/ messages and MISO actions/ messages de-conflicted<br>• Initial list of talking points<br>• IRC actions to disseminate approved messages/ talking points |

## Table 4.1. Mission Analysis (continued)

| *MDMP Sub-Step* | *Inputs* | *IO Officer Actions* | *IO Officer Outputs* |
|---|---|---|---|
| *Develop Proposed Problem Statement and Mission Statement* | • Initial IO mission<br>• Initial IO objectives<br>• Approved themes and messages | • List issues and determine primary obstacles that impede achieving the desired end state in the information environment<br>• Recommend possible initial objectives for inclusion in the restated mission | • Input to proposed problem statement<br>• Essential tasks<br>• Restated mission<br>• Revised or additional initial objectives recommended for inclusion in the restated mission<br>• Updated synchronization of themes and messages with actions |
| *Present Mission Analysis Briefing* | • IO running estimate.<br>• Unit standard operating procedure | • Prepare to brief IO portion of mission analysis | • IO portion of mission analysis briefing |
| *Develop and Issue Initial Commander's Intent* | • Higher HQ commander's intent<br>• Results of mission analysis<br>• IO running estimate | • Develop recommended input to the commander's intent and narrative | • Recommend input to the commander's intent and narrative |
| *Develop and Issue Initial Planning Guidance* | • Higher HQ OPLAN or OPORD<br>• Results of mission analysis<br>• IO running estimate | • Develop recommended input to the commander's guidance<br>• Combine the refined EEFIs with the provisional OPSEC measures to produce the planning guidance | • Recommended input to the commander's guidance<br>• Recommended OPSEC planning guidance<br>• Recommended military deception guidance, to include guidance on using deception in support of OPSEC, if appropriate<br>• Recommended IO targeting guidance |

**Table 4.1. Mission Analysis (continued)**

| *MDMP Sub-Step* | *Inputs* | *IO Officer Actions* | *IO Officer Outputs* |
|---|---|---|---|
| *Issue a Warning Order* | • Commander's intent and guidance<br>• Approved restated mission and initial objectives<br>• Mission analysis products | • Prepare input to the warning order. Input may include —<br>- Early tasking to subordinate units<br>- Initial mission statement<br>- OPSEC planning guidance<br>- Reconnaissance and surveillance tasking<br>• Military deception guidance | • Input to mission, commander's intent, commander's critical information requirements, and concept of the operations |

**COA** course of action
**EEFI** essential element of friendly information
**G-2** assistant chief of staff, intelligence
**G-3** assistant chief of staff, operations
**G-5** assistant chief of staff, plans
**HQ** headquarters
**IO** information operations
**IPB** intelligence preparation of the battlefield
**IR** information requirements
**IRC** information related capability
**MISO** military information support operations
**OPLAN** operations plan
**OPORD** operations order
**OPSEC** operations security
**PA** public affairs
**PIR** priority intelligence requirement
**S-2** battalion or brigade intelligence officer
**S-3** battalion or brigade operations staff officer
**S-5** battalion or brigade plans staff officer

# COURSE OF ACTION DEVELOPMENT

4-79. After the mission analysis briefing, the staff begins developing COAs for analysis and comparison based on the restated mission, commander's intent, and planning guidance. During COA development, the staff prepares feasible COAs that integrate the effects of all combat power elements to accomplish the mission. Based on the unit's approved mission statement, the IO officer develops a distinct scheme of IO, IO objectives, and IRC tasks for each COA.

4-80. The IO officer is involved early in COA development. The focus is on determining how to achieve decisive advantage in and through the information environment at the critical times and places of each COA. Depending on the time available, planning products may be written or verbal.

## ASSESS RELATIVE COMBAT POWER

4-81. IO synchronization of IRCs enhances the combat power, constructive and destructive, of friendly forces in numerous ways. Some examples include:

- Military deception influences application (or misapplication) of threat forces and capabilities at places and times that favor friendly operations.
- Countering the effects of propaganda degrades threat propaganda efforts by exposing lies and providing accurate information.
- MISO and civil military operations favorably influence foreign audiences by emphasizing the positive actions of U.S. forces.
- Movement and maneuver destroys or disrupts threat communicators, controls territory through which information flows, and influences affected populations.
- Electronic warfare jams threat communications and command and control signals.
- Fires destroys threat communication infrastructure.

4-82. The IO officer ensures that the staff considers IO when analyzing relative combat power. IO can be especially valuable in reducing resource expenditures by other combat power elements. For example, commanders can use electronic warfare to jam a communications node instead of using fires to destroy it.

4-83. IO contributions are often difficult to factor into numerical force ratios. With IO officer support, staff planners consider the effects of IO on the intangible factors of military operations as they assess relative combat power. Intangible factors include such things as the uncertainty of war and the will of friendly forces and the threat. Varied approaches and methods may be used to achieve IO effects. One method is to increase the relative combat power assigned to forces who effectively employ organic IRCs. For example, strict OPSEC discipline by friendly forces increases the difficulty the threat has in collecting information. Units with a Theater IO Group OPSEC support detachment may further increase their relative combat power as a result of this augmentation.

## Generate Options

4-84. Options are expressed as COAs. Given the increasing impact of the information environment on operations and the threat's use of information-focused warfare to gain advantage, staffs recognize that, in certain COAs, IO may be the main effort.

4-85. The IO officer assists the staff in considering the ways that IO can support each COA. This requires the IO officer to determine which IRCs to employ and the trade-offs associated with each. In brainstorming options, the IO officer thinks first in an unconstrained manner, then refines available options based on the running estimate and knowledge of available assets and those that are anticipated. During this sub-step, the IO officer also develops input to military deception COAs, if applicable. The main output of this effort is an initial scheme of IO by phase for each COA.

## Array Forces

4-86. The staff arrays forces to determine the forces necessary to accomplish the mission and to develop a knowledge base for making decisions concerning concepts of operations. The IO officer ensures planners consider the impact of available IRCs on force ratios as they determine the initial placements. IRCs may reduce the number of maneuver forces required or may increase the COA options available. Planners consider the deception story during this step because aspects of it may affect unit positioning.

4-87. Although the staff considered IRC availability when developing COAs, this step allows them to further validate if the required capabilities are present and, if not, determine if they can be obtained and positioned in time to achieve required effects. It also enables the IO officer to determine if available IRCs are properly positioned and task-organized.

## Develop a Broad Concept

4-88. The broad concept concisely expresses the "how" of the commander's visualization and will eventually provide the framework for the concept of operations and summarizes the contributions of all warfighting functions (FM 6-0). The IO officer develops schemes of IO and IO objectives for each COA that nest with the broad concept. With input from IRC representatives, the IO officer considers how IRCs can achieve the IO objectives.

4-89. IO schemes of support are further expressed in terms of the weighted efforts required to support the overall concept of operations. Depending on proportion of offense, defense, and stability tasks, the IO officer determines the best mix of attack, defend, and stability IO efforts needed to ensure achievement of objectives. The IO officer then determines which IRCs to allocate to each effort and possible tasking conflicts.

4-90. During this sub-step, the IO officer develops control measures, critical and defended asset lists, and additional EEFIs for each COA, as well as determines OPSEC vulnerabilities and measures. Most importantly, the IO officer produces five essential, often time-intensive, outputs. These are—

- COA worksheets.
- Synchronization matrix.
- Target nominations.

- Risk assessment.
- Measures of performance and effectiveness.

## COA Worksheets

4-91. The IO officer employs COA worksheets to prepare for COA analysis and focus IRC efforts. These worksheets can be narrative or graphical or a combination of both. The IO officer prepares one worksheet for each IO objective in each scheme of IO. IO worksheets include the following information, as a minimum:

- A description of the COA.
- The scheme of IO in statement form.
- The IO objective in statement form.
- Information concerning IRC tasks that support the objective, listed by IRC.
- Anticipated adversary counteractions for each IRC task.
- Measures of performance and effectiveness for each IRC task.
- Information required to assess each IRC task.

4-92. The COA worksheet needs to show how each IRC contributes to the IO objective and the scheme of IO for that COA. When completed, the work sheets help the IO officer tie together the staff products developed to support each COA. IO planners also use the worksheets to focus task development for all IRCs. They retain completed work sheets for use during subsequent steps of the MDMP.

## Synchronization Matrix

4-93. The IO officer develops an IO synchronization matrix for each COA to determine when to execute IRC tasks. IO synchronization matrices show estimates of the time it takes for friendly forces to execute an IRC task; the adversary to observe, process and analyze the effect(s) of the executed task; and the adversary to act on those effect(s). The IO officer synchronizes IRC tasks with other combined arms tasks. The G-2 (S-2) and G-3 (S-3) time lines are used to reverse-plan and determine when to initiate IRC tasks. Due to the lead time required, some IRC tasks must be executed early in an operation. Regardless of when the IRC tasks start, they are still synchronized with other combined arms tasks. Many IRC tasks are executed throughout an operation; some are both first to begin and last to end. IO synchronization matrices vary in format, depending on commander preference and unit standard operating procedures. At a minimum, the synchronization matrix should include—

- IO objectives.
- IRC tasks.
- The operational timeline to execute the IRC tasks.
- The depiction of how IRC synchronization integrates with lines of operations or lines of effort.

## Target Nominations

4-94. The IO officer uses information derived during mission analysis, IPB products, and the high-value target list to nominate high-pay-off targets (HPTs) for each friendly COA. HPTs are selected to be added to the high-payoff target list. HPTs are developed in conjunction with the IRC tasks employed to affect them. Targets attacked by nonlethal means, such as jamming or MISO broadcasts, may require assessment by means other than those normally used in battle damage assessment. The IO officer submits IRs for this information to the G-2 (S-2) when nominating them. If these targets are approved, the IRs needed to assess the effects on them become PIRs that the G-2 (S-2) adds to the information collection plan. If the command does not have the assets or resources to answer the IO IRs, the target is not engaged unless the attack guidance specifies otherwise or the commander so directs. The targeting team performs this synchronization.

## Risk Assessment

4-95. The assessment of IO-associated risk during COA development and COA analysis focuses primarily on hazards related to executing the scheme of IO and its associated IRC tasks. However, the IO officer assesses all hazards as they emerge. The IO officer also monitors identified hazards and evaluates the effectiveness of controls established to counter them.

4-96. The IO officer examines each COA and its scheme of IO to determine if they contain hazards not identified during mission analysis. The IO officer then develops controls to manage these hazards, determines residual risk, and prepares to test the controls during COA analysis. The IO officer coordinates controls with other staff sections as necessary. Controls that require IRC tasks to implement are added to the IO COA worksheet for the COA.

4-97. The IO officer considers two types of hazards associated with the scheme of IO: those associated with the scheme of IO itself and its supporting IRC tasks; and those from other aspects of the concept of operations that may affect execution of IO. The IO officer identifies as many of these hazards as possible so the commander can consider them in decisions.

4-98. Some hazards result from the need to focus IO efforts. These hazards require commanders to take prudent risks. Some examples include:

- As part of a military deception operation, the commander limits camouflage, concealment, and deception measures applied to elements they want the adversary to detect. The commander accepts the risk of the threat targeting these elements.
- The commander concentrates cybersecurity efforts on a few critical mission command nodes, accepting the risk that other nodes may be degraded.
- The commander elects to destroy an adversary communications node that is also a valuable intelligence source. The commander accepts the risk of operating without that intelligence.

4-99. Hazards also result from unintended actions by the threat and other forces/groups in response to friendly IO. In addition, unintended consequences of other tactical activities can affect IO. Examples include:

- An electronic attack may disrupt friendly as well as threat communications.
- In a stability operation, efforts to influence a mayor to support U.S. forces instead of simply not opposing them may boost the popularity of an anti-U.S. rival, risking loss of long-term local political support.

4-100. Thorough planning can reduce, but will never eliminate, unintended consequences. The IO officer identifies possible unintended consequences that cause effects within the information environment and focuses on those most likely to affect mission accomplishment.

4-101. The IO officer considers the effects of IO-related hazards on the local populace and infrastructure as well as on friendly forces. The IO officer assesses these hazards, develops controls, determines residual risks, and advises the commander on risk mitigation measures. These unintended consequences could be caused by an IRC or by other activity that causes effects in the IE.

4-102. The commander alone accepts or rejects risk. The IO officer advises the commander concerning risk associated with IO-related hazards and recommends controls to mitigate this risk. The commander decides what risk to accept. An example of using IO for accident risk mitigation is the synchronized use of civil military operations and MISO, in coordination with public affairs, to warn the local populace of the accident hazards associated with military operations. When risks are attributable to IRC tasks, the IO officer assigns risk mitigation measures to the responsible unit and places them in the IO appendix's coordinating instructions.

4-103. The IO officer produces a list of IO-related hazards and assessments of the associated risks. This list becomes the IO input to the G-3 (S-3) risk assessment matrix. (For detailed information on assessing risk levels, see ATP 5-19.)

## Measures of Performance and Effectiveness

4-104. Measures of performance and measures of effectiveness drive information requirements necessary to measure the degree to which operations accomplish the unit's mission. As COA development continues, the IO officer considers how to assess IO effectiveness, by determining:

- IRC tasks that require assessment.
- Measures of performance for IRC tasks and measures of effectiveness for IO objectives, as well as baselines to measure the degree of change, and associated IO-related targets.
- The information needed to make the assessment.

- How to collect the information.
- Who or what will collect the information.
- How the commander will use the information to support decisions.

4-105. The responses to these considerations are recorded on the IO COA worksheets and added to the IO portion of the operations assessment plan. Information required to assess IO effects becomes IRs. The IO officer submits IRs for the COA that the commander approves to the G-2 (S-2). The IO officer establishes measures of performance and effectiveness based on how IRC tasks contribute to achieving one or more IO objectives. If a task's results are not measurable, the IO officer eliminates the task.

### ASSIGN HEADQUARTERS

4-106. Headquarters are typically assigned based on their ability to integrate the warfighting functions. Their capacity to plan, prepare, execute, and assess IO varies, depending on such variables as organic capabilities, mission essential tasks, and training. When commanders determines that the decisive operation or a shaping operation is IO-dominant, they turn to the IO officer to assess potential mission command vulnerabilities and ways to mitigate them. Higher headquarters, in particular, conduct this assessment for subordinate headquarters being assigned IO-dominant missions and provides additional assets, as required.

### DEVELOP COURSE OF ACTION STATEMENTS AND SKETCHES

4-107. The G-3 (S-3) prepares a COA statement and supporting sketch for each COA for the overall operation. Together, the statement and sketch cover who, what, when, where, how, and why for each subordinate unit. They also state any significant risks for the force as a whole. The IO officer provides IO input to each COA statement and sketch. At a minimum, each COA statement and sketch should include its associated scheme of IO. COA statements may also identify select IO objectives and IRC tasks when they address specific commander concerns or priorities.

### CONDUCT COURSE OF ACTION BRIEFING

4-108. Given the increasing impact of the information environment on operations, commanders benefit from ensuring the IO officer is present during all MDMP briefings. For this specific briefing, the IO officer is able to provide essential rationale for the scheme of IO and respond to IO-related questions from the commander or G-3 (S-3).

### SELECT OR MODIFY COURSE OF ACTION FOR CONTINUED ANALYSIS

4-109. Whether the commander selects a given COA or COAs, modifies COAs, or creates a new COA altogether, the IO officer prepares for COA analysis and war-gaming. If the commander rejects all COAs, the IO officer develops new schemes of support, mindful of the commander's revised planning guidance.

4-110. Table 4-2 provides a summary of the inputs, actions and outputs required of the IO officer/element. Only those sub-steps within COA development with significant IO activity are listed.

**Table 4-2. Course of action development**

| *MDMP Sub-Step* | *Inputs* | *IO Officer Actions* | *IO Officer Outputs* |
|---|---|---|---|
| *Assess Relative Combat Power* | • IPB or combined information overlay<br>• Task organization<br>• IO running estimate<br>• Vulnerability assessment | **For each COA —**<br>• Analyze IRC effects on friendly and threat capabilities, vulnerabilities, and combat power | **For each COA —**<br>• Description of the potential effects of relative combat power stated by IRC |

| *MDMP Sub-Step* | *Inputs* | *IO Officer Actions* | *IO Officer Outputs* |
|---|---|---|---|
| *Generate Options* | • Commander's intent and guidance<br>• IPB or combined information overlay<br>• Friendly, neutral, and enemy information related capabilities, resources, and vulnerabilities | • Determine different ways for IO to support each COA<br>• Determine IRCs to employ.<br>• Determine how to focus IRCs on the overall objective<br>• Determine IO's role in the decisive and shaping operations for each COA<br>• Determine possible tradeoffs among IRCs<br>• Develop input to military deception COAs (deception stories) | • Scheme of IO for each COA<br>• Input to military deception COAs |
| *Array Forces* | • Restated mission<br>• Commander's intent and guidance<br>• IPB or combined information overlay<br>• Input to military deception plan or concept | • Allocate IRCs for each scheme<br>• Identify requirements for additional IRCs<br>• Examine effect of possible military deception COAs on force positioning<br>• Identify military deception means | • Initial IRC location and task organization<br>• Additional IRC requirements |

**Table 4-2. Course of action development (continued)**

| *MDMP Sub-Step* | *Inputs* | *IO Officer Actions* | *IO Officer Outputs* |
|---|---|---|---|
| *Develop a Broad Concept* | • COAs<br>• IPB or combined information overlay<br>• High value target list<br>• IO mission statement<br>• Initial scheme of IO for each COA | **For each COA —**<br>• Develop scheme of IO<br>• Develop objectives<br>• Develop control measures<br>• Identify and prioritize IRC tasks<br>• Nominate selected HPTs<br>• Determine initial IO task execution timeline<br>• Refine input to risk assessment<br>• Develop IO portion of assessment plan<br>• Identify additional EEFIs<br>• Identify and assess OPSEC indicators to determine vulnerabilities<br>• Develop OPSEC measures to shield vulnerabilities<br>• Determine residual risk associated with each vulnerability after OPSEC measures are applied<br>• Determine feedback required for assessment of military deception COAs | **For each COA —**<br>• Refined scheme, objectives, and control measures; IRC tasks; and tasks to subordinate units<br>• IO COA worksheets<br>• Synchronization matrices<br>• Execution time line<br>• IO-related high-payoff target nominations<br>• Critical and defended asset lists<br>• Input to risk management plan, including residual risk associated with each OPSEC vulnerability<br>• Success criteria to support assessment<br>• Additional EEFIs<br>• OPSEC vulnerabilities<br>• OPSEC measures to shield vulnerabilities |
| *Assign Headquarters* | • IPB/combined information overlay<br>• IO running estimate<br>• IO vulnerability assessment<br>• IO tasks by IRC and subordinate unit | **For each COA —**<br>• Assess mission command strengths and weaknesses to determine vulnerabilities of specific headquarters regarding ability to execute IO<br>• Assess mission command strengths and weaknesses to determine vulnerabilities of subordinate commands<br>• Reevaluate critical and defended asset lists | **For each COA —**<br>• Recommendations for allocation of G-3 (S-3) IO personnel to headquarters in light of mission command vulnerability assessment<br>• Recommendations of grouping of IRCs to subordinate commands in light of mission command vulnerability assessment<br>• Updated critical and defended asset lists<br>• Initial list of IRCs to tasks assigned |

**Table 4-2. Course of action development (continued)**

| *MDMP Sub-Step* | *Inputs* | *IO Officer Actions* | *IO Officer Outputs* |
|---|---|---|---|
| *Develop COA Statements and Sketches* | • COA statement<br>• A scheme of IO and objectives for each COA | • Submit input for each COA statement and sketch to G-3 (S-3)<br>• Prepare scheme statement and sketch for each COA | • Input for each COA statement and sketch<br>• Scheme of IO and sketches for each COA, stating the most important objectives |
| **COA** course of action<br>**EEFI** essential element of friendly information<br>**HPT** high-payoff target | **IO** information operations<br>**IPB** intelligence preparation of the battlefield<br>**IRC** information-related capability | **IPB** intelligence preparation of the battlefield<br>**OPSEC** operations security | |

# COURSE OF ACTION ANALYSIS AND WAR-GAMING

4-111. COA analysis (war-gaming) enables commanders and staffs to identify difficulties or coordination problems as well as probable consequences of planned actions for each COA being considered. It helps them think through the tentative plan. War-gaming is a disciplined process that staffs use to envision the flow of battle. Its purpose is to stimulate ideas and provide insights that might not otherwise be discovered. Effective war-gaming allows the staff to test each COA, identify its strengths and weaknesses, and alter it if necessary. During war-gaming, new hazards may be identified, the risk associated with them assessed, and controls established. OPSEC measures and other risk control measures are also evaluated.

4-112. War-gaming helps the IO officer synchronize IRC operations and helps the staff integrate IO into the overall operation. During the war game, the IO officer addresses how each IRC contributes to the scheme of IO for that COA and its associated time lines, critical events, and decision points. The IO officer revises the schemes of IO as needed during war-gaming.

4-113. The IO officer uses the synchronization matrices and worksheets for each COA as scripts for the war game. The IRCs are synchronized with each other and with the concepts of operations for the different COAs. To the extent possible, the IO officer also includes planned counter-actions to anticipated threat reactions.

4-114. During preparation for war-gaming, the IO officer gives the G-2 (S-2) likely threat information-related actions and reactions to friendly IO, to include possible threat responses in the information environment to friendly operations. The IO officer also continues to provide input to the G-2 (S-2) for HPT development and selection.

4-115. Before beginning the war game, staff planners develop criteria to evaluate the effectiveness and efficiency of each COA during COA comparison. These criteria are listed in paragraph 3c of the IO running estimate and become the outline for the COA analysis in paragraph 4. The IO officer develops the criteria for evaluating the schemes of IO. Using IO-specific criteria allows the IO officer to explain the advantages and disadvantages of each COA. Evaluation criteria that may help discriminate among various COAs could include:

- Lead time required for implementation.
- The number of decision points that require support.
- The cost of achieving an IO objective versus the expected benefits.
- The risk to friendly assets posed by threat information activities.

4-116. During war-gaming the IO officer participates in the action-reaction-counteraction process. For example, the action may be patrols designed to enforce curfew; the threat reaction is messaging accusing U.S. forces of causing damage and casualties; the counteraction is assigning combat camera to document U.S. force patrols and interactions with the indigenous population and incorporating the documentation with another IRC in order to provide appropriate content to the target audience. The IO officer uses the synchronization matrices and COA worksheets to insert IRC tasks into the war game at the time planned. A complete COA worksheet allows the IO officer to state the organization performing the task and its location. The IO officer remains flexible throughout the process and is prepared to modify input to the war game as it develops. The IO officer is also prepared to modify the scheme of IO, IO objectives, and IRC tasks to mitigate possible threat actions discovered during the war game. The IO officer notes any branches and sequels identified during the war game. Concepts of support for these branches or sequels are developed as time permits.

4-117. The results of COA analysis are a refined scheme of IO and associated products for each COA. During war-gaming, the IO officer refines IRs, EEFIs, and HPTs for each COA, synchronizing them with that COA's concept of operations. Staff planners normally record war-gaming results, including IRC effects, on the G-3 (S-3) synchronization matrix. The IO officer may also record the results on the COA worksheets. These help the IO officer subsequently synchronize IRCs. The worksheets and synchronization matrices provide the basis for IO input to paragraph 3 of the OPLAN/OPORD, paragraph 3 of the IO and IRC appendices.

4-118. Table 4-3 on page 4-27 provides a summary of the inputs, actions and outputs required of the IO officer during course of action analysis.

# COURSE OF ACTION COMPARISON

4-119. During COA comparison, the staff compares feasible COAs to identify the one with the highest probability of success against the most likely adversary COA and the most dangerous adversary COA. Each staff section evaluates the advantages and disadvantages of each COA from the staff section's perspective, and presents its findings to the staff. The staff outlines each COA in terms of the evaluation criteria established before the war game and identifies the advantages and disadvantages of each with respect to the others. The IO officer records this analysis in paragraph 4 of the IO estimate.

4-120. The IO officer determines the COA that IO can best support based on the evaluation criteria established during war-game preparation. The results of this comparison become paragraph 5 of the IO estimate.

4-121. Table 4-4 on page 4-28 provides a summary of the inputs, actions and outputs required of the IO officer during course of action comparison. Table 4-3. Course of action analysis (war game)

**Table 4-3. Course of action analysis (war game)**

| *MDMP Step* | *Inputs* | *IO Officer Actions* | *IO Officer Outputs* |
|---|---|---|---|
| *Course of Action Analysis* | • Updated running estimate.<br>• IPB/combined information overlay<br>• Updated assumptions<br><br>**For each COA —**<br><br>• Scheme of IO and objectives for each COA sketch<br>• Execution timeline | • Develop evaluation criteria for each COA<br>• Gather the tools<br>• List all friendly IRCs<br>• List assumptions<br>• Synchronize tasks performed by different IRCs and subordinate commands<br>• Coordinate IO with cyber electromagnetic activities<br>• Integrate scheme of IO into the concept of operations for each COA<br>• Synchronize scheme of IO with higher and adjacent headquarters<br>• Identify enemy information warfare capabilities and likely actions and reactions<br>• War game friendly IRCs against enemy vulnerabilities and display the results<br>• War game friendly IRC impacts on various audiences and populations and display the results<br>• War game enemy information warfare capabilities against friendly vulnerabilities and display the results<br>• Synchronize and de-conflict targets<br>• Determine whether modifications to the COA result in additional EEFIs or OPSEC vulnerabilities; if so recommend OPSEC measures to shield them<br>• Assign attack measures to HPTs.<br>• Test OPSEC measures<br>• Determine decision points for executing tasks<br>• War game each military deception COA<br>• Identify each military deception COA's potential branches; assess risk to the COA<br>• List the most dangerous or beneficial branch on the decision support template or synchronization matrix<br>• Participate in the war game briefing (optional) | • Potential decision points<br>• Initial assessment measures<br>• Updated assumptions<br>• An evaluation of each military deception COA in terms of criteria established before the war game<br><br>**For each COA —**<br><br>• An evaluation in terms of criteria established before the war game<br>• Recorded input to war game results<br>• Refined scheme of IO<br>• Refined tasks<br>• Refined input to attack guidance matrix and target support matrix<br>• IRs and requests for information identified during war game<br>• Refined EEFIs and OPSEC vulnerabilities and OPSEC measures<br>• Paragraph 4 of the running estimate<br>• Input to the G-3 (S-3) synchronization matrix<br>• Input to the HPTL |

**COA** course of action
**EEFIs** essential elements of friendly information
**HPT** high-payoff target
**HPTL** high-payoff target list
**IO** information operations
**IPB** intelligence preparation of the battlefield
**IR** information requirement
**IRC** information-related capability
**OPSEC** operations security
**MDMP** military decisionmaking process

**Table 4-4. COA comparison**

| *MDMP Task* | *Inputs* | *IO Officer Actions* | *IO Officer Outputs* |
|---|---|---|---|
| *Course of Action Comparison* | • Updated IO running estimate<br>• Refined COAs<br>• COA evaluation criteria<br>• COA evaluations from COA analysis<br>• Updated assumptions | • Compare the COAs with each other to determine the advantages and disadvantages of each<br>• Determine which COA is most supportable from an IO perspective<br>• Determine if any OPSEC measures require the commander's approval | • Advantages and disadvantages for each COA<br>• Most supportable COA from an IO perspective<br>• Input to COA decision matrix<br>• Updated assumptions<br>• Paragraph 4, IO running estimate |
| **COA** course of action | **IO** information operations | **MDMP** military decisionmaking process | **OPSEC** operations security |

# COURSE OF ACTION APPROVAL

4-122. After completing the COA comparison, the staff identifies its preferred COA and recommends it to the commander in a COA decision briefing, if time permits. The concept of operations for the approved COA becomes the concept of operations for the operation itself. The scheme of IO for the approved COA becomes the scheme of IO for the operation. Once a COA is approved, the commander refines the commander's intent and issues additional planning guidance. The G-3 (S-3) then issues a WARNORD and begins orders production.

4-123. The WARNORD issued after COA approval contains information that executing units require to complete planning and preparation. Possible IO input to this WARNORD includes:

- Contributions to the commander's intent/concept of operations.
- Changes to the CCIRs.
- Additional or modified risk guidance.
- Time-sensitive reconnaissance tasks.
- IRC tasks requiring early initiation.
- A summary of the scheme of IO and IO objectives.

4-124. During the COA decision briefing, the IO officer is prepared to present the associated scheme of IO for each COA and comment on the COA from an IO perspective. If the IO officer perceives the need for additions or changes to the commander's intent or guidance with respect to IO, they ask for it.

4-125. Table 4-5 on page 4-29 provides a summary of the inputs, actions and outputs required of the IO officer during course of action approval.

# ORDERS PRODUCTION, DISSEMINATION, AND TRANSITION

4-126. Based on the commander's decision and final guidance, the staff refines the approved COA and completes and issues the OPLAN/OPORD. Time permitting, the staff begins planning branches and sequels. The IO officer ensures input is placed in the appropriate paragraphs of the base order and its annexes, especially the IO appendix to the operations annex. When necessary, the IO officer or appropriate special staff officers prepare appendixes for one or more IRCs [(See Appendix A for an annotated format of appendix 15 (Information Operations) to Annex C (Operations)].

4-127. Table 4-6 provides a summary of the inputs, actions and outputs required of the IO officer during course of action approval.

**Table 4-5. Course of action approval**

| *MDMP Step* | *Inputs* | *IO Officer Actions* | *IO Officer Outputs* |
|---|---|---|---|
| *Course of Action Approval* | • Updated IO running estimate<br>• Evaluated COAs<br>• Recommended COAs<br>• Updated assumptions | • Provide input to COA recommendation<br>• Re-evaluate input to the commander's intent and guidance<br>• Refine scheme of IO, objectives, and tasks for approved COA and update synchronization matrix<br>• Prepare input to the WARNORD<br>• Participate in the COA decision briefing<br>• Recommend the COA that IO can best support<br>• Request decision on executing any OPSEC measures that entail significant resource expenditure or high risk | • Finalized scheme of IO for approved COA<br>• Finalized tasks based on approved COA<br>• Input to WARNORD<br>• Updated synchronization matrix |
| **COA** course of action **IO** information operations **MDMP** military decisionmaking process **WARNORD** warning order | | | |

**Table 4-6. Orders production, dissemination and transition**

| *MDMP Task* | *Inputs* | *IO Officer Actions* | *IO Officer Outputs* |
|---|---|---|---|
| *Orders Production, Dissemination and Transition* | • Approved COA<br>• Refined commander's guidance<br>• Refined commander's intent<br>• IO running estimate<br>• Execution matrix<br>• Finalized mission statement, scheme of IO, objectives, and tasks | • Ensure input is placed in tasks to subordinate units and coordinating instructions<br>• Produce Appendix 14 (MILDEC) to Annex C (Operations)<br>• Produce Appendix 15 (IO) to Annex C (Operations)<br>• Produce Appendix 3 (OPSEC) to Annex E (Protection)<br>• Coordinate tasks with IRC staff officers<br>• Conduct other staff coordination.<br>• Refine execution matrix<br>• Transition from planning to operations | • Synchronization matrix<br>• Approved Paragraph 3.k. (10)<br>• Approved Appendix 14 to Annex C<br>• Approved Appendix 15 to Annex C<br>• Approved Appendix 3 to Annex E<br>• IO input to AGM and TSM<br>• Subordinates understand the IO portion of the plan or order |
| **AGM** attack guidance matrix **COA** course of action **IO** information operations **IRC** information-related capability **MDMP** military decisionmaking process **MILDEC** military deception **OPSEC** operations security **TSM** trunk signaling mission | | | |

This page intentionally left blank.

# Chapter 5
# Preparation

5-1. Preparation consists of those activities performed by units and Soldiers to improve their ability to execute an operation (ADP 5-0). Preparation creates conditions that improve friendly force opportunities for success. Because many IO objectives and IRC tasks require long lead times to create desired effects, preparation for IO often starts earlier than for other types of operations. Initial preparation for specific IRCs and IO units (such as 1st IO Command or a Theater IO Group) may begin during peacetime.

5-2. Peacetime preparation by units or capabilities involves building contingency plan databases about the anticipated area of operations. These databases can be used for IO input to IPB and to plan IO to defend friendly intentions, such as network protection and operations security (OPSEC). IO portions of contingency plans are continuously updated. Normal IO working group participants maintain their own data to provide the IO officer with the latest information.

5-3. During peacetime, IO officers prepare for future operations by analyzing anticipated area(s) of operations' information environment and likely threat information capabilities. Examples of factors to consider include, but are not limited to—

- Religious, ethnic, and cultural mores, norms, and values.
- Non-military communications infrastructure and architecture.
- Military communication and command and control infrastructure and architecture.
- Military training and level of proficiency (to determine susceptibility to denial, deception, and IO).
- Literacy rate.
- Formal and informal organizations exerting influence and leaders within these organizations.
- Ethnic factional relationships and languages.

5-4. Preparation includes assessing unit readiness to execute IO. Commanders and staffs monitor preparations and evaluate them against criteria established during planning to determine variances. This assessment forecasts the effects these factors have on readiness to execute the overall operation as well as individual IRC tasks.

5-5. Preparation for IO takes place at three levels: staff (IO officer), IRC units or elements, and individual. The IO officer helps prepare for IO by performing staff tasks and monitoring preparations by IRC units or elements. These units perform preparation activities as a group for tasks that involve the entire unit, and as individuals for tasks that each soldier and leader must complete.

5-6. Chapter 3 of ADRP 5-0 provides a comprehensive overview of preparation activities. The activities most relevant to conducting IO include—

- Improve situational understanding.
- Revise and refine plans and orders.
- Conduct coordination and liaison.
- Initiate information collection.
- Initiate security operations.
- Initiate troop movements.
- Initiate network preparation.
- Manage and prepare terrain.
- Conduct confirmation briefs.
- Conduct rehearsals.

## IMPROVE SITUATIONAL UNDERSTANDING

5-7. The IO officer/element must understand and share their understanding of the information environment with the commander and staff. During preparation, information collection begins, which helps to validate assumptions and improve situational understanding. Coordination, liaison, and rehearsals further enhance this understanding. Given the information environment's complexity, this task is never-ending and depends on everyone, not just the IO officer, to update and refine understanding of the information environment.

## REVISE AND REFINE PLANS AND ORDERS

5-8. Plans are not static; the commander adjusts them based on new information. This information may be the result of analysis of unit preparations, answers to IO IRs, and updates of threat information capacity and capability.

5-9. During preparation, the IO officer adjusts the relevant portions of the operation plan (OPLAN) or operation order (OPORD) to reflect the commander's decisions. The IO officer also updates the IO running estimate so that it contains the most current information about adversary information activities, changes in the weather or terrain, and friendly IRCs.

5-10. The IO officer ensures that IO input to IPB remains relevant throughout planning and preparation. To do this, they ensure that IO input to the information collection plan is adjusted to support refinements and revisions made to the OPLAN/OPORD.

5-11. IO preparation begins during planning. As the IO appendix begins to take shape, IO officer coordination with other staff elements is vital because IO affects every other warfighting function. For example, planning an attack on a command and control (C2) high-payoff target requires coordination with the targeting team. A comprehensive attack offering a high probability of success may involve air interdiction and therefore needs to be placed on the air tasking order. It may involve deep attack: rocket and missile fires have to be scheduled in the fire support plan. Army jammers and collectors have to fly the missions when and where needed. The IO officer ensures the different portions of the OPLAN/OPORD contain the necessary coordinating instructions for these actions to occur at the right time and place.

5-12. Effective IO is consistent at all echelons. The IO officer reviews subordinate unit OPLANs/OPORDs to ensure IO has been effectively addressed and detect inconsistencies. The IO officer also looks for possible conflicts between the command's OPLAN/OPORD and those of subordinates. When appropriate, the IO officer reviews adjacent unit OPLANs/OPORDs for possible conflicts. This review allows the IO officer to identify opportunities to mass IO effects across units.

5-13. OPLAN/OPORD refinement includes developing branches and sequels. Branches and sequels are normally identified during war-gaming (COA analysis). However, the staff may determine the need for them at any time. The G-3 (S-3) prioritizes branches and sequels. The staff develops them as time permits. The IO officer participates in their development as with any other aspect of planning.

5-14. A key focus during preparation is on assessment of the current state of the information environment. This assessment is performed to establish baselines, which are subsequently used when assessing whether IO objectives and IRC tasks were effective in creating desired effects.

## CONDUCT COORDINATION AND LIAISON

5-15. IO requires all units and elements to coordinate with each other continuously, as well as liaise. Coordination begins during planning; however, input to a plan alone does not constitute coordination. Coordination involves exchanging the information needed to synchronize operations. The majority of coordination takes place during preparation. It is then that the IO officer follows through on the coordination initiated during planning. Exchanging information is critical to successful coordination and execution. Coordination may be internal or external and is enhanced through liaison.

## Internal Coordination

5-16. Internal coordination occurs within the unit headquarters. The IO officer initiates the explicit and implicit coordinating activities with other staff sections, as well as within the IO element, if one exists. Much of this coordination occurs during IO working group meetings; however, IO working group members do not wait for a meeting to coordinate. They remain aware of actions that may affect, or be affected by, their functional responsibilities. They initiate coordination as soon as they become aware of a situation that requires it. The IO officer remains fully informed of IO-related coordination. The IO officer corrects or resolves problems of external coordination revealed by command and staff visits and information gathering. During internal coordination, the IO officer resolves problems and conflicts and ensures that resources allocated to support IO arrive and are distributed. Examples of internal coordination include, but are not limited to:

- Deconflicting military information support operations (MISO) with public affairs activities and products.
- Monitoring the progress of answers to IO RFIs.
- Monitoring RFIs to higher headquarters by the G-3 (S-3) current operations.
- Checking the air tasking order for missions requested by the IO officer/element.
- Monitoring the movements and readiness of IRCs.
- Determining space asset status and space weather implications.
- Participating in the integration of IO-related targets into the targeting process.
- Continuous monitoring and validation of OPSEC procedures, particularly in preparation for military deception. This could include a short statement on physical security, particularly during movement.

5-17. The IO officer remains mindful that training is conducted during planning and preparation. This training occurs as new soldiers and IRCs are integrated into the command and its battle rhythm. Additionally, the IO officer provides training to subordinate elements, as requested, to fill gaps in their IO capacity.

5-18. Internal coordination is especially important to ensure requisite staff support to various IRCs in order to enhance their readiness and effectiveness. Examples include but are not limited to—

- Electronic warfare (EW).
  - G-2 (S-2)—Coordinates intelligence gathering in support of the EW mission. Recommend the use of EW against adversary systems that use the electromagnetic spectrum.
  - G-3 (S-3)—Coordinates and prioritizes EW targets.
  - G-4 (S-4)—Coordinates distribution of EW equipment and supplies, less cryptographic support.
  - IO officer—Coordinates EW tasks with those of other IRCs and assists with preparation of the cyberspace electromagnetic activities appendix.
  - EW officer—Monitors the preparation of military intelligence units to support EW missions; prepare cyber effects request forms and electronic attack request forms; monitors other staff functions that support or affect EW.
- MISO.
  - G-2 (S-2)—Prepares intelligence estimate and analysis of the area of operation.
  - G-3 (S-3)—Requests additional MISO units as required.
  - IO officer—Identifies requirements for additional MISO units to the G-3 (S-3).
  - G-4 (S-4)—Prepares logistic support of MISO.
  - Psychological Operations (PSYOP) officer—Prepares the MISO appendix to Annex C. Prepares the MISO estimate.
- OPSEC.
  - G-2(S-2)—Provides data on threat intelligence collection capabilities.
  - IO officer—Determines the EEFIs.
  - G-4 (S-4)—Advises on the vulnerabilities of supply, transport, and maintenance facilities, and lines of communications.

  - G-5 (S-5)—Determines availability of civilian resources for use as guard forces.
  - OPSEC officer—Prepares the OPSEC estimate and appendix.
  - Provost marshal—Advises on physical security measures.
- Military deception.
  - G-2 (S-2)—Determines adversary surveillance capabilities.
  - G-3 (S-3)—Coordinates movement of units participating in military deception.
  - G-4 (S-4)—Coordinates logistic support to carry out assigned deception tasks.
  - G-9 (S-9)—Coordinates host-nation support to implement the military deception plan.
  - Military deception officer—Prepares to monitor execution of military deception operation.

### EXTERNAL COORDINATION

5-19. External coordination includes coordinating with or among subordinate units and higher headquarters, as well as IO support units, IRCs, and resources that may not be under the unit's control during planning but are necessary to execute the plan. External coordination also includes coordinating with adjacent units or agencies. (Adjacent refers to any organization that can affect a unit's operations in and through the information environment.) This coordination is necessary to integrate IO throughout the force. Examples of external coordination include:

- Assessing unit OPSEC posture.
- Making sure the military deception operation is tracking with preparation for the overall operation.
- Periodically validating assumptions.
- Ensuring military deception operations are synchronized with those of higher, lower, and adjacent units.

5-20. The IO officer remains aware of the effectiveness of cybersecurity tasks taken by the G-6 (S-6). Proper protection of plans and orders, and refinements to them, are essential during operations.

5-21. Coordination with joint, interorganizational, and multinational partners is essential to the conduct of IO, as these entities and organizations affect the information environment and are affected by it. The IO working group is the primary means for this coordination but direct, face-to-face coordination is frequently necessary to ensure unity of effort.

### LIAISON

5-22. Establishing and maintaining liaison is one of the most important means of external coordination. The IO officer may perform direct liaison but units may select another staff member to be part of the liaison team. Establishing liaison during planning enhances subsequent coordination during preparation and execution.

5-23. Practical liaison can be achieved through personal contact between IO officers or between the IO officer and agencies/organizations involved in affecting the information environment. This coordination is accomplished through exchanging personnel, through agreement on mutual support between adjacent units or organizations, or by a combination of these means. Liaison should, when possible, be reciprocal between higher, lower, and adjacent units/organizations. Liaison must be reciprocal between IO sections when U.S. forces are operating with or adjacent to multinational partners.

5-24. Liaison also has a force protection mission. Where host-nation security forces retain some operational capability, liaison is vital to coordinate actions. They provide intelligence and other related information about conditions in-theater.

## INITIATE INFORMATION COLLECTION

5-25. Execution requires accurate, up-to-date situational awareness. During preparation, the IO officer updates IRs to ensure the most current information possible. The IO officer also works with the G-2 (S-2) to update collection asset taskings necessary to assess IO.

## INITIATE SECURITY OPERATIONS

5-26. Security operations serve to protect the force from surprise and threat attacks during preparation. While often considered in terms of specific missions that physically screen, guard, cover, or provide area or local security, security operations should also include IRC tasks that provide these same protections in the informational and cognitive dimensions of the information environment. Military deception, OSPEC, space operations, and cyberspace operations all support security operations. Not including these IRC effects into plans potentially puts the force at risk.

## INITIATE TROOP MOVEMENTS

5-27. During preparation, IRCs are positioned or repositioned, as necessary, to ensure they can fulfill their assigned tasks. IO unit augmentation and integration also occurs during preparation.

## INITIATE NETWORK PREPARATION

5-28. IO supports the commander's ability to optimize the information element of combat power. In terms of establishing and readying the network, units must think in terms of both technical and human networks. Technical networks have to be set up, engineered, tailored, and tested to meet the specific needs of each operation. Similarly, human networks have to be initiated, cultivated, and refined during preparation. The IO officer coordinates the establishment of networks that help shape the information environment favorable to friendly objectives. The goal of establishing each category of network is to ensure the availability, reliability, accuracy, and speed of information to facilitate shared understanding and decision making.

## MANAGE AND PREPARE TERRAIN

5-29. *Terrain management* is the process of allocating terrain by establishing areas of operation, designating assembly areas, and specifying locations for units and activities to deconflict activities that might interfere with each other (ADRP 5-0). While terrain is physical and geographic, it is a subset of the operational and information environments. When commanders designate areas of operation, they are simultaneously assigning responsibility to specific portions of the information environment. One of the most important reasons for managing physical terrain is to avoid fratricide. The same rationale exists for the information environment: to avoid information fratricide. For example, the IO officer can ensure control measures are established to deconflict EW activities with MISO efforts to inform the local populace through radio broadcasts.

5-30. Analysis of the information environment during IPB leads to an understanding of aspects of the information environment in which friendly forces have an advantage and in which they are disadvantaged. During preparation, the IO officer, in concert with the IO working group and its members, undertake actions to exploit the advantages and overcome the disadvantages. For example, if cellular phone communication is essential to strengthen coordination between U.S. forces and an indigenous ally and cell towers are non-existent or degraded, mobile towers could be deployed.

## CONDUCT CONFIRMATION BRIEFINGS

5-31. A confirmation brief is a briefing subordinate leaders give to the higher commander immediately after the operation order is given. It is the leaders' understanding of the commander's intent, their specific tasks, and the relationship between their mission and the other units in the operation. The IO officer assists subordinate commanders and their IO representatives with these briefings when the commander's intent and specific tasks are IO-focused or have aspects related to IO. They also assist subordinate commanders to deduce IO implied tasks and to understand the information environment in their area of operations.

## CONDUCT REHEARSALS

5-32. The IO officer participates in unit rehearsals to ensure IO is integrated with overall operation and to identify potential problems during execution. The IO officer may conduct further rehearsals of tasks and actions to ensure coordination and effective synchronization of IRCs. Before participating in a rehearsal, the IO officer reviews the plans or orders of subordinate and supporting commands.

# Chapter 6
# Execution

6-1. Execution of IO includes IRCs executing the synchronization plan and the commander and staff monitoring and assessing their activities relative to the plan and adjusting these efforts, as necessary. The primary mechanism for monitoring and assessing IRC activities is the IO working group. There are two variations of the IO working group. The first monitors and assesses ongoing planned operations and convenes on a routine, recurring basis. The second monitors and assesses unplanned or crisis situations and convenes on an as-needed basis.

## INFORMATION OPERATIONS WORKING GROUP

6-2. The IO working group is the primary means by which the commander, staff and other relevant participants ensure the execution of IO. The IO working group is a collaborative staff meeting led by the IO officer, and periodically chaired by the G-3 (S-3), executive officer, chief of staff or the commander. It is a critical planning event integrated into the unit's battle rhythm. Figure 6-1 on page 6-2 provides a possible template for the conduct of the IO working group that can be applied at the tactical through strategic levels. Core and other participants are not static; they will fluctuate by level and by mission/situation.

### PURPOSE

6-3. The IO working group is the primary mechanism for ensuring effects in and through the information environment are planned and synchronized to support the commander's intent and concept of operations. This means that the staff must assess the current status of operations relative to the end state and determine where efforts are working well and where they are not. More specifically, they must ensure targets are identified and nominated at the right place and time to achieve decisive results. The IO working group occurs regularly in the unit's battle rhythm and always before the next targeting working group. The only exception is a crisis IO working group (also referred to as consequence management or crisis action working group), which occurs as soon as feasible before or after an event or incident that will significantly alter the information environment and give the threat operational advantage unless handled quickly and adeptly.

### INPUTS/OUTPUTS

6-4. The example in figure 6-1 is not exhaustive. In terms of inputs, it identifies those documents, products, and tools that historically and practically have provided the IO working group the information necessary to achieve consensus and make informed recommendations to the G-3 (S-3) and commander. The outputs listed are those considered essential to ensuring the staff can effectively conduct IO.

6-5. One tool that the IO working group uses to affirm and adjust the synchronized employment of IRCs is the IO synchronization matrix. An updated synchronization matrix is the working group's key output and essential input to the next targeting meeting.

### AGENDA

6-6. Like other aspects of the IO working group, the proposed agenda is flexible to the needs of the commander and the staff/participants. Figure 6-1 breaks the meeting down by weighted effort, recognizing that some members of the working group may not need to participate in all parts and that classification levels may adjust depending on the capabilities or assets under consideration and discussion. For example, the public affairs officer/representative will likely be present for Parts 1, 2 and possibly 3, but not for Part 4. Another possible agenda format is by time horizon and yet another by phase of the operation.

| Purpose | Agenda |
|---|---|
| Prioritize, request, and synchronize information-related capabilities and IO augmentation to optimize effects in and through the IE.<br><br>**Battle Rhythm:**<br>• Before targeting work group | **Part 1:** Operations and Intelligence Update<br>• Intelligence update<br>• Information environment update<br>• Operations update or significant activities<br>• Review plans, future operations, and current operations<br>• Assessment update (information requirements, indicators)<br>• Calendar update, due outs, and responsibilities from previous meeting<br><br>**Part 2:** Stabilize<br>**Part 3:** Protect and defend<br>**Part 4:** Attack<br>(Parts 2–4:) • Review and update synch matrix • Guidance and comments |

| Inputs/Outputs | | Structure/Participants |
|---|---|---|
| **Inputs:**<br>• Higher headquarters orders and guidance<br>• Commander's intent, concept of operations and narrative<br>• Information-related capabilities status (running estimates)<br>• Intelligence collection assets<br>• Combined information overlays, intelligence preparation of the battlefield<br>• Media monitoring analysis<br>• Cultural calendar<br>• Engagements schedule<br>• Audience analysis<br>• Scheme of IO and synchronization matrix<br>• Commander's objectives for IO<br>• Success criteria: measures of effectiveness and performance | **Outputs:**<br>• Updated scheme of IO<br>• Updated IO synchronization matrix<br>• Key leader engagement recommendations<br>• Refined themes and messages<br>• Refined operational products<br>• Target nominations<br>• Updated combined information overlay<br>• Plans and orders update<br>• Information requirements | **Lead:** IO Officer<br>(chair: G-3 (S-3), XO, DCO, or CDR)<br><br>**Core participants:** Military information support operations, G-2 (S-2), subordinate unit representatives, G-3 (S-3), fires, G-9 (S-9), operations security, public affairs<br><br>**Other participants:** G-6 (S-6), cyber electromagnetic activities, space operations, military deception planner, combat camera, foreign area officer or cultural advisor, special forces liaison, knowledge management officer, G-4 (S-4), engineer, chaplain, staff judge advocate, chaplain and unified action partners (mission and situation dependent) |

| | | | |
|---|---|---|---|
| **CCIR** commander's critical information requirements<br>**CDR** commander<br>**DCO** defense coordinating officer<br>**EEFI** essential elements of friendly information<br>**G-2** assistant chief of staff, intelligence<br>**G-3** assistant chief of staff, operations | **G-4** assistant chief of staff, logistics<br>**G-6** assistant chief of staff, signal<br>**G-9** assistant chief of staff, civil affairs operations<br>**IE** information environment<br>**IO** information operations | **IPB** intelligence preparation of the battlefield<br>IRCs information-related capabilities<br>**OPSEC** operations security<br>**S-2** battalion or brigade intelligence staff officer<br>**S-3** battalion or brigade operations staff officer | **S-4** battalion or brigade logistics staff officer<br>**S-6** battalion or brigade signal staff officer<br>**S-9** battalion or brigade civil affairs operations staff officer |

**Figure 6-1: Example template for an IO working group**

6-7. Consistent across all agenda formats are the operational and intelligence updates. These updates are designed to ground participants in the current situation and threat, examine how well operations are meeting the concept of operations and determine whether results are advancing the unit toward the desired end state.

## STRUCTURE/PARTICIPANTS

6-8. The IO officer leads and routinely chairs the IO working group. Staff members typically participating in the working group include personnel from the warfighting functional cells (as appropriate to the mission), the coordinating cells, the special staff, IRC managers (organic and augmenting), subordinate unit IO officers, and augmenting IO units or teams. Table 6-1 on page 6-4 provides an example listing of the participants as well as sample responsibilities.

## IO WORKING GROUP IN ANTICIPATION OF/RESPONSE TO CRISIS OR SIGNIFICANT INCIDENT

6-9. The IO working group convenes as soon as feasible before or after an event. Anyone can request the convening of the IO working group to deal with crisis or incident through the IO officer who, in consultation with the G-3 (S-3) and commander, determines the merits of the request and those personnel who should comprise the working group's initial membership. The working group's purpose is to determine the additional measures, activities, and effects that must be undertaken or generated in order to sustain operational advantage in the information environment. The group also seeks to mitigate possible negative consequences resulting from crisis events or incidents, particularly those that would adversely affect U.S. and coalition credibility. Its membership is more ad-hoc than the routine IO working group but also situation dependent.

# IO RESPONSIBILITIES WITHIN THE VARIOUS COMMAND POSTS

6-10. IO execution involves monitoring and assessing IO as the operation unfolds and requires coordination among the tactical command post (CP) and main CP, which can be challenging. Each monitors different parts of the operation and not all have an assigned functional area 30 or IO officer. Continuous exchange of information among those assigned responsibility for IO at these CPs is essential to ensuring the effective execution of IO.

6-11. The tactical CP directs IO execution and adjusts missions as required. The IO representative or responsible agent—

- Maintains the IO portion of the common operational picture to support current operations.
- Maintains information requirement status.
- Coordinates preparation and execution of IO with maneuver and fires.
- Recommends adjustments to current IO.
- Tracks IRCs and recommends repositioning, as required.
- Tracks applicable targets in conjunction with the G-2 (S-2).
- Nominates targets for attack.
- Provides initial assessment of effectiveness.

6-12. The main CP plans, coordinates, and integrates IO. It—

- Creates and maintains IO aspects of the common operational picture.
- Maintains the IO estimate.
- Incorporates answers to IRs and requests for information into the IO estimate.
- Maintains a current IO order of battle.
- Deconflicts IO internally and externally.
- Requests/coordinates IO support with other warfighting function representatives, outside agencies, higher headquarters, and augmenting forces.
- Identifies future objectives based on successes or failures of current operations.

**Table 6-1. Roles and responsibilities of IO working group representatives**

| *Representative* | *Responsibility* |
|---|---|
| ***Information Operations*** | • Distribute read-ahead packets<br>• Lead working group<br>• Establish and enforce agenda<br>• Lead information environment update<br>• Recommend commander's critical information requirements<br>• Keep records, track tasks, and disseminate meeting notes |
| ***Cyber Electromagnetic Activities*** | • Provide cyber electromagnetic activities-related information and capabilities to support information operations analysis and objectives<br>• Coordinate, synchronize and deconflict information operations efforts with cyberspace electromagnetic activities efforts or cyberspace electromagnetic activities efforts with information operations efforts |

**Table 6.1. Roles and responsibilities of IO working group representatives (continued)**

| *Representative* | *Responsibility* |
|---|---|
| ***Military Information Support Operations*** | • Advise on both psychological effects (planned) and psychological impacts (unplanned)<br>• Advise on use of lethal and nonlethal means to influence selected audiences to accomplish objectives<br>• Develop key leader engagement plans<br>• Monitor and coordinate assigned, attached, or supporting military information support unit actions<br>• Identify status of influence efforts in the unit, laterally, and at higher and lower echelons<br>• Provide target audience analysis |
| ***G-2 (S-2)*** | • Provide an intelligence update<br>• Brief information requirements and priority information requirements<br>• Develop the initial information collection plan<br>• Provide foreign disclosure-related guidance and updates |
| ***G-3 (S-3)*** | • Provide operations update and significant activity update<br>• Task units or sections based on due outs<br>• Update fragmentary orders<br>• Maintain a task tracker |
| ***Subordinate unit information operations*** | • Identify opportunities for information operations support to lines of effort<br>• Provide input to assessments<br>• Provide input to information environment update |
| ***Public Affairs*** | • Develop media analysis products<br>• Develop media engagement plan<br>• Provide higher headquarters strategic communication plan<br>• Provide changes to themes and messages from higher headquarters<br>• Develop command information plan |
| ***G-9 (S-9)*** | • Provides specific country information<br>• Ensures the timely update of the civil component of the common operational picture through the civil information management process<br>• Advise on civil considerations within the operational environment<br>• Identify concerns of population groups within the projected joint operational area/area of operations and potential flash points that can result in civil instability<br>• Provide cultural awareness briefings<br>• Advise on displaced civilians movement routes, critical infrastructure, and significant social, religious, and cultural shrines, monuments, and facilities<br>• Advise on information impacts on the civil component<br>• Identify key civilian nodes |
| ***Information-related capabilities representatives*** | • Serve as subject-matter expert for their staff function or capability<br>• Identify opportunities for information-related capability support to lines of effort or operations |

| | | |
|---|---|---|
| **G-2** assistant chief of staff, intelligence | **G-9** assistant chief of staff, civil affairs operations | **S-3** battalion or brigade operations staff officer |
| **G-3** assistant chief of staff, operations | **S-2** battalion or brigade intelligence staff officer | **S-9** battalion or brigade civil affairs operations staff officer |

6-13. The IO officer monitors IRCs and keeps the G-3 (S-3) informed on overall IO status. The IO officer also recommends to the G-3 (S-3) changes to IRC taskings for inclusion in fragmentary orders, as warranted.

# ASSESSING DURING EXECUTION

6-14. Assessment precedes and guides the other activities of the operations process. It involves continuous monitoring of the current situation and evaluation of the current situation against the desired end state to determine progress and make decisions and adjustments.

6-15. The IO officer compiles information from all CPs, the G-2 (S-2), and higher headquarters to maintain a continuous IO assessment in the IO estimate. The primary objective of assessment is to determine whether IO is achieving planned effects. As the situation changes, the IO officer and G-3 (S-3) make sure IO remains fully synchronized with the overall operation.

6-16. Assessment is continuous; it precedes and guides every operations process activity and concludes each operation or phase of an operation. During planning, the commander and staff determine those IO objectives to be assessed, measures of performance and effectiveness, and the means of obtaining the information necessary to determine effectiveness. During orders production, the IO officer uses this information to prepare the IO portion of the overall assessment plan. During execution, the IO officer uses established measures of performance and effectiveness, as well as baselines and indicators, to assess IO objectives.

## MONITORING IO

6-17. The IO officer monitors IRCs to determine progress towards achieving the IO objectives. Once execution begins, the IO officer monitors the threat and friendly situations to track IRC task accomplishment, determine the effects of IO during each phase of the operation, and detect and track any unintended consequences.

6-18. Monitoring the execution of defend-weighted tasks is done at the main CP because it is the focal point for intelligence analysis and production, and because the headquarters mission command nodes are monitored there. The IO officer works closely with the intelligence cell, G-2 (S-2), and IO working group representatives to provide a running assessment of the effectiveness of threat information efforts and keeps the G-3 (S-3) and various integrating cells informed.

6-19. With G-2 (S-2), G-3 (S-3), and fire support representatives, the IO officer monitors attack-weighted IO execution in the tactical CP and the main CP. For example, during combined arms maneuver, the IO officer is concerned with attacking threat command and control nodes with airborne and ground-based jammers, fire support, attack helicopters, and tactical air. After preplanned IO-related HPTs have been struck, the strike's effectiveness is assessed. Effective IO support of current operations depends on how rapidly the tactical CP can perform the targeting cycle to strike targets of opportunity. The G-3 (S-3) representative in the tactical CP keeps the main CP informed of current operations, including IO.

6-20. To organize and portray IO execution, the IO officer and working group use several tools, to include:

- IO synchronization matrix.
- Decision support template.
- High-payoff target list.
- Critical asset list and defended asset list.

6-21. IO officer and working group use either the synchronization matrix from the IO appendix or an extract containing current and near-term IO objectives and IRC tasks, depending on the complexity of the operation. The synchronization matrix is used to monitor progress and results of IO objectives and IRC tasks and keep IO execution focused on contributing to the overall operation. The decision support template produced by the G-3 (S-3) is used by the IO officer to monitor progress of IO in relation to decision points and any branches or sequels. The IO officer maintains a list or graphic (for example, a link and node diagram) that tracks the status of IO-related HPTs identified during planning. The IO officer uses the critical asset list and defended asset list to monitor the status of critical friendly information nodes and the status of critical systems supporting IO, for example: electronic warfare systems, military information support operations (MISO) assets, and deep attack assets.

### EVALUATING IO

6-22. During execution, the IO officer works with the intelligence cell and integrating cells to obtain the information needed to determine individual and collective IO effects. Evaluation not only estimates the effectiveness of task execution, but also evaluates the effect of the entire IO effort on the threat, other relevant audiences in the area of operations, and friendly operations. Task execution is evaluated using measures of performance. Task effectiveness is evaluated using measures of effectiveness, which compare achieved results against a baseline. Additional information on assessment and the unique considerations involved in assessing IO are found in chapter 8.

6-23. Based on the IO effects evaluation, the IO officer adjusts IO to further exploit enemy vulnerabilities, redirects actions yielding insufficient effects, or terminates actions after they have achieved the desired result. The IO officer keeps the G-3 (S-3) and commander informed of IO effects and how these impact friendly and adversary operations. Some of the possible changes to IO include:

- Strike a target or continue to protect a critical asset to ensure the desired effect.
- Execute a branch or sequel.

## DECISION MAKING DURING EXECUTION

6-24. Decision making during execution includes:

- Executing IO as planned.
- Adjusting IO to a changing friendly situation.
- Adjusting IO to an unexpected enemy reaction.

### EXECUTING IO AS PLANNED

6-25. Essential to execution is a continuous information flow among the various functional and integrating cells. The IO officer tracks execution with intelligence and current operations cells, as well as with the targeting staff. The IO officer, in concert with the IO working group, maintains a synchronization matrix. This matrix is periodically updated and provided to the headquarters' functional and integrating cells. Using the matrix, the IO officer and working group keep record of completed IRC tasks. As tasks are completed, the IO officer passes the information to the intelligence cell. The IO officer and working group use this information to keep IO synchronized with the overall operation.

6-26. The IO officer determines whether the threat commander and other identified leaders are reacting to IO as anticipated during course of action analysis. The IO officer, in concert with the IO working group, looks for new threat vulnerabilities and for new IO-related targets. The IO officer proposes changes to the operation order (OPORD) to deal with variances throughout execution. The G-3 (S-3) issues FRAGORDs pertaining to IO, as requested by the IO officer. These FRAGORDs may implement changes to the scheme of IO, IO objectives, and IRC tasks. The IO officer updates the IO synchronization matrix and IO assessment plan to reflect these changes.

6-27. Given the flexibility of advanced information systems, the time available to exploit new threat command and control vulnerabilities may be limited and requires an immediate response from designated IRCs. Actions to defeat threat information efforts need to be undertaken before exploitation advantage disappears. The G-3 (S-3) may issue a verbal FRAGORD when immediate action is required.

### ADJUSTING IO TO A CHANGING FRIENDLY SITUATION

6-28. As IO is executed, it often varies from the plan. Possible reasons for a variance include:

- An IO task is aborted or assets redirected.
- An IO-related target did not respond as anticipated.
- The threat effectively countered an IO attack.
- The threat successfully disrupted friendly mission command.
- The initial plan did not identify an emergent IO-related target or target of opportunity.

6-29. The IO officer's challenge is to rapidly assess how changes in IO execution affect the overall operation and to determine necessary follow-on actions. Based on the commander's input, the IO officer, in coordination with the rest of the headquarters' functional and integrating cells, considers COAs, conducts a quick COA analysis, and determines the most feasible COA.

6-30. If the selected COA falls within the decision-making authority of the G-3 (S-3), IO execution can be adjusted without notifying the commander. When changes exceed previously designated limits, the IO officer obtains approval from the commander. At this point, a more formal decision-making process may be required before issuing a FRAGORD, especially if a major adjustment to the operation order (OPORD) is needed. In such a case, the IO officer, working with the G-3 (S-3), participates in a time-constrained military decisionmaking process (MDMP) to develop a new COA.

### ADJUSTING IO TO AN UNEXPECTED THREAT REACTION

6-31. The threat may react in an unexpected manner to IO or to the overall operation. If threat actions diverge significantly from those anticipated when the OPORD was written, the commander and staff look first at branch and sequel plans. If branch or sequel plans fail to adequately address the new situation, a new planning effort may be required.

6-32. The IO officer prepares branches that modify defend weighted efforts when threat actions cause new friendly vulnerabilities, or when friendly attack or stabilize efforts prove ineffective. The intelligence and current operations integration cells work with the IO officer to maintain a running assessment of threat capability to disrupt friendly mission command, and look for ways to lessen friendly vulnerabilities. Concurrently, they look for opportunities to reestablish IO effectiveness. Under these conditions, the IO officer determines the adequacy of existing branches and sequels. If none fit the situation, they create a new branch or sequel and disseminate it by FRAGORD.

6-33. If a new plan is needed, time available dictates the length of the decision-making process and the amount of detail contained in an order. The IO officer may only be able to recommend the use of IRCs that can immediately affect the overall operation: for example, electronic warfare, and MISO. Other IRCs proceed as originally planned and are adjusted later, unless they conflict with the new plan.

## OTHER EXECUTION CONSIDERATIONS

6-34. Other considerations include, but are not limited to—

- IO execution begins early.
- IO execution requires flexibility.

### IO EXECUTION BEGINS EARLY

6-35. Potential adversary and enemy commanders begin forming perceptions of a situation well before they encounter friendly forces. Recognizing this fact, commanders establish a baseline of IO that is practiced routinely in garrison and training. Selected IRCs (for example, MISO, OPSEC, combat camera, and military deception) begin contributing to an IO objective well before a deployment occurs. To support early execution of the overall operation, IO planning, preparation, and execution frequently begin well before the staff formally starts planning for an operation.

### IO EXECUTION REQUIRES FLEXIBILITY

6-36. Actions by threat decision makers sometimes take surprising turns, uncovering unanticipated weaknesses or strengths. Similarly, friendly commanders may react unexpectedly in response to threat activities. Flexibility is key to success in IO execution. Effective commanders and well-trained staffs are flexible enough to expect the unexpected and exploit threat vulnerabilities/friendly strengths and protect against threat strengths/friendly vulnerabilities.

This page intentionally left blank.

# Chapter 7
# Targeting Integration

7-1. Targeting is the process of selecting and prioritizing targets and matching the appropriate response to them, considering operational requirements and capabilities (JP 3-0). IO is integrated into the targeting cycle to produce effects in and through the information environment that support objectives. The targeting cycle facilitates the engagement of the right target with the right asset at the right time. The IO officer or representative is a part of the targeting team, responsible to the commander and staff for all aspects of IO.

## TARGETING METHODOLOGY

7-2. Army targeting methodology is based on four functions: decide, detect, deliver, and assess (D3A) (see Figure 7-1, page 7-2). The decide function occurs concurrently with planning. The detect function occurs during preparation and execution. The deliver function occurs primarily during execution, although some IO-related targets may be engaged while the command is preparing for the overall operation. The assess function occurs throughout.

7-3. The targeting process is cyclical. The command's battle rhythm determines the frequency of targeting working group meetings. IO-related target nominations are developed by the IO officer and by the IO working group, which validates all IO-related targets before they are nominated to the targeting working group. Therefore, the IO working group is always scheduled in advance of the targeting working group.

## DECIDE

7-4. The decide function is part of the planning activity of the operations process. It occurs concurrently with the military decisionmaking process (MDMP). During the decide function, the targeting team focuses and sets priorities for intelligence collection and attack planning. Based on the commander's intent and concept of operations, the targeting team establishes targeting priorities for each phase or critical event of an operation. The following products reflect these priorities—

- High-payoff target list.
- Information collection plan.
- Target selection standards.
- Attack guidance matrix.
- Target synchronization matrix.

7-5. The high-payoff target list is a prioritized list of targets whose loss to the enemy will significantly contribute to the success of the friendly course of action. High-payoff targets (HPTs) are those high-value targets (HVTs) identified during COA development and validated in subsequent steps that must be acquired and successfully attacked for the success of the friendly commander's mission. Examples of IO-related HPTs are threat command and control nodes and intelligence collection assets/capabilities.

7-6. The information collection plan, prepared by the G-3 (S-3) and coordinated with the entire staff, synchronizes the four primary means information collection to provide intelligence to the commander. The G-2 (S-2) ensures all available collection assets provide the required information. Information requirements submitted by the IO officer can require longer lead times to detect targets and dwell times to assess the effects of IRCs directed against these targets.

| | Operations Process Activity | Targeting Process Function | Targeting Task |
|---|---|---|---|
| ASSESSMENT | PLANNING | DECIDE | **Mission Analysis**<br>Develop IO-related HVTs<br>Provide IO input to targeting guidance and targeting objectives<br><br>**COA Development**<br>Designate potential IO-related HPTs<br>Contribute to the threat and vulnerability assessment<br>Deconflict and coordinate potential HPTs<br><br>**COA Analysis**<br>Develop high priority target list<br>Establish target selection standards<br>Develop AGM<br>Determine criteria of<br>• Successful BDA<br>• Requirements<br><br>**Orders Production**<br>Finalize high-payoff target list<br>Finalize target selection standards<br>Finalize AGM<br>Submit IO information requirements/requests for information to G-2 (S-2) |
| | PREPARATION EXECUTION | DETECT | • Execute collection plan<br>• Update PIRs/IO IRs as they are answered<br>• Update high-payoff target list and AGM |
| | | DELIVER | • Execute attacks in accordance with the AGM |
| | | ASSESS | • Evaluate effects of attacks<br>• Monitor targets attacked with nonlethal IO |

AGM attack guidance matrix; BDA battle damage assessment; COA course of action; HPT high-payoff target; HVT high-value target; IO Information operations; PIR priority intelligence requirements

**Figure 7-1. The operations process, targeting cycle and IO-related tasks**

7-7. Target selection standards establish criteria for deciding when targets are located accurately enough to attack. These criteria are often more complicated for IO, especially when attempting to identify actors and audiences with precision.

7-8. The attack guidance matrix addresses how and when targets are to be engaged and desired effects of the engagement. For IO-related targets, effects are diverse, running the gamut from destruction of assets to changed behaviors.

7-9. The target synchronization matrix is a list of HPTs by category and the agencies responsible for detecting them, attacking them, and assessing the effects of the attacks. It combines data from the high-payoff target list, information collection plan and attack guidance matrix.

7-10. The targeting team develops or contributes to these products throughout the MDMP. The commander approves them during COA approval. The IO officer ensures they include information necessary to engage IO-related targets. IO-related vulnerability analyses done by the G-2 (S-2) and IO officer provide a basis for deciding which IO-related targets to attack.

## Mission Analysis

7-11. The two targeting-related IO products of mission analysis are a list of IO-related HVTs and recommendations for the commander's targeting guidance. The IO officer works with the G-2 (S-2) during IPB to develop IO-related HVTs, and with other members of the targeting team to develop IO targeting guidance recommendations.

## Intelligence Preparation of the Battlefield

7-12. IPB includes preparing templates that portray threat forces and assets unconstrained by the environment. The intelligence cell adjusts threat templates based on terrain and weather to create situational templates that portray possible threat COAs. These situational templates allow the intelligence to identify HVTs. The IO officer works with the intelligence cell throughout IPB to identify threat information-related capabilities and vulnerabilities and other key groups in the area of operations. These capabilities and vulnerabilities become IO-related HVTs.

## Targeting Guidance

7-13. Issued within the commander's guidance is targeting guidance. This guidance describes the desired effects the commander wants to achieve. IO targeting focuses on HVTs that support critical, information-related threat capabilities that underpin their objectives and are vulnerable to friendly IO exploitation.

7-14. The IO officer develops input to targeting guidance based on the initial mission and available and anticipated IRCs. The IO officer identifies the functions, capabilities, or units to be attacked; the effects desired; and the purpose for the attack. The IO officer uses the targeting guidance to select IO-related HPTs from among identified HVTs. These HPTs are confirmed during COA analysis.

7-15. Targeting guidance is developed separately from IO objectives. IO objectives are generally broad in scope. They encompass all IO weighted efforts (attack, defend, stabilize). The IO officer develops recommendations for targeting guidance that supports achieving objectives.

7-16. When developing IO input to the targeting guidance, the IO officer considers the time required to achieve effects and the time required to determine results. Some IRCs require targeting guidance that allows for the acquisition, engagement, and assessment of targets while the unit is preparing for the overall operation. For example, the commander may want to psychologically and electronically isolate the enemy's reserve before engaging it with fires. Doing this requires electronic attack of threat command and control systems and military information support operations (MISO) directed at the threat 24 to 48 hours before lethal fires are initiated. Successfully achieving IO objectives for this phase of the operation requires targeting guidance that gives IO-related targets the appropriate priority.

# COURSE OF ACTION DEVELOPMENT

7-17. Feasible COAs, that integrate the effects of all elements of combat power, are developed by the staff. The IO officer prepares a scheme of IO that identifies objectives and IRC tasks for each COA. The IRC tasks are correlated with targets on the HVT list. A single IRC or multiple IRCs can be planned against a single HVT.

7-18. For each COA, the IO officer identifies HVTs that will support attainment of an IO objective. IO-related HVTs that subsequently support friendly IO objectives, and that can be engaged by IRCs, become HPTs. The targeting team also performs target value analysis, coordinates and deconflicts targets, and establishes assessment criteria. The IO officer participates in each of these tasks.

## Target Value Analysis

7-19. The targeting team performs target value analysis for each COA the staff develops. The initial sources for target value analysis are target spreadsheets and target sheets. Target spreadsheets (target folders) identify target sets associated with adversary functions that could interfere with each friendly COA or that are key to adversary success. IO-related targets can be analyzed as a separate target set or incorporated into other target sets. The IO officer establishes any IO-specific target sets. Each target set is assigned a priority based on its contribution to the success of a friendly objective, its impact on an enemy or adversary COA, and friendly capability to service the target.

7-20. The targeting team uses target spreadsheets during the war game to determine which HVTs to attack. The IO officer ensures that target spreadsheets include information on threat capabilities and IO-related HVTs and that the IO target set, if designated, is assigned a value appropriate to IO's relative importance to each friendly COA. If an IO target set is not designated, the IO officer ensures that IO-related targets are assigned an appropriate priority within the target sets used.

7-21. Target sheets contain the information required to engage a specific target. Target sheets state how attacking the target affects the threat's operation. The IO officer prepares target sheets for HVTs to analyze them from an IO planning perspective. These HVTs are expressed as target subsets, such as decision makers. Information requirements concerning them include:

- What influences these decision makers.
- How they communicate.
- With whom they communicate.
- Weaknesses, susceptibilities, accessibility, feasibility, and pressure points.

## Deconflicting and Coordinating Targets

7-22. The IO officer and working group consider the possible consequences of attacking any target or target set. Their purpose is to identify possible duplication or attenuation of effects. The attack of physical targets always has second- and third-order effects (informational and cognitive) that could diminish or enhance their value to the overall operation. For example, fires that result in the collateral deaths of civilian non-combatants can have a negative cognitive effect, while using fires to destroy the enemy's fiber network so that it relies on radio communications vulnerable to jamming can have a positive informational effect. Also, the effects achieved by one IRC might compete with or diminish the effects of another IRC. Thus, IRC synchronization and the integration of IO into other lines of effort requires methodical coordination and deconfliction efforts.

7-23. IO working group members consider all targets from their various perspectives. Deconfliction in this context means ensuring that engaging a target does not produce effects that interfere with the effects of other IRC tasks or IO-related targets, or otherwise inhibit mission accomplishment. Coordination ensures that the effects of engaging different targets complement each other and further the commander's intent.

7-24. IO officers at different echelons may seek to engage the same targets and, possibly, desire different effects. Therefore, IO-focused targeting includes coordinating and deconflicting targets with higher and subordinate units before the targeting working group meets. Some IO-related targets may also be nominated by other staff elements. The IO officer presents the effects required to accomplish the IO objective associated with those targets when the targeting team determines how to engage them. IO officers must also coordinate and deconflict targets with unified action partners whose doctrinal use of IRCs and policies governing their employment differ. Such coordination extends the planning horizon and may limit how IRCs are integrated.

7-25. One way to achieve this coordination and deconfliction is by beginning parallel planning as early as possible in the MDMP. This means that the IO officer and the targeting team should share all pertinent information with subordinate units and adjacent and higher headquarters.

## Assessment Criteria

7-26. Generally, the effects of lethal attacks can be evaluated quickly using readily observable and quantifiable criteria, such as the percentage of the target destroyed. Assessing nonlethal attacks often requires monitoring the target over time, using a mix of quantitative and qualitative criteria. Establishing meaningful measures of performance and effectiveness for IO-related targets requires formulating a theory or logic of change in relation to IO objectives and the desired end state. The IO officer and working group essentially ask: will successful attack of a specific target or target set contribute to the attainment of the objective and what will the observable actions or activities leading to the desired outcome look like? The logic of change is expressed in terms of the anticipated causal chain that begins when the target is engaged. (See chapter 8 for more detail on the theory or logic of change.)

7-27. IO-related targets attacked by means such as jamming or MISO broadcasts require assessment by means other than those used in battle damage assessment. The IO officer develops post-attack or post-engagement assessment criteria for these targets and determines the information needed to determine how well they have been met. The IO officer prepares IO IRs or RFIs for this information. If these targets are approved, the IO IRs for the approved targets may be recommended to the commander as priority intelligence requirements. If the command does not have the assets to answer these IO IRs, the target is not engaged unless the attack guidance specifies otherwise or the commander so directs.

## COURSE OF ACTION ANALYSIS

7-28. COA analysis (war-gaming) is a disciplined process that staffs use to visualize the flow of a battle. During the war game, the staff decides or determines—

- Which HVTs are HPTs.
- When to engage each HPT.
- Which system or capability to use against each HPT.
- The desired effects of each attack, expressed in terms of the targeting objectives.
- Which HPTs require battle damage assessment or post-attack/engagement assessment. The IO officer submits IRs for IO-related targets to the G-2 (S-2) for inclusion in the collection plan.
- Which HPTs require special instructions or require coordination.

7-29. Based on the war game, the targeting team produces the following draft targeting products for each COA:

- High-payoff target list.
- Target selection standards.
- Attack guidance matrix.
- Target synchronization matrix.

### High-Payoff Target List

7-30. During mission analysis, the IO officer identifies potential targets, which are vetted by the IO working group. The IO officer takes nominated targets to the next targeting working group and works within that body to get these targets onto the high-payoff target list and approved by the targeting board.

### Target Selection Standards

7-31. Target selection standards are applied to enemy activities to decide whether the activity can be engaged as a target. Target selection standards are usually disseminated as a matrix. Military intelligence analysts use target selection standards to determine targets from combat information and pass them to fire support assets for attack. Attack systems' managers, such as fire control elements and fire direction centers, use target selection standards to determine whether to attack a potential target. The intelligence and fires cells determine target selection standards. The IO officer ensures that they consider IO-related targets and establish appropriate standards for engaging them.

7-32. For nonlethal attacks or engagements, the IO officer may have to develop descriptive criteria to supplement or replace criteria developed by the fires cell. For example, target selection standards during a security cooperation operation may describe what constitutes a hostile crowd, such as: a group larger than 25 people, armed with sticks or other weapons, and with leaders using radios or cellular telephones to direct it.

### Attack Guidance Matrix

7-33. The targeting team recommends attack guidance based on the results of the war game. Attack guidance is normally disseminated as a matrix. An attack guidance matrix includes the following information, listed by target set or HPT:

- Timing of attacks (expressed as immediate, planned, or as acquired).
- Attack system assigned.
- Attack criteria (expressed as neutralize, suppress, harass, or destroy).
- Restrictions or special instructions.

7-34. Only one attack guidance matrix is produced for execution at any point in the operation; however, each phase of the operation may have its own matrix. To synchronize effects, all lethal and nonlethal attack systems, including MISO and electronic attack, for example, are placed on the attack guidance matrix. The attack guidance matrix is a synchronization and integration tool. It is normally included as part of the fire support annex. However, it is not a tasking document. Attack tasks for unit assets, including IRCs, are identified as taskings to subordinate units and agencies in the body or appropriate annexes or appendixes of the OPLAN/ OPORD.

### Target Synchronization Matrix

7-35. The target synchronization matrix lists HPTs by category and the agencies responsible for detecting them, attacking them, and assessing the effects of the attacks. It combines data from the high-payoff target list, information collection plan, and attack guidance matrix. A completed target synchronization matrix allows the targeting team to verify that assets have been assigned to each targeting process task for each target. The targeting team may prepare a target synchronization matrix for each COA, or may use the high-payoff target list, target selection standards, and attack guidance matrix for the war game and prepare a target synchronization matrix for only the approved COA.

## Course of Action Comparison and Approval and Orders Production

7-36. After war-gaming all the COAs, the staff compares them and recommends one to the commander for approval. When the commander approves a COA, the targeting products for that COA become the basis for targeting for the operation. The targeting team meets to finalize the high-payoff target list, target selection standards, attack guidance matrix, and input to the information collection plan. The team also performs any additional coordination required. After accomplishing these tasks, targeting team members ensure that targeting factors that fall within their functional areas are placed in the appropriate part of the OPLAN/OPORD.

# DETECT

7-37. This function involves locating HPTs accurately enough to engage them. It primarily entails execution of the information collection plan. All staff agencies, including the IO officer, are responsible for passing to the G-2 (S-2) information collected by their assets that answer IRs. Conversely, the G-2 (S-2) is responsible for passing combat information and intelligence to the agencies that identified the IRs. Sharing information allows timely evaluation of attacks, assessment of IO, and development of new targets. Effective information and knowledge management are, therefore, essential.

7-38. The information collection plan focuses on identifying HPTs and answering PIRs. These are prioritized based on the importance of the target or information to the commander's concept of operation and intent. When designated by the commander, PIRs can include requirements concerning IO; obtaining answers to these requirements will assist the IO officer in assessing IO. Thus, there is some overlap between detect and assess functions. Detecting targets for nonlethal attacks may require information collection support from higher headquarters. The targeting team adjusts the high-payoff target list and attack guidance matrix to meet changes as the situation develops. The IO officer submits new IO IRs/RFIs as needed.

7-39. During the detect function, the IO officer updates the high-payoff target list and target synchronization matrix. In addition to the information collection plan, the IO officer will use other information sources, particularly culturally-attuned ones that have unique access to or knowledge of the information environment and its various audiences. Examples include atmospheric teams; cultural attaches or advisors; joint, interorganizational or multinational partner cultural experts; interpreters, or indigenous leaders.

# DELIVER

7-40. This function occurs primarily during execution, although some IO-related targets may be engaged while the command is preparing for the overall operation. The key to understanding the deliver function is to know which assets are available to perform a specific function or deliver a specific effect and to ensure these assets are ready and capable. Examples of delivery methods include but are not limited to:

- Corps/division/brigade commander.
- Provincial reconstruction team member or other unified action partner.
- Host nation government leader.

- Loudspeaker.
- Media broadcast.
- Social media posts and videos.
- Patrols.

7-41. During this step, the IO officer executes relevant portions of the target synchronization matrix. As IO-related delivery means and methods are multi-faceted and often involve human interaction, this step includes recording the delivery act and keeping detailed accounts or notes of actions taken or the proceedings, discussions, and commitments involved. The IO officer will ensure that required reporting procedures are explained and disseminated in the operations order or as part of the unit's standard operating procedures.

## ASSESS

7-42. There are multiple types and levels of assessment. Assessment within D3A specifically focuses on whether the commander's targeting guidance was met for a specific target. From an IO perspective, such guidance may speak in terms of influence or degraded decision making, which are difficult to quantify. In the case of engagements, for example, assessment will help determine whether messages were retained by the target, whether these messages resulted in changed behavior, and whether reengagement may be necessary. An ongoing consideration in the information environment is that there may be a significant lag between the time of delivery, the effect taking place, and determination of an effect.

7-43. During this step, the IO officer and IRCs evaluate measures of effectiveness and performance to determine if desired effects were achieved. If not, it recommends re-engagement or other actions.

## OTHER TARGETING METHODOLOGIES

7-44. The D3A method is employed for deliberate targeting. Other methodologies exist to deal with different mission sets and types of units. They are not meant to replace D3A, but complement it. These other methodologies include:

- Find, fix, track, target, engage, and assess.
- Find, fix, finish, exploit, analyze, and disseminate.

### FIND, FIX, TRACK, TARGET, ENGAGE, AND ASSESS

7-45. This methodology is employed primarily for dynamic targeting, which is targeting that prosecutes targets identified too late, or not selected for action in time to be included in deliberate targeting (JP 3-60). An emergent target of opportunity or a change in the situation may necessitate a change to a planned target. These targets still require confirmation, verification, validation, and authorization, but in a shorter timeframe than deliberate targeting allows. Dynamic targeting focuses on time-sensitive targets and HPTs. From an IO perspective, many targets may be time-sensitive. Examples include: a hard-to-reach or inaccessible key leader, a flash mob, an accident requiring combat camera documentation, or a denial-of-service attack or other disruption to communication flow. (See ATP 3-60.1, Appendix A.)

### FIND, FIX, FINISH, EXPLOIT, ANALYZE, AND DISSEMINATE

7-46. This methodology is particularly useful in targeting high-value individuals. A high-value individual is a person of interest who is identified, surveilled, tracked, influenced, or engaged. Though typically used by special operations forces, find, fix, finish, exploit, analyze, and disseminate helps maneuver leaders at all levels with aligning intelligence and operations assets for pinpoint targeting of personalities and exploiting vulnerabilities in a given network. (See ATP 3-60, Appendix B).

This page intentionally left blank.

# Chapter 8
# Assessment

8-1. Assessment precedes and guides the other activities of the operations process. It is also part of targeting. In short, assessment occurs at all levels and within all operations and has a role in any process or activity. The purpose of assessment is to improve the commander's decision making and make operations more effective. Assessment is a key component of the commander's decision cycle, helping to determine the results of unit actions in the context of overall mission objectives. Assessment provides information about the current state of the operational environment, the progress of the operation, and recommendations to mitigate or overcome discrepancies between actual and predicted progress. It also reveals how specific capabilities, such as IRCs, contribute to this progress. Commanders adjust operations based on assessment results to ensure objectives are met and the military end state is achieved.

## ASSESSMENT PRIORITIZATION

8-2. Assessment has little value unless it meets the needs of its users. It does this by supporting two critical aspects of mission command: shared understanding and decision making. When prioritized and resourced adequately, assessment facilitates a more detailed shared understanding among the commander, staff, and other stakeholders about how the operation is progressing. Regardless of the level or frequency of assessment data collection, staffs will provide the commander ongoing assessment updates.

8-3. Staff assessments, along with those received from higher headquarters or unified action partners, combine with the commander's personal assessment to create an overall assessment, which informs the commander's subsequent decisions. The commander may decide to stay the current course or to issue a FRAGORD to reprioritize missions or tasks, terminate or initiate activities, or redirect resources or the allocation of forces to achieve overall mission objectives. The commander can also direct the development of a new operational approach or plan, if necessary.

8-4. IO contributes to overall operations assessment by examining efforts in and through the information environment. IO-focused assessment is an integral part of the unit's assessment plan, which is discussed broadly in ADRP 5-0 and in detail in FM 6-0. ADRP 5-0 provides overarching guidance on assessment; however, there are unique considerations to the assessment of IO that commanders and staffs take into account.

## ASSESSMENT RATIONALE

8-5. Assessment or evaluation is a judgment of merit of an action or operation as to whether it achieved its intended outcome(s). It supports planning, improves effectiveness and efficiency of operations, and enforces accountability. These three purposes correspond to three types of evaluation: formative, process, and summative.

8-6. Formative evaluation supports planning by examining whether an operation or program is being designed to meet its intended purpose. In terms of IO, it involves testing messages, determining baselines, analyzing audiences, and developing the logic by which the operation will create influence.

8-7. Process evaluation occurs primarily during execution and serves to enhance effectiveness and efficiency, as well as facilitate in-process decision making. In terms of IO, it assesses whether the scheme of IO is being executed as planned. If the scheme is not going as planned, process evaluation facilitates decisions that lead to corrective action.

8-8. Summative evaluation occurs post-execution and supports decision making and accountability. While process evaluation supports decisions that adjust activities or efforts as the operation unfolds, summative evaluation supports decisions about the overall operation and whether it achieved the commander's intent. It leads to the determination of those aspects of the operation to sustain and those to eliminate or curtail should a similar operation be undertaken in the future.

8-9. In addition to supporting users such as the IO officer, the IO working group, IRC managers, other staff sections, and the commander, operations assessment feeds higher headquarters assessment and, oftentimes, external entities, such as governmental leadership. IO efforts, in particular, often elicit congressional scrutiny and commander-led assessment ensures units are ready to demonstrate the effectiveness of their influence efforts.

8-10. Assessment is most valuable when operations or operational efforts are not working as planned because it helps the commander and staff figure out why and take corrective action. Units should avoid using assessment to justify decisions already made or merely to check the box. Assessment without the intent to employ its results is a waste of time and resources.

# PRINCIPLES THAT ENHANCE THE EFFECTIVENESS OF IO ASSESSMENT

8-11. Assessment effectiveness is enhanced when it adheres to the following principles or best practices:

- Uses clear, realistic and measurable objectives.
- Begins with planning.
- Employs an explicit logic of the effort.
- Is continual and consistent over time.
- Is iterative.
- Is prioritized and resourced.

8-12. Assessment is more effective when IO objectives are specific, measurable, achievable, relevant and time-bound. Creating clear, realistic, and measurable objectives can be challenging early on, as initial guidance from higher might lack clarity. The IO officer asks clarifying questions but also proactively establishes the most specific, measurable, achievable, relevant, and time-bound objectives possible and provides them to higher headquarters for review and refinement. The IO officer also tests its objective statements with relevant stakeholders, most especially the IRCs that contribute to the attainment of these objectives.

8-13. Because IO creates effects in and through the information environment to influence, disrupt, corrupt, or usurp threat and other audience behavior and decision making, it is necessary to understand what the desired behavior looks like. This understanding drives the planning necessary to achieve the desired outcome. In other words, effective planning for IO cannot occur unless assessment is part of the operations process from the beginning.

8-14. Unlike fires, whose effects are rapidly discernable, effects in the information environment may not be immediate and their causality can be difficult to determine. An essential part of planning and assessing IO is the need to develop an explicit logic of the effort for each objective or effect. The logic of the effort makes explicit how specific efforts lead to the attainment of objectives. The value of this logic is that its assumptions are made explicit and can become hypotheses that can then be tested and, if necessary, refined. Figure 8-1 on page 8-3 provides a simple example of a logic statement and how it evolves when its hypothesis is tested. More complex examples would include additional threat counter-measures that would test each successive hypothesis and the refinement of the IRC mix necessary to create as foolproof a logic as possible, balanced against risk, available assets, time, and cost.

8-15. Since IO objectives are primarily articulated in terms of a change in one (or more) dimensions of the information environment, a baseline is required to assess progress toward or attainment of the objective. A baseline captures the current state of a person, place, or thing.

8-16. Because evaluation is essential to planning, operational effectiveness and efficiency, and decision making and accountability, it is continual. More important for IO assessment is the fact that objectives are often measured in terms of patterns or trends in behavior. If assessment is not continual and consistent, these patterns or trends become difficult or impossible to detect and measure.

8-17. IO assessment is iterative because, in most instances, IO is iterative. Rarely does a single capability produce a singular and decisive effect that is readily and fully measurable. Effects in the information environment take time to unfold and become fully visible. Indicators are used to show progress towards the desired cumulative outcome, but because progress takes time, things change. The environment changes, the logic of change changes, and the indicators of progress change. In the face of these changes, measures are iteratively refined, corrected and reapplied.

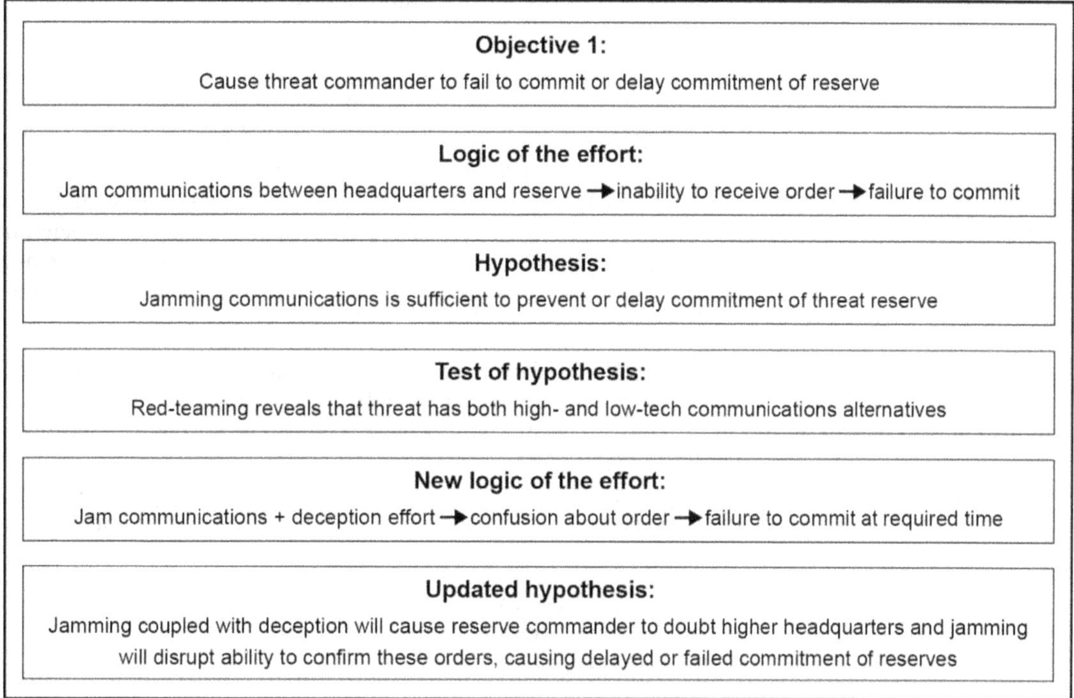


**Figure 8-1. Logic of the effort example**

8-18. To be effective, assessment requires commander emphasis, prioritization, and allocation of resources. This requirement does not mean that every activity, event, or operation requires an equal investment in or level of assessment. Through their guidance and direction, commanders make clear their assessment priorities and ensure that IO assessment receives due emphasis and support.

# IO ASSESSMENT CONSIDERATIONS

8-19. Assessment of IO in general and of specific effects in the information environment require careful development of measures of effectiveness and performance, as well as identification of indicators that will best signal achievement of these measures and desired outcomes. Assessment in the information environment is not easy and adherence to the following considerations will aid in making IO assessment more effective.

## MEASURES OF EFFECTIVENESS

8-20. A *measure of effectiveness* is a criterion used to assess changes in system behavior, capability, or operational environment that is tied to measuring the attainment of an end state, achievement of an objective, or creation of an effect (JP 3-0). Measures of effectiveness help measure changes in conditions, both positive and negative. They are commonly found and tracked in formal assessment plans.

8-21. Time is a factor when assessing IO and developing measures of effectiveness. The attainment of IO objectives leading to the commander's desired end state often requires days or months to realize. It is essential, therefore, to have a baseline from which to measure change and also to time-bound the change. Time-bounding makes clear how long it will take before the change is observed. It helps to set necessary expectations, foster patience, and avoid a rush to judgment. If a behavioral objective is anticipated to take considerable time, assessment planning may choose to break the objective into smaller increments, each with more immediate observable outcomes. Finally, it is also important to analyze and understand the cultural relevance of time in the area of operations and account for and adapt to it.

8-22. Developing informational, behavioral and sentiment baselines often requires significant time and resource investments. Sentiment baselines, such as those determined through surveys or interviews, may require contracted labor to accomplish. The IO officer must factor in the lead time necessary to contract a third-party, provide it time to develop the survey instrument, administer the survey, and tabulate and report on the results.

8-23. Commanders and staffs, particularly the IO officer, must account for the order of effects when assessing IO or, more broadly, any effect. For example, an effect in the physical dimension (1st order) can resonate in unexpected ways in the informational and cognitive dimensions (2nd and 3rd orders). During Operation Enduring Freedom, night raids, while operationally necessary to root out insurgents, caused significant backlash among the indigenous population, local leaders, and the national government. Part of the IO officer's task is to anticipate second- and third-order effects and conduct a risk analysis to determine if potential higher-order effects outweigh the benefits of achieving lower-order effects. The aim is to amplify intended consequences in all dimensions of the information environment, while mitigating unintended consequences.

8-24. Units must account for directness of effect and understand the difference between causational linkages and correlational ones. Certain effects, even desired ones, may not be directly tied to friendly efforts in the information environment; however, friendly forces may still be held accountable for these effects and must react appropriately. This fact underlines the importance of developing a logic of the effort for each IO objective. This logic explicitly states how synchronized IRCs will lead to the desired change expressed in the objective. The logic also differentiates planned activities from other possible contributing factors and articulates expected outputs and outcomes.

8-25. Effectiveness in the cognitive dimension typically requires variety and repetition. Rarely does a single tactic, task, method, action, or message change behavior. Assessment plans must therefore build in varied actions and repeated messages and measure their cumulative effect.

## Measures of Performance

8-26. A *measure of performance* is a criterion used to assess friendly actions that is tied to measuring task accomplishment (JP 3-0). Measures of performance help answer questions such as "Was the action taken?" or "Were the tasks completed to standard?" A measure of performance confirms or denies that a task has been properly performed. Measures of performance are commonly found and tracked at all echelons in execution matrixes. They are also commonly used to evaluate training.

8-27. There is no definitive number of tasks to support a given objective; therefore, there is no definitive number of measures of performance to support any given measure of effectiveness. Again, variety and repetition necessitate that multiple tasks typically support each objective and the corresponding measure of performance is the means to confirm or deny that each task is executed in the first place and properly performed.

8-28. Delivery, especially means of delivery, is a critical consideration when developing IRC tasks and their associated measures of performance, particularly when it comes to message delivery. No matter how well-crafted the message, if delivery assets are unavailable or only available in insufficient number, the objective will likely not be achieved. Means of delivery should also be considered in terms of accessibility and acceptability to the target audience. For example, if only a small percentage of the population listens to radio or watches television then these means should not be the only means of delivery considered.

## Indicators

8-29. An *indicator* is an item of information that provides insight into a measure of effectiveness or measure of performance (ADRP 5-0). Indicators take the form of reports from subordinates, surveys and polls, and information requirements. Indicators help to answer the question "What is the current status of this measure of effectiveness?" A single indicator can inform multiple measures of effectiveness.

8-30. Not everything observed is an indicator and not every indicator is a sign of progress. Indicators of psychological effects or changes in sentiment are not always easy to detect or may not be markers of the desired behavior change. The upshot of these facts is that establishing indicators requires rigorous effort in order to select those observable and measurable signs or signals that are reflective of changed behavior. Often behavior change is incremental and being able to detect the intervening steps to large-scale behavior change is essential to measuring progress. Again, in-depth knowledge is required of those targets or audiences for whom behavior change is required to achieve the commander's desired end state.

8-31. Measuring progress requires the ability to detect both micro and macro indicators simultaneously. The IO officer must, therefore, coordinate with the G-2 (S-2) in order to know what collection assets are available and the types of information that each provides and how this information helps create actionable knowledge. Soldiers are a vital collection asset. The IO officer should invest time to train all Soldiers on observation techniques that enable them to spot and discriminate meaningful indicators and ways to report what they see.

8-32. The IO officer should employ a variety of means to identify indicators, validate or corroborate conclusions about them, and measure progress. Some of the more commonly used sources are:

- Information collection assets
- Military Information Support Operations (MISO) teams
- Soldier and leader engagements
- Civil-military operations
- Polling and surveys (which primarily measure attitudes, not motivations)
- Media monitoring and analysis
- Patrol and spot reports
- Information sharing with unified action partners
- Conversations with local leaders, partners, and trusted agents
- Passive monitoring (atmospherics)

8-33. Figure 8-2 portrays the relationship between objectives (the change that needs to happen) and measures of performance, indicators, and measures of effectiveness. The logic of the effort is shown as a relationship between available, selected, and synchronized IRCs and the effects expected over time. While the figure suggests that this logic is generic, it is not. It is unique to every objective and combination of IRCs.

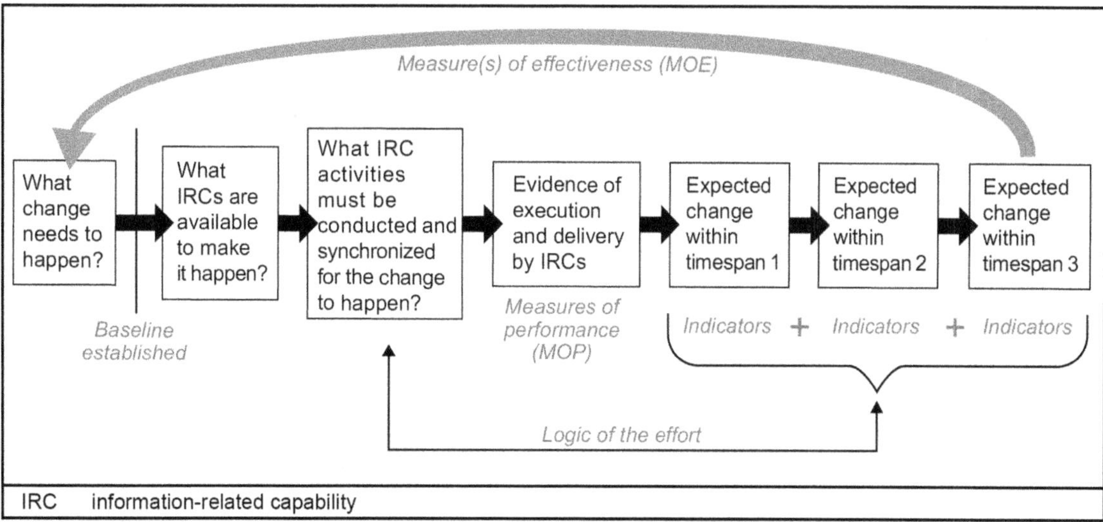


**Figure 8-2. Logic flow and components of an IO objective**

This page intentionally left blank.

# Chapter 9
# Brigade and Below Information Operations

9-1. IO integration and synchronization activities are essential to mission success at all levels. At brigade and below, units synchronize fewer IRCs but their effects are more immediate and, proportionately, more integral to achieving unit objectives. Brigade and below and especially small-unit operations require Soldiers to be ready and capable of effectively engaging the local populace while part of patrols, convoys, and tactical actions. Brigade and below operations also take advantage of effects being achieved by IRCs at higher levels and makes them relevant to a unit's area of operations.

9-2. As an example, IO considerations during patrols expand the purpose of patrols beyond combat operations and reconnaissance. Patrols always create effects in the information environment. In addition to gathering information, patrols can execute psychological actions, deliver messages, disseminate information, and influence target audiences through presence and direct interaction. Lower-echelon units must therefore shape this presence to reinforce the commander's intent. Their presence is further shaped and amplified through the use of available higher-echelon IRCs, such as military information support operations (MISO), public affairs, and civil affairs operations. Individual Soldiers must be able to engage the local population and deliver messages in such a way that they influence target and audience behavior in accordance with objectives.

## PRESENCE, PROFILE, AND POSTURE

9-3. Presence, profile and posture are interrelated terms that define and describe a unit's visual, aural, and oral presentation to others. Everything a unit or Soldier does speaks, in some manner, to those who witness or hear it. Presence, profile and posture are an active means by which units can shape sentiments through physical, visual, and audible actions.

### PRESENCE

9-4. Presence, the act of being physically present, always sends a message. Presence can be menacing or reassuring, depending on the situation. Absence, or the lack of presence, can create perceptions that work for or against the unit's aims. Being very conscious and deliberate about being present or absent can be a powerful form of influence and should not be left to chance. Once units determine that presence is required, or that there is no choice but to be present, how they convey that presence is important. Both profile and posture address the way that units, patrols, and Soldiers are present.

### PROFILE

9-5. Profile is about the degree of presence, both in terms of quantity and quality. Quantity is reflected in how much a unit is present, as in its footprint or task organization. Quality speaks to the nature of that presence, as in its current capability, as well as its reputation.

9-6. During the conduct of offensive- and defensive-focused operations, a unit tends to optimize its profile, not simply in number of forces but in terms of all assets or effects it can bring to bear. Here is where an information-related capability (IRC) like military deception can play a significant role. It allows commanders to make their force appear larger or more substantial than it is. In contrast, during stability-focused operations, the aim is often to keep one's profile to a minimum—to conduct an operation with the smallest force necessary to ensure force protection but not appear unduly threatening. Therefore, a unit's profile may be both minimized and optimized through partnership efforts with local national security forces.

9-7. Quality of presence significantly affects perceptions or sentiments, either positively or negatively, and requires continual vigilance. Soldiers and leaders must be conscious of their personal profile and actively work to build and preserve their credibility.

### POSTURE

9-8. Posture is an expression of attitude. Whether active or passive, threatening or non-threatening, or defensive or welcoming. Posture dictates how units or Soldiers appear to others and how they act towards them.

9-9. Posture is determined by the operational environment and necessity. For example, if force protection is paramount, a unit might decide to wear full protection and appear more aggressive in its stance and movements. If persuading the local population to support an upcoming change to the way biometrics are gathered is paramount, a unit might decide to wear soft hats and no body armor.

9-10. The relationship between posture and profile enables one to counterbalance the other. A unit at a numerical disadvantage can compensate through an aggressive posture. Conversely, a unit with more than enough forces can soften its posture, appropriate to the situation.

## SOLDIER AND LEADER ENGAGEMENTS

9-11. Like presence, profile and posture, Soldier and leader engagement (SLE) is an IRC that every unit inherently has at its disposal and for which it is responsible to employ. Patrols conduct deliberate SLE as part of their mission but must be ready to conduct dynamic SLEs; that is, unplanned engagements with local audiences with whom they come in contact during the routine conduct of the patrol. While these interactions may be impromptu, they still benefit from prior planning and training. Themes, messages, and talking points provide Soldiers with the necessary guidance to communicate with target audiences, whether deliberately engaged or inadvertently encountered.

9-12. Planning for dynamic SLEs is integral to planning the patrol. It involves anticipating individuals and groups that the patrol might encounter and developing appropriate response scenarios. Further, it involves reviewing and, to the extent necessary, memorizing the commander's intent, desired end state and narrative, and the messages and talking points that support them. Perhaps most important of all, it means having Soldiers rehearse the response scenarios to a point where they can engage local foreign audiences with confidence, competence, and nuance.

## LEVERAGING OTHER IRCS

9-13. At the brigade level, the S3 coordinates with IRC experts and other members on the staff to support tactical-level operations and produce desired effects in and through the information environment. These capabilities are generally requested through the target nomination process and coordinated with the higher headquarters. Common IRCs include, but are not limited to:

- MISO.
- Civil Affairs Operations.
- Combat Camera.
- Electronic Warfare.
- Space Operations.
- Cyberspace operations.
- Military Deception.
- Special Technical Operations.

### MILITARY INFORMATION SUPPORT OPERATIONS (MISO)

9-14. A MISO detachment typically supports a brigade combat team. The detachment commander and non-commissioned officer in charge serve on the brigade combat team staff as planners and coordinators of influence activities. They employ subordinate tactical teams to conduct engagement activities, execute psychological actions, deliver messages, use loudspeakers for message delivery and tactical military deception, and for collecting information on the operational environment. Product development and production is a company-level and above function and requires coordination for dedicated support or tailored messages and are subject to applicable or required authorities within the given area of operations.

## Civil Affairs Operations

9-15. When planning a patrol, consideration must be given to civil affairs operations that may be ongoing or recently completed in the area that the patrol will occur. Spotlighting or reinforcing these operations, whether through talking points or by presence at the project site, can help reinforce their benefits.

9-16. Civil affairs operations units often develop novelty items that resonate with indigenous audiences, such as school supplies, radios, and sports equipment or apparel. Patrols can employ these items to increase the effects of their engagements and interactions favorably. Commanders can facilitate the development and use of these items by providing access to funding sources and implementing streamlined approval processes. However, these items simply provide the venue to engage an audience and deliver the desired message. They are not the sole purpose of Soldier and leader engagements.

## Combat Camera

9-17. Combat camera provides several benefits to patrols. First, combat camera can record engagements for historical purposes. Second, combat camera images can be used for future public affairs or MISO products. They can also be used to counter threat propaganda. If combat camera assets are not available, units can designate one or more Soldiers to use unit-issued or personal cameras; however, the unit must have a procedure in place for the review, clearance, and disposition of any images taken.

## Technical and Special Capabilities

9-18. Electronic warfare assets can be coordinated to support operations by jamming, broadcasting, or spoofing to gain information environment effects that support and reinforce maneuver actions. Space assets can be requested to assist with reconnaissance, surveillance, communications, and imagery support. Requests for assets may have to go through the S-2 or S-6, depending on the specific capability and its intended use.

9-19. Tactical military deceptions can be employed to influence a threat decision maker to take actions that give the friendly force a position of relative advantage. Special technical operations can be employed to create effects within the unit's area of operations that cannot be accomplished by available assets or that would cause too great a risk. Effects in cyberspace may be requested to protect, exploit, or deny the threat the ability to collect or disseminate information in and through cyberspace.

This page intentionally left blank.

# Appendix A
# IO Input to Operation Plans and Orders

A-1. Commanders and staffs use Appendix 15 (Information Operations) to Annex C (Operations) to operation plans and orders to describe how information operations (IO) will support operations described in the base plan or order. The IO officer is the staff officer responsible for this appendix.

A-2. The Appendix 15 (Figure A-1) that appears on pages A-2 through A-4 is a guide and should not limit the information contained in an actual Appendix 15. Appendix 15 should be specific to the operation being conducted; thus, the content of actual Appendix 15s will vary greatly.

*[CLASSIFICATION]*

*Place the classification at the top and bottom of every page of the OPLAN or OPORD. Place the classification marking at the front of each paragraph and subparagraph in parentheses. See AR 380-5 for classification and release marking instruction.*

**Copy ## of ## copies**
**Issuing headquarters**
**Place of issue**
**Date-time group of signature**
**Message reference number**

*Include heading if attachment is distributed separately from the base order or higher-level attachment.*

**APPENDIX 15 (INFORMATION OPERATIONS) TO ANNEX C (OPERATIONS) TO OPERATION PLAN/ORDER [number] [(code name)] — [issuing headquarters] [(classification of title)]**

(U) **References:** *Refer to higher headquarters' OPLAN or OPORD and identify map sheets for operation (optional). Add any other specific references to IO, if needed.*

**1.** (U) **Situation.** *Include information affecting information operations (IO) that paragraph 1 of the OPLAN or OPORD does not cover or that needs expansion.*

a. (U) Area of Interest. *Describe the information environment as it relates to IO. Refer to Tab 1 (Combined Information Overlay) to Appendix 15 (Information Operations) to Annex C (Operations) as required.*

b. (U) Area of Operations. *Refer to Appendix 2 (Operation Overlay) to Annex C (Operations).*

(1) (U) Information Environment. *Describe the physical, informational, and cognitive dimensions of the information environment that affect IO. Refer to Tab 1 (Combined Information Overlay) to Appendix 15 (Information Operations) to Annex C (Operations) as required.*

(2) (U) Weather. *Describe aspects of weather that impact information operations. Refer to Annex B (Intelligence) as required.*

c. (U) Enemy Forces. *List known and templated locations and activities of enemy information units for one echelon up and two echelons down. List enemy maneuver and information-related capabilities that will impact friendly operations. State probable enemy courses of action and employment of enemy information assets. Describe the informational and cognitive dimensions of the information environment that affect enemy actions. Refer to Tab 1 (Combined Information Overlay) to Appendix 15 (Information Operations) to Annex C (Operations) as required.*

d. (U) Friendly Forces. *Outline the higher headquarters' plan as it pertains to IO. List designation, location, and outline of plan of higher, adjacent, and other functional area assets that support or impact the issuing headquarters or require coordination and additional support. Identify friendly IO/IRC assets and resources that affect subordinate commander IO planning. Identify friendly forces IO vulnerabilities. Identify friendly foreign forces with which subordinate commanders may operate. Identify potential conflicts within the information environment, especially if conducting joint or multinational operations. Identify and deconflict IRC employment and information environment effects.*

e. (U) Interagency, Intergovernmental, and Nongovernmental Organizations. *Identify and describe other organizations in the area of operations that may impact the conduct of IO or implementation of IO-specific equipment and tactics.*

f. (U) Civil Considerations. *Describe critical aspects of the civil situation that impact IO. See Tab C (Civil Considerations) to Appendix 1 (Intelligence Estimate) to Annex B (Intelligence) and Annex K (Civil Affairs Operations) as required. Also refer to Tab 1 (Combined Information Overlay) to Appendix 15 (Information Operations) to Annex C (Operations) as required.*

**[page number]**
**[CLASSIFICATION]**

**Figure A-1. Appendix 15 (IO) to Annex C (Operations)**

[CLASSIFICATION]
**APPENDIX 15 (INFORMATION OPERATIONS) TO ANNEX C (OPERATIONS) TO OPERATION PLAN/ORDER [number] [(code name)] — [issuing headquarters] [(classification of title)]**

g. (U) Attachments and Detachments. *List IRCs or IO units only as necessary to clarify task organization. Examples include Tactical MISO Teams, Mobile Public Affairs Detachments, and Visual Information Teams. Refer to Annex A (Task Organization) as required.*

h. (U) Assumptions. *List any IO-specific assumptions.*

**2. (U) Mission.** *State the IO mission.*

**3. (U) Execution.**

a. (U) Scheme of Support. *Describe how IO supports the commander's intent and concept of operations. Establish the priorities of support to units for each phase of the operation. Establish IO objectives to employ IRCs to achieve the desired endstate. Describe how IO weighted efforts will support offense, defense, and stability tasks. Identify target sets and effects, by priority. Describe the general concept for the integration of IO. List the staff sections, elements, and working groups responsible for aspects of IO. Include IO collection methods for information developed in staff sections, elements, and working groups outside the IO element and working group. Ensure subordinate units and higher headquarters receive the IO synchronization plan. Describe the plan for the integration of unified action and nongovernmental partners and organizations. Refer to Annex C (Operations) as required. This section is designed to provide insight and understanding of how IO is integrated across the operational plan.*

b. (U) Assessment. *Describe the priorities for assessment and identify the measures of performance and effectiveness and indicators used to assess information operations objectives against end state conditions. Refer to Annex M (Assessment) as required.*

c. (U) Tasks to Subordinate Units. *List IO tasks assigned to specific subordinate units not contained in the base order.*

d. (U) Coordinating Instructions. *List only IO instructions applicable to two or more subordinate units not covered in the base order. Identify and highlight any IO-specific rules of engagement, risk reduction control measures, environmental considerations, coordination requirements between units, and CCIRs and EEFIs that pertain to IO.*

**4. (U) Sustainment.** *Identify priorities of sustainment for IO key tasks and specify additional instructions as required. Refer to Annex F (Sustainment) as required.*

a. (U) Logistics. *Use subparagraphs to identify priorities and specific instruction for logistics pertaining to IO. See Appendix 1 (Logistics) to Annex F (Sustainment) and Annex P (Host-Nation Support) as required.*

b. (U) Personnel. *Use subparagraphs to identify priorities and specific instruction for human resources support pertaining to IO. See Appendix 2 (Personnel Services Support) to Annex F (Sustainment) as required.*

c. (U) Health System Support. *See Appendix 3 (Army Health System Support) to Annex F (Sustainment) as required.*

**5. (U) Command and Signal.**

a. (U) Command.

(1) (U) Location of Commander. *State the location of key IO leaders.*

(2) (U) Liaison Requirements. *State the IO liaison requirements not covered in the unit's SOPs.*

**[page number]**
[CLASSIFICATION]

**Figure A-1. Appendix 15 (IO) to Annex C (Operations) (continued)**

[CLASSIFICATION]
**APPENDIX 15 (INFORMATION OPERATIONS) TO ANNEX C (OPERATIONS) TO OPERATION PLAN/ORDER [number] [(code name)] — [issuing headquarters] [(classification of title)]**

b. (U) Control.

(1) (U) Command Posts. *Describe IO integration into command posts (CPs), including the location of each CP and its time of opening and closing.*

(2) (U) Reports. *List IO-specific reports not covered in SOPs. See Annex R (Reports) as required.*

c. (U) Signal. *Address any IO-specific communications requirements. See Annex H (Signal) as required.*

**ACKNOWLEDGE:** *Include only if attachment is distributed separately from the base order.*

[Commander's last name]
[Commander's rank]

*The commander or authorized representative signs the original copy of the attachment. If the representative signs the original, add the phrase "For the Commander." The signed copy is the historical copy and remains in the headquarters' files.*

**OFFICIAL:**
[Authenticator's name]
[Authenticator's position]

*Use only if the commander does not sign the original attachment. If the commander signs the original, no further authentication is required. If the commander does not sign, the signature of the preparing staff officer requires authentication and only the last name and rank of the commander appear in the signature block.*

**ATTACHMENT:** List lower-level attachments (tabs and exhibits).
Tab A–Combined Information Overlay
Tab B- Information-Related Capabilities Synchronization Matrix
Tab C–Presence, Posture, and Profile
Tab D–Combat Camera
Tab E–Soldier and Leader Engagement

**DISTRIBUTION:** *Show only if distributed separately from the base order or higher-level attachments.*

**[page number]**
**[CLASSIFICATION]**

**Figure A-1. Appendix 15 (IO) to Annex C (Operations) (continued)**

# Glossary

## SECTION I – ACRONYMS AND ABBREVIATIONS

| | |
|---|---|
| **AGM** | Attack guidance matrix |
| **C2** | command and control |
| **CCIRs** | commander's critical information requirements |
| **CO** | cyberspace operations |
| **COA** | course of action |
| **CP** | command post |
| **D3A** | decide, detect, deliver, and assess |
| **EEFI** | essential elements of friendly information |
| **EW** | electronic warfare |
| **FRAGORD** | fragmentary order |
| **G-1** | assistant chief of staff, personnel |
| **G-2** | assistant chief of staff, intelligence |
| **G-3** | assistant chief of staff, operations |
| **G-4** | assistant chief of staff, logistics |
| **G-5** | assistant chief of staff, plans |
| **G-6** | assistant chief of staff, signal |
| **G-9** | assistant chief of staff, civil affairs operations |
| **HPT** | high-payoff target |
| **HVT** | high-value target |
| **IPB** | intelligence preparation of the battlefield |
| **IO** | information operations |
| **IR** | information requirement |
| **IRC** | information-related capability |
| **MDMP** | military decisionmaking process |
| **MISO** | military information support operations |
| **OPLAN** | operation plan |
| **OPORD** | operation order |
| **OPSEC** | operations security |
| **PSYOP** | psychological operations |
| **WARNORD** | warning order |

## SECTION II – TERMS

**combat power**

(Army) The total means of destructive, constructive, and information capabilities that a military unit or formation can apply at a given time. (ADRP 3-0)

**commander's communication synchronization**

A process to coordinate and synchronize narratives, themes, messages, images, operations, and actions to ensure their integrity and consistency to the lowest tactical level across all relevant communication activities. Also called CCS. (JP 3-61)

**commander's critical information requirement**

An information requirement identified by the commander as being critical to facilitating timely decision making. Also called CCIR. (JP 3-0)

**commander's intent**

A clear and concise expression of the purpose of the operation and the desired military end state that supports mission command, provides focus to the staff, and helps subordinate and supporting commanders act to achieve the commander's desired results without further orders, even when the operation does not unfold as planned. (JP 3-0)

**concept of operations**

(Army) A statement that directs the manner in which subordinate units cooperate to accomplish that mission and establish the sequence of actions the force will use to achieve the end state. (ADRP 5-0)

**cyberspace**

A global domain within the information environment consisting of the interdependent networks of information technology infrastructures and resident data, including the Internet, telecommunications networks, computer systems, and embedded processors and controllers. (JP 3-12)

**cyberspace operations**

The employment of cyberspace capabilities where the primary purpose is to achieve objectives in or through cyberspace. Also called CO. (JP 3-0)

**decisive action**

The continuous, simultaneous combinations of offensive, defensive, and stability or defense support of civil authorities tasks. (ADRP 3-0)

**end state**

The set of required conditions that defines achievement of the commander's objectives. (JP 3-0)

**essential element of friendly information**

(Army) A critical aspect of a friendly operation that, if known by the enemy, would subsequently compromise, lead to failure, or limit success of the operation and therefore should be protected from enemy detection. Also called EEFI. (ADRP 5-0)

**indicator**

(Army) In the context of assessment, an item of information that provides insight into a measure of effectiveness or measure of performance. (ADRP 5-0)

**information environment**

The aggregate of individuals, organizations, and systems that collect, process, dissseminate, or act on information. (JP 3-13)

***information fratricide**

Adverse effects on the information environment resulting from a failure to effectively synchronize the employment of multiple information-related capabilities which may impede the conduct of friendly operations or adversely affect friendly forces.

**information operations**

The integrated employment, during military operations, of information-related capabilities in concert with other lines of operation to influence, disrupt, corrupt, or usurp the decision-making of adversaries and potential adversaries while protecting our own. Also called IO. (JP 3-13)

**information-related capability**

A tool, technique, or activity employed within a dimension of the information environment that can be used to create effects and operationally desirable conditions. Also called IRC. (JP 3-13).

**line of effort**

(Army) A line that links multiple tasks using the logic of purpose rather than geographical reference to focus efforts toward establishing operational and strategic conditions. Also called LOE. (ADRP 3-0)

**line of operations**

(Army) A line that defines the directional orientation of a force in time and space in relation to the enemy and links the force with its base of operations and objectives. (ADRP 3-0)

**measure of effectiveness**

(DOD) A criterion used to assess changes in system behavior, capability, or operational environment that is tied to measuring the attainment of an end state, achievement of an objective, or creation of an effect. Also called MOE. (JP 3-0)

**measure of performance**

(DOD) A criterion used to assess friendly actions that is tied to measuring task accomplishment. Also called MOP. (JP 3-0)

**message**

A narrowly focused communication directed at a specific audience to support a specific theme. Also called MSG. (JP 3-61)

**military deception**

Actions executed to deliberately mislead adversary military, paramilitary, or violent extremist organization decision makers, thereby causing the adversary to take specific actions (or inactions) that will contribute to the accomplishment of the friendly mission. (JP 3-13.4)

**mission command**

(Army) The exercise of authority and direction by the commander using mission orders to enable disciplined initiative within the commander's intent to empower agile and adaptive leaders in the conduct of unified land operations. (ADP 6-0)

**narrative**

Overarching expression of context and desired results. (JDN 2-13)

**operational environment**

A composite of the conditions, circumstances, and influences that affect the employment of capabilities and bear on the decisions of the commander. Also called OE. (JP 3-0)

**planning**

The art and science of understanding a situation, envisioning a desired future, and laying out effective ways of bringing that future about. (ADP 5-0)

**running estimate**

The continuous assessment of the current situation used to determine if the current operation is proceeding according to the commander's intent and if planned future operations are supportable. (ADP 5-0)

***Soldier and leader engagement**

Interpersonal Service-member interactions with audiences in an area of operations. Also called SLE.

**targeting**

(DOD) The process of selecting and prioritizing targets and matching the appropriate response to them, considering operational requirements and capabilities. (JP 3-0)

**terrain management**

The process of allocating terrain by establishing areas of operation, designating assembly areas, and specifying locations for units and activities to deconflict activities that might interfere with each other. (ADRP 5-0)

**theme**

Unifying idea or intention that supports the narrative and is designed for broad application to achieve specific objectives. (JDN 2-13)

# References

All URLs accessed on 9 September 2016.


## REQUIRED PUBLICATIONS

These documents must be available to intended users of this publication.

*Department of Defense Dictionary of Military and Associated Terms*. 15 October 2016.

ADRP 1-02. *Terms and Military Symbols*. 16 November 2016.

## RELATED PUBLICATIONS

These documents contain relevant supplemental information.

### JOINT PUBLICATIONS

Most joint publications are available online: http://www.dtic.mil/doctrine/new_pubs/jointpub.htm

JDN 2-13. *Commander's Communication Synchronization*. 16 December 2013.

JP 3-0. *Joint Operations*. 11 August 2011.

JP 3-12. *Cyberspace Operations*. 5 February 2013. This publication is available at https://jdeis.js.mil/jdeis/index.jsp?pindex=2

JP 3-13. *Information Operations*. 27 November 2012.

JP 3-13.4. *Military Deception*. 26 January 2012.

JP 5-0. *Joint Operation Planning*. 11 August 2011.

JP 3-60. *Joint Targeting*. 31 January 2013

JP 3-61. *Public Affairs*. 17 November 2015.

### ARMY PUBLICATIONS

Most Army doctrinal publications are available online: http://armypubs.army.mil/

ADP 5-0. *The Operations Process*. 17 May 2012.

ADP 6-0. *Mission Command*. 17 May 2012.

ADRP 3-0. *Unified Land Operations*. 16 May 2012.

ADRP 5-0. *The Operations Process*. 17 May 2012.

AR 350-2. *Operational Environment and Opposing Force Program*. 19 May 2015.

AR 380-5.*Department of the Army Information Security Program*. 29 September 2000.

ATP 2-01.3. *Intelligence Preparation of the Battlefield*. 10 November 2014.

ATP 3-60. *Targeting*. 7 May 2015.

ATP 3-60.1. *Dynamic Targeting, Multi-Service Tactics, Techniques, and Procedures for Dynamic Targeting.* {MCRP 3-16D; NTTP 3-60.1; AFTTP 3-2.3} 10 September 2015.

ATP 3-90.1. *Armor and Mechanized Infantry Company Team*. 27 January 2016.

ATP 3-90.37. *Countering Improvised Explosive Devices*. 29 July 2014.

ATP 5-0.1. *Army Design Methodology*. 1 July 2015.

ATP 5-19. *Risk Management*. 14 April 2014.

FM 6-0. *Commander and Staff Organization and Operations*. 5 May 2014.

FM 27-10. *The Law of Land Warfare*. 18 July 1956.

# RECOMMENDED READINGS

ADP 3-0 *Unified Land Operations*. 10 October 2011.

ADRP 6-0. *Mission Command.* 17 May 2012.

FM 6-02. *Signal Support to Operations*. 22 January 2014.

FM 7-100.1. *Opposing Force Operations*. 27 December 2004.

TC 7-100. *Hybrid Threat*. 26 November 2010.

TC 7-100.2. *Opposing Force Tactics*. 9 December 2011.

TC 7-100.3. Irregular Opposing Forces. 17 January 2014.

TC 7-100.4. *Hybrid Threat Force Structure Organizational Guide*. 4 June 2015.

## OTHER PUBLICATIONS

*Assessing and Evaluating Department of Defense Efforts to Inform, Influence, and Persuade: Desk Reference*. Copyright © 2015. Christopher Paul, Jessica Yeats, Colin P. Clarke, & Miriam Matthews. RAND National Defense Research Institute. http://www.rand.org/content/dam/rand/pubs/research_reports/RR800/RR809z1/RAND_RR809z1.pdf

*Assessing and Evaluating Department of Defense Efforts to Inform, Influence, and Persuade: Handbook for Practitioners*. Copyright © 2015. Christopher Paul, Jessica Yeats, Colin P. Clarke, & Miriam Matthews. RAND National Defense Research Institute. http://comm.eval.org/HigherLogic/System/DownloadDocumentFile.ashx?DocumentFileKey=45b2d092-0c76-4a81-a13a-f1f0087c2dce

*Assessing and Evaluating Department of Defense Efforts to Inform, Influence, and Persuade: An Annotated Reading List*. Copyright © 2015. Christopher Paul, Jessica Yeats, Colin P. Clarke, & Miriam Matthews. RAND National Defense Research Institute. http://www.rand.org/content/dam/rand/pubs/research_reports/RR800/RR809z3/RAND_RR809z3.pdf

*Dominating Duffer's Domain: Lessons for the 21st-Century Information Operations Practitioner (*Report written for the Marine Corps Information Operations Center) Copyright © 2015. Christopher Paul and William Marcellino. RAND National Defense Research Institute.

# PRESCRIBED FORMS

None

# REFERENCED FORMS

Unless otherwise indicated, DA Forms are available on the Army Publishing Directorate (APD) web site: http://armypubs.army.mil.

DA Form 2028. *Recommended Changes to Publications and Blank Forms*.

# Index

Entries are by paragraph number.

**FM 3-13**
**6 December 2016**

By order of the Secretary of the Army:

**MARK A. MILLEY**
*General, United States Army*
*Chief of Staff*

Official:

**GERALD B. O'KEEFE**
*Administrative Assistant to the*
*Secretary of the Army*
1634003

## DISTRIBUTION:

*Active Army, Army National Guard, and U.S. Army Reserve*: To be distributed in accordance with the initial distribution number (IDN) 115425 requirements for FM 3-13.

# Information Operations

**ANNEX 3-13 INFORMATION OPERATIONS**

# CATALOG OF DOCTRINE TOPICS

ANNEX 3-13 INFORMATION OPERATIONS

## INTRODUCTION TO INFORMATION OPERATIONS

Last Updated: 28 April 2016

The purpose of information operations (IO) is to affect adversary and potential adversary decision making with the intent to ultimately affect their behavior in ways that help achieve friendly objectives. Information operations is defined as "the integrated employment, during military operations, of information-related capabilities [IRCs] in concert with other lines of operation to influence, disrupt, corrupt, or usurp the decision making of adversaries and potential adversaries while protecting our own."[1] Deliberate targeting of an adversary's decision making process is enabled by understanding the cognitive factors related to that process, the information that they use, and how they receive and send information. IO is an integrating function, which means that it incorporates capabilities to plan, execute, and assess the information used by adversary decision makers, with the intent of influencing, disrupting, corrupting, or usurping that process. This is not the same as integrating non-lethal capabilities and activities, which may or may not have a behavior-related objective as their primary purpose.

The decision-making process can be modeled with a cycle of steps referred to as the observe, orient, decide, act (OODA) loop.[2] The steps of this model occur within the information environment and consist of three targetable dimensions: 1) informational, 2) physical, and 3) cognitive.

The information dimension represents the content of the information used by the decision maker. Once someone applies meaning to any data element, the data element is transduced into information. This distinction is subtle; but the impact is profound.

Not all data is transmitted by electronic means. A handwritten note or the sound of an explosion conveys data, but the predetermined meaning applied to either the data on the note, or acoustical data will cause the recipient to act or not to act.

The cognitive dimension is where the decision maker transforms the data from the physical dimension into meaningful information. While we can't directly target the adversary's cognitive processes, we can indirectly target them through the information

---

[1] Joint Publication (JP) 3-13, *Information Operations*.

[2] Annex 3-0, *Operations and Planning*.

and physical dimensions. This is accomplished by understanding the adversary's culture, organization, and individual psychology, which enables us to affect the adversary's OODA loop and ultimately their behavior.[3]

IO is fundamental to the overall military objective of influencing an adversary. IO involves synchronizing effects from all domains during all phases of war through the use of kinetic and non-kinetic actions to produce lethal and non-lethal effects. The planning and execution processes begin with the commander's operational design that guides planners as they coordinate, integrate, and synchronize the IRCs and other lines of operation. IO planning should be integrated into existing planning processes, such as the joint operation planning process (JOPP). IO planning is not a standalone process. In fact, JP 5-0 clearly identifies IO as a key output resulting from course of action development.

Additionally, IO is complementary to the practices, processes, and end goals of an effects-based approach to operations. IO facilitates targeting development and intelligence requirements, and matches actions with intended messages. Through planning, execution, and assessment processes, IO provides the means to employ the right capabilities (kinetic and non-kinetic) to achieve the desired effects to meet the combatant commander's objectives while supporting the commander's communication synchronization strategy.

## INFORMATION OPERATIONS DEFINITIONS AND DESCRIPTIONS

**Commander's Communication Synchronization[4]:** Commander's communication synchronization (CCS) is the Department of Defense's primary approach to implementing United States Government (USG) strategic communication guidance as it applies to military operations. The CCS is the joint force commander's (JFC's) approach for integrating all IRCs, in concert with other lines of effort and operation. It synchronizes themes, messages, images, and actions to support the JFC's objectives. Commander's intent should be reflected in every staff product. Air Force component commanders should similarly conduct their own commander's communication synchronization program. This component level communication synchronization coordinates themes, messages, images, and actions to support the commander, Air Force forces' objectives

**Information Environment**. The information environment is defined as "the aggregate of individuals, organizations, and systems that collect, process, disseminate, or act on information."[5] The information environment is comprised of the physical, informational, and cognitive dimensions. IO primarily focuses on affecting the cognitive dimension, where human decision making occurs, through the physical and information dimensions.

---

[3] JP 3-13, *Information Operations*.

[4] Joint Doctrine Note 2-13, *Commander's Communication Synchronization*.

[5] JP 3-13, *Information Operations*.

**Information-Related Capabilities**. IRCs are defined as "tools, techniques, or activities using data, information, or knowledge to create effects and operationally desirable conditions within the physical, informational, and cognitive dimensions of the information environment."[6] IRCs create both lethal and nonlethal effects. When IRCs are employed with the primary purpose of affecting the cognitive dimension, it is typically considered IO. IRCs may also include activities such as counterpropaganda, engagements, and shows-of-force, as well as techniques like having the host nation designated as the lead for night raids or not using dogs to search houses. IRCs can be employed individually or in combination to create lethal and non-lethal effects supporting a wide range of missions and objectives.

**Informational Dimension**. The informational dimension encompasses where and how information is collected, processed, stored, disseminated, and protected. It is the dimension where the command and control (C2) of military forces is exercised and where the commander's intent is conveyed.

**Physical Dimension**. The physical dimension is composed of C2 systems, key decision makers, and supporting infrastructure that enable individuals and organizations to create effects. The physical dimension includes, but is not limited to, human beings, C2 facilities, newspapers, books, microwave towers, computer processing units, laptops, smart phones, tablet computers, and any other objects that are subject to empirical measurement. The physical dimension is not confined solely to military or nation-based systems and processes; it is a defused network connected across national, economic, and geographical boundaries."

**Cognitive Dimension**. The cognitive dimension encompasses the minds of those who transmit, receive and respond to, or act on information. These elements are influenced by many factors, including individual and cultural beliefs, norms, vulnerabilities, motivations, emotions, experiences, morals, education, mental health, identities, and ideologies.

**Target Audience**. A target audience is defined as "an individual or group selected for influence."[7]

---

[6] JP 3-13, *Information Operations*.
[7] JP 3-13, *Information Operations*.

ANNEX 3-13 INFORMATION OPERATIONS

## ROLE OF INFORMATION OPERATIONS THROUGHOUT THE RANGE OF MILITARY OPERATIONS AND PHASES OF WAR

Last Reviewed: 28 April 2016

Information operations (IO) presents viable options to combatant commanders (CCDRs) for conducting operations throughout the range of military operations (ROMO) and all phases of war. IO enables forces to achieve objectives and possibly deter aggression. It enables the use of information-related capabilities (IRCs) in restricted, contested, or politically sensitive areas where traditional air, land, and sea operations may not be permitted. Historically, commanders have employed various IRCs to prevent escalation and enable security.

For example during a humanitarian assistance operation, a commander may influence host nation and even regional cooperation through the integration of public affairs (PA) activities and military information support operations (MISO) messaging designed to facilitate safe and orderly humanitarian assistance among the local populace. During a major operation, the commander may influence region-wide perceptions as well as local behavior through integration of electronic warfare (EW), MISO, and cyberspace operations (CO) with other kinetic or non-kinetic missions against key targets. Examples of other IRCs employed across the ROMO can be seen in figure on IO and the ROMO.

IRCs Employed Across the ROMO

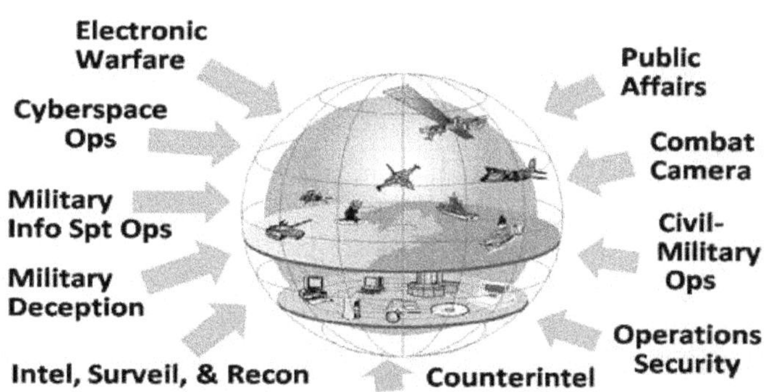


**IRCs Employed Across the ROMO**

ANNEX 3-13 INFORMATION OPERATIONS

## POLICY AND LEGAL CONSIDERATIONS FOR INFORMATION OPERATIONS

Last Updated: 28 April 2016

As in all military operations, the law of armed conflict applies to information operations (IO). Questions may arise about the legality of targeting systems with dual-use functionality that support an adversary's military and civilian populace. Likewise, targeting military systems without consideration to collateral effects may result in legally or politically unacceptable indirect effects on the civilian population. Similarly, rules of engagement (ROE) in a given area of responsibility may further constrain the integrated employment of IRCs. Commanders, in coordination with legal advisors, should request mission-specific ROE from the appropriate senior authority (e.g., combatant commanders, Secretary of Defense etc.) as required. However, due to the sensitive nature of targeting anything prior to hostilities, commanders may not want to risk inadvertent escalation. Since the operational complexity of applying IRCs is furthered by diverse legal concerns, legal advisors should be included in IO planning.

See Annex 1-04, *Legal Support to Commanders* for additional information.

ANNEX 3-13 INFORMATION OPERATIONS

## AIRMAN'S PERSPECTIVE ON INFORMATION OPERATIONS

Last Updated: 28 April 2016

Air Force information operations (IO) primarily exists at the air component level as part of the joint IO effort under the joint force commander (JFC) and combatant commander (CCDR). "At the operational level of war, IO ensures synchronized messaging from all IRCs and ensures information-related capabilities (IRCs) complement each other and do not detract from or interfere with any IO-related/messaging objectives. It includes informing and attempting to affect behavior and decision making as it applies to all relevant non-US audiences. IO should not be confused with integrating non-lethal capabilities. IO planners should be aware of capabilities for creating both lethal and non-lethal effects, as well as plans to ensure any cognitive effects they have will enhance and not detract from IO-related/messaging objectives. IO planners work with all other planners and IRC liaisons, using standard planning and execution steps of the joint operation planning process for air, air tasking cycle, and targeting cycle to accomplish commander's objectives. IO-specific by-products include items such as synchronization matrices, coordinated narratives and themes, and target audience analysis. There is no separate IO plan.

The targeting of a select audience's decision-making process is not new for Airmen. In addition to the requisite understanding of the information content and connectivity used by targeted decision makers, the Air Force has developed an analysis capability called behavioral influence analysis (BIA). BIA provides an understanding of the decision makers' behavior to include culture, organization, and individual psychology (e.g., perceptual patterns, cognitive style, reasoning and judgment, and decision selection processes). It is this knowledge, coupled with an Airman's ability to strike information-related targets that is the essence of Air Force IO. The integrated employment of capabilities to affect information content and connectivity of an adversary provides military advantage to friendly forces.

Air Force IO also includes the integrated planning, employment, monitoring, and assessment of themes, messages, and actions (verbal, visual, and symbolic) as part of the commander's communication synchronization (CCS) at the component level. The CCS will include pertinent portions of the joint force commander's or combatant commander's communication strategy, which may include communication synchronization themes and messages as well as any relevant component commander's themes and messages. At the air component level, Air Force IO planners should ensure these themes, messages, and actions (e.g., IRCs) are integrated across all lines of operation.

---

ANNEX 3-13 INFORMATION OPERATIONS

## INFORMATION-RELATED CAPABILITIES (IRCs)

Last Updated: 28 April 2016

In 2011, the definition of information operations (IO) was revised to eliminate references to specific capabilities and describe those generically as information-related capabilities (IRCs). As a result, the Air Force no longer distinguishes and categorizes IO capabilities with terms like "core capabilities", "influence operations," or "integrated control enablers." The Air Force now references tools, techniques, and activities when used to affect the information environment.

The distinction of IO's role as an integrating function merits emphasis. IO is not a capability in and of itself. IO does not "own" individual capabilities but rather plans and integrates the use of IRCs, tools, techniques, and activities in order to create a desired effect—to affect adversary, neutral, and friendly decision making, which contributes towards a specified set of behaviors. IRCs can be employed by themselves or in combination to conduct or support a wide range of missions. For example, IO planners should help ensure electronic attack (EA), offensive space control, air attacks, and cyberspace operations are coordinated and deconflicted from the perspective of cognitive/behavioral effects. The coordination process should also strive to resolve conflict between actions and messages. Individually, IRCs have wider application than IO employment. What unites capabilities as IRCs is a common IO battlespace—the information environment—whether those capabilities operate in it or affect it. Numerous Air Force capabilities have potential to be employed for IO purposes. See figure on IO Employment of IRCs.

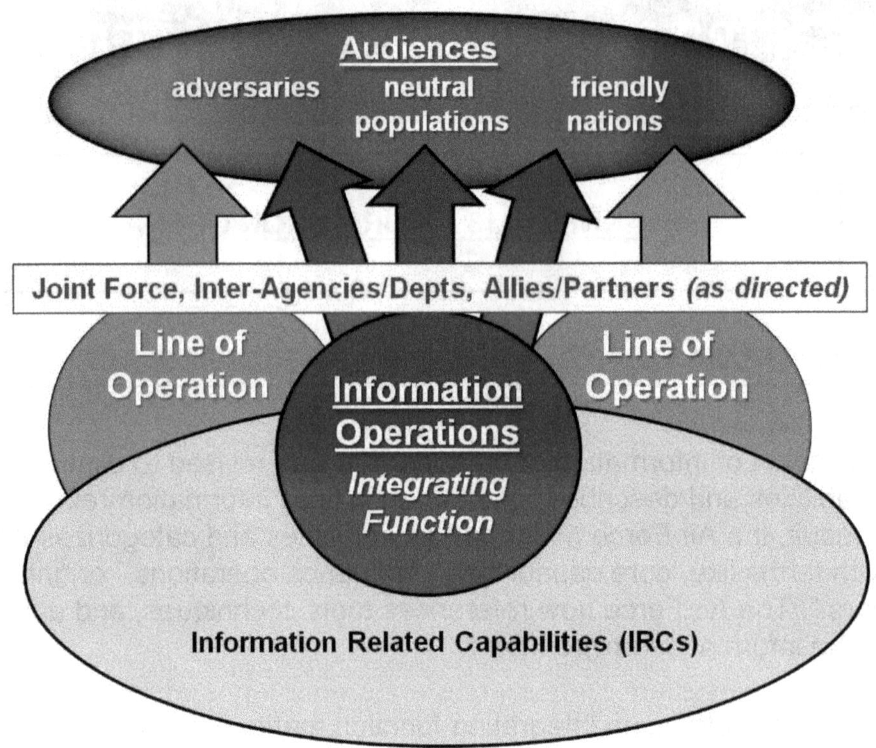


**IO Employment of IRCs**

---

ANNEX 3-13 INFORMATION OPERATIONS

## INFORMATION-RELATED CAPABILITIES: ELECTRONIC WARFARE (EW)

Last Updated: 28 April 2016

Electronic warfare (EW) is defined as "military action involving the use of electromagnetic and directed energy to control the electromagnetic spectrum [EMS] or to attack the enemy."[1] EW consists of three divisions: electronic attack (EA), electronic protection (EP), and electronic warfare support (ES). EW contributes to the success of information operations by using offensive and defensive tactics and techniques in a variety of combinations to shape, disrupt, and exploit adversarial use of the EMS while protecting friendly freedom of action in that spectrum. During combat operations, the commander, Air Force forces (COMAFFOR)/joint force air component commander (JFACC) is usually designated as EW control authority (EWCA) and jamming control authority for the employment of EW assets, associated policy, and processes in the joint operations area. The COMAFFOR/JFACC typically stands up an EW coordination cell to employ EA to negate an adversary's effective use of the EMS by degrading, neutralizing, or destroying combat capability. To deconflict intended effects, the following activities should be closely coordinated: EA, EP, ES, offensive cyberspace operations, offensive space control, military deception, operations security, and intelligence.

See Annex 3-51, *Electronic Warfare*, for more information on EW.

---

[1] JP 3-13.1, *Electronic Warfare*.

ANNEX 3-13 INFORMATION OPERATIONS

## INFORMATION-RELATED CAPABILITIES: MILITARY INFORMATION SUPPORT OPERATIONS (MISO)

Last Updated: 28 April 2016

Military information support operations (MISO) are defined as "planned operations to convey selected information and indicators to foreign audiences to influence their emotions, motives, objective reasoning, and ultimately the behavior of foreign governments, organizations, groups, and individuals in a manner favorable to the originator's objectives."[1] MISO may attempt to either induce change in foreign attitudes and behavior or reinforce existing attitudes and behavior. MISO at the combatant command level usually resides in the combatant commander's (CCDR) J39 directorate or in a military information support task force (MISTF), which includes a MISO planner as a member of the joint IO cell or joint IO staff.

The final approving authority for themes normally resides at the national level but is usually delegated to a geographic CCDR or joint task force commander during times of crisis. At the Air Force component level, MISO planners may be part of the joint force air component commander (JFACC's) IO team, or may be retained as part of the commander, Air Force forces' (COMAFFOR's) staff. It is essential for the MISO planner to represent COMAFFOR/JFACC requirements to MISTF for integration into the joint force commander's overall plan. Additionally, MISO planners should closely coordinate with military deception, operations security , public affairs, and other information-related capability leads to ensure the integrity and consistency of themes, messages, images, and actions.

[1] JP 3-13.2, *Military Information Support Operations*.

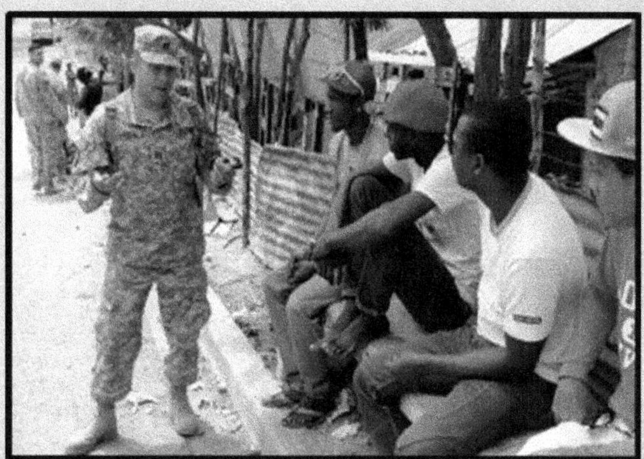

Capt. Abraham Alvarenga of the 102nd Group Support Battalion, 71st Theater Information Group assigned to Task Force Larimar, visits the Dominican Republic's Barahona province, May 7, 2014. The Military Information Support Operations group interviewed members of the community regarding the general and specialized medical services they received at no cost during the annual bilateral humanitarian exercise known as Beyond the Horizon. Such face-to-face communications are critical to MISO's mission today.

## INFORMATION-RELATED CAPABILITIES: MILITARY DECEPTION

Last Updated: 28 April 2016

Military deception (MILDEC) is defined as "actions executed to deliberately mislead adversary military, paramilitary, or violent extremist organization decision makers, thereby causing the adversary to take specific actions (or fail to take actions) that will contribute to the accomplishment of the friendly mission."[1] Deception operations can span all levels of war and can include, at the same time, both offensive and defensive components. During planning, MILDEC can be integrated into the early phases of an operation. The MILDEC role during the early phases of an operation will be based on the specific situation of the operation or campaign to help set conditions that will facilitate phases that follow. Deception can distract the adversary from legitimate friendly military operations and can confuse and dissipate adversary forces. MILDEC affects the adversary's information systems, processes, and capabilities to create desired behavior. MILDEC planners require adversary and potential adversary decision maker analysis for a sufficiently detailed understanding of how the information environment supports the adversary's decision-making process.

Each information-related capability (IRC) has a part to play in successful MILDEC credibility over time, so information operations (IO) facilitates close coordination with military information support operations (MISO), operations security (OPSEC), public affairs (PA), and commander's communication synchronization (CCS) personnel within the joint IO cell or staff. Whereas MISO, PA, and CCS activities may share a common specific audience with MILDEC, only MILDEC actions are designed to mislead. There is a delicate balance between successful deception efforts and media access to ongoing operations. Inappropriate media access may compromise deception efforts. Conversely, MILDEC must not intentionally target or mislead the news media, the US public, or Congress. Deception activities potentially visible to the US public should be closely coordinated with PA operations so as to not compromise operational considerations or diminish the credibility of PA operations in the national media. Due to the sensitive nature of MILDEC plans and objectives, a strict need-to-know policy should be enforced. Additionally, approval authorities for conducting MILDEC actions are typically at the joint force commander-level or above, so the approval action may require sufficient lead time for staffing.

---

[1] JP 3-13.4, *Military Deception*.

Army Field Manual 90-2, *"Battlefield Deception,"* (October 1988) revealed that the Army was revitalizing its deception capabilities, leading up to the greatest modern use of tactical deception in 1991 — Operation DESERT STORM. During DESERT STORM, a signal company mimicked traffic for the XVIII and V Corps headquarters to make it appear that they were stationary, when in fact they were moving into position for the "left hook," a flanking maneuver through the western Iraqi desert. The enemy focused on an amphibious training demonstration put on by the Marine Corps, causing Iraqi forces to reinforce the coastline, facing away from the main attack.

ANNEX 3-13 INFORMATION OPERATIONS

# INFORMATION-RELATED CAPABILITIES: OPERATIONS SECURITY

Last Updated: 28 April 2016

Operations security (OPSEC) is defined as "a process of identifying critical information and subsequently analyzing friendly actions attendant to military operations and other activities."[1] OPSEC denies adversaries critical information and observable indicators about friendly forces and intentions. OPSEC identifies any unclassified activity or information that, when analyzed with other activities and information, can reveal protected and important friendly operations, information, or activities. A critical information list should be developed and continuously updated in peacetime as well as conflict. The critical information list helps ensure military personnel and media are aware of non-releasable information.

The information operations (IO) team enables the OPSEC planner to maintain situational awareness of friendly information and actions and to assist other air operations center planners in incorporating OPSEC considerations during the planning process. Once the OPSEC process identifies vulnerabilities, other information-related capabilities (e.g., military deception, military information support operations, electronic warfare, cyberspace operations) can be used to ensure OPSEC requirements are satisfied.

---

[1] JP 3-13.3, *Operations Security*.

ANNEX 3-13 INFORMATION OPERATIONS

## INFORMATION-RELATED CAPABILITIES: PUBLIC AFFAIRS

Last Reviewed: 28 April 2016

Public affairs (PA) provides information operations (IO) with an open and credible means to reach key public audiences. PA consists of public information, command information, and civic engagement activities that are directed toward both the external and internal publics with interest in the DOD.[1] The external public may include allied, neutral, and adversary audiences. Truth is foundational to the credibility of all public affairs operations. Timely and agile dissemination is essential to help achieve desired information effects. PA plays a significant role throughout the range of military operations, with PA being one of the most prominent information-related capabilities (IRCs) used prior to the outset of hostilities and during stability operations. While PA cannot provide false or misleading information, it must be aware of the intent of other IRCs such as military deception, military information support operations (MISO) and operations security to lessen the chance of compromise. PA integration with other IRCs is vital to ensure the capabilities complement rather than conflict with each other.

Rather than providing an advantage to an adversary, the carefully coordinated release of operational information in some situations can intimidate an adversary, deter conflict, and counter adversary propaganda while also maintaining or building support for military operations.

### Counterpropaganda

Counterpropaganda operations involve those efforts to negate, neutralize, diminish the effects of, or gain an advantage from adversary propaganda efforts.[2] Counterpropaganda operations are normally handled through PA channels; however, several other IRCs can support that activity. In addition to PA activities to refute adversary propaganda, there may be electronic warfare or cyberspace operations denying adversary use of propaganda outlets. MISO contributes to counterpropaganda missions by amplifying key themes and messages among specific foreign audiences, some of which may be inaccessible by PA operations. Timing and initiative in the information environment is vital to defeating propaganda, particularly when addressing incidents involving collateral damage or friendly force mistakes. Rapidly providing

[1] JP 3-61, *Public Affairs*.

[2] Annex 3-61, *Public Affairs Operations*.

accurate, available information to the public may help disarm adversary attempts to exploit friendly actions for their propaganda value. MISO planners may also assist PA with conducting propaganda analysis.

**Combat Camera (COMCAM)**

COMCAM is a specialized directed imagery capability in support of strategic, operational, and planning requirements during wartime operations, worldwide crisis, contingencies, joint exercises, humanitarian operations, and other events of significant national interest involving the DOD. COMCAM acquires, processes, and distributes classified and unclassified still and motion imagery. PA typically has oversight responsibility for COMCAM activities, although COMCAM may support other IRC operations. COMCAM teams are uniquely organized, trained (including fully certified/qualified aircrew members) and equipped for rapid global response to provide documentation of air and ground operations and provide visual products for use by IRCs. Commanders use these products for communication needs, operational planning, decision making, operational assessment, and to satisfy requirements for historical documentation of operations. Where rapid global response, aerial imagery, special forces operations, or combat maneuver and capability are not required, traditional visual information resources, not COMCAM, should be used.

See Annex 3-61, *Public Affairs Operations*, for more information on PA, Counterpropaganda, or COMCAM.

---

**ANNEX 3-13 INFORMATION OPERATIONS**

## INFORMATION-RELATED CAPABILITIES: AUDIENCE ENGAGEMENTS

Last Reviewed: 28 April 2016

Audience engagements are an important contributor to information operations (IO) because of their ability to convey key messages where they are needed to assist in accomplishing military objectives. Engagements permit interface directly with a specific audience through traditional methods of information exchange. Engagements are broadly described as interactions that take place between military personnel and audiences.[1] Audiences may be key leaders or mass populations, and those audiences may be military or civilian. Engagements may be in person or virtual (e.g., a teleconference), impromptu encounters or planned events, such as during civil-military operations (CMO).

**Civil-Military Operations**

CMO are engagement opportunities of particular interest to IO planners. In CMO, military personnel perform functions normally provided by the local government, placing them in direct contact with civilian populations. This level of interface results in CMO having a significant effect on perceptions of the local populace and on relations with the military, as they work with governmental and nongovernmental organizations. CMO principally engage with friendly and neutral populations but may also reach adversaries. While CMO activities occur in conjunction with other military actions, they may present the only engagement opportunity with certain audiences.[2] Forces involved in engagement opportunities such as medical, engineering, or security force assistance may not have a habitual working relationship with IO efforts, so IO planners should be pro-active with their coordination. CMO can enable broader IO objectives and ensure consistency with the commander's communication strategy.

---

[1] JP 3-13, *Information Operations*.
[2] JP 3-57, *Civil-Military Operations*.

ANNEX 3-13 INFORMATION OPERATIONS

## INFORMATION-RELATED CAPABILITIES: INTELLIGENCE, SURVEILLANCE, AND RECONNAISSANCE

Last Reviewed: 28 April 2016

Information operations (IO) planning, execution, and assessment rely heavily on tailored intelligence, surveillance, and reconnaissance (ISR). While information-related capabilities (IRCs) separately rely on ISR support for their array of individual application, IO integrated employment of IRCs requires concerted, tailored ISR support in its own right. ISR is defined as "an activity that integrates the planning and operation of sensors, assets, and processing, exploitation, and dissemination systems in direct support of current and future operations. This is an integrated intelligence and operations function."[1] The IO team's affiliation with the Air Force forces (AFFOR) operations directorate and the combat operations division of the air operations center (AOC) enables an inherent close coordination for the operations aspect of ISR. Similarly, the IO team maintains habitual coordination with the AFFOR intelligence directorate or AOC ISR division for the intelligence aspect of ISR. The intelligence directorate or ISR division may opt to establish an IO intelligence integration (IOII) function to dedicate intelligence support to IO.

Establishment of a dedicated IOII function satisfies IO's needs, which require advanced and timely coordination to establish baseline characterizations of the information environment, analyze current intelligence for nuanced IO application, develop detailed targeting packages, and conduct complex effects assessments. Furthermore, the IOII element is a conduit for translating and internally coordinating IO's requirements with the intelligence collection management and production cells.

See Annex 2-0, *Global Integrated ISR Operations*, for more information.

---

[1] JP 2-01, *Joint and National Intelligence Support to Military Operations*.

ANNEX 3-13 INFORMATION OPERATIONS

# INFORMATION-RELATED CAPABILITIES: COUNTERINTELLIGENCE

Last Updated: 28 April 2016

Counterintelligence (CI) is defined as "information gathered and activities conducted to identify, deceive, exploit, disrupt, or protect against espionage, other intelligence activities, sabotage, or assassinations conducted for or on behalf of foreign powers, organizations or persons or their agents, or international terrorist organizations or activities."[1] Air Force Office of Special Investigation oversees all Air Force CI activities.

CI support to information operations (IO) includes identifying threats within the information environment through CI collections and analysis and assessing those threats through reactive and proactive means. Threat documentation through intelligence, surveillance, and reconnaissance (ISR) processes and CI products are the primary methods of notifying commanders. CI has the capability to neutralize and exploit threats through investigation and operations. Successful CI and operations security (OPSEC) activities deny adversaries useful information on friendly forces. CI typically has a close working relationship with information-related capabilities (IRCs) such as ISR and OPSEC but may not have the same habitual relationship with other IRCs. IO planners should ensure collaboration with CI professionals to maximize CI integration with other IRCs such as military information support operations, military deception, and cyberspace operations.

---

[1] JP 2-0, *Joint Intelligence*.

# INFORMATION-RELATED CAPABILITIES: SPACE OPERATIONS

Last Updated: 28 April 2016

Two mission areas of space operations concern the information environment—global space mission operations and space control.

Global space mission operations capitalize on the information environment to provide force-enhancing capabilities, which include: intelligence, surveillance, and reconnaissance; launch detection; missile tracking; environmental monitoring; satellite communications; and positioning, navigation, and timing.

Space control is defined as "operations to ensure freedom of action in space for the United States and its allies and, when directed, deny an adversary freedom of action in space." Defensive space control operations are defined as "operations conducted to preserve the ability to exploit space capabilities via active and passive actions, while protecting friendly space capabilities from attack, interference, or unintentional hazards." Offensive space control is defined as "those operations prevent an adversary's hostile use of United States/third-party space capabilities and services or negate (deceive, disrupt, degrade, deny, or destroy) an adversary's efforts to interfere with or attack United States/allied space systems."

See Annex 3-14, *Space Operations*, for more information.

ANNEX 3-13 INFORMATION OPERATIONS

## INFORMATION-RELATED CAPABILITIES: CYBERSPACE OPERATIONS

Last Updated: 28 April 2016

Cyberspace operations (CO) are defined as "the employment of cyberspace capabilities where the primary purpose is to achieve objectives in or through cyberspace."[1] CO use specific cyberspace capabilities to create effects that support operations across all domains. In contrast, information operations (IO) integrates information-related capabilities (IRCs) with its focus on the decision making of adversaries and allies alike. When employed in support of IO, CO include offensive and defensive capabilities exercised through cyberspace, as an integrated aspect of a larger effort to affect the information environment. CO may be employed independently or in conjunction with other IRCs to create effects in the adversary's battle space and ensure US forces' freedom of maneuver in the information environment.

See Annex 3-12, *Cyberspace Operations*, for more information.

---

[1] JP 3-0, *Joint Operations*.

**ANNEX 3-13 INFORMATION OPERATIONS**

## INFORMATION-RELATED CAPABILITIES: SIGNATURE MANAGEMENT

Last Updated: 28 April 2016

Signature management (SM) is a process used to profile day-to-day observable activities and operational trends at wings/installations and at each of their resident or associate units. SM incorporates the analytical methods of OPSEC creating synergies and resource efficiencies for the wing/installation OPSEC program. These result in identifying details that can be used in efforts to defend or exploit operational advantages at a given military installation and inherent to a unit's operational mission.

When an air component commander's military deception (MILDEC) plan requires Air Force wings and installations to present specified observable activities, the air component commander's MILDEC planner determines the actions required by the supporting unit(s) and communicates those requirements to the wing or installation Signature Management Officer (SMO) or NCO (SMNCO).

Wing and installations do not directly plan or execute MILDEC on their own, but are tasked by the operational MILDEC planner or OPSEC planner to accomplish S M tasks that directly support the operational MILDEC plan. The SMO defines the local operating environment and captures process points that present key signatures, observables, indicators, and profiles with critical information value. This process, known as the base profiling process, is the deliberate effort to identify functional areas and the observables, signatures, and indicators they produce and how they contribute to the overall signature of day-to-day activities and operational trends. Ultimately, this provides the correct presentation of forces when tasked to support the operational MILDEC plan.

ANNEX 3-13 INFORMATION OPERATIONS

## OTHER INFORMATION OPERATIONS CAPABILITIES

Last Reviewed: 28 April 2016

Information operations (IO) planners should consider all available options and/or combinations of lethal and non-lethal, kinetic and non-kinetic means in order to achieve the desired lethal and/or non-lethal effects.

Modern military operations require the ability to engage a target audience with a combination of lethal and non-lethal means, to produce both lethal and non-lethal effects. Non-kinetic and non-lethal means are not reserved only for friendly or neutral audiences. The ability to influence and affect an adversary through non-lethal means may prove to be a better option. For example, well-crafted military information support operations products may be the best solution to convey the intended message through a variety of print and electronic media to select audiences, which may also free-up conventional, kinetic assets to pursue other objectives.

Lethal actions are those taken through "physical, material means like bombs, bullets, rockets, and other munitions."[1] Kinetic actions are those designed to produce effects using the forces and energy of moving bodies and directed energy, including physical damage to, alteration of, or destruction of targets. Kinetic actions can have lethal or non-lethal effects.[2] Non-kinetic and -lethal actions include logical, electromagnetic, or behavioral means, such as gathering intelligence to understand how an adversary's cyber networks function in order to prioritize targeted nodes or a public affairs operation to inform friendly, neutral and/or adversarial audiences. Non-lethal options offer the capability to create effects and achieve influence without destroying targets, which may be more advantageous to the overall objectives.

**Special Technical Operations**

IO planners should maintain close coordination with the special technical operations element to integrate, synchronize, and deconflict operations, as appropriate.

For additional information, see JP 3-13, *Information Operations*.

---

[1] Annex 3-60, *Targeting*.

[2] Annex 3-0, *Operations and Planning*

ANNEX 3-13 INFORMATION OPERATIONS

## COMMAND AND CONTROL OF INFORMATION OPERATIONS PLANNERS AND INFORMATION-RELATED CAPABILITY FORCES

Last Updated: 28 April 2016

Information-related capability (IRC) forces and information operations (IO) planners are assigned to geographic and functional combatant commands (CCMDs) who employ forces in support of worldwide operations. The functional CCMDs provide IRC support to joint operations in all geographic area of responsibilities (AORs), as required. Thus, the command and control (C2) structure established for integrating IRCs should be robust enough to account for these various operating areas.

The combatant commander (CCDR) develops a theater campaign plan to accomplish ongoing and enduring theater objectives, including those involving IO. The CCDR may establish a joint task force (JTF) commanded by a joint force commander (JFC) to accomplish specific tasks or carry out a particular contingency. The CCDR or subordinate JFC normally designates a joint force IO officer to accomplish broad IO oversight functions. The joint force IO officer heads the JTF IO cell, when designated.

Primary and supporting components are designated by the JFC. If deemed appropriate, the CCDR or subordinate JFC may choose to use service component assets as part of IO integration into their planning efforts. Air Force IO planners and information-related capabilities are typically presented by the commander, Air Force forces to the CCDR or other JFC through either an Air Force component major command or a component numbered Air Force. In addition to IO support to CCDR objectives and messaging requirements, Air Force forces should also use their capabilities, tools, techniques and activities to support component objectives and leadership's messaging objectives.

**ANNEX 3-13 INFORMATION OPERATIONS**

## COMMAND RELATIONSHIPS AND INFORMATION OPERATIONS

Last Updated: 28 April 2016

When a theater requests information-related capabilities (IRCs) from organizations with global responsibilities, the Secretary of Defense (SecDef) will specify a command relationship between the functional combatant commander (FCC) and the geographic combatant commander (GCC) - normally a support relationship. This will be employed at appropriate levels within both the supporting and supported commands. These support relationships fall into four categories: general, mutual, direct, and close support.[1]

For IRCs providing effects via a support relationship, it is important for both supported and supporting commanders to document their requirements in an "establishing directive." The establishing directive should specify the purpose of the support relationship, the effect(s) desired, and the scope of the action(s) to be taken. Additional information includes:

- The IRCs allocated to the supporting commander's effort.
- The time, place, level, and duration of the supporting commander's effort.
- The relative priority of the supported commander's effort.
- The degree of authorities exercised by the supported and supporting commanders over the effort, to include processes for reconciling competing requirements and resolving emergency events expeditiously, as required.

To facilitate a support relationship, there should be an appropriate level of coordination between the involved commanders. This facilitates planning the detailed integration of IRCs and their effects with theater operations, and enables theater warfighters to coordinate directly at either the same or differing organizational levels. A direct liaison authorized relationship[2] should be established for coordination between the theater and functional IO planners.

---

[1] JP 1, *Doctrine for the Armed Forces of the United States*, Chapter IV, Section 6.

[2] DIRLAUTH is explained in JP 1, Chapter V, Section 9c.

If the desired effects produced by IRCs of a functional combatant command are focused primarily on a single area of responsibility, the SecDef may direct the FCC to attach IRC forces to the GCC of that theater. In these situations, the SecDef normally attaches the required forces with specification of operational control (OPCON)[3] to the GCC. An example may be the SecDef directing the Commander, US Strategic Command to attach space forces to a GCC. The GCC, in turn, normally attaches gained forces to the appropriate Service component commander with specification of OPCON. The theater commander, Air Force forces (COMAFFOR) is the Service component commander for Air Force IRC forces. The functional component commander for many IRCs is usually the in-theater joint force air component commander.

If the COMAFFOR is formally designated as the supported commander for IRC operations, the JFC normally delegates related coordinating authorities down to the COMAFFOR to coordinate joint IRC operations and integrate theater and global IRCs and their effects. The COMAFFOR is well suited to coordinate many Air Force IRC operations because of the COMAFFOR theater-wide perspective, ability to exercise command and control of IRC forces, and subject-matter expertise on the AFFOR staff and the air operations center IO team. Senior IRC or IO advisors on the COMAFFOR's staff may be assigned the responsibilities of executing IRC authorities on behalf of the COMAFFOR. Examples of coordinating authorities include space coordinating authority and counterintelligence coordinating authority.[4]

---

[3] See JP 1, Chapter IV, Section 4.

[4] For a description of these coordinating authorities, see Annex 3-14, *Space Operations*, and JP 2-01.2, *Counterintelligence and Human Intelligence in Joint Operations*.

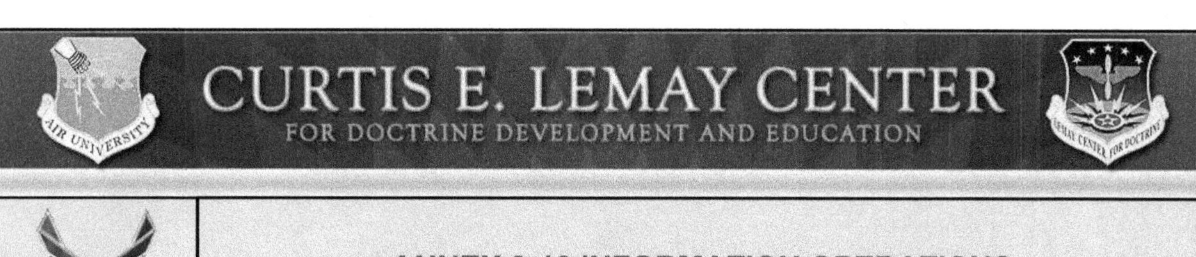


# ORGANIZATION OF INFORMATION OPERATIONS

Last Reviewed: 28 April 2016

Air Force information-related capability (IRC) planners operating in-theater under the operational control (OPCON) of the commander, Air Force forces (COMAFFOR) are typically assigned or attached to an air expeditionary task force (AETF). Within the AETF, IRC forces are normally attached to an air expeditionary wing, group, or squadron. The COMAFFOR normally exercises command and control (C2) of the AETF through an A-staff and an air operations center (AOC). See Annex 3-30, *Command and Control*, for further discussion of C2 mechanisms.

The Air Force embeds information operations (IO) and IRC expertise within the AFFOR staff, AOC IO team or the joint force commander's (JFC's) IO staff or cell to facilitate IRC integration and operations. Component staffs address component objectives and the desired effects required to achieve them. Also, the Air Force may augment other staffs with IO and IRC expertise to assist with tasking IRCs in-theater and integrating global IRCs and effects. IO planning should be coordinated during planning at the JFC and air component level, by AFFOR and AOC staffs. Planners at both levels should coordinate adaptive planning processes with supporting commands for IO.

As an example, US Air Forces Central Command's combined air operations center established a non-lethal effects team and non-lethal effects duty officer, similar to the IO team and IO duty officer. It was organized to focus primarily on integrating electronic warfare, cyberspace, and space effects into the JFC's operation, as opposed to integrating all non-lethal effects. The processes and organizational constructs by which non-lethal effects are integrated are based on individual commander's requirements and thus vary widely across AOCs.

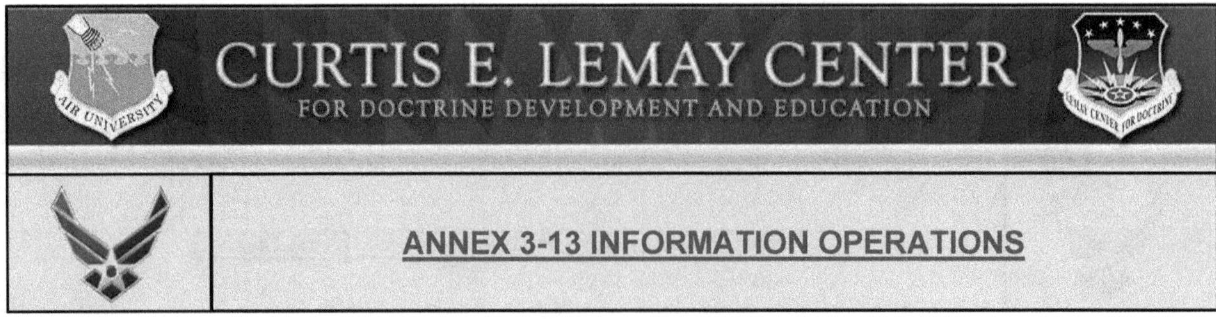


# PRESENTATION OF INFORMATION OPERATIONS PLANNERS AND INFORMATION-RELATED CAPABILITY FORCES

Last Updated: 28 April 2016

When directed, the Air Force presents information operations (IO) planners and information-related capability (IRC) forces to combatant commanders (CCDRs) to meet national-level and theater-level taskings.

The IO staff and planning function for a theater component is typically presented as a function within an air operations center (AOC) and on the commander, Air Force forces' (COMAFFOR's) staff. The AFFOR and AOC IO planners typically serve as a focal point for coordinating requirements for reachback support from IRCs outside of theater and should ensure their plans and support are in line with joint IO across the joint operations area.

An AOC normally includes an IO team that coordinates with all of the AOC divisions and with counterpart IO elements at other commands and task forces. The IO team may be attached to the AOC's strategy division and coordinate with the other AOC divisions, or the IO team may report direct to the AOC commander as a cross-cutting specialty team. Also within the AOC, an IO duty officer is typically assigned to work alongside other specialty duty officers for the senior duty officer or directly for the chief of combat operations.

**Service and Functional IO Responsibilities**

IO planners and IRC specialists on the Service and functional component staffs fill critical roles needed to successfully integrate IRC tasks and effects into theater operations. AFFOR and AOC specialists share a common effort in support of the commander's objectives and complement each other's responsibilities. The two staffs coordinate regularly to ensure consistency in focus and that their respective responsibilities and external relationships are appropriately deconflicted.

In general, the AFFOR IO staff coordinates planning actions at the joint force commander or CCDR level. In addition to internal AFFOR coordination, the AFFOR IO staff coordinates with the AOC IO team, component MAJCOM and NAF staffs, the joint staff, and functional and geographic combatant command staffs to:

- Request IRC forces and IO support (e.g., request for forces).

- Establish supporting-supported command relationships and authorities for IO planning and IRC tasking (e.g., direct liaison authorized [DIRLAUTH], electronic warfare coordinating authority).

- Facilitate deployment, beddown, and redeployment of unit-level IRC forces (e.g., deployment order, time-phased force and deployment data).

- Provide IO and IRC input on strategic/campaign-level operation planning documents (e.g., theater campaign plans, concept plans, operation orders).

In contrast, the AOC IO staff coordinates planning and tasking actions at the joint task force (JTF)-level. In addition to internal AOC coordination, the AOC IO team coordinates with IRC contacts on air expeditionary task force (AETF) staffs, IO contacts on JTF staffs, and IO contacts on other theater component staffs to:

- Provide input on operation planning documents (e.g., annexes/appendices, joint air operations plan, air operations directive).

- Coordinate themes, messages, and actions, approvals (e.g., rules of engagement, airspace control order), tasking orders (e.g., air/space/cyber tasking order), targeting lists (joint integrated prioritized target list, restricted target list, no-strike list).

- Submit requirements for analytical and targeting needs (e.g., telecom studies, patterns of life).

- Develop assessment criteria (e.g., measures of performance/effectiveness).

Example forums (or mechanisms) for coordination and commander's updates may be the joint targeting coordination board, joint collection management board, and battlestaff update brief.

**Reachback and Federated Support for IO**

Commanders and their staffs should consider leveraging other resources and capabilities available through reachback and federation to support theater IO and IRC activities. There are many Service, joint, Department of Defense, interagency, and national organizations referenced in this publication that can provide additional support to theater IO efforts. For instance, the National Air and Space Intelligence Center and the 363d Intelligence Surveillance Reconnaissance Group may be able to provide behavioral analysis and targeting products to meet IRC operational requirements. The AOC combat plans, strategy, and ISR divisions should be the main organizations in-theater requesting additional support. The need to establish command relationships for requesting reachback support may vary depending on the purpose and extent of support. If any formal relationship is needed for developing plans, DIRLAUTH is usually appropriate. Command relationships for executing operations may range from nothing formal required (i.e., standard tasking processes are sufficient) to formal establishment of tactical control (i.e., for dedicated, responsive support). Support established by formal agreement is termed “federated.”

---

ANNEX 3-13 INFORMATION OPERATIONS

## PLANNING AND INFORMATION OPERATIONS

Last Updated: 28 April 2016

Properly integrated employment of Information-related capabilities (IRCs) can create desired effects that accomplish objectives at tactical, operational, and strategic levels. Information operations (IO) is a critical military function because it presents viable options to commanders for conducting operations across the range of military operations (ROMO), not just during hostilities. IRCs can be used in restricted, contested, or politically sensitive areas where traditional air, land, and sea operations may not be permitted. The employment and phasing of IRCs may vary based on mission or availability, but the function of IO has broad application and effects. IO should be incorporated seamlessly and early throughout the operation planning, execution, and assessment processes, because of its broad application and effects and also because of its inherent challenges. The large number of potential IRCs that may be applied and the complexity of integration require extensive coordination. While IO requires early and extensive planning, there should not be a separate IO planning process or IO plan from the standard joint operation planning process (JOPP) and products. IO planners should provide appropriate inputs during each step of the JOPP for air (JOPPA) and the air tasking cycle.

Multiple IRCs can be integrated into planning across the ROMO. IO integration of IRCs is planned within the framework of the JOPP. IO planning should be integrated into the joint force commander's (JFC's) deliberate and crisis action planning. Moreover, IRCs should be integrated throughout the plans, then developed and executed by all supporting commands. Supporting component planning should be consistent with campaign plans, operation plans (OPLANs) and operation orders (OPORDs) developed by the JFC.

Multiple annexes in operation planning products contain IO contributions to the overall effort and should be reviewed by the IO planner. Development of these annexes is the supported commander's responsibility but requires coordinated effort between the JFC, supporting combatant commands, and component level staffs.[1]

### Deliberate Planning

During deliberate planning, theater planners normally incorporate IO planning into theater campaign plans (TCPs) and OPLANs. However, IO requirements should be

[1] JP 5-0, *Joint Operation Planning*, provides a list of joint operation planning products.

considered as part of the overall campaign or operational plan, and thought should be given to use of IO during operational design; such requirements should not simply be limited to a single appendix or single phase of an OPLAN. IO planning should be embedded throughout the planning process so that IRCs are appropriately integrated into every phase of the commander's plan. The majority of deliberate planning occurs within the Air Force Service component, AFFOR; consequently, IO and IRC planners should be embedded throughout the AFFOR staff, especially the A-3 and A-5. Planners should ensure IO is thoroughly addressed in a campaign support or contingency support plan's primary annex, Annex C, Operations (Appendix 3), and should coordinate closely with other lead planners to ensure IO is tied into all relevant annexes.

**Reachback support**

Reachback support may be requested to provide IRC-specific expertise or information to augment theater planning. This cooperation facilitates a comprehensive and realistic development of force requirements in support of theater OPLANs. Likewise, IRC requirements and IO planning considerations should be included in functional combatant commander's plans supporting theater operations. Planners should also ensure deployable IRCs are included in the time phased force and deployment data. Integration of IRCs is the responsibility of the geographic combatant commander and the commander, Air Force forces (COMAFFOR). The need to establish formal command relationships for reachback, or federated, support may vary depending on the purpose and extent of support.

**Crisis Action Planning**

Because of the time-sensitive nature of crisis action planning, it may be challenging to address IRC requirements if not previously identified. Certain IRCs may need substantial lead time for coordination up to the Secretary of Defense (SecDef)-level due to their political sensitivity or because they are controlled by other organizations such as national agencies, civil organizations, or even commercial enterprises. The end result of crisis action planning produces OPORDs and fragmentary orders that can be executed to satisfy SecDef direction.

Again, commanders should consider IO options throughout operational design and planning, and IRCs should be fully integrated into the development of all courses of action (COAs). During COA development, IO planners should identify tasks for IRCs in support of theater objectives and examine the role and contributions of IRCs in the various phases of the OPLAN. Knowledge of global and theater IRCs will enable the commander to make an informed decision. IO planners should also be embedded in red teams during COA wargaming.

**Plan Development**

Theater planning can help integrate IRCs and effects throughout the JFC's TCP or OPLAN. For OPLANs, this is normally accomplished through the JOPPA, which combines the mission activities and desired effects into a coherent plan to support the

JFC's overall plan.[2] The result is the joint air operations plan (JAOP). Again, there is no separate IO planning process or plan. The JAOP should include the integration of all allocated and assigned theater IRCs and all requests for theater support from global-mission IRCs. Theater IRCs, and effects derived from deployed and organic theater IRCs under the COMAFFOR's control, should be integrated into day-to-day operations through the air tasking order. The majority of JAOP development occurs within the air operations center (AOC); consequently, IO planning and IRC expertise should be embedded throughout the AOC. Finally, IO and IRC planners may coordinate with functional operations centers to synchronize and deconflict the development of their planning products such as the joint space operations plan and the space operations directive.

**Planning Factors**

As an integrating function, the IO planner is typically not responsible for the specific employment planning of the provided IRC. For instance, the electronic warfare (EW) coordination cell plans and employs EW capabilities, the intelligence, surveillance, and reconnaissance (ISR) collection manager and platform liaison plans and employs ISR capabilities, and the AFFOR A6 is responsible for planning theater communications. Some IRC assets are controlled at the national level due to their global access and multi-mission capabilities, yet they provide tactical effects and capabilities as well. Additionally, because they operate over a vast information environment, resources may not always be available for use.

**Global-Theater Integration**

Many IRCs have global requirements for national defense, requests from multiple theaters, and are continuously employed or executing tasking orders. This requires timely deconfliction and integration with other elements of the theater operation. Integrating various IRCs is accomplished through deliberate coordination processes between the theater AOCs and functional operations centers. The employment of IRCs at the operational level is accomplished through tasking orders that deconflict and integrate the full range of capabilities with theater operations. Theater IO and IRC planners should coordinate with functional operations centers to synchronize and deconflict the ATO with functional tasking orders, such as the joint space tasking order and cyber tasking order.

**Joint Intelligence Preparation of the Operational Environment (JIPOE)**

JIPOE provides commanders at all levels with knowledge of the information environment to effectively conduct planning. Knowledge of the information environment enables commanders to anticipate future conditions, establish priorities, and exploit emerging opportunities. JIPOE is a continuous analytical process to describe the operational environment, evaluate the adversary and other actors, and help determine adversary COAs. IO and IRC planners especially require detailed analysis of the information environment, including:

---

[2] See JP 3-30, *Command and Control for Joint Air Operations*, and Annex 3-0, *Operations and Planning*, for more information on the JOPPA and products such as the JAOP and air operations directive.

- Command and control networks, organizations, and infrastructure.

- Media infrastructure.

- Cultural demographics of the population and subgroups.

- Key decision makers and their behavioral patterns, decision-making processes, and advisors/relationships.

- Adversary exploitation of the information environment.

- Key communicators.

Given the long lead times often required for producing IO-relevant intelligence, requirements should be identified as early as possible in the planning process. An established IO-intelligence relationship will help with understanding types of information available and better defining requirements.

**Sequencing and Phasing of IO**

Understanding the sequence of operations over time is critical to effective planning. Commanders and planners often use phasing as a way to arrange and conduct a complex operation in manageable parts. The main purpose of phasing is to integrate and synchronize related activities, thereby enhancing flexibility and unity of effort during execution. The commander determines the number and actual phases of an operation. Phases in a plan are sequential, but during execution there will often be some simultaneous and overlapping execution of the activities within the phases.

During the shaping and/or deterrence phase(s) (often "phase 0 or phase 1" of an operation in OPLANs[3]), joint IO is often the main means by which the combatant commander or JFC can deter aggression and prevent escalation of hostilities. Often, the objective is to convince adversaries that planned or potential COAs that threaten the United States' vital interests are so undesirable that they give up hostile plans and choose COAs more favorable to US objectives. While conducting operations intended to seize the initiative from an adversary, IO efforts may still be focused on garnering support for unified actions and establishing conditions conducive to political solutions to the situation. At the same time, the JFC must prepare IO for potential hostilities, including recognizing and preempting dangers inherent in the information environment.

During portions of an operation devoted to seizing the initiative and dominating an enemy, IO planning will likely involve developing advantages across the information environment to facilitate execution of component missions (such as gaining and maintaining air superiority and other major combat). Normally, the objective in these

---

[3] See JPs 3-0, *Joint Operations* and 5-0, *Joint Operation Planning* for a discussion of the joint phasing model.

phases is to break the enemy's will for organized resistance, reduce casualties and collateral damage, act as a force multiplier, and hasten and smooth transition to post-conflict operations.

During the stabilization phase(s) of an operation, IO once again may become the main effort. It should be flexible enough to simultaneously support stabilization and combat operations. The objective is to change the perceptions and behaviors towards favoring US and multinational objectives, support the peacetime elements of friendly policy, and assess the impact of current operations on the ability to transfer overall regional authority to a legitimate civil entity. During phases devoted to legitimizing civil authority, IO should help influence the attitudes of local and regional populations to regard friendly civil authority objectives favorably.

**Planning for Effects**

All planners, including IO and IRC planners, should approach planning problems using an effects-based perspective. The IO planner's focus is not just about the integrated employment of IRCs, but more so on creating desired effects to achieve military objectives. Therefore, an effects based approach to operations (EBAO) is an ideal approach to IO planning. IO focuses primarily on affecting the cognitive dimension of the information environment. Effects can manifest at the tactical, operational, and strategic levels depending on the message or action, so IO and IRC planners should consider that any tactical action can result in strategic effects.[4]

**Direct and Indirect Effects**

IO planners should consider the indirect effects that IRCs may create beyond the direct effects. Indirect effects from IRC actions tend to resonate more with the audience and manifest in desired behavior and decision making. However, they take time to manifest and are more difficult to identify, characterize, and attribute. Because indirect effects take time to manifest and are more difficult to assess, IO planners should coordinate requirements and planning early and manage the commander's expectations for timing of approval and results.

Additionally, IO planners should not overlook the importance of pre-planning certain responses to proactively counter actions an adversary is known to take. For example, if an adversary is known to exploit damaged areas by publishing falsified or misleading images, or providing those images to media outlets, IO planners could account for such actions before the mission is executed, during the targeting process. For any mission occurring in an area known for this type of exploitation, IO planners could request friendly assets in the area collect post-event imagery to ensure an accurate image is available should the need arise. Such a response would serve as a counterpropaganda effort before the adversary's attempts gained any ground.

**Unintended Effects**

---

[4] See Annex 3-0, *Operations and Planning*, for a description of effects and EBAO.

All actions have the potential to generate unintended effects or consequences, whether caused by error, inadequate planning, or unforeseen circumstances. Examples of an unintended direct effect may be collateral damage from an air strike or collateral interference from electronic jamming. Examples of unintended indirect effects may be a local village unwilling to provide a safe area for downed airmen or a host nation government denying access to airspace. All planners, including IO planners and IRC planners, should possess a deeper understanding of indirect behavioral effects and should proactively coordinate on plan annexes and target lists to identify potential risks of unintended effects; as well as consult with political and legal advisors, CCS representatives, and targeteers for information regarding rules of engagement and prohibited/restricted targets lists.

**Targeting**

Targeting is defined as "the process of selecting and prioritizing targets and matching the appropriate response, considering operational requirements and capabilities."[5] Targeting supports the process of linking the desired effects to actions and tasks. The IO and IRC planner should participate in all aspects of the joint targeting cycle, to include developing targets for nomination to the joint force target list.

See Annex 3-60, *Targeting*, for further information.

---

[5] JP 3-60, *Joint Targeting*.

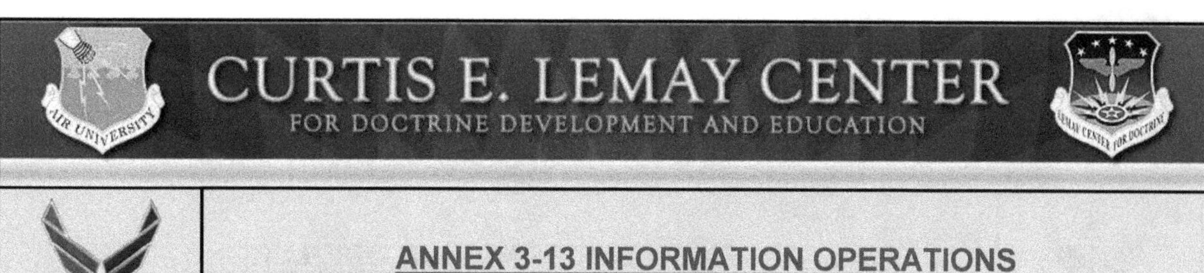


## EXECUTION AND INFORMATION OPERATIONS

Last Updated: 28 April 2016

Execution is a dynamic combination of theater and global operational processes requiring timely integrated employment of information-related capabilities (IRCs) throughout the joint operation plan.

The commander, Air Force forces (COMAFFOR) tasks IRC forces to execute operations via the tasking process, which is a part of the joint operation planning process for air (JOPPA). Within the air operations center (AOC), information operations (IO) and IRC specialists coordinate integration of IRC forces, mission, targets, and effects into theater operations via the joint air tasking cycle. Depending on the supporting IRC force, owning command, and relationship, the air tasking order (ATO) alone may constitute all the tasking information and coordination required to task an IRC force. However, tasking an IRC force will likely require IO and IRC specialists to coordinate with other theater operations centers or functional operations centers, which typically generate corresponding tasking orders of their own. Properly generated and coordinated taskings are vital to successful integration of theater and global operations. Not all operations, actions, and activities (OAAs) however, are captured in an ATO (e.g. engagements, exchanges, Red Horse projects, cyberspace operations). IO planners should maintain awareness of OAAs that have cognitive/behavioral impacts and integrate them into planning efforts

For assigned and attached IRC forces in-theater, execution of operations is tasked via the ATO. IO and IRC specialists primarily coordinate with tasking leads in the AOC's combat operations division and situationally advise external points of contact. For theater IRC forces assigned but not attached to the COMAFFOR, IO and IRC specialists coordinate with other theater operations centers to task those theater forces. For assigned IRC forces operating from outside of theater, this involves global IRCs, IO, and IRC specialists coordinating with functional operations centers to task those global forces through their corresponding tasking cycles (e.g., joint space tasking cycle) and tasking orders (e.g., joint space tasking order, cyber tasking order).

See Annex 3-0, *Operations and Planning*, for further information.

## ASSESSMENT AND INFORMATION OPERATIONS

Last Updated: 28 April 2016

Assessment is the determination of the overall effectiveness of operations and should be an iterative process. Because of the information operations (IO) planner's integrating nature and focus on affecting the cognitive domain, it is challenging to assess the success of IO. Information-related capability (IRC) effects, especially second- and third-order effects, may not manifest themselves until later in time. Consequently, measurements of effectiveness may be absent or incomplete. Additionally, identifying a cause and effect relationship can often be difficult. IO planners should generate valid measures for all desired effects and coordinate with the intelligence community to ensure that measures chosen are observable by the available collection capability. The employment of IRCs should be assessed to determine if they have been effective in achieving the commander's objectives. Assessment should include observable changes in the specific audience, methods of detection, and the relationship between cause and effect. The ambiguities and limitations resident within the information environment require frequent adjustment of operational planning considerations to ensure desired effects are generated while avoiding specifically designated or unintended negative consequences.

The commander, Air Force forces is normally responsible for evaluating results of IO. There are two primary types of assessments accomplished, operational and tactical. The operational-level assessment is usually executed within the strategy division of the air operations center (AOC). The tactical assessment is generally performed by the intelligence, surveillance, and reconnaissance division (ISRD) of the AOC.

Assessment at the operational level focuses on both performance and effects via measures of performance (MOPs) and measures of effectiveness (MOEs), respectively. MOPs and MOEs can both be measured either quantitatively or qualitatively. MOPs are criteria used to assess friendly accomplishment of IRC tasks and mission execution (e.g., if the desired effect is to decrease the number of violent crimes, then the MOP is to increase security or police forces within the target population). They help determine if delivery methods are actually reaching the intended specific audience. In contrast, MOEs are criteria used to assess changes in system behavior, capability, or operational environment to determine whether IO actions being executed are creating desired effects, thereby accomplishing the commander's objectives (e.g., the number of weapons caches voluntarily turned over, increase in the number of cooperative projects between the military and the civil population, or decreased number of violent crimes).

Operational-level planners and analysts should develop an intimate understanding of the linkage between IRCs and the intended effect. This requires direct feedback from those closest to observing the intended effects, such as the IRC specialists executing IO missions or the supported warfighters. IO assessment may also require coordination of collection requirements with the AOC ISRD.

A more detailed explanation of assessing operations can be found in JP 5-0, *Joint Operation Planning* or Annex 3-0, *Operations and Planning*.

---

NAVY WARFARE PUBLICATION

# NAVY INFORMATION OPERATIONS

EDITION FEBRUARY 2014

DEPARTMENT OF THE NAVY
OFFICE OF THE CHIEF OF NAVAL OPERATIONS

DISTRIBUTION RESTRICTION:
APPROVED FOR PUBLIC RELEASE;
DISTRIBUTION IS UNLIMITED.

NAVY WARFARE DEVELOPMENT COMMAND
1528 PIERSEY STREET BLDG O-27
NORFOLK VA 23511-2723

PRIMARY REVIEW AUTHORITY:
NAVY INFORMATION OPERATIONS COMMAND
NORFOLK (NIOC-N)

| URGENT CHANGE/ERRATUM RECORD | | |
|---|---|---|
| NUMBER | DATE | ENTERED BY |
| | | |
| | | |
| | | |

0411LP1142913

INTENTIONALLY BLANK

DEPARTMENT OF THE NAVY
NAVY WARFARE DEVELOPMENT COMMAND
1528 PIERSEY STREET BLDG O-27
NORFOLK VA 23511-2723

21 May 2014

# LETTER OF PROMULGATION

1. NWP 3-13 (FEB 2014), Navy Information Operations, is UNCLASSIFIED. Handle in accordance with the administrative procedures contained in NTTP 1-01 (APR 2005), The Navy Warfare Library.

2. NWP 3-13 (FEB 2014) is effective upon receipt and supersedes NWP 3-13 (JUN 2003), Navy Information Operations. Destroy superseded material without report.

3. NWP 3-13 (FEB 2014) provides information operations (IO) guidance to Navy commanders, planners, and operators to exploit and shape the information environment (IE) and apply information-related capabilities (IRC) to achieve military objectives. It reinforces the integrating functionality of IO to incorporate IRC and engage in the IE to provide a military advantage to the friendly Navy force. This NWP offers a framework of fundamental principles, practices, techniques, procedures, and terms that guides a commander in employing IRC to accomplish the mission.

4. NWP 3-13 (FEB 2014) is approved for public release; distribution is unlimited.

SCOTT B. JERABEK

INTENTIONALLY BLANK

PUBLICATION NOTICE

ROUTING

1. NWP 3-13 (FEB 2014), NAVY INFORMATION OPERATIONS, provides information operations guidance to Navy commanders, planners, and operators to exploit and shape the information environment and apply information-related capabilities to achieve military objectives. This publication reinforces the integrating functionality of information operations to incorporate information-related capabilities and engage in the information environment to provide a military advantage to the friendly Navy force. It is effective upon receipt.

2. This publication replaces NWP 3-13 (JUN 2003), Navy Information Operations.

Navy Warfare Library Custodian

Navy Warfare Library publications must be made readily available to all users and other interested personnel within the U.S. Navy.

*Note to Navy Warfare Library Custodian*

This notice should be duplicated for routing to cognizant personnel to keep them informed of changes to this publication.

INTENTIONALLY BLANK

# CONTENTS

*Page No.*

# LIST OF ILLUSTRATIONS

*Page No.*

INTENTIONALLY BLANK

# PREFACE

Information operations is the integrated employment, during military operations, of information-related capabilities in concert with other lines of operation to influence, disrupt, corrupt, or usurp the decisionmaking of adversaries and potential adversaries while protecting our own. Delivering current, relevant, and accurate doctrine to Navy planners and operators is essential. There are operational and tactical implications of this revision, including potential organizational and process adjustments in the maritime operations center.

Report administrative discrepancies by letter, message, or e-mail to:

COMMANDER
NAVY WARFARE DEVELOPMENT COMMAND
ATTN: DOCTRINE
1528 PIERSEY STREET BLDG O-27
NORFOLK VA 23511-2723

NWDC_NRFK_FLEETPUBS@NAVY.MIL

## ORDERING PRINTED COPIES

Order printed copies of a publication using the print-on-demand (POD) system. A command may requisition a publication using the standard military standard requisitioning and issue procedure (MILSTRIP) process on the Naval Supply Systems Command Web site called the Naval Logistics Library (https://nll.ahf.nmci.navy.mil). An approved requisition is forwarded to the specific Defense Logistics Agency (DLA) site at which the publication's electronic file is officially stored. Commands may also order publications through the Navy Doctrine Library System Web site (https://ndls.nwdc.navy.mil) by visiting publication-specific metadata Web pages and selecting the hyperlink on the stock number, which is linked to the Naval Logistics Library Web site. Users may be prompted to create an account to complete the ordering process. Currently, three copies are printed at no cost to the requester.

## CHANGE RECOMMENDATIONS

Procedures for recommending changes are provided below.

## WEB-BASED CHANGE RECOMMENDATIONS

Recommended changes to this publication may be submitted to the Navy Doctrine Library System, accessible through the Navy Warfare Development Command (NWDC) Web site at: https://ndls.nwdc.navy.smil.mil or https://ndls.nwdc.navy.mil.

## URGENT CHANGE RECOMMENDATIONS

When items for changes are considered urgent, send this information by message to the primary review authority, info NWDC. Clearly identify and justify both the proposed change and its urgency. Information addressees should comment as appropriate. See the sample for urgent change recommendation message format on page 13.

## ROUTINE CHANGE RECOMMENDATIONS

Submit routine recommended changes to this publication at any time by using the routine change recommendation letter format on page 14. Mail it to the address below or post the recommendation on the Navy Doctrine Library System site.

COMMANDER
NAVY WARFARE DEVELOPMENT COMMAND
ATTN: DOCTRINE
1528 PIERSEY STREET BLDG O-27
NORFOLK VA 23511-2723

## CHANGE BARS

Revised text is indicated by a black vertical line in the outside margin of the page, like the one printed next to this paragraph. The change bar indicates added or restated information. A change bar in the margin adjacent to the chapter number and title indicates a new or completely revised chapter.

## WARNINGS, CAUTIONS, AND NOTES

The following definitions apply to warnings, cautions, and notes used in this manual:

**WARNING**

An operating procedure, practice, or condition that may result in injury or death if not carefully observed or followed.

**CAUTION**

An operating procedure, practice, or condition that may result in damage to equipment if not carefully observed or followed.

**Note**

An operating procedure, practice, or condition that requires emphasis.

## WORDING

Word usage and intended meaning throughout this publication are as follows:

"Shall" indicates the application of a procedure is mandatory.

"Should" indicates the application of a procedure is recommended.

"May" and "need not" indicate the application of a procedure is optional.

"Will" indicates future time. It never indicates any degree of requirement for application of a procedure.

FM ORIGINATOR

TO *(Primary Review Authority)*//JJJ//

INFO COMNAVWARDEVCOM NORFOLK VA//

COMUSFLTFORCOM NORFOLK VA//JJJ//

COMUSPACFLT PEARL HARBOR HI//JJJ//

*(Additional Commands as Appropriate)*//JJJ//

BT

CLASSIFICATION//N03510//

MSGID/GENADMIN/*(Organization ID)*//

SUBJ/URGENT CHANGE RECOMMENDATION FOR *(Publication Short Title)*//

REF/A/DOC/NTTP 1-01//

POC/*(Command Representative)*//

RMKS/ 1. IAW REF A URGENT CHANGE IS RECOMMENDED FOR *(Publication Short Title)*

2. PAGE ______ ART/PARA NO ______ LINE NO ______ FIG NO ______

3. PROPOSED NEW TEXT *(Include classification)*

4. JUSTIFICATION.

BT

***Ensure that actual message conforms to MTF requirements.***

Urgent Change Recommendation Message Format

DEPARTMENT OF THE NAVY
NAME OF ACTIVITY
STREET ADDRESS
CITY, STATE XXXXX-XXXX

5219
Code/Serial
Date

FROM: *(Name, Grade or Title, Activity, Location)*
TO: *(Primary Review Authority)*

SUBJECT: ROUTINE CHANGE RECOMMENDATION TO *(Publication Short Title, Revision/Edition, Change Number, Publication Long Title)*

ENCL: *(List Attached Tables, Figures, etc.)*

1. The following changes are recommended for NTTP X-XX, Rev. X, Change X:

a. CHANGE: (Page 1-1, Paragraph 1.1.1, Line 1)
Replace "…the ~~National Command Authority~~ President and Secretary of Defense establish~~es~~ procedures for the…"
REASON: SECNAVINST ####, dated ####, instructing the term "National Command Authority" be replaced with "President and Secretary of Defense."

b. ADD: (Page 2-1, Paragraph 2.2, Line 4)
Add sentence at end of paragraph "See Figure 2-1."
REASON: Sentence will refer reader to enclosed illustration.
Add Figure 2-1 (see enclosure) where appropriate.
REASON: Enclosed figure helps clarify text in Paragraph 2.2.

c. DELETE: (Page 4-2, Paragraph 4.2.2, Line 3)
Remove "Navy Tactical Support Activity."
"…~~Navy Tactical Support Activity, and~~ the Navy Warfare Development Command ~~are~~ is responsible for…"
REASON: Activity has been deactivated.

2. Point of contact for this action is *(name, grade or title, telephone, e-mail address).*

*(SIGNATURE)*
NAME

Copy to:
COMUSFLTFORCOM
COMUSPACFLT
COMNAVWARDEVCOM

Routine Change Recommendation Letter Format

# CHAPTER 1

# Introduction

## 1.1 PURPOSE

This Navy warfare publication (NWP) provides information operations (IO) guidance to Navy commanders, planners, and operators to exploit and shape the information environment (IE) and apply information-related capabilities (IRC) to achieve military objectives. This publication reinforces the integrating functionality of IO to incorporate IRC and engage in the information environment to provide a military advantage to the friendly Navy force.

Like all Navy doctrine, this NWP should not impede a commander's exercise of innovation and mission command. This NWP offers a framework of fundamental principles, practices, techniques, procedures, and terms that guide a commander in employing IRC to accomplish the mission.

## 1.2 SCOPE

This NWP provides doctrine for the planning, preparation, execution, and assessment of IO for Navy operations. This NWP applies across the levels of war, mainly directed at the operational level of war. It fits between joint force commander-level guidance in Joint Publication (JP) 3-13, Information Operations; Navy tactical-level guidance in Navy Tactics, Techniques, and Procedures (NTTP) 3-13.2, Information Operations Warfare Commander (IWC) Manual; and other information-related NTTPs. The Navy typically executes IRC at the tactical level; but operational-level synchronization can optimize IO's integrative power.

## 1.3 BACKGROUND

Long before man walked the Earth, the survival of thinking creatures depended on exploiting information. Successful predators developed techniques to approach their quarry without alarming them, while potential prey with the best camouflage lived long enough to pass that trait to another generation. Social animals learned the importance of using influence, prestige, and fear to advance their survival. As humans moved from hunting packs to tribes and then to nations, information advantages contributed to survival and triumph in battle.

Modern advances in technology have increased the role of information in warfare; there are many instances of maritime IO that predate electronic communications and steam propulsion. For example, Napoleon's army was a potent land force but his navy struggled to match the British Royal Navy at sea. The French invested in an extensive network of semaphore stations capable of relaying visual signals up to 200 miles in an hour. This produced an information advantage, improving Napoleon's already effective command and control (C2) and passing observation reports along the coast to alert ships and reduce the Royal Navy's ability to achieve surprise. Among the Royal Navy's commanders was Lord Thomas Cochrane of the brig HMS *Speedy*. Cochrane was especially skilled in applying deception and surprise to defeat more-capable enemies and to capture unsuspecting prize ships. In 1808, one of Cochrane's raiding parties attacked a semaphore station and set it afire as the French signalmen retreated. After the British withdrew, the French were relieved to find charred remains of their codebooks, assuming the attackers did not realize their value. In reality, Cochrane had copied the codes and passed it along to his superiors, enabling the British to decode the semaphore traffic and to insert false messages. Even in the days of fighting sail, maritime commanders integrated network intrusion, disruption, intelligence, and deception to create information effects and achieve desired goals.

The United States Navy's doctrinal concept of an integrating information function began in 1986 with a tactical memorandum on command, control, and communication countermeasures, described as the combination of electronic warfare (EW), military deception (MILDEC), operations security (OPSEC), and physical destruction. In 1989, then-Chief of Naval Operations (CNO) Admiral Carlisle A.H. Trost designated space and electronic warfare as a warfare mission area, defined in a 1992 CNO policy paper as "the destruction or neutralization of enemy space and electronic warfare targets. As warfare support, it is the enhancement of friendly force battle management through the integrated employment and exploitation of the electromagnetic spectra and the medium of space."

This integrating function was redefined through the years under terms such as "command and control warfare" and "information warfare" before becoming IO in 2005. Evolving joint and Navy doctrine has refined IO as a discrete warfare area, not just a supporting function or enabling capability, and the IE as a valuable and contested part of the battle space.

## 1.4 KEY DEFINITIONS

In January 2011, Secretary of Defense (SecDef) Memo 12401-10 redefined information operations as the integrated employment, during military operations, of information-related capabilities in concert with other lines of operation to influence, disrupt, corrupt, or usurp the decisionmaking of adversaries and potential adversaries while protecting our own.

JP 3-13 defines these terms:

1. An information-related capability is a tool, technique, or activity employed within a dimension of the IE that may be used to create effects and operationally desirable conditions. (Chapter 3 discusses IRC in detail.)

2. The information environment is the aggregate of individuals, organizations, and systems that collect, process, disseminate, or act on information. The IE includes physical, informational, and cognitive dimensions.

3. The target audience (TA) is an individual or group selected for influence. Influence is the act or power to produce a desired outcome or end on a TA.

Integration is the arrangement of military forces and their actions to create a force that operates by engaging as a whole.

Discussion of IRC and its effects sometimes requires contrast with conventional noninformation military capabilities such as bombs, missiles, and bullets. This NWP refers to lethal effects to describe the observable physical damage intentionally caused by explosions or the dynamic motion of objects, and a lethal weapon is a device designed to cause such damage. JP 1-02, Department of Defense Dictionary of Military and Associated Terms, defines a nonlethal weapon as "a weapon that is explicitly designed and primarily employed so as to incapacitate personnel or materiel, while minimizing fatalities, permanent injury to personnel, and undesired damage to property and the environment."

# CHAPTER 2

# Information Operations Fundamentals

## 2.1 WAYS, ENDS, MEANS

As a model of military operations, ends are a commander's intended outcomes resulting in or supporting the desired strategic end state. Ways are the sequence of actions (methods and tactics and procedures, practices, and strategies) to achieve the ends. Means are the resources required to execute the ways such as troops, weapons systems, money, political will, and time. In this model of military operations, IRC is a means to create effects that induce an intended sequence of events that support strategic ends, either by supporting a friendly sequence of actions or undermining an adversary's sequence of actions.

The means of national power can only be effective when all elements focus on moving toward a feasible and clearly defined end state. In his book, "On War", German general and military theorist Carl von Clausewitz wrote, "War is thus an act of force to compel our enemy to do our will." Military objectives must cause a realistic change in the adversary's behavior or capability as a means to achieve that desired national/theater strategic end state; this is true whether using lethal fires or IRC. Planners must define the audience or target and how to apply IRC for the best results. MILDEC may manipulate adversary decision makers to act in a way advantageous to friendly military objectives. The general populace may be open to influences that may shift allegiance toward a more favorable leadership. A cyberspace or electronic attack might disrupt the adversary's C2. Lethal effects or military information support operations (MISO) can sap adversary combatants of their will to fight or send them into an irrational rage; friendly force planners must be careful to decide which option best suits the current mission.

Actions intended to influence a target audience focus on altering the perceptions and behaviors of leaders, groups, or entire populations to affect behaviors, protect operations, and project accurate information to achieve desired effects. These effects should result in a change in the adversary's behavior decision cycle and align with the commander's objectives.

## 2.2 INFORMATION SUPERIORITY

JP 1-02 defines information superiority as "the operational advantage derived from the ability to collect, process, and disseminate an uninterrupted flow of information while exploiting or denying an adversary's ability to do the same." The concept should not imply an impossible goal of friendly force information perfection against total information denial for the enemy. It simply means the commander operates with less friction from the fog of war than the opposing commander does.

Just as it is impossible to sustain global maritime superiority, it is not always practical or desirable to maintain continuous information superiority. While ideal, "an uninterrupted flow of information" should not be required or even assumed. Commanders and their staffs need to make information a priority and their units must capitalize on the synergy between information and other lines of operation, apply IRC, and expend resources when it is necessary for mission success.

## 2.3 AUTHORITIES, RESPONSIBILITIES, AND LEGAL CONSIDERATIONS

Navy forces typically operate under a component commander or joint task force commander attached to a combatant commander (CCDR) or a subordinate joint force commander (JFC). A JFC executes unified actions to apply all of the instruments of national power to affect adversary political, military, economic, social, infrastructure, and information systems.

### 2.3.1 Authorities

The authority to employ IRC derives from Title 10, U.S. Code, Armed Forces. While Title 10 does not address IO separately, it provides the legal basis for the roles, missions, and organization of the Department of Defense (DOD) and the Services. Title 10, Section 16, gives command authority over assigned forces to the CCDR, which provides that individual with the authority to organize and employ commands and forces, assign tasks, designate objectives, and provide authoritative direction over all aspects of military operations.

DOD policy delegates authority to DOD components. DOD Directive 3600.01 series, Information Operations, is the principal IO policy document. Its counterpart, Chairman of the Joint Chiefs of Staff Instruction 3210.01C, Joint Information Operations Proponent, provides joint policy regarding the use of IRC, professional qualifications for the joint IO force, as well as joint IO education and training requirements. These two documents delineate the CCDR's authority to conduct joint IO and to delegate operational authority to a subordinate JFC, as appropriate.

The nature of IO is such that the exercise of operational authority inherently requires a detailed and rigorous legal interpretation of authority or legality of specific actions. Commanders at all levels should involve their staff judge advocates in the development of IO policy and the conduct of IO.

### 2.3.2 Responsibilities

JP 3-13 describes responsibilities for Undersecretary of Defense for Policy, Undersecretary of Defense for Intelligence, and the Joint Staff. The Joint Information Operations Warfare Center ensures IRC integration in support of IO and provide IO subject matter experts to the Joint Staff and the combatant commands (CCMD).

The Chairman of the Joint Chiefs of Staff (CJCS), as the principal military advisor to the President, Secretary of Defense, and the National Security Council, is responsible for developing and providing U.S. military policies, positions, and strategies that support DOD IO operational planning as part of the interagency process. CJCS IO functions include:

1. Validate capability based IO requirements through the Joint Requirements Oversight Council.

2. Develop and maintain joint doctrine for IO and IRC in joint operations.

3. Ensure all joint education, training, plans, and operations include, and are consistent with, IO policy, strategy, and doctrine.

The Deputy Director for Global Operations (J38) serves as the CJCS's focal point for IO and coordinates with the Joint Staff, CCMD, and other organizations that have direct or supporting IO responsibilities.

The Unified Command Plan provides guidance to CCDR and assigns missions and force structure as well as geographic or functional areas of responsibility (AORs). CCDRs integrate, plan, coordinate, and execute IO when conducting campaigns and identify and prioritize IO requirements. The CCDRs also integrate IO into appropriate security cooperation plans and activities.

In addition to these responsibilities, Commander, United States Special Operations Command is also responsible for integrating and coordinating MISO, including providing other CCDRs with MISO planning and execution capabilities. Commander, United States Strategic Command (CDRUSSTRATCOM) is responsible for acting as an advocate for joint electromagnetic spectrum operations (JEMSO), cyberspace operations (CO), and space operations. As the joint EW advocate, CDRUSSTRATCOM is focused on enhancing interoperability and providing other CCDRs with EW capabilities and expertise in support of their missions. As CO advocate, CDRUSSTRATCOM is responsible for synchronizing CO planning. CCDR's responsibilities include:

1. Plan, exercise, and conduct IO in support of national goals and objectives as directed by the Joint Strategic Capabilities Plan (JSCP).

2. Integrate capabilities into deliberate and crisis action planning to conduct IO in accordance with appropriate policy and doctrine to accomplish their Unified Command Plan-assigned missions.

3. Develop a process within the component command and joint task force (JTF) staffs that effectively integrates the various capabilities and activities to conduct IO.

4. Incorporate IO tactics, techniques, and procedures into exercises, modeling and simulation, and training events using the joint mission-essential task process.

5. Develop and support intelligence requirements information operations activities under all pertinent operational plans.

6. Develop, maintain, and prioritize IO requirements.

7. Incorporate IO into flexible deterrent options such as military exercises and shows of force.

Service component commanders derive responsibilities from their parent Service. These responsibilities include recommending to the JFC the proper employment of the Service IRC in support of joint IO. If deemed appropriate, the CCDR or JFC may also choose to conduct IO using Service component capabilities.

1. Develop IO doctrine and tactics and organize, train, and equip forces with capabilities to conduct IO. Ensure the Services' forces and planning capabilities effectively support the combatant commanders through the appropriate Service component commanders.

2. Conduct research, development, testing and evaluation, and procurement of capabilities that meet validated Service and joint IO requirements.

3. Incorporate IO into Service school curricula and into appropriate training and education activities.

Like Service component commands, functional component commands have authority over forces or—in the case of IO—IRC, as delegated by the establishing authority (normally a CCDR or JFC). Functional component commands may also be tasked to plan and execute IO as an integrated part of joint operations.

### 2.3.3 Legal Considerations for Information Operations

Military activities in the information environment, like all military operations, are conducted in accordance with law and policy. The conduct of IO often involves legal and policy questions requiring not just local review but often, national-level coordination and approval. The U.S. Constitution, U.S. legal codes, and international laws set boundaries and establish precedence for all military activity, to include IO. JP 3-13 provides further discussion of legal considerations in the conduct of joint IO.

The staff judge advocate should be involved in IO planning and execution. Legal considerations include, but are not limited to, an assessment of:

1. The different legal limitations placed on IO in peacetime, crisis, and conflict (to include war). Legal analysis of intended wartime targets requires traditional Law of War analysis.

2. The legal aspects of transitioning from defensive to offensive operations.

3. Special protection for international civil aviation, international banking, and cultural or historical property.

4. Actions that are expressly prohibited by international law or convention. Examples include, but are not limited to:

    a. Destruction resulting from space-based attack[1]

---

[1] Convention on International Liability for Damage Caused by Space Objects

b. Violation of a country's neutrality by an attack launched from a neutral nation[2]

c. MISO broadcasts from the sea, which may constitute unauthorized broadcasting[3].

## 2.4 EMPLOYMENT OF INFORMATION-RELATED CAPABILITIES

Information is how an organization develops situational awareness, makes decisions, and executes orders. Figure 2-1 depicts the adversary decision-making process through the IE and the effects of IRC upon it.

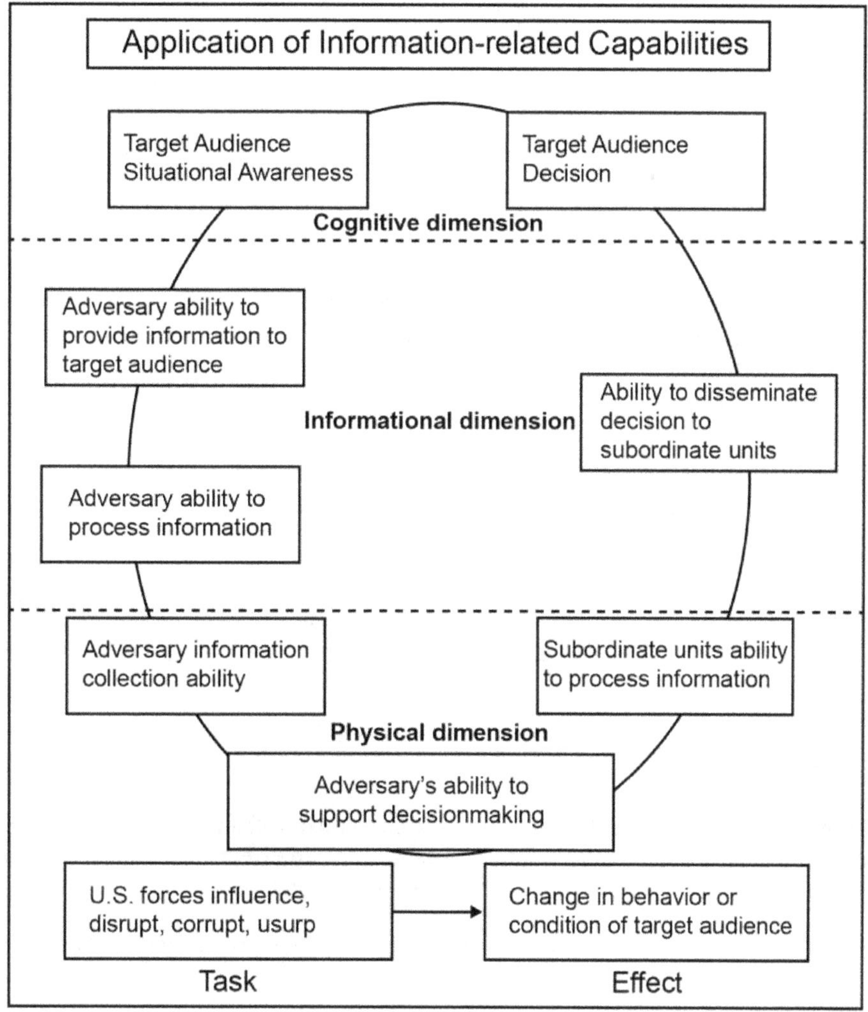


Figure 2-1. Applying Information-related Capabilities from Task to Effect

2 Hague Convention V

3 United Nations Convention on the Law of the Sea

### 2.4.1 Effects

An effect is the physical or behavioral state of a system that results from an action, a set of actions, or another effect. The success of the Navy force is defined by its ability to create the effects necessary to achieve military objectives, whether at the strategic, operational, or tactical levels. Commanders should clearly articulate the objectives or goals of a given military operation. Effects should then flow from objectives as a product of the military operations designed to help achieve those objectives.

Based on clear objectives, planners should design specific operations to achieve a desired outcome and then identify the optimum capability for achieving that outcome. There are second-order and third-order effects that should also be taken into consideration. Many of the variables in IO planning also have human dimensions that are difficult to measure, may not be directly observable, and for which it may be difficult to acquire feedback. At all times, planners should analyze effects from the point of view of the culture and social makeup of the country or location of upcoming operations. Information assessment is inherently challenging and has a lower degree of accuracy than conventional battle damage assessment. Nevertheless, the planning for IO should focus on operational objectives and the effects produced. Operational assessment allows the commander to evaluate IO and adjust specific information operations to evolving combat situations to increase its effectiveness.

Strategic effects can be created by a wide variety of military actions at all levels of war. IO can create effects at the strategic level and require coordination with other instruments of national power. In addition, tactical-level IO events have the potential to create strategic effects. Influence operations are often designed to affect a nation's leaders or population. Communications networks are often an integral part of national (strategic) infrastructure and may be vulnerable to attack. Those strategic vulnerabilities present in our adversaries may also be present at home. As a result, our strategic defense is highly dependent on the IRC that create information and maritime superiority.

IO at the strategic level of war is directed by the President or SecDef and is planned in coordination with other agencies or organizations outside the DOD. Such operations should be coordinated among supporting Navy units, the CCDR's IO team or cell, the JTF commander's IO team or cell, and other supporting components to ensure unity of effort and prevent conflict with ongoing operational-level efforts. Examples of how IO can achieve strategic effects include:

1. Promote durable relationships and partnerships to influence both friendly and adversarial behavior toward achieving national objectives.

2. Institute appropriate protective and defensive measures to ensure friendly forces can continuously conduct IO across the entire spectrum of conflict. Such measures create effects that deny adversaries knowledge of or the ability to access or disrupt friendly information operations.

3. Reduce adversary leadership resistance to U.S. national objectives by affecting their resolve or confidence.

4. Negatively impact an adversary's ability to lead by affecting their communications with their forces or their understanding of the operating environment.

5. Employ actions that reduce friendly vulnerabilities to physical and cyberspace attacks.

Operational-level effects can be created by a wide variety of military actions at all levels of war. The Service or functional component commander conducts IO within the assigned AOR or joint operation area. IO at this level uses military assets and capabilities to achieve operational effects through the design, organization, integration, and conduct of campaigns and major operations. IO plans between and among supported and supporting commands should be coordinated closely to prevent redundancy, mission degradation, and fratricide. Specific operational effects IO can achieve at this level may include:

1. Hindering an adversary's ability to strike by incapacitating their information systems and creating confusion

2. Slowing or stopping an adversary's operational tempo by causing hesitation, confusion, and misdirection

3. Reducing an adversary's command and control capability
4. Influencing adversary and neutral perceptions of leaders, military forces, and populations away from adversary objectives and toward U.S. objectives
5. Disrupting the adversary commander's ability to mass and synchronize combat power
6. Employing actions that reduce friendly vulnerabilities to physical and cyberspace attacks
7. Protecting forces during humanitarian assistance, disaster response, and noncombatant evacuation operations
8. Protecting friendly force C2 and information.

Tactical tasks are actions intended to create desired effects or preclude undesired effects supporting tactical objectives. The Navy or maritime component commander directs tactical IO execution. The primary focus of IO at the tactical level of war is to deny, degrade, deceive, disrupt, or destroy an adversary's use of information directly related to conducting military operations. Tactical IO includes protecting friendly information and information systems.

Figure 2-2 depicts three generic information tasks and possible effects and IRC used to achieve them.

### 2.4.2 Influence Target Audiences

A detailed understanding of adversary decision maker(s), planning, and integration with operations is required for conducting operations focused on affecting the perceptions and behaviors of leaders, groups, or populations. U.S. forces employ capabilities to affect behaviors, protect operations, communicate the commander's intent, and project accurate information to create desired effects across the cognitive dimension. Effects result in a change in behavior or a change in the adversary's decision cycle so that it aligns with the commander's objectives. The principal military capabilities to support accomplishment of influence objectives include MISO, MILDEC,

| Task | Influence Target Audiences | Disrupt, Degrade Adversary Command and Control Systems | Protect Friendly Information and Information Systems |
|---|---|---|---|
| Effects | Inform and educate target audiences<br>Influence adversary and neutral perceptions toward U.S. objectives | Exploit adversary C2 systems<br>Disrupt adversary decision-making cycle<br>Misdirect reconnaissance collection efforts | Assure own-force communications<br>Deny friendly force intelligence to hostile collection |
| IRC | Commander's communications strategy<br>Public affairs (PA)<br>Engagement<br>Military information support operations<br>Civil-military operations<br>Intelligence<br>Counterintelligence | Lethal effects<br>Electronic attack<br>Electronic support<br>Offensive cyberspace operations<br>Intelligence<br>Counterintelligence<br>Military deception | Information assurance<br>Electronic spectrum management<br>Electronic protection<br>Defensive cyberspace operations<br>Operations security<br>Physical security<br>Intelligence<br>Counterintelligence<br>Emission control<br>Information operations condition |

Figure 2-2. Information Tasks, Effects, and Information-related Capabilities

OPSEC, counterintelligence, counterpropaganda, and public affairs. The commander's communication strategy (CCS) is one key to shaping influence operations.

Understanding the target audience is key to all influence endeavors. Logically, the first step in the influence process is to decide who or what to influence. The second step is to develop a detailed target audience analysis (TAA) that properly matches influence objectives.

The methodology to conduct TAA achieves four overarching objectives.

1. Precisely identify the optimal target audiences.

2. Measure the ability to influence an audience.

3. Identify the best process to influence that audience.

4. Produce and deploy the triggers that effectively and measurably impact the audience.

The TAA should construct a robust profile of the audience to determine how an appropriately conceived and developed message campaign can influence it. Because there is no universal model of communications applicable to all groups and cultures, tailor all communication efforts to the local dynamics with respect to the behaviors they are meant to change. Select and integrate the ways and means to achieve desired effects and influence objectives. Operations are executed and assessed to see if effects and objectives were met. Chapter 3 describes influence capabilities. See JP 3-13 for further discussion of the influence paradigm.

### 2.4.3 Disrupting or Degrading Adversary Command and Control Systems

The adversary force, like all organizations, relies on communications and information networks to make and implement decisions. Small cells can limit communications to face-to-face encounters and couriers; this is excellent OPSEC but limits the size and complexity of operations. Some adversaries mirror the way U.S. forces use the electromagnetic spectrum (EMS) and computer networks as the backbone of elaborate special-purpose military information architectures. Adversaries across the range of sophistication also use civilian telecommunications, particularly cell phones and the Internet, to gather intelligence, disseminate information, shape perceptions, and direct operations.

The integrated use of lethal effects, EW, and CO supported by intelligence disrupt and exploit adversary C2. The fires cell synchronizes physical attack, electronic attack (EA), and offensive cyberspace operations (OCO) against adversary C2.

### 2.4.4 Protect Friendly Information and Information Systems

Information and information systems protection includes active and passive measures that protect and defend friendly information and information systems to ensure timely, accurate, and relevant friendly information to support command and control of Navy forces. It denies enemies the opportunity to exploit friendly information and information systems for their own purposes. The secure and uninterrupted flow of data and information allows Navy forces to multiply their combat power and synchronize maritime power projection with other joint capabilities. Numerous threats to that capability exist in the operational environment. Information protection includes information assurance (IA), defensive cyberspace operations (DCO), electronic protection (EP), OPSEC, physical security, and intelligence. All these capabilities are interrelated and integrated to protect information and information systems.

INTENTIONALLY BLANK

# CHAPTER 3

# Information-Related Capabilities

## 3.1 OVERVIEW

Older definitions of IO focused heavily on a set list of core capabilities. This led to stovepipe thinking and weakened the integrating effect. As SecDef Memo 12401-10, Strategic Communication and Information Operations in the DOD, explains, "successful IO requires the identification of IRC most likely to achieve desired effects and not simply the employment of a capability. Modifying the definition also effects a needed change to the existing notion that the core capabilities must be overseen by one entity. Capability integration does not necessitate ownership."

An IRC can be effective as part of an operation if it can answer the question "Why did you do that?" with a specific effect or a military advantage that helps achieve the commander's goal and supports movement towards mission success and a desired end state.

## 3.2 DESCRIPTION OF INFORMATION-RELATED CAPABILITIES

An IRC is defined as a tool, technique, or activity employed within a dimension of the information environment that can be used to create effects and operationally desirable conditions (JP 1-02). Planners may find the following list useful to identify traditional IRC but it should not limit one's vision of possible resources.

1. Core capabilities (including the original "five pillars")

    a. EW

    b. Cyberspace operations

    c. MISO

    d. MILDEC

    e. OPSEC

    f. PA

    g. Civil-military operations (CMO)

    h. Defense support to public diplomacy

    i. Physical (lethal) attack

    j. IA

    k. Physical security

    l. Combat camera (visual information)

m. Intelligence

n. Counterintelligence.

JP 3-13 lists the following examples of IO capabilities integrated in joint IO.

1. Strategic communication (SC), discussed in paragraph 3.2.1.
2. Joint interagency coordination group. As a capability, this allows joint commanders to interface with organizations across the diplomatic, informational, military, and economic spectrum, including other U.S. Government (USG) departments, other governments, private sector entities, and nongovernmental organizations.
3. PA, discussed in paragraph 3.2.2.
4. CMO.
5. CO, discussed in paragraph 3.2.3.
6. IA.
7. Space operations.
8. MISO, discussed in paragraph 3.2.5.
9. Intelligence.
10. MILDEC, discussed in paragraph 3.2.6.
11. OPSEC.
12. Special technical operations (STO).
13. JEMSO, which are EW and joint EMS management operations used to exploit, attack, protect, and manage the electromagnetic (EM) operational environment to achieve the commander's objectives. Traditional EW terminology best describes Navy operations, but the JEMSO construct may be more useful to operational-level planners.
14. Key leader engagement.

Within the Navy, the Information Dominance Corps has extended the IRC concept across the functions of intelligence (N2), assured C2, and meteorology and oceanography. The Center for Naval Analyses study, Structures for Information Operations Warfare Commander and Information Dominance Afloat (September 2013), examines existing models of conducting IO and the impact of adopting an information dominance warfare model. This NWP does not endorse the study's recommendations but encourages further debate and a broad vision of how the Navy integrates and employs available IRC to best satisfy mission requirements.

Recent DOD IO policy and doctrine (Secretary of Defense Memo 12401-10, JP 3-13, and DOD Directive 3600.01) stress influence at the strategic and operational levels as the focus of IO. Navy doctrine has typically emphasized the disrupt, corrupt, or usurp tactical information superiority aspects of IO as well as the protect functions. As an integrating function, IO should embrace information's impact on operations as a whole and not stress a single aspect at the cost of another. Navy planners should make IRC choices based on their echelon, mission, and available capabilities—not on a preconceived checklist.

### 3.2.1 Strategic Communication and Commander's Communication Strategy

Strategic communication is focused Government efforts to understand and engage key audiences to create, strengthen, or preserve conditions favorable for the advancement of USG interests, policies, and objectives through the use of coordinated programs, plans, themes, messages, and products synchronized with the actions of all instruments of national power.

SC is a national strategic-level initiative of the USG under the auspices of the Department of State. The Joint Staff director of communication provides SC guidance to the CCMD via different products, such as guidance for development of the theater campaign plan, JSCP tasking, or a warning order (WARNORD), that specifically directs crisis action planning. These products facilitate planning during the initiation phase in the joint operation planning process (JOPP). (JOPP is covered in chapter 5.) Navy commanders synchronize maritime operations toward a unified action supporting SC.

Although lethal weapons can create significant influence effects, IRC—such as PA, MISO, and defense support to public diplomacy—can prove invaluable to inform and influence.

The CCDR develops a theater campaign plan containing theater security cooperation guidance, which should include long-term information objectives during phase 0 operations throughout the AOR.

A JFC develops a CCS based on the SC guidance, narratives, themes, and messages. CCS is a commander's strategy for coordinating and synchronizing themes, messages, images, and actions to support strategic communication-related objectives and ensure the integrity and consistency of themes and messages to the lowest tactical level through integrating all relevant communication activities.

In support of the JFC strategy, Navy planners conduct detailed mission analysis and operational-level planning to develop a maritime strategy that describes the Navy role in the overarching plan. Using the maritime operations center (MOC) construct of cross-functional team (CFT), missions are developed across the three planning horizons—future plans, future operations, and current operations—to fully integrate IRC.

A recent example of the Navy's successful employment of CCS was evidenced during Operation UNIFIED RESPONSE following the 2010 Haiti earthquake. As part of the plan to contribute to UNIFIED RESPONSE, each afloat unit embarked Navy PA professionals to provide near-real-time coordination while underscoring the critical role the sea service played in providing humanitarian assistance and disaster relief. Although not a combat operation, the effect was significant in achieving broader strategic objectives and building international consensus to the relief effort.

### 3.2.2 Public Affairs

PA is directed toward the external and internal public with interest in the DOD. PA conducts three basic functions: public information, command information, and community engagement activities. These functions support the commander's intent and concept of operations (CONOPS). PA performs a primary coordination role of public information in the military.

PA supports Navy operations by communicating factual and accurate unclassified information about military activities to various audiences. The timely release of official information aids in the pursuit of unified action while bolstering public support. Credible, well-timed information can mitigate the impact of an adversary's efforts. PA personnel at all levels offer invaluable advice to leaders on the possible outcomes of military actions, identify the potential impact on the public information realm, and serve as key resources to assess achieving desired effects. For more information on PA, refer to JP 3-61, Public Affairs.

### 3.2.3 Cyberspace Operations

Cyberspace is a global domain within the information environment consisting of the interdependent networks of information technology infrastructures and resident data, including the Internet, telecommunications networks, computer systems, and embedded processors and controllers. CO is the employment of cyberspace capabilities in which the primary purpose is to achieve objectives in or through cyberspace. A cyberspace capability is a device, computer program, or technique—including any combination of software, firmware, or hardware—designed to create an effect in cyberspace.

#### 3.2.3.1 Cyberspace Domain and Information Environment

Cyberspace crosses geographic and geopolitical boundaries. Much of it resides outside U.S. control and it is tightly integrated with the operation of national critical infrastructures and key assets as well as with the conduct of commerce, governance, and national security. CO integrates with other capabilities to gain and protect an operational advantage and to place adversaries at a disadvantage. The Navy needs assured security within its networks. Commanders seek to gain and retain the degree of freedom of action in cyberspace that is required at a particular place and time to accomplish mission objectives, yet still deny the same freedom to adversaries. Commanders should also be prepared to operate in a degraded or denied cyberspace.

#### 3.2.3.2 Cyberspace Functional Operations

United States Strategic Command (USSTRATCOM), United States Cyber Command (USCYBERCOM), and Fleet Cyber Command (FLTCYBERCOM)/Commander, 10th Fleet (COMTENTHFLT) plan, coordinate, synchronize, and conduct activities to direct operations and defense of specified DOD networks. They also prepare for and conduct military operations in support of the JFC's mission. Timely intelligence and threat indicators from traditional and advanced sensors, vulnerability information from DOD and non-DOD sources, and accurate assessment inform CO missions.

CO includes OCO, DCO, and DOD information network operations. The successful execution of CO requires the synchronized employment of offensive and defensive capabilities underpinned by effective and timely operational preparation of the environment and secure operation of supporting data networks.

DOD information network operations include the employment of manual and automated methods to preserve and sustain the availability, confidentiality, integrity, and nonrepudiation of military information networks. They are actions taken to design, build, secure, operate, maintain, and sustain DOD networks. These include proactive actions that address the entire DOD information network, including such actions as configuration control and patching, IA measures, user training, physical security and secure architecture design, operation of host-based security systems and firewalls, and encryption of data at rest. The U.S. military reliance on cyberspace is well understood by adversaries. For that reason, JFC planning to ensure resiliency in the face of cyberspace threats is essential.

OCO is categorized as the employment of cyberspace operations to support the JFC operational requirements and the defense of DOD networks. OCO conduct activities that actively gather information, manipulate, disrupt, deny, degrade, or destroy computers, information systems, or networks through cyberspace.

Support operations involve forces and actions required to operate, sustain, and secure the DOD information network as well as cyberspace activities that support all military operations. Support operations do not include DCO in response to specific threats directed at the DOD information network but rather those that constitute steady-state IA to establish and operate secure networks. For additional information, see JP 3-12, Cyberspace Operations.

#### 3.2.3.3 Command and Control of Cyberspace Operations

CO requires a coordinated effort to synchronize forces toward a common objective. The C2 structure simultaneously supports actions at the theater or joint operations area level and at the global level. Global CO should be integrated and synchronized with capabilities under control of the JFC. Command and control of forces that conduct most CO activities, as defined by the execute order, authorizes actions based on threats that meet particular conditions and triggers (executed either manually or automatically); the nature of the threat requires an immediate response. These conditions are addressed by the campaign/operation plans that include DCO, OCO, and DOD information network operations. The affected CCDR is the supported commander for CO in their AOR.

A secure, resilient, and flexible C2 architecture enables commanders to maintain unity of effort in employment of their forces at the critical times and places. CO requires coordination of theater operations with global operations, creating a dynamic supported/supporting C2 arrangement. The supported commander integrates CO into specific joint operations, campaign plans and CONOPS, operation plans (OPLANs), and operation orders. C2 of DOD information network operations and DCO may require predetermined and preauthorized actions based on meeting particular conditions and triggers.

The Navy likely enters a conflict as part of a joint or combined task force, not as a single-Service force. The specific C2 elements the JFC selects depends on the type and scale of operation, the cyberspace presence or sophistication of the adversary, and the types of cyberspace targets identified.

CO planners face the same considerations and challenges that are present in planning for military operations as well as some unique considerations. A full understanding of an adversary's posture and capabilities in cyberspace involves not only understanding the underlying network infrastructure but also requires profiles on system users and administers a clear understanding of what friendly forces and capabilities might be targeted and how and an understanding of applicable domestic, foreign, and international laws and policy. CO planners use JOPP to implement the JFC's guidance and intent.

Targeting is included in the coordination of CO. Targeting integrates and synchronizes fires within joint operations through the process of selecting and prioritizing desired effects and matching the appropriate capabilities to those effects, given operational requirements and limitations; targeting links the desired effects of fires to specific tasks at the joint force component level. Planners should specify the scope, level, start time, and duration of the desired effects. Targets are selected from the three components of cyberspace, including physical network, logical network, and cyber-persona. The process identifies and coordinates multiple activities across multiple components.

Cyberspace capabilities operate and create effects within cyberspace. They may be as simple as the type of computer operating system being used by an adversary or as complex as the exact serial number of the latest update installed, what system resources are available, or what other applications are expected to be running (or not running) when the cyberspace capability executes on target. CO planners work with the supported command to identify, validate, and vet targets for OCO and enabling operations. Using available all-source analysis and the JFC's normal targeting processes, the targeting staffs develop and maintain the joint integrated prioritized target list and supporting documents.

CO capabilities are typically integrated with the commander's other capabilities to gain the advantage, to protect and maintain that advantage, and to place adversaries at a disadvantage. Commanders seek to gain and retain the degree of freedom of action in cyberspace required at a particular place and time to accomplish mission objectives, yet deny the same to adversaries. They are also prepared to operate in a degraded or denied cyberspace.

### 3.2.4 Electronic Warfare

EW is military action involving the use of EM and directed energy to control the EMS or to attack the enemy. EW consists of three divisions: EA, EP, and electronic warfare support (ES). Figure 3-1 provides an overview, and the following sections describe the specific functional areas of EW.

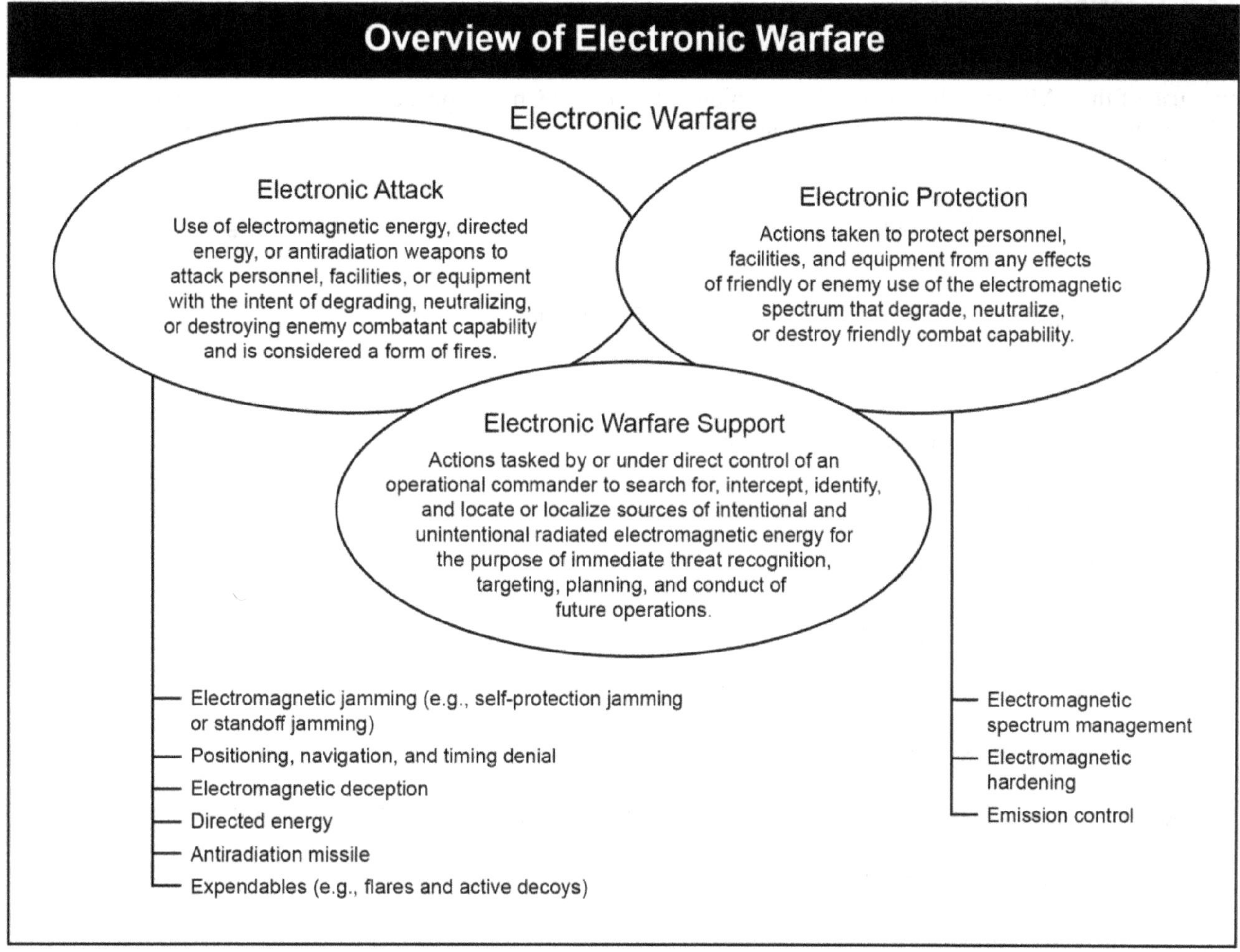


Figure 3-1. Overview of Electronic Warfare

### 3.2.4.1 Electronic Warfare Support

ES involves actions tasked by, or under direct control of, an operational commander to search for, intercept, identify, and locate or localize sources of intentional and unintentional radiated EM energy for the purpose of immediate threat recognition, threat avoidance, targeting, planning, and conduct of future operations. ES responds to and supports immediate operational requirements. ES is the Navy's most powerful tool to assess the EM environment for timely information vital to mission success.

ES and signals intelligence (SIGINT) often share the same or similar assets and resources and may be tasked simultaneously to collect information that meets both requirements. Under certain circumstances, data collected for intelligence may meet immediate operational requirements. Information collected for ES purposes is normally also processed by the appropriate parts of the intelligence community for further exploitation after the operational commander's ES requirements are met. As such, information collected from the EMS may serve two purposes: as ES, unprocessed information used by operational forces to develop and maintain situational awareness for an operationally defined timeframe or particular campaign phase; as SIGINT, retained and processed under appropriate intelligence authorities in response to specified intelligence requirements. In cases in which planned ES operations conflict with intelligence collection efforts, the commander with tasking authority (i.e., JFC, joint force maritime component commander (JFMCC), or tactical commander) decides which mission has priority.

### 3.2.4.2 Electronic Protection

EP involves actions taken to protect personnel, facilities, and equipment from any effects of friendly, neutral, or enemy use of the EMS as well as natural phenomena that degrade, neutralize, or destroy friendly combat capability. EP focuses on system or process attributes or capabilities. Inherent hardware features minimize the impact of unplanned or undesired EM signals on an EM-dependent system's operation. EP processes are designed to eliminate, reduce, or mitigate the impact of the same unplanned or undesired EM signals. These features and processes combine to allow friendly capabilities to function as intended in contested and congested EM operating environments.

EP includes actions taken to ensure friendly use of the EMS, to include:

1. Frequency agility in a radio
2. Variable pulse repetition frequency in radar
3. Receiver/signal processing
4. Spread spectrum technology
5. Spectrum management processes
6. Frequency coordination measures (e.g., joint restricted frequency list)
7. Global Positioning System antijam measures
8. Selective opacity (i.e., the phenomenon of not permitting the passage of EM radiation) of optical apertures
9. Emission control (EMCON) procedures
10. Wartime reserve modes.

EP is not force protection or self-protection. EP is use of EM energy or physical properties to preserve an EMS-dependent system from direct or environmental EM effects, thereby allowing the system to continue operating against both enemy EA and friendly EM interference. For example, a platform may deploy a decoy (flare, chaff, or active radio frequency) to misdirect an incoming missile. This is EA, since the decoy attacks the missile's ability to use the EMS to reach the intended target. If a missile's guidance system employs flare rejection or chaff discrimination logic or operates radar outside the frequency range of active decoys, those are examples of EP as they ensure the missile's use of the EMS. Although defensive EA actions and EP protect personnel, facilities, capabilities, and equipment, EP protects from the effects of EA (friendly or adversary) or electromagnetic interference, while defensive EA is primarily used to protect against lethal attacks by denying adversary use of the EMS to target, guide, or trigger weapons.

### 3.2.4.3 Electronic Attack

Electronic attack refers to the division of EW involving the use of EM energy, directed energy, or antiradiation weapons to attack personnel, facilities, or equipment with the intent of degrading, neutralizing, or destroying enemy combat capability and is considered a form of fires (see JP 3-09, Joint Fire Support). EA includes actions taken to prevent or reduce an enemy's effective use of the EMS through employment of systems or weapons that use EM energy (e.g., jamming in the form of EM disruption, degradation, denial, and deception). EA includes both active EA, in which EA systems or weapons radiate in the EMS, as well as passive EA (nonradiating/re-radiating) such as chaff. It also includes employment of systems or weapons that use radiated EM energy (to include directed energy) as their primary disruptive or destructive mechanism. Examples include lasers, electro-optical, infrared, and radio frequency weapons such as high-power microwave or those employing an electromagnetic pulse.

#### 3.2.4.4 Electromagnetic Battle Management

Electromagnetic battle management (EMBM) is the dynamic monitoring, assessing, planning, and directing of JEMSO in support of the commander's scheme of maneuver. EMBM proactively harnesses multiple platforms and diverse capabilities into a networked and cohesive sensor/decision/target/engagement system and protects friendly use of the EMS while strategically denying benefits to the adversary.

Once a plan is approved and an operation is under way, the preponderance of EW staff effort shifts to EMBM. EMBM includes continuous monitoring of the EM operating environment, EMS management, and dynamic reallocation of EW assets based on emerging operational issues. Normally, personnel on watch in the joint operations center perform this monitoring. These watch personnel, stationed at a dedicated EW watch station, are normally tasked to alert other EW or staff personnel to carry out specific coordinating actions, including preplanned responses consistent with established rules of engagement. For more information about EW, refer to JP 3-13.1, Electronic Warfare, and NTTP 3-51.1, Navy Electronic Warfare.

### 3.2.5 Military Information Support Operations

MISO are planned to convey selected information and indicators to foreign audiences to influence their emotions, motives, objective reasoning, and, ultimately, the behavior of foreign governments, organizations, and individuals in a manner favorable to the originator's objectives. Specifically trained Service members conduct these operations.

MISO plays a fundamental role in a commander's communication efforts through the planned use of directed programs specifically designed to support USG and DOD activities and policies. MISO practitioners follow a deliberate process that: 1) aligns a commander's objectives with an analysis of the environment; 2) selects a relevant target audience and develops focused, culturally and environmentally attuned messages and actions; 3) employs sophisticated media delivery means; and 4) produces observable, measurable behavioral responses. When viewed as part of a joint operation, MISO provides fundamental capability sets to support campaign objectives through appropriate planning and execution of component tactical actions.

There is a basic distinction between psychological impact and MISO. Military actions, such as strikes or shows of force, have a psychological impact; however, they are differentiated from MISO unless their specified purpose is to influence a target audience's perceptions and subsequent behavior.

MISO, in conjunction with SC and PA, establish and reinforce foreign perceptions of U.S. military, political, and economic power and resolve. In conflict, MISO can degrade the enemy's relative combat power, reduce civilian interference, minimize collateral damage, and maximize local support for operations.

The principal considerations for effective MISO employment include early planning and sustained employment; integration of MISO with the communication strategies of the USG and multinational partners; use of indigenous assets, command emphasis, and resourcing; responsive MISO approval process; and quantifiable and timely assessment criteria.

At the operational level, MISO plays a central role in achieving the commander's information objectives by shaping, inducing, or influencing an adversary's attitudes and behavior. The CCDR's or component commander's J39 staff section is the nexus of IO synchronization in plan development and assessment.

From a maritime perspective, the MOC IO cell identifies and draws on available dissemination assets, product reproduction capabilities, and planning resources. The IO cell collaborates with joint MISO experts, civil affairs representatives and, in some cases, State Department representatives to identify maritime audiences, develop themes and products, and plan dissemination.

PA and MISO activities are separate and distinct functions that support and reinforce one another. Doing so requires coordination and synchronization. Commanders ensure that appropriate coordination between MISO and PA activities is consistent with DOD principles of information, policy or statutory limitation, and security.

The following factors should be considered when synchronizing strategic communication, communication strategy, PA, and IO:

1. Unity of effort among disparate communities
2. Maintain good situational awareness among stakeholders
3. Coordinate activities to avoid or mitigate unintended consequences.

For more information on MISO, refer to JP 3-13.2.

### 3.2.6 Military Deception

MILDEC is the collective term for actions intended to mislead adversary decision makers, thereby causing the adversary to take specific actions or inactions that contribute to the accomplishment of the friendly mission. MILDEC may be employed at the strategic, operational, or tactical levels; can be incorporated into a supported or supporting operation; and can be performed in every phase of military operations. When successfully executed, MILDEC is invaluable in saving lives and resources and can expedite the end of hostilities.

MILDEC targets enemy decision makers. MILDEC goals and objectives contribute to the success of the commander's mission. The deception objective is a concise statement of what the MILDEC causes the adversary to do or not do. It is expressed in terms of the adversary's action or inaction, which directly leads to the purpose or condition stated in the MILDEC goal. The deception target is the adversary decision maker with the authority to make the decision that achieves the deception objective to reinforce or change their behavior in our favor.

Successful MILDEC execution includes thorough planning and attention to detail. In addition to a detailed series of event coordination, a detailed knowledge of the adversary's decision makers and their authorities, behaviors (expected reactions), and tactics is critical. To conduct a MILDEC operation, planners develop:

1. Deception mission analysis
2. Deception planning guidance
3. Staff deception estimate
4. Commander's deception estimate
5. CJCS estimate review, if required
6. Deception plan development
7. Deception plan review and approval.

Deception event sequence, synchronization, and timing must work in concert so the adversary has the time to observe, analyze, and decide on a course of action (COA) based on those observations. Six principles provide guidance for planning and executing MILDEC.

1. Focus. The deception must target the adversary decision maker capable of causing the desired action or inaction.
2. Objective. To shape a decision maker's perception, causing the adversary to take (or not take) specific actions.
3. Centralized planning and control. More than in many other military activities, MILDEC should be centrally planned and directed. Consistency is crucial to success.
4. Security. Deny adversary's knowledge of a force's intent to deceive and execution of that intent.

5. Timeliness. A deception operation requires careful timing.
6. Integration. Fully integrate each MILDEC with the operation it supports.

MILDEC can achieve different objectives in support of the desired ends.

1. Mask friendly maneuver
2. Reinforce enemy perception of friendly strengths, weaknesses, and intentions
3. Distract the enemy
4. Overwhelm adversary intelligence collection and analysis capabilities
5. Disrupt their decision-making process (render adversaries unable to decide or force a quick response)
6. Create false appearances of friendly capabilities (strengths/weaknesses)
7. Force an unanticipated maneuver/reaction
8. Force the adversary to cancel a planned action
9. Confuse the enemy as to your force strength, activity, location, timeline, equipment, or intent
10. Disrupt your enemy's ability to synchronize or coordinate a counterattack
11. Demoralize the enemy
12. Increase your enemy's proverbial fog of war
13. Achieve surprise.

The MOC IO cell includes a MILDEC planner who is responsible for incorporating MILDEC into operational-level plans.

# CHAPTER 4

# Information Operations Organizational Relationships and Forces

## 4.1 ADMINISTRATIVE AND OPERATIONAL RELATIONSHIPS

Navy forces typically operate under a component commander or joint task force commander as assigned/attached to a CCDR or a subordinate JFC. A JFC uses the concept of unified actions—the synchronization, coordination, and/or integration of activities of Governmental and nongovernmental entities with military operations to achieve unity of effort—to apply all of the instruments of national power (diplomatic, information, military, and economic) to affect adversary capabilities and behavior.

Force providers organize, man, train, and equip Navy forces so that they are ready to deliver IRC to achieve desired effects and attain a commander's objectives. They are assigned to force employers who determine IO objectives to support the commander's plan and plan, integrate, and employ IRC to achieve desired effects and objectives in joint operations. Navy commanders perform C2 functions for all roles of warfare. At the operational level, Navy component commanders (NCCs) or numbered fleet commanders (NFCs) command assigned forces and carry out C2 functions through the MOC to dynamically plan, direct, monitor, and assess operations. The MOC IO cell plans, integrates, and coordinates the employment of IRC.

### 4.1.1 U.S. Fleet Forces Command and U.S. Pacific Fleet

Administratively, NFCs, United States Fleet Forces Command (USFF), and United States Pacific Fleet (USPACFLT) serve as the Navy component command to CCDR. USFF supports both the CNO and CCDR worldwide. USFF also provides responsive, relevant, sustainable Navy forces that are ready for tasking to United States Northern Command through Commander, Task Force EIGHT ZERO. The command provides operational and planning support to CCMD and integrated warfighter capability requirements to the CNO.

In collaboration with USPACFLT, USFF organizes, mans, trains, maintains, and equips Navy forces; develops and submits budgets; and executes readiness and personnel accounts to develop required and sustainable levels of fleet readiness. Additionally, USFF serves as the unified voice for fleet training requirements and policies to generate combat-ready Navy forces per the fleet response plan using the fleet training continuum (FTC).

Navy forces proceed through the basic and integrated training phases of the fleet response training program. USFF and its subordinates provide the training means and coordinate with Commander, Navy Cyber Forces (NCF) and other type commanders (TYCOMs) to train and assess the readiness of personnel and forces to deploy ready to employ their IRC to achieve desired effects. Figure 4-1 illustrates the alignment of Navy IO organizations.

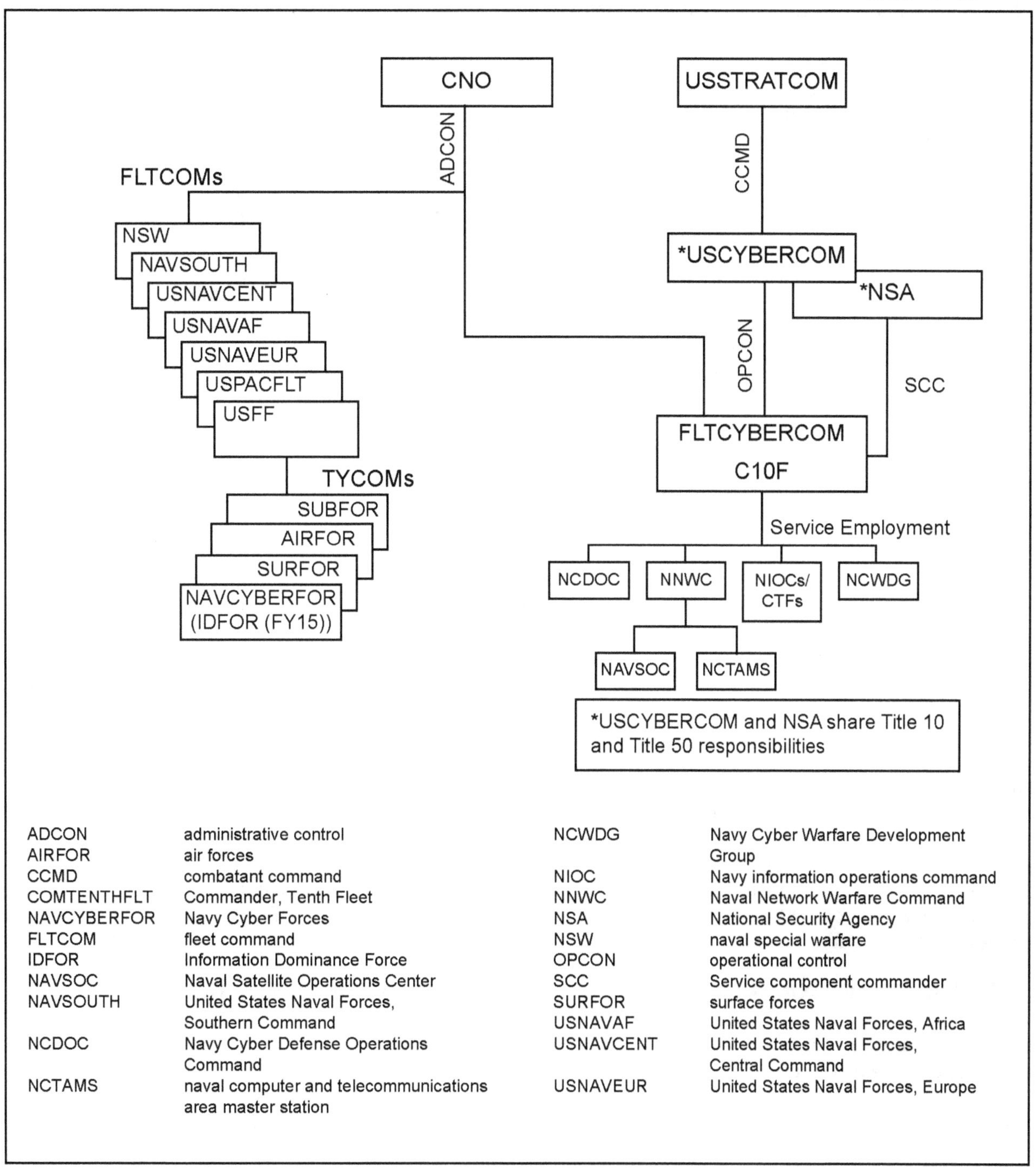
CNO
ADCON
FLTCOMs
NSW
NAVSOUTH
USNAVCENT
USNAVAF
USNAVEUR
USPACFLT
USFF
TYCOMs
SUBFOR
AIRFOR
SURFOR
NAVCYBERFOR
(IDFOR (FY15))
USSTRATCOM
CCMD
*USCYBERCOM
*NSA
OPCON
SCC
FLTCYBERCOM
C10F
Service Employment
NCDOC
NNWC
NIOCs/
CTFs
NCWDG
NAVSOC
NCTAMS
*USCYBERCOM and NSA share Title 10 and Title 50 responsibilities
ADCON administrative control
AIRFOR air forces
CCMD combatant command
COMTENTHFLT Commander, Tenth Fleet
NAVCYBERFOR Navy Cyber Forces
FLTCOM fleet command
IDFOR Information Dominance Force
NAVSOC Naval Satellite Operations Center
NAVSOUTH United States Naval Forces, Southern Command
NCDOC Navy Cyber Defense Operations Command
NCTAMS naval computer and telecommunications area master station
NCWDG Navy Cyber Warfare Development Group
NIOC Navy information operations command
NNWC Naval Network Warfare Command
NSA National Security Agency
NSW naval special warfare
OPCON operational control
SCC Service component commander
SURFOR surface forces
USNAVAF United States Naval Forces, Africa
USNAVCENT United States Naval Forces, Central Command
USNAVEUR United States Naval Forces, Europe

Figure 4-1. Navy Administrative and Operational Alignment

### 4.1.2 U.S. Fleet Cyber Command/U.S. Tenth Fleet

FLTCYBERCOM is an echelon II command and reports as the Navy component command to USSTRATCOM and USCYBERCOM. USCYBERCOM and the National Security Agency (NSA) are commanded by the same person, which helps in coordinating Title 10 and Title 50, War and National Defense, responsibilities and authorities. Navy operational cyberspace forces are assigned to the echelon III COMTENTHFLT, who is dual-hatted as Commander, FLTCYBERCOM. Several organizations are operationally assigned to COMTENTHFLT: Navy Cyber Defense Operations Command, Navy Network Warfare Command, Navy information operations commands (NIOCs), Navy Cyber Warfare Development Group, Naval Satellite Operations Center, and naval computer and telecommunications area master stations.

FLTCYBERCOM serves as the central operating authority for Navy networks, SIGINT, IO, EW, and space capabilities in support of forces afloat and ashore. It directs Navy CO globally to deter and defeat aggression and ensures freedom of action to achieve military objectives in and through cyberspace. As COMTENTHFLT, the command provides operational support to Navy commanders worldwide supporting information and computer, EW, and space operations. In addition to joint and Service reporting, the command also serves as the Navy's Service Cryptologic Element, reporting to the Central Security Service.

### 4.1.3 Navy Cyber Forces Command

Type commanders man, train, and equip their assigned forces. Both USFF and USPACFLT have air, surface, and subsurface TYCOMs. NCF is the TYCOM for afloat Navy cyber forces and is assigned under USFF and supports USPACFLT. NCF has subordinate and supporting commands that assist in the scheduling, planning, and execution of requisite cyberspace training. NCF works closely with the air, surface, and subsurface TYCOMs who own the platforms to monitor and ensure that assigned units are properly manned for operational readiness. They coordinate with the Bureau of Naval Personnel to ensure manning levels are met. NCF further monitors the material readiness of their assigned forces. They coordinate with maintenance facilities and other technical support to maintain the material readiness of all equipment/assets in the highest state of readiness. Training is critical for the readiness and ability of forces to employ IO capabilities. As the complexity of the equipment and the sophistication of tactics continue to rise, the need for maximum effectiveness in the use of that equipment mandates thoroughly trained operators who are prepared to respond when needed.

These organizations carry out a number of supporting tasks important to the Navy force ability to accomplish assigned tasks and missions. The tactics for all IRC should be developed and exercised to effectively deliver the right capability at the right time and place to achieve the desired results. Extensive intelligence and targeting support should also be carried out and integrated into the FTC so Navy forces are fully ready to employ their IRC when they report for duty.

## 4.2 COMMAND AND CONTROL STRUCTURE FOR INFORMATION OPERATIONS

At the operational level, NCC and NFC provide maritime capabilities in support of the CCDR and JFCs. Figure 4-2 provides the organizational alignment for the numbered fleets and the combatant commands.

The NFC prepares IO plans to protect the information grids, shape the operating environment, and exploit adversary vulnerabilities. The NFC employs tactical assets in the form of a carrier strike group (CSG), amphibious ready group (ARG), or independent units within the theater. These assets shape the theater in support of the unified combatant commander's theater campaign plan (TCP) and provide IO support to joint planning and operations.

COMTENTHFLT provides manning and equipment augmentation and reachback support to the NFC and their forces to support the effective employment of IRC for the assigned missions and tasks. COMTENTHFLT ensures coordination with intelligence activities and IO to protect the information and information systems to support Navy forces and the ability to employ IRC.

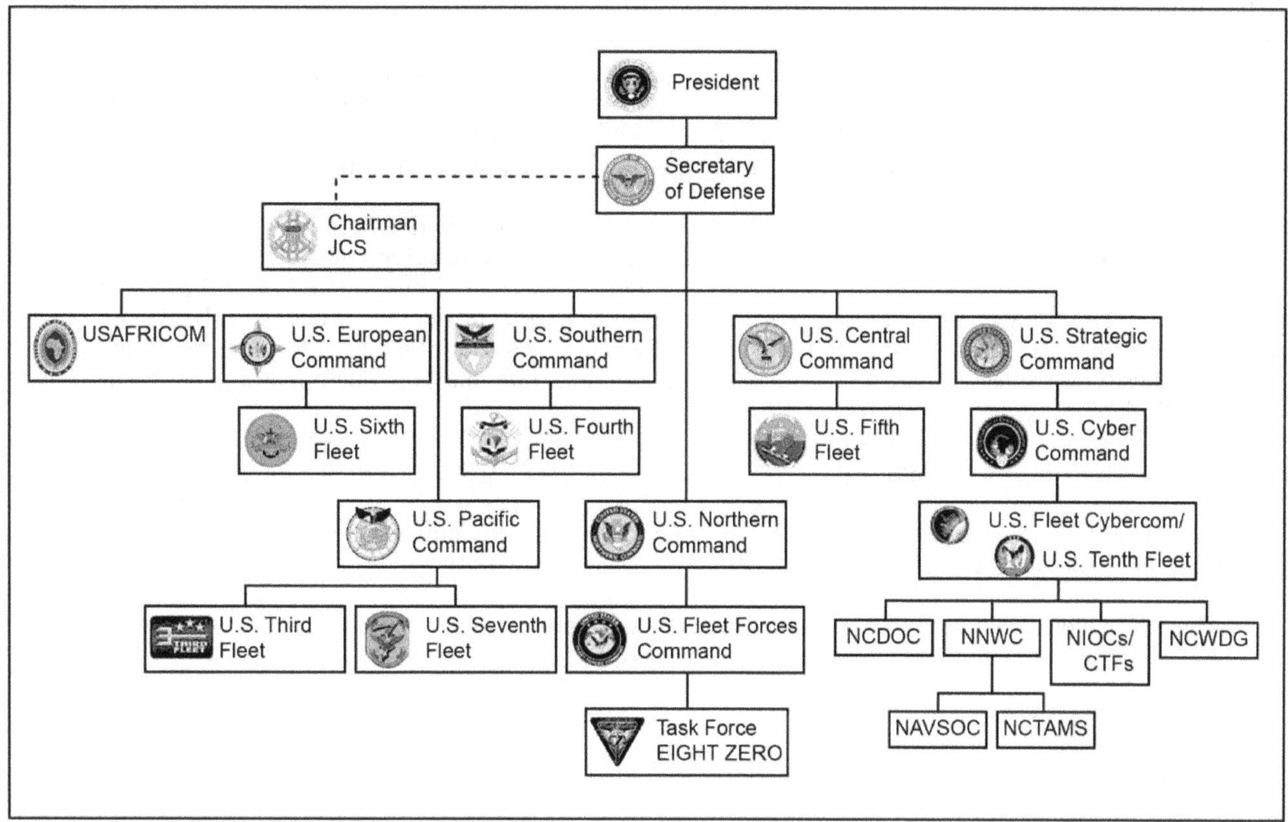


Figure 4-2. Organizational Alignment for Numbered Fleets and Combatant Commands

## 4.3 INFORMATION OPERATIONS COMMAND AND CONTROL ROLES AND RELATIONSHIPS

In consultation with subordinate commanders, the NFC/NCC determines the IRC/forces necessary to meet operational requirements. The NFC/NCC's daily guidance and event-based campaign plan drive these requirements. The IO cell integrates, coordinates, synchronizes, and deconflicts the use of IRC to support actions to achieve desired effects in support of the commander's plan. IO planners task available forces/capabilities in support of the plan. The intent is that IRC be apportioned to accomplish the tasks and objectives in support of the maritime commander's plan. Capabilities not required by the Navy component are made available for tasking by the JTF to support the JFC's mission and campaign plan.

In peacetime, the major command (such as USFF) or the numbered fleet MOC has a standing IO staff, typically designated N39, along with an IO cell staffed across disciplines as required by operations to plan IO and coordinate IRC. The MOC IO cell integrates into the structure within the MOC. The IO cell provides the IO expertise to plan, employ, and assess IO and employs IRC prior to the initiation of hostilities, transition to conflict, and reconstitution. The JFMCC IO cell has representation as appropriate within each planning cell throughout the MOC.

During peacetime, the MOC coordinates (when tasked) with Service-, joint-, and national-level organizations to plan and achieve effects to deter or, if deterrence fails, influence, shape, and prepare the operating environment for effective follow-on maritime operations. To maintain proper expertise, the N39/IO cell also trains and exercises to support the MOC's wartime missions. In addition, N39 develops and reviews the IO portion of operational plans and uses existing intelligence analysis to support peacetime operations through transition to conflict while maintaining close working relationships with external IO-related activities. Successful military operations carefully integrate all IRC to support the commander's objectives and plans. The N39/IO cell chief considers the use of all IRC to support other lines of operation as well as IO as a line of operation when appropriate.

During the transition to conflict, reconstitution phases of a campaign plan, and upon full activation of the MOC, the N39/IO cell provides the Navy's key IO expertise. The MOC typically is the main organizational structure through which the full set of IRC are integrated and synchronized through IO. Based on the commander's direction and guidance, the N39/IO cell supports the design and execution of portions of the campaign that use IO and the IRC to accomplish the commander's objectives. The IO team's primary focus is to plan and integrate IRC into the commander's maritime operation plan (OPLAN) and is closely associated with STO.

IO cell members within the MOC integrate IO planning, execution, coordination, targeting, monitoring, adjustment, and assessment. They work within the MOC organization to develop rules of engagement (ROE) necessary to support IO and fuse target nominations into attack plans and tasking orders. The IO cell should ensure the ROE and IO operating requirements and authorizations are considered. The IO cell should coordinate IO-specific intelligence requests and requirements with the N2. The fusion of the IO cell's disciplines into the MOC promotes timely integration of IRC with other force options into maritime operations and the air tasking order (ATO) planning and execution processes.

### 4.3.1 Numbered Fleet Commander

The IO coordination and integration process for the Navy, Service, or functional component commander or a NFC serving as a JTF commander may include:

1. The JFC develops theater campaign objectives and normally designates a joint force IO officer for broad IO oversight functions. When designated, the joint force IO officer heads the JFC J39/IO cell.

2. The JFC IO team (composed of select representatives from each staff element, Service component, and supporting agencies responsible for integrating the capabilities and disciplines of IO) develops IO options in support of JFC objectives. Detailed execution is left to the components to accomplish through tactical actions and tasks. The component commanders should set the priority, effects, and timing for all IO in the overall operation.

3. Navy and other components address component objectives and the desired effects required to achieve them. The JFC designates primary and supporting components.

4. The MOC IO team completes maritime component tasks, as determined by the JFC's objectives, the component objectives, and the commander's intent for planning and integration. The IO team helps integrate IRC into the maritime OPLAN and ATO.

5. The MOC IO cell members meet regularly to develop and coordinate IO in the COAs. The IO cell should seamlessly integrate the planning results through the MOC CTF into the maritime OPLAN and the ATO/tasking process for commander's approval.

The IO cell should ensure the ROE and operating requirements and authorizations, such as special target lists, are considered. The team should coordinate and follow up on IO-specific intelligence requests and requirements through the N2/staff and stay in contact with the appropriate assets to resolve problems and coordinate requirements and tasking. Likewise, the team chief should help ensure target deconfliction.

The NFC's MOC IO cell, at the operational level of war:

1. Prepares IO plans to shape the operational environment

2. Protects information, information systems, and Navy and DOD networks

3. Disrupts adversary C2

4. Exploits adversary vulnerabilities

5. Ensures the most effective use of EMS resources.

The NFC's IO cell maintains awareness of all IRC in military operations. The NFC employs tactical assets, such as CSGs, ESGs, and ARGs, within the theater in support of the unified combatant commander's TCP. The NFC may serve as the Navy component commander or JFMCC during major combat operations supporting a JFC.

Only the NFC has the authority to reassign, redirect, or reallocate a subordinate's forces. When a subordinate unit (such as a CSG or ARG) does not have the organic IRC to support an assigned mission, the IO cell coordinates tasking of available IRC based on the NFC's/NCC's IRC apportionment decision.

### 4.3.2 Numbered Fleet Commander Maritime Operations Center Information Operations Cell

The MOC is the organizational and procedural means by which the NFC carries out C2 of assigned forces and coordinates with higher authority to support assigned missions. The mission of the MOC IO cell is to coordinate and integrate employment of IRC during military operations. The IO cell within a MOC functions as the core organizational construct for an NCC, NFC, or JFMCC to support operational-level IO planning, execution, and assessment. The MOC IO cell can also serve as the core construct for a JTF joint IO cell. The MOC IO cell coordinates with other component operations centers.

The MOC has a permanent IO staff billeted according to the role being filled, the mission, overall manning of the command, and the commander's desires. It can be augmented in response to the changing complexity of operations. The IO staff forms the core of the IO cell, a more fluid organization that stands up as needed, and may draw on MOC assets in response to any aspect of an operation.

The IO staff and select command representatives or liaison officers make up the IO cell. The IO cell provides planners to the operational planning teams made up of future plans and future operations cells. The IO cell maintains a presence in current operations. The IO cell meets to ensure IO-related activities developed across the operational planning teams do not conflict and can be supported with available assets. The IO cell ensures the plan incorporates all the salient IO capabilities, needs, and details and ensures the IO actions are integrated with the overall maritime and JTF scheme of maneuver. The IO representative to the operational planning teams provides guidance to the specialists within the IO cell to develop actions to support the scheme of maneuver. The IO cell integrates these actions into composite plans and, with the IO cell chief's approval, presents the IO plan to future plans and operations cells as required.

The combination of qualified MOC IO staff, augmentation, potential cyberspace support elements, and reachback to FLTCYBERCOM/COMTENTHFLT allows IO to integrate dynamically into the MOC. This ensures the MOC IO cell is supported by and supports military operations as required. IO cell functions include:

1. Support current operations. Perform continuous planning, execution, and assessment of integrated IO and IO-related activities in support of the combatant commander's goals and objectives. Also, direct the execution of IO activities in support of the current scheme of maneuver and to achieve information superiority.

2. Integrate and coordinate IO into the campaign plan. As the experts in IO, the cell recommends priorities to achieve IO objectives identified during the planning process and coordinates plans with higher headquarters, other components and subordinates, and assigned assets or units. Members also participate in targeting board and fires cell to prioritize, nominate, and deconflict targets and to provide alternative means to prosecute targets.

3. Conduct assessment. Using measures of effectiveness (MOEs) and measures of performance (MOPs), evaluate and compare the target's behavior against expectations and, if required, determine how to modify plans or how to reengage the target for the desired effect.

The IO cell develops and synchronizes IO plans and supports planning efforts within future plans and operations, current operations, assessment cells, and other CTF as required to support the mission. The IO cell consists of the IO cell chief, the IO officer, and personnel with expertise in the areas of planning, targeting, and IRC. These unique skill sets, along with an IO support team as shown in figure 4-3, should be present in or readily available to the IO cell. The Operations officer is key to integrating IO into future and current operations and is responsible for balancing the resource requirements within the staff during selection and execution of a course of action.

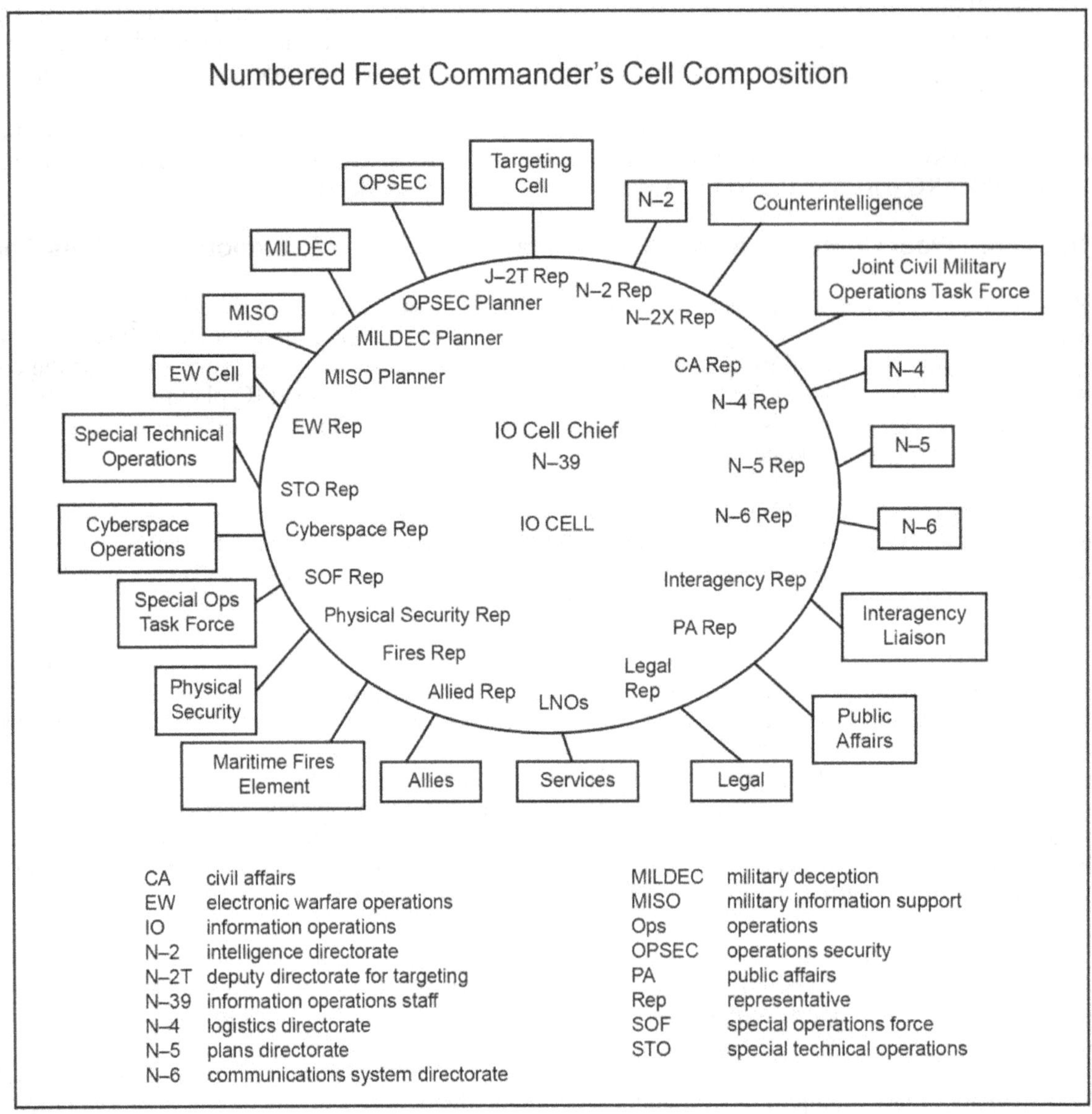


Figure 4-3. Notional Information Operations Cell Composition

IO planners work closely with various staff and warfare area planners to identify target audiences and target sets that can be affected with IRC to support the full range of the maritime commander's objectives. The MOC receives information from a broad range of sources, including national, operational, and tactical units and sensors that can be used as the basis for the assessment, planning, execution, and changes in force employment during environment shaping or upon execution of an OPLAN.

The IO cell responsibilities listed below vary with the complexity and level of operations and the role of the staff as either a Service or functional component command. The IO cell:

1. Coordinates the overall IO portion of the plan for the NFC.

2. Protects the force against hostile information, information systems, and electronic attacks as well as hostile propaganda and deception.

3. Directs maritime force IRC to support the NFC's concept of operations.

4. Integrates IO into all force plans and evolutions and coordinates this effort with JTF, subordinate headquarters, and other components.

5. Controls force emitters and releases control of applicable systems through EMCON guidance to subordinate commanders.

6. Controls all force information and information systems and releases control of applicable systems through information operations condition (INFOCON) guidance to subordinate commanders.

7. Maintains, protects, and shapes the desired force operations profile and signature and ensures the development of favorable tactical situations.

8. Directs maritime force IRC.

9. Uses information provided by theater and national assets to task and direct forces in support of IO.

10. Directs assets involved in environment awareness and shaping efforts, IO support to tactical missions, and IO execution and monitoring, to include targeting assets, directing units in localization and engaging information targets, and countersurveillance and countertargeting.

11. Coordinates with PA, visual information, and CMO to ensure their efforts are compatible with IO for operational effectiveness (e.g., protecting critical operational indicators and countering adversary propaganda).

12. Presents targets that require lethal engagement to achieve IO objectives to the appropriate joint boards, centers, and cells. This includes target nominations to the joint target list, maritime target list, and draft joint integrated prioritized target list.

13. Coordinates with theater IO cell to recommend or deconflict targets for information attack and to determine potential effects of theater IO activities on force operations.

14. Provides joint targeting coordination board (JTCB) with liaison officers knowledgeable on targets nominated by the IO cell and IO weapons capabilities.

15. Coordinates planning of airborne EW operations with the electronic warfare coordination cell (EWCC).

16. Determines assignment of jamming control authority in conjunction with JTF IO and joint force air component commander (JFACC) EWCC.

17. Conducts effects assessment of IO capabilities and operational assessment of IO support to the commander and JTF IO cell objectives.

18. Provides input to the commander's objectives, guidance, and intent.

### 4.3.3 Composite Warfare Commander

The officer in tactical command (OTC) assigns the composite warfare commander (CWC) authority and ascribed functions for the overall direction and control of the force. The OTC retains the power to negate any particular action by the CWC. The OTC may designate more than one CWC in a maritime OA. For example, with multiple CSGs or ARGs operating within a maritime OA, each group may have its own CWC. In some cases, they may all operate under a single CWC.

The CWC has five subordinate warfare commanders.

1. Air and missile defense commander

2. Antisubmarine warfare commander

3. Information operations warfare commander (IWC)

4. Strike warfare commander
5. Surface warfare commander.

Refer to NWP 3-56, Composite Warfare Doctrine, for further information about the CWC construct.

### 4.3.4 Information Operations Warfare Commander

Under the direction of the CWC, the IWC shapes and assesses the IE, achieves and maintains information superiority, develops and executes IO plans in support of CWC objectives, and supports other warfare commanders. As such, the IWC is responsible to the CWC for all IO within the strike group. The IWC also integrates IO into all plans and evolutions and coordinates this effort with theater, fleet, and JTF IO planners and disseminates IO data to the force.

The IWC also ensures targeting board awareness of IO objectives to maximize mission effectiveness of IRC and supporting lethal and nonlethal effects. The IWC coordinates with the MOC IO cell to recommend or deconflict targets for attack and to determine potential effects of theater IO activities on CSG and ARG operations.

The IWC is responsible to the strike group commander for planning and executing IRC, including protecting the force against hostile operations within the EMS and cyberspace. The IWC establishes and maintains the tactical picture through spectrum awareness, mission-oriented planning, and directing and monitoring plans. The IWC assists the commander to control all force emitters and information systems by recommending and executing EMCON, River City, and INFOCON.

Typical functions the CWC assigns to an IWC include:

1. Assist OTC or CWC in force IO planning and integration.
2. Assist OTC or CWC in force EW planning and integration.
3. Coordinate and control force ES assets and ensure ES information dissemination within the force.
4. Coordinate and control force EA assets.
5. Recommend the force EMCON profile to OTC, including responding to changes in the tactical situation. This includes coordinating with the antisubmarine warfare commander to manage acoustic emissions.
6. Assist OTC or CWC to establish a communications security own force monitoring plan.
7. Formulate and promulgate, as force spectrum manager, the force afloat EMS operations program.
8. Coordinate with airspace control authority, air resource element coordinator, and helicopter element coordinator for support aircraft.
9. Coordinate with the cryptologic resource coordinator for the employment of ES and SIGINT equipment in support of force tactical intelligence requirements.
10. Direct the use of force expendable decoy resources.
11. Develop preplanned responses for countersurveillance, counterinfluence, and countertargeting.
12. Integrate real-time ES contact reports with indications and warnings to recommend force defensive measures and readiness conditions to OTC or CWC.
13. Monitor force actions and communications to ensure alignment with previously directed SC objectives.

Refer to NTTP 3-13.2, Information Operations Warfare Commander Manual, for further information.

#### 4.3.5 Carrier Strike Group and Amphibious Ready Group Commanders

The CSG and ARG employ individual unit or small group tactics to execute IRC as tasked by the NFC or Navy/naval/maritime component commander. The CSG and ARG units routinely execute operational environment (OE) shaping plans developed by the NFC. They share the information derived from conducting OE awareness with other force consumers through the DOD information networks.

The Navy normally organizes assigned/attached forces as part of a task force, typically aligned through an NFC. The afloat senior commander is normally designated as the OTC or CWC. As part of a joint command structure, the NFC may be designated as a JTF commander or a JFMCC under a CCDR, JFC, or commander of another JTF. Further, an NCC may also be tasked as a JFMCC or be assigned by the CCDR to provide Service support to a JFC or a joint task force commander.

An IO team from Navy Information Operations Command-Norfolk (NIOC–N), VA, or NIOC San Diego, CA, supports the ARG and embarked Marine air-ground task force (MAGTF) commander with IO planning and execution. Augmentees from FLTCYBERCOM activities may be part of the afloat IO planning team and support for ARG IO evolutions. During open-ocean transits and approaches to the littorals, the ARG planning team focuses on exchanging current IO data with the appropriate theater MOC IO cell and other ARGs and units to maintain a current regional picture for the ARG commander. During littoral operations, the planning team focuses on EMCON support to amphibious operations and defense of the amphibious task force. This shift in focus requires a shift in reporting priorities and liaison efforts from the EW modules of other ARG ships to MAGTF elements located ashore or afloat.

# CHAPTER 5

# Information Operations and Planning

## 5.1 INTRODUCTION

The planning process allows the commander and staff to plan and execute operations effectively, to ensure that the employment of forces is linked to objectives, and to integrate IO seamlessly with the actions of a joint force. The planning process assists commanders and their staffs in analyzing operational environment effects and distilling a multitude of planning information in order to provide the commander with a coherent framework to support decisions. The process is thorough and helps apply clarity, sound judgment, logic, and professional expertise.

Just as all maritime operations are integrated within the broader context of joint operations and campaigns, so IO is integrated with joint planning to ensure a successful military operation, setting the necessary conditions for the strategic end state. It is critical that Navy efforts correctly align maritime forces and their capabilities with joint requirements.

The Navy's core capabilities across the phases of an operation are shown in figure 5-1. IRC can support all the Navy's core capabilities and should be identified and developed during planning, execution, and transitions between phases. IRC can be included along the planning horizons for current operations, future operations, and future plans.

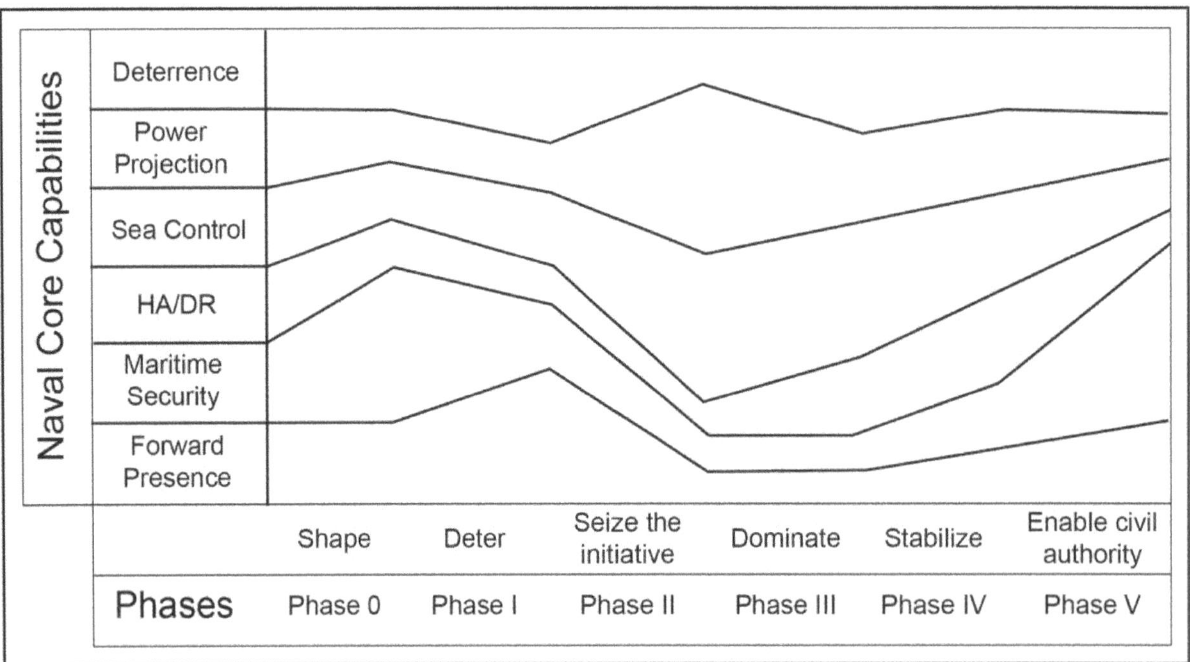


Figure 5-1. Notional Application of Navy Core Capabilities Across the Six-phase Campaign Model Continuum

The Navy force provides unique options to the joint commander, each useful in executing IO, including:

1. Forward deployment and prompt response
2. Sustained presence
3. A maneuverable base with freedom of movement in international waters
4. A scalable force with flexible capabilities.

## 5.2 OPERATION PLANNING

Operational-level planners should have a thorough knowledge of JP 5-0, Joint Operation Planning, and NWP 5-01, Navy Planning. Prior to developing any operational plan, it is necessary to understand strategic guidance and the sources of strategic direction. Planners should derive purpose and focus from all available sources, including the JSCP, Guidance for Employment of the Force, Global Force Management Implementation Guidance, and others. Strategic guidance provides the shape of the desired strategic and military end states to a plan or order. This process enables unified action, a concept describing the synchronization, coordination, and integration of the activities of Governmental and nongovernmental entities with military operations to achieve unity of effort. For additional information on unified action, see JP 1.

Operation planning has a close relationship with policy and strategic guidance. Comprehensive policy can clarify planning. Consequently, deliberate or crisis action planning correctly informs policy. The planning process provides a common basis for discussion, execution, and change for the joint force, its subordinate and higher headquarters, the joint planning and execution community, and national leadership. It establishes the necessary scope and scale to enable inclusion of IRC into a plan in order to develop an integrated product to meet the commander's intent.

### 5.2.1 Applicability to Navy Planners

Effective Navy planners are knowledgeable in joint planning and are experts in how the Navy's unique maritime capabilities can contribute to joint mission success. Further, they comprehend the necessity to integrate IO and IRC throughout plan development, supported by IO planners, when even greater expertise is required.

The JFMCC is the JFC's maritime warfighter, designated to control joint operations at sea. The authority for operational-level planning and employment of maritime forces and assets rests with the JFMCC.

JFMCC planning duties and responsibilities may include, but are not limited to:

1. Develop a maritime OPLAN to best support joint force objectives
2. Develop maritime COAs within the framework of the JFC-assigned objective mission, the forces available, and the commander's intent
3. Coordinate JFMCC planning with higher, lower, adjacent, and multinational headquarters
4. Determine JFMCC forces required and coordinate deployment planning in support of the selected COAs
5. Coordinate the planning and execution of maneuver operations with other missions.

Members of the MOC N39 cell and subsequently formed operational planning teams (OPTs) benefit from this knowledge and approach.

### 5.2.2 Operational Design

Operational design is the conception and construction of the framework that underpins a campaign or major OPLAN and its subsequent execution. The modern OE is characterized by complexity and uncertainty and compels solutions that stress innovation and agility. Effective operational design requires the ability to comprehend imprecise information, ambiguity, and continual plan refinement while developing branch plans and sequels for future operations.

Joint and Navy doctrine emphatically state a commander's role in operational design. The commander is the central figure in operational design, not just because of the commander's education and experience, but also because the commander's judgment and decisions are required to guide the staff through the process. Generally, the more complex a situation, the more critical a commander's early involvement becomes as the plan takes shape.

A commander's wisdom is essential to developing the operational approach, which is necessary to establish the necessary conditions for COA development. This applies to the JFC and to the JFMCC as well. In a nuanced and complex OE, which includes the maritime segment of the joint operations area, considering, evaluating, and employing IRC along with their relevance to the ends, way, and means, are fundamental actions for the commander and planning staff.

The commander's intent is essential for the planning team. This brief statement includes the purpose and the desired end state and addresses risk. It reflects an understanding of the strategic direction, the OE, and any impediments (i.e., risk and uncertainty) to mission accomplishment.

Planners apply elements of operational design to provide the conceptual framework that underpins the operation or campaign plans and their subsequent execution. The application of operational design and operational art refines the problem and further reduces uncertainty while adequately ordering complex problems to allow facilitating more detailed planning. Additionally, it connects strategy and tactics by accounting for operational-level plans, orders, and assessment. Operational design may precede the planning process and offer initial planning considerations that include military end state, center of gravity, lines of effort, decisive points, etc.

### 5.2.3 Operational Art

Operational art is the cognitive approach by commanders and staffs—supported by their skill, knowledge, experience, creativity, and judgment—to develop strategies, campaigns, and operations to organize and employ military forces by integrating ends, ways, and means.

In spite of the way it is always presented and taught, combat planning does not lend itself to cookbook solutions, scientific models, or simple linear processes. Developing a solution requires study of the interplay of hundreds, if not thousands, of independent variables—some easily predicted, some wildly unexpected. An adaptable enemy does not fall victim to the same tactic more than once.

It is critical for staff planners to comprehend the elements of operational art and assist the commander as necessary. The use and application of operational art is a commander's technique. It is the creative thinking used to design strategies, campaigns, and major operations and to organize and employ military force. It allows commanders to understand the challenges facing them and to conceptualize approaches for achieving their strategic objectives. The thought process helps commanders and their staffs to lessen the ambiguity and uncertainty of a complex operational environment, understand the military problem set, and visualize how best to effectively employ the military element of national power in order to accomplish an assigned mission. This is the essence of operational art and, when employed correctly, it enables pursuit of unified action.

Operational design extends operational art's vision with a creative process that helps commanders and planners answer the ends–ways–means risk questions. The elements of operational design are individual tools that help the JFC and staffs visualize and describe the broad operational approach. Operational art, operational design, and operation planning processes form a synergy to produce the plan to underpin a joint operation.

### 5.2.4 Intelligence Support

IO, like all other military activities, benefits from robust intelligence support. Information operations intelligence integration (IOII) is the integration of intelligence disciplines and analytic methods to characterize and forecast, identify vulnerabilities, determine effects, and assess the information environment. IOII uses a joint concept explored further in JP 3-13.

IOII is critical to the planning, execution, and assessment of IO and the use of IRC. SIGINT is a category of intelligence comprising, either individually or in combination, all communications intelligence, electronic intelligence, and foreign instrumentation signals intelligence, however transmitted.

IO requires unique and detailed intelligence never before asked of intelligence collection agencies and activities. Intelligence preparation of the operational environment is vital to successful IO. Support from non-DOD and non-U.S. sources may also be required. Commanders dedicate intelligence personnel and capabilities to support IO planning and execution to ensure IO activities and IRC effectively support operations.

The combatant command's IO cell is the primary focal point for supporting the JTF and component commanders with IO products that support IO planning, execution, and assessment. It provides analysis of an adversary's IO capabilities and intentions and helps support the indications and warning process. A CCDR can request a national intelligence support team stand-up, composed of intelligence and communications experts from other intelligence agencies as required.

Cyber intelligence is the tracking, analyzing, and countering of digital security threats. This type of intelligence is a blend of physical espionage and defense with modern information technology. Cyber intelligence efforts help combat computer viruses, hackers, and terrorists who use the Internet to gain sensitive information. Aggressively fighting these threats is as significant a part of this field as protecting parties from them. Intelligence activities are critical to IO planning, execution, and assessment. Commanders draw on the resources they need to conduct effective IO in support of the CCDR and put it to best use.

### 5.2.5 Operation Planning Process

The joint operation planning process is an orderly, analytical process that consists of a logical set of steps to analyze a mission, select the best course of action, and produce a joint OPLAN or order. JOPP is an iterative process that structures the efforts of the commander and staff to develop plans appropriate to the military problem set at hand. Planners at all echelons apply analytical rigor and follow developmental steps to ensure a familiar and repeatable process and develop unity of effort. The principles of JOPP are relevant and adhered to during deliberate planning as well as crisis action planning, with the amount of time available for planning being the key distinction between the two.

Within the Navy, commanders are expected to operate independently while following their superior commander's intent; to act when an opportunity presents itself and to feel comfortable in conditions of ambiguity. These are attributes honed by mutual trust and confidence and years of experience at sea. This description of disciplined initiative is also known as mission command in joint doctrine. While the concept may be new to other Services, it is how the Navy has historically commanded. To ensure that planning does not stifle mission command, Navy planning focuses more on the purpose of operations rather than the details of how subordinates execute the tasks and avoids overly restrictive command and control concepts. The commander's intent cannot be a staff product; rather, if must be a true embodiment of the commander's vision and the centerpiece of the commander's discussions with subordinate commanders. Nonetheless, the terminology, products, and concepts of the Navy planning process are consistent with joint planning and joint doctrine and are compatible with other Services' doctrine.

Collecting information and building situational awareness to support the commander's planning and decision-making process supports the initiation of planning and is critical to all steps in the process. The following vignette provides a framework and context to step through the milestones in the planning process (figure 5-2).

Operation Synergy

In response to a crisis in Country TEAL, the Commander, U.S. Ocean Command (CDRUSOCEANCOM, the geographic combatant command in whose area of responsibility TEAL is located), received a CJCS planning order to develop courses of action based on staff estimates. TEAL's government has traditionally countered U.S. initiatives to establish normal diplomatic relations and has a long history of arms purchases from Country ORANGE, to include antiship cruise missile and ballistic missile components. After recent elections, significant numbers of citizens who supported the opposition party were killed by TEAL's armed forces, producing regime instability and a growing humanitarian crisis. CDRUSOCEANCOM's Navy component command is Commander, U.S. Eleventh Fleet (COMELEVENTHFLT). ELEVENTHFLT's additional responsibilities include a be-prepared-to function to serve as a JTF headquarters and JFMCC. Since TEAL is an island nation, a plan that focuses on a maritime-centric COA receives particular scrutiny.

The desired political goal is to end the humanitarian crisis and keep hostilities from spreading through the region by restoring regime stability while encouraging future strides toward democracy and openness to U.S. diplomacy. The CCDR's vision for military objectives in the information environment includes both immediate tactical elements to ensure a military advantage and long-term influence elements to shape a more positive narrative. The JFMCC forces include Navy ships and aircraft with immense combat power along with IRC. There is a challenge for the members of the OPT in the JFMCC (MOC) IO cell in their deliberations to develop a line of operation that involves integrating disparate capabilities into a plan and then coordinating and synchronizing their use during the plan's execution; in other words, identifying the intended effects and aligning the appropriate capabilities to achieve those effects.

There are essentially three broad tasks to consider and each includes numerous subordinate activities:

1. Protect friendly information and information systems. Both pro-regime and antiregime elements, in theater and globally, oppose U.S. involvement in the dispute, and both sides have shown skill and enthusiasm in attacking the Navy in the information environment. Possible IRC to counter these attacks include an effective OPSEC posture and efficient IA and DCO techniques.
2. Disrupt or degrade adversary C2 systems. The JFMCC can de-escalate internal violence and protect U.S. forces by attacking the adversary's C2 nodes using lethal fires and IRC, including EA and OCO, and executing MILDEC.
3. Influence a target audience(s). The JFMCC's plan contains a significant influence dimension and considers identifying key adversary operational- and tactical-level decision makers and leadership. Exploring the method to develop encounters and perceptions necessary to shape deeds that support achieving the desired military end state is essential, (e.g., key leader engagement, MILDEC, defense support to public diplomacy, etc.). This dimension also contains use of MISO with the aim of altering TA behavior and developing and implementing an effective commander's communication strategy to align key themes and messages to support the desired outcome.

Because of careful evaluation of available IRC and their judicious employment, the JFMCC planners brief COMELEVENTHFLT)/JFMCC and CDRUSOCEANCOM on the approach and objectives, seeking guidance and the authority to continue to plan development to respond to the crisis in TEAL. As the operation progresses and knowledge of the joint OE becomes clearer, the plan must be refined, integrate the available IRC in every phase to deliver an operational advantage that conforms with strategic guidance, and consistent with the goals of the U.S. strategic end state.

Figure 5-2. Example: Planning Process

### 5.2.5.1 Planning Initiation

Planning initiation is the critical first step in the planning process, whether in deliberate planning or in response to an emerging situation in crisis action planning. The JFC typically provides initial planning guidance based on current understanding of the operational environment, the problem, and the initial operational approach for the campaign or operation. It could specify time constraints, outline initial coordination requirements, or authorize movement of key capabilities within the JFC's authority. Receipt of the JFC's initial planning guidance is essential for JFMCC and other component commanders to begin their respective staff planning tasks in response to an initiating directive (e.g., a WARNORD or other planning document).

#### 5.2.5.2 Mission Analysis

As the name implies, the mission analysis portion of planning is an intensely methodical review of the operation. This is a time for the commander and staff to carefully study the assigned tasks and identify other tasks, resources, and coordination requirements necessary for mission accomplishment. If appropriate IRC were not considered before this point in the planning sequence, this is a critical time to begin the integration process by identifying candidates for inclusion in each phase of the operation. When the commander is tasked, planners consider the following questions:

1. What is the purpose of the assigned mission?
2. What tasks must my command perform to accomplish the mission?
3. What are the limitations on my force's actions?
4. What assets are needed to support my operation?

Staff mission analysis activities, whether accomplished in the mission analysis process by members of joint planning group (JPG) or OPT, may include:

1. Analyze higher headquarters planning activities and strategic guidance
2. Review commander's initial planning guidance, including initial understanding of the operational environment, of the problem, and description of the operational approach
3. Determine known facts and develop planning assumptions
4. Determine and analyze operational limitations
5. Determine specified, implied, and essential tasks
6. Develop mission statement
7. Conduct initial force allocation review
8. Develop risk assessment
9. Develop mission success criteria
10. Develop commander's critical information requirements
11. Prepare staff estimates
12. Prepare and deliver mission analysis brief
13. Publish commander's updated planning guidance.

This is joint doctrine common to all Services and a process that is relevant to all circumstances; it may be truncated or modified based on time constraints. Mission analysis concludes with a formal briefing and issuing the commander's refined planning guidance containing:

1. Approved mission statement
2. Key elements of the OE

3. Clear statement of the problem to be solved
4. Key assumptions
5. Key operational limitations
6. Discussion of the national strategic end state
7. Termination criteria
8. Military end state
9. Military objectives
10. Commander's initial thoughts on the conditions necessary to achieve objectives
11. Acceptable or unacceptable levels of risk in key areas
12. The commander's operational approach.

#### 5.2.5.3 Course of Action Development

A COA is a unique choice presented to the commander to accomplish an assigned mission. To be complete, a COA should be based on the operational approach and include the fundamental answers of who, what, where, when, why, and how an action takes place. Similarly, the essential tasks from the draft mission statement are common to all COAs. As with mission analysis, COA development draws on key inputs to influence a number of outputs. COAs may be separate and distinct throughout the operational domains (air, land, maritime, space, and cyberspace), the information environment, or through some combination.

JP 5-0 and NWP 5-0 cover techniques to develop COAs. IRC may be best coordinated by using the joint functions of C2, intelligence, fires, movement and maneuver, protection, and sustainment. Each of these functional areas provides sufficient opportunity to address inclusion of specific IRC and the role that maritime forces assume in their eventual execution. Additionally, Navy planners should consider three key questions during COA development to best employ assigned maritime forces and nest the plan under a broader joint construct:

1. How do land forces, maritime forces, air forces, and special operations forces integrate across the joint functions to accomplish their assigned tasks?
2. What are the major ways in which space operations can support operations across the joint functions?
3. How can the joint forces conduct IO to support joint operations?

Apply a validity test to each tentative (i.e., an option not yet approved or working) COA using the following assessment criteria: adequate, feasible, acceptable, distinguishable, and complete.

#### 5.2.5.4 War Gaming

War gaming facilitates COA analysis and, depending on the time available, can be accomplished through a range of options. War gaming techniques generally begin with a detailed narrative to describe how events unfold; the "sketch note," which adds an operational sketch and commentary to the graphic; and a computer-assisted modeling and simulation undertaking. Any option is appropriate and is evaluated against an adversary's most probable and most dangerous COA.

The war game represents an ideal opportunity to include IRC using the aforementioned criteria. While techniques to conduct the war game may vary—including a red cell to offer an opposing view along with a white cell chaired by a senior staff leader to ensure objectives are met and efficiency is retained throughout the process—they are key components to success when evaluating the results.

#### 5.2.5.5 COA Comparison

The next step in COA development is to compare possible COAs but not against one another. Rather, evaluate each independently against the desired mission outcome within the given established criteria. There are numerous approaches to conduct a comparison, but the most important consideration is the element of consistency in evaluation. The goal is to create a matrix using numerical (and possibly weighted) criteria to aid the commander's selection of the COA best suited to accomplish the assigned mission.

#### 5.2.5.6 COA Approval

It is prudent and customary to conduct a formal briefing for the commander and headquarters staff to select a COA for approval. This presentation provides the commander with an opportunity to obtain responses to any unanswered questions, include additional guidance from higher headquarters, or alter the approach if required. Once a decision is made on a COA, refined planning commences. It informs a decision statement to facilitate the JFC's commander's estimate and plan or order development.

## 5.3 TARGETING

The purpose of targeting is to achieve specific desired effects at the strategic, operational, and tactical levels of war. A target is a specific area, object, audience, function, or facility subject to military action on which an effect is directed. Targeting is a process of matching a target in the cognitive, informational, or physical domain with lethal or nonlethal capabilities. Targeting involves giving the commander recommendations for an attack on targets that may help achieve military objectives and providing options to achieve desired effects.

Clear objectives and commander's guidance are the foundations of the targeting process. Objectives are developed, and commander's guidance is normally provided, at the national, theater, and component levels. At the operational level, IO targeting nominations originate from IO planners integrated into the MOC and JTF targeting processes for approval and coordination. They are significantly influenced by in-depth intelligence analysis. IO planners use established targeting processes and methodologies to recommend targets for which IO can be used to support the theater campaign plan. Some other considerations include:

1. Early identification of critical elements with respect to specific targets is essential for successful IO. Understanding the nature of the threat helps defend and protect against adversary IO.

    a. Employ IRC to achieve military objectives when appropriate. IRC may target a key element of a specific, critical adversary target set.

    b. Understanding the nature of the threat helps defend and protect against adversary IO. An IO threat should be defined in terms of a specific adversary's intent, capability, and opportunity to influence the elements of the friendly information environment critical to achieving objectives.

    c. An IO threat is an adversary that is organized, resourced, and motivated to affect decision makers. Hackers, criminals and organized crime, insiders, industrial and economic espionage, and, in some cases, terrorism constitute a general threat to the protected information environment. This general threat requires monitoring for indications of a specific IO threat and subsequently may require additional defensive IO measures.

2. C2 remains a substantial target for IO. Commercial communications systems linked to friendly and adversary C2 systems offer unique challenges to offensive targeting and defensive protection.

3. Examples of key areas of warfare support comprising potential offensive target sets and requiring protection include, but are not limited to logistics, intelligence, and non-C2 communications systems. An adversary's offensive capabilities may target friendly commercial infrastructures, just as friendly offensive capabilities may target an adversary's commercial infrastructures.

Targeting is a familiar process for JFMCC staffs, similar to offering excess sorties to the JFACC staff for additional mission availability to be apportioned in the ATO. Sequential tasking provides the commander with supplemental capability to facilitate mission accomplishment. Within the MOC N39 IO cell, similar opportunities exist to integrate IRC into the JPG/OPT planning sequence. These may represent a distinct line of operation or a line of effort and may fall into a special technological capability based on the nature of employment.

A target is an entity or object considered for possible engagement or action. It may be an area, complex, installation, force, equipment, capability, function, individual, group, system, entity, or behavior identified for possible action to support the commander's objectives, guidance, and intent. JP 3-60, Joint Targeting, describes four principles that are applied throughout the targeting cycle to create desired effects while diminishing undesired collateral effects.

1. Focused. The function of targeting is to achieve the JFC's objectives through target engagement within the parameters set by the CONOPS, the operational limitations within the plans and orders (to include fragmentary orders), the ROE, the Law of War, and agreements concerning the sovereignty of national territories. Every target nominated should contribute to attaining the JFC's objectives.

2. Effects-based. The art of targeting seeks to create desired effects with the least risk and least expenditure of time and resources.

3. Interdisciplinary. Joint targeting entails participation from all elements of the JFC's staff, component commanders' staffs, other agencies, departments, organizations, and multinational partners. IO expert participation is central for processes involving IRC and lethal effects on information systems and is useful in ensuring lethal actions are aligned with the commander's influence objectives.

4. Systematic. The joint targeting cycle is designed to create effects in a systematic manner. It is a rational, iterative process that methodically analyzes, prioritizes, and assigns assets against targets systematically.

IO planners consider all instruments of the adversary's national power to determine how best to achieve stated objectives by affecting information and information systems. Successful integration of IRC into the targeting process is fundamental to the success of the campaign. IO may call for targeting adversary human decision processes (human factors), information, and information systems used to support decisionmaking or adversary morale with a variety of lethal and nonlethal means. The selection of IO actions should be consistent with national objectives, applicable international conventions, ROE, and other guidance.

The joint force IO cell is another source for target requirements and should be closely integrated to deconflict redundant targeting, consider intelligence gain versus loss assessments, and provide inputs to the restricted target list and no-strike list. IO planners coordinate and integrate IO at all levels. Most destructive IO attacks either support strategic attacks or are considered strategic attacks or interdiction operations themselves. Therefore, planners, operators, and targeteers should carefully consider prospective IO target nominations when making apportionment decisions.

The maritime targeting cell includes IO planners who assist the staff planners in developing the JFMCC input to the joint integrated prioritized target list and in issuing subsequent task orders. The IO planners conduct frequent liaison with the JTCB IO planner counterparts to coordinate and synchronize target selection planning.

The JFMCC staff is responsible for identifying potential target sets to be presented and adjudicated at the JFC's JTCB. With respect to specific IO-related targets, the JFMCC assigns the nomenclature of high-value and high-payoff as applicable to those candidate targets. Target sets in which lethal effects may have desired IO results may include microwave towers or communications antennae and power generators or transformers.

Similarly, IRC, like OCO and EA, can disrupt adversary systems, impacting combat capabilities in the physical domain.

Figure 5-3 identifies the six phases of the joint targeting cycle. It is imperative the JFMCC planners comprehend the entire cycle and the specific requirements associated with each of the phases to ensure IRC are correctly identified, considered, war-gamed, and ultimately written into the plan from the operational to tactical level. For additional information on targeting, refer to NTTP 3-13.1 and JP 3-60.

## 5.4 ASSESSMENT

Assessment is a continuous process that measures the overall effectiveness of employing joint force capabilities during military operations, the determination of the progress toward accomplishing a task, creating a condition, or achieving an objective. Assessment considerations are identified during mission analysis. As the commander's critical information requirements are developed, key indicators are derived from identifying essential information that ultimately measures progress made (or lost) towards an objective.

A measure of effectiveness (MOE) is a criterion used to assess changes in system behavior, capability, or OE that ties to measuring the attainment of an end state, achievement of an objective, or creation of an effect. A measure of performance (MOP) is a criterion used to assess a friendly action that ties to measuring task accomplishment.

Both MOP (task assessment: Are we doing things right?) and MOE (Are we doing the right things?) are important to the commander. Establish decisive points based on progress made in the areas of through monitoring and evaluating and then recommending or directing action. Altering the collection plan, adjusting MOE indicators, or changing IRC employment are viable options based on the assessment of progress. A detailed, practical discussion of assessment contained in JP 5-0, Appendix D, may help create the JFMCC IO assessment plan. See NTTP 3-32.01, Operational Assessment, for additional information.

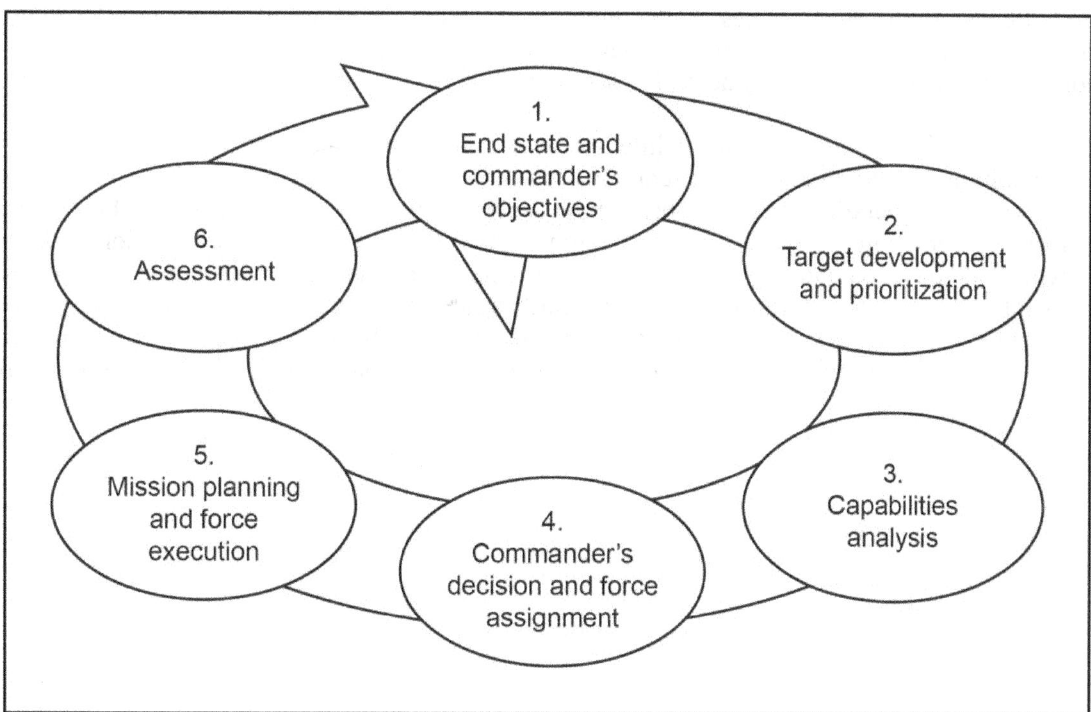


Figure 5-3. Six Phases of the Joint Targeting Cycle

## 5.5 COORDINATION WITH PARTNERS

Although the Navy is always prepared to undertake unilateral military action, coordination with navies of other nations has become typical. Multination participation can be vital for mission accomplishment and can strengthen partnerships. This participation may include long-standing alliances, such as the North Atlantic Treaty Organization, or a hybrid coalition of nations with conflicting histories and interests but working together for a specific common purpose.

### 5.5.1 Multinational and Coalition Considerations

IO concepts, doctrine, procedures, and capabilities are recognized by U.S. allies and coalition members. Naturally, there are disparate views based on national interests, interpretation, doctrine, and culture, which require coordination and conflict resolution on friction points by the multinational force commander and staff. Navy planners would be wise to recognize that coalition capabilities complement U.S. expertise, forming synergy by the significant regional and operational acumen they contribute.

The NATO alliance has a substantive and authoritative IO policy. It is based on the premise that civil-military cooperation is founded in close, interactive relationships among partner nation militaries. NATO military public information and IO have a definitive relationship. Although there is a distinct separation in function, plans and actions are well coordinated. Formalized terms of reference provide overarching guidance and consensus where possible. For additional information, see AJP 3-10, Allied Joint Doctrine for Information Operations.

### 5.5.2 Interorganizational Coordination

Interorganizational coordination is defined as the interaction among elements of the DOD; engaged U.S. Government agencies; state, territorial, local and tribal agencies; foreign military forces and government agencies; intergovernmental organizations; nongovernmental organizations; and the private sector. With the amalgamation of disparate cultures, objectives, resources, talent, and experience coming together to contribute a solution to a complex problem set, near-precise and consensus-level guidance is essential. Joint doctrine exists to provide such a foundation for coordination of military activities within the military end state.

The significance for JFMCC planners is that, while interagency coordination primarily takes place at the CCDR headquarters, additional coordination may be required at the component command level. Depending on the scenario and phase of an operation, maritime forces and capabilities may be assigned additional tasks to achieve military and strategic end states. Some organizations' representatives are present in the OE prior to and following military activities and their livelihood and purpose may be impacted by planned operations or by unintended consequences. This is particularly true for nongovernmental organizations and private sector interests, many of which prefer not to coordinate actions, fearing that their objectives may be jeopardized by close association with military actors. For additional information, see JP 3-08, Interorganizational Coordination during Joint Operations.

INTENTIONALLY BLANK

# REFERENCES

NTTP 3-13.2, Information Operations Warfare Commander Manual

NTTP 3-51.1, Navy Electronic Warfare

NWP 3-53, Navy Psychological Operations

NWP 3-56, Composite Warfare Doctrine

SecDef Memo 12401-10, Strategic Communication and Information Operations in the DOD

JP 3-08, Interorganizational Coordination during Joint Operations

JP 3-09, Joint Fire Support

JP 3-12, Cyberspace Operations

JP 3-13, Information Operations

JP 3-13.1, Electronic Warfare

JP 3-60, Joint Targeting

JP 3-61, Public Affairs

JP 5-0, Joint Operation Planning

Center for Analyses Study, Structures for Information Warfare and Information Dominance Afloat (September 2013)

Chairman of the Joint Chiefs of Staff Instruction 3210.01 series, Joint Information Operations Policy

DOD Directive 3600.01 series, Information Operations

Title 10, U.S. Code, Armed Forces

Title 50, U.S. Code, War and National Defense

INTENTIONALLY BLANK

# GLOSSARY

**functional component commands.** A command normally, but not necessarily, composed of forces of two or more Military Departments which may be established across the range of military operations to perform particular operational missions that may be of short duration or may extend over a period of time. See also component; Service component command. (JP 1-02. Source: JP 1)

**information environment.** The aggregate of individuals, organizations, and systems that collect, process, disseminate, or act on information. (JP 1-02. Source: JP 3-13)

**information operations-information-related capability.** A tool, technique, or activity employed within a dimension of the information environment that can be used to create effects and operationally desirable conditions. Also called IRC. (JP 1-02. Source: JP 3-13)

**integration.** 1. In force protection, the synchronized transfer of units into an operational commander's force prior to mission execution. (JP 1-02. Source: JP 1) 2. The arrangement of military forces and their actions to create a force that operates by engaging as a whole. (JP 1-02. Source: JP 1)

**strategic level of war.** The level of war at which a nation, often as a member of a group of nations, determines national or multinational (alliance or coalition) strategic security objectives and guidance, then develops and uses national resources to achieve those objectives. See also operational level of war; tactical level of war. (JP 1-02. Source: JP 3-0)

**target audience.** An individual or group selected for influence. Also called TA. (JP 1-02. Source: JP 3-13)

INTENTIONALLY BLANK

# LIST OF ACRONYMS AND ABBREVIATIONS

| | |
|---|---|
| **AOR** | area of responsibility |
| **ARG** | amphibious ready group |
| **ATO** | air tasking order |
| **C2** | command and control |
| **CCDR** | combatant commander |
| **CCMD** | combatant command |
| **CCS** | commander's communication strategy |
| **CDRUSSTRATCOM** | Commander, United States Strategic Command |
| **CJCS** | Chairman Joint Chiefs of Staff |
| **CMO** | civil-military operations |
| **CNO** | Chief of Naval Operations |
| **CO** | cyberspace operations |
| **COA** | course of action |
| **COMTENTHFLT** | Commander, Tenth Fleet |
| **CONOPS** | concept of operations |
| **CSG** | carrier strike group |
| **CTF** | cross-functional team |
| **CWC** | composite warfare commander |
| **DCO** | defensive cyberspace operations |
| **DOD** | Department of Defense |
| **EA** | electronic attack |
| **EP** | electronic protection |
| **EM** | electromagnetic |
| **EMBM** | electromagnetic battle management |
| **EMCON** | emission control |

| | |
|---|---|
| **EMS** | electromagnetic spectrum |
| **ES** | electronic warfare support |
| **EW** | electronic warfare |
| **EWCC** | electronic warfare coordination cell |
| **FLTCYBERCOM** | Fleet Cyber Command |
| **FTC** | fleet training continuum |
| **IA** | information assurance |
| **INFOCON** | information operations condition |
| **IO** | information operations |
| **IOII** | information operations intelligence integration |
| **IRC** | information-related capability |
| **IWC** | information operations warfare commander |
| **JEMSO** | joint electromagnetic spectrum operations |
| **JFACC** | joint force air component commander |
| **JFC** | joint force commander |
| **JFMCC** | joint force maritime component commander |
| **JOPP** | joint operation planning process |
| **JP** | joint publication |
| **JPG** | joint planning group |
| **JSCP** | Joint Strategic Capabilities Plan |
| **JTCB** | joint targeting coordination board |
| **JTF** | joint task force |
| **MAGTF** | Marine air-ground task force |
| **MILDEC** | military deception |
| **MISO** | military information support operations |
| **MOC** | maritime operations center |
| **MOE** | measure of effectiveness |
| **MOP** | measure of performance |

| | |
|---|---|
| **NATO** | North Atlantic Treaty Organization |
| **NCC** | Navy component commander |
| **NCF** | Navy Cyber Forces |
| **NFC** | numbered fleet commander |
| **NIOC** | Navy Information Operations Command |
| **NTTP** | Navy tactics, techniques, and procedures |
| **NWP** | Navy warfare publication |
| **OCO** | offensive cyberspace operations |
| **OE** | operational environment |
| **OPLAN** | operation plan |
| **OPSEC** | operations security |
| **OPT** | operational planning team |
| **OTC** | officer in tactical command |
| **PA** | public affairs |
| **ROE** | rules of engagement |
| **SC** | strategic communication |
| **SecDef** | Secretary of Defense |
| **SIGINT** | signals intelligence |
| **STO** | special technical operations |
| **TA** | target audience |
| **TAA** | target audience analysis |
| **TCP** | theater campaign plan |
| **WARNORD** | warning order |
| **USCYBERCOM** | United States Cyber Command |
| **USFF** | United States Fleet Forces Command |
| **USG** | United States Government |
| **USPACFLT** | United States Pacific Fleet |
| **USSTRATCOM** | United States Strategic Command |

INTENTIONALLY BLANK

LIST OF EFFECTIVE PAGES

| Effective Pages | Page Numbers |
|---|---|
| FEB 2014 | 1 thru 14 |
| FEB 2014 | 1-1, 1-2 |
| FEB 2014 | 2-1 thru 2-8 |
| FEB 2014 | 3-1 thru 3-10 |
| FEB 2014 | 4-1 thru 4-10 |
| FEB 2014 | 5-1 thru 5-12 |
| FEB 2014 | Reference-1, Reference-2 |
| FEB 2014 | Glossary-1, Glossary-2 |
| FEB 2014 | LOAA-1 thru LOAA-4 |
| FEB 2014 | LEP-1, LEP-2 |

INTENTIONALLY BLANK

MCWP 3-40.4

# Marine Air-Ground Task Force Information Operations

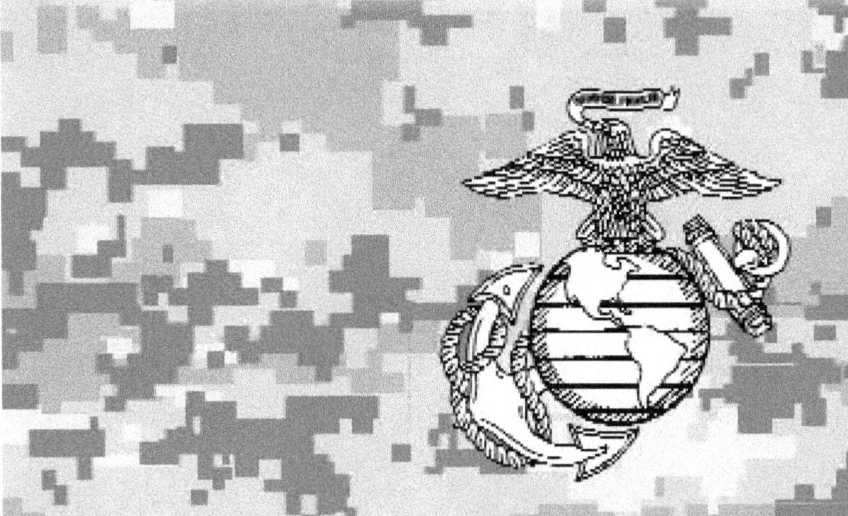

US Marine Corps

DISTRIBUTION STATEMENT A: Approved for public release; distribution is unlimited.

PCN 143 000140 00

**To Our Readers**

**Changes:** Readers of this publication are encouraged to submit suggestions and changes through the Universal Need Statement (UNS) process. The UNS submission process is delineated in Marine Corps Order 3900.15_, *Marine Corps Expeditionary Force Development System*, which can be obtained from the on-line Marine Corps Publications Electronic Library:

http://www.marines.mil/News/Publications/ELECTRONICLIBRARY.aspx.

The UNS recommendation should include the following information:

- Location of change
  - Publication number and title
  - Current page number
  - Paragraph number (if applicable)
  - Line number
  - Figure or table number (if applicable)
- Nature of change
  - Addition/deletion of text
  - Proposed new text

**Additional copies:** If this publication is not an electronic only distribution, a printed copy may be obtained from Marine Corps Logistics Base, Albany, GA 31704-5001, by following the instructions in MCBul 5600, *Marine Corps Doctrinal Publications Status.* An electronic copy may be obtained from the United States Marine Corps Doctrine web page:

https://www.doctrine.usmc.mil.

**Unless otherwise stated, whenever the masculine gender is used, both men and women are included.**

DEPARTMENT OF THE NAVY
Headquarters United States Marine Corps
Washington, D.C. 20380-1775

1 July 2013

FOREWORD

Marine Corps Warfighting Publication (MCWP) 3-40.4, *Marine Air-Ground Task Force Information Operations*, operationalizes the *Marine Corps Operating Concept for Information Operations*. This publication contains doctrine for employment of the various information-related capabilities integrated as information operations in support of the Marine air-ground task force (MAGTF).

The purpose of this publication is to provide MAGTF commanders and their staffs guidance in planning, preparing, executing, and assessing information operations in support of the MAGTF's operational objectives. It gives Marines a warfighter's orientation to information operations, providing a basis to understand the relevance of information operations and a framework to implement information operations.

This publication is intended for Marines assigned to a MAGTF that are responsible for information operations planning.

Reviewed and approved this date.

BY DIRECTION OF THE COMMANDANT OF THE MARINE CORPS

RICHARD P. MILLS
Lieutenant General, U.S. Marine Corps
Deputy Commandant for Combat Development and Integration

Publication Control Number: 143 000140 00

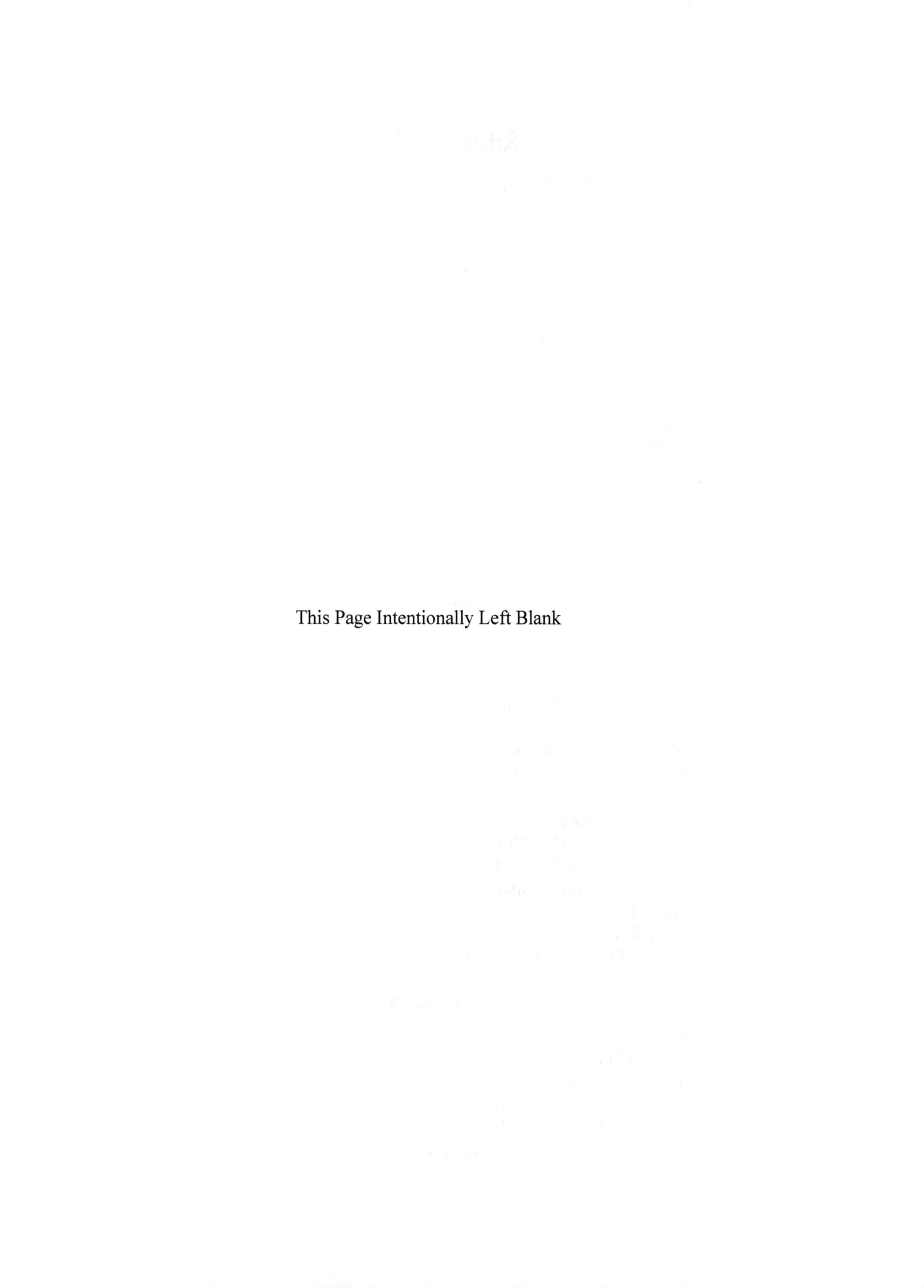

This Page Intentionally Left Blank

# Marine Air-Ground Task Force Information Operations

## Table of Contents

### Chapter 1. Fundamentals



### Chapter 2. Integration and Planning



### Chapter 3. Key Information-Related Capabilities

## Chapter 4. Information Operations Intelligence Integration



## Appendices



## Glossary

## References and Related Publications

This Page Intentionally Left Blank

# Chapter 1
# Fundamentals

As defined in Marine Corps Reference Publication (MCRP) 5-12C, *Marine Corps Supplement to the Department of Defense Dictionary of Military and Associated Terms*, information operations (IO) are the integration, coordination, and synchronization of all actions taken in the information environment to affect a relevant decisionmaker in order to create an operational advantage for the commander. The Marine air-ground task force (MAGTF) executes IO as an inherent element of all operations to enable and enhance the overall ability to conduct successful military actions. In order to apply information operations across a range of military operations, the MAGTF commander integrates his military actions, forces, and capabilities throughout the operational environments (air, land, maritime, and space domains and information environment). These efforts can create and/or sustain desired and measurable effects on the adversary's leaders, forces (regular or irregular), information, and information systems and other audiences; while protecting and defending the MAGTF commander's forces, information, and information systems.

As with other elements of combat power, there is no universal formula for the application of information operations; therefore, information operations should be viewed as an element of combat power, focusing on when and where it best supports MAGTF operations. The factors of mission, enemy, terrain and weather, troops and support available—time available and, when required, civilian considerations are the major determinants.

Information operations are primarily concerned with affecting decisions and decisionmaking processes while at the same time defending friendly decisionmaking processes in order to achieve information superiority. Information operations affect and defend decisionmaking based on six fundamental assumptions:

- Decisionmakers generally value the quality of information they receive.
- The influences of geography, language, culture, religion, organization, experience, and personality of the decisionmaker impact the relative value placed upon the information received.
- Decisions are made based on the information available at the time.
- It is possible, with finite resources, to understand the relevant aspects of the information environment to include the processes decisionmakers use to make decisions.
- It is possible to affect the information environment in which specific decisionmakers act through psychological, electronic, or physical means.
- It is possible to measure the effectiveness of IO actions in relation to an operational objective.

Although each of these assumptions is an important enabling factor for information operations they may not all be true for every operation. For any specific operation where one or more of these assumptions are not met, the risk assessment provided to the commander would be adjusted accordingly.

Marines deploy as unique, task-organized MAGTFs and their ability to task-organize and integrate the necessary combat power to achieve the objective is part of their expeditionary mindset. Therefore, the integration of information operations into the Marine Corps Planning Process (MCPP) is critical.

## Legal Considerations

Information operations may involve complex legal and policy issues requiring careful review. Similar to operations in the physical environment, MAGTF activities in the information environment are bounded by policy, societal values, and a fundamental respect for human dignity. Marines, whether operating physically from bases or locations overseas or from within the boundaries of the United States, are required by law and policy to act in accordance with US law and other standards of conduct (e.g., law of war [often called the law of armed conflict], rules of engagement). Because of the potential numerous legal issues associated with information operations, it is critical to obtain a legal analysis of the proposed operation within the context of the applicable law, ideally through the judge advocate's participation within an IO planning cell. This individual should be consulted early and often to ensure compliance and eliminate potential delay. If, based on lack of capacity, a judge advocate cannot be a permanent member, an open and continuous dialogue must be established with the staff judge advocate (SJA).

## Information Environment

The information environment is the aggregate of individuals, organizations, and systems that collect, process, disseminate, or act on information. (Joint Publication [JP] 1-02, *Department of Defense Dictionary of Military and Associated Terms*) Therefore, a solid understanding of the information environment must be achieved before any planning can begin. Refinement of the command's understanding of the information environment continues throughout the planning process and the execution of operations. The information environment consists of three interrelated dimensions: cognitive, informational, and physical. Table 1-1 represents a typical view of the three interrelated dimensions and some of their characteristics.

**Table 1-1. Dimensions of the Information Environment.**

| | |
|---|---|
| **Cognitive Dimension** | Exists in the minds of human beings.<br>Consists of individual and collective consciousness.<br>Exists where information is used to shape perceptions and make decisions.<br>Significant characteristics include values, beliefs, perceptions, awareness, and decisionmaking. |
| **Informational Dimension** | Created by the interaction of the physical and cognitive dimensions.<br>Exists where information is collected, processed and disseminated.<br>Significant characteristics are information content and flow. |
| **Physical Dimension** | Consist of the tangible, real world.<br>Exists where information environment overlaps with the physical world.<br>Consists of individuals, organizations, information systems, and the physical networks that connect them.<br>Significant characteristics include terrain, weather, civilian information infrastructure, media, populace, and third party organizations. |

### Cognitive Dimension

The cognitive dimension consists of the beliefs of a person or persons whose decisions can impact the commander's end state and is the hardest dimension to assess. The key to understanding this dimension is understanding that decisions are made based on culture, life experiences, relationships, outside events, ideology, and the influences of those inside and outside a decisionmaker's group. Added to these variables are the perceptions that are built on information collected on current events and the plans and beliefs of others. Ultimately, the commander must determine how a targeted decisionmaker will act on his beliefs and perceptions and how that action will impact the commander's end state.

### Informational Dimension

The informational dimension consists of the content of information and the way it flows to and from a decisionmaker to form a message. The content of the message is the idea or thought that is conveyed to key audiences. The message must flow so its intended audience can actually hear, read, or see it.

### Physical Dimension

The physical dimension consists of both key individuals and human networks and a technical and physical infrastructure that supports the information flow to its intended audience:

- Key individuals are those that provide access to audiences of interest, have the ability to influence target audiences, or may be the audience of interest themselves.
- Human networks are groups that support the process and dissemination of information to an audience. They can also shape the beliefs of others based on their own ideology and goals.
- Technical infrastructure is what is needed to produce, process, receive, send, and store information so that the decisionmaker can interact with others and make decisions.
- The physical infrastructure supports the flow of information and is what houses the technical infrastructure, as well as key individuals and human networks.

## Use of Information

Part of understanding a target audience's information environment is to understand how the target audience leverages information within that environment. When assessing a target audience's use of information, it is important not to mirror the discussion with US abilities. Depending on the sophistication of the audience, they may or may not have the same capabilities as the United States. An IO planner must fully validate any assumptions about a target audience's capabilities to leverage information prior to the end of the planning phase. The IO planner's analysis of an adversary target audience's methods of leveraging information must address the target audience's ability to protect, collect, and project information:

- How will the target audience leverage information within their operational environment in order to achieve their goals?
- How will the target audience protect information that is deemed critical (information required to make decisions without being interrupted)?
- How will the target audience collect—either overtly or covertly—information on its adversaries so they can make decisions that best support their goals?
- How will the target audience project information to others in order to persuade others to support their goals?

## Information Superiority

Information superiority is the operational advantage derived from the ability to collect, process, and disseminate an uninterrupted flow of information while exploiting or denying an adversary's ability to do the same. (JP 1-02) Obtaining the operational advantage described within the definition of information superiority is the overarching focus of information operations. Just as each mission's end state is different, so is information superiority. For example, during combat operations, information superiority can gain surprise over the adversary or prevent the adversary from employing its reserve forces. During counterinsurgency operations, information superiority can gain populace support for friendly operations or prevent adversary freedom of information flow. In each case, information superiority is defined specifically for the mission in terms of what advantage is sought for the MAGTF.

Gaining information superiority over the adversary should always be the main effort of information operations. To achieve information superiority, the MAGTF uses information to actively attack the adversary and to shape the information environment to the MAGTF's advantage. This duality of operations is analogous to fire and maneuver where fires equate to attacking the adversary's ability to use information and maneuver equate to actions that seize and retain information nodes for the purpose of gaining a positional advantage. To be effective, information operations must balance activities that shape the information environment with those that attack the adversary. Through a combination of both, the MAGTF seeks information superiority over its opponent.

The MAGTF will rarely achieve absolute and universal information superiority. The actions of opposing forces, as well as the information content and flow in the operational area, are not static. Therefore, information superiority is a localized and transitory condition over the adversary. The MAGTF seeks information superiority at certain times and places, usually at or before the decisive point of the operation.

## Information-Related Capabilities

Military operations are not planned for the purpose of employing any particular capability. Mission requirements (such as campaign objectives, the operational environment, and adversary and friendly forces) dictate what capabilities a commander uses and how they are employed. Information operations are no different.

Although often described as a discrete set of capabilities, information operations are really much more. The capabilities used for information operations should be selected based on mission requirements. Such a capability is, according to JP 1-02, a capability, function, or activity that uses data, information, or electromagnetic spectrum to produce lethal or nonlethal effects in the physical or informational dimensions with an expressed intent to cause deliberate effects within the cognitive dimension of the information environment.

Some information-related capabilities (IRCs), such as electronic warfare (EW), military information support operations (MISO), combat camera (COMCAM), and cyberspace operations, require trained specialists and equipment. However, each element of a MAGTF must be able to employ other capabilities, such as operations security (OPSEC), military deception (MILDEC), key leader engagements, and a rewards program to support its operations. Refer to chapter 3 for a discussion on capabilities relevant to information operations.

## Information Operations Effects

Commanders use IRCs to create or produce effects that contribute to the achievement of military objectives. Numerous common terms, such as the following, are used but have unique meanings when describing IO effects:

- *Destroy.* Destroy is to damage a system or entity so badly that it cannot perform any function or be restored to a usable condition without being entirely rebuilt.
- *Disrupt.* Disrupt is to break or interrupt the flow of information.
- *Degrade.* Degrade is to reduce the effectiveness or efficiency of an adversary's command and control (C2) or communications systems and information collection efforts or means. Information operations can also degrade the morale of a unit, reduce the target's worth or value, or reduce the quality of an adversary's decisions and actions.
- *Deny.* Deny is to prevent the adversary from accessing and using critical information, systems, and services.
- *Deceive.* Deceive is to cause a person to believe what is not true. Military deception seeks to mislead an adversary's decisionmakers by manipulating their perception of reality.
- *Exploit.* Exploit is to gain access to an adversary's C2 systems to collect information or to plant false or misleading information.
- *Influence.* Influence is to cause others to behave in a manner favorable to US forces.
- *Isolate.* Isolate is to seal off both physically and psychologically an adversary from its sources of support, to deny an adversary freedom of movement, and prevent an adversary unit from having contact with other adversary forces.
- *Protect.* Protect is to take action to guard against espionage or capture of sensitive equipment and information.
- *Restore.* Restore is to bring information and information systems back to their original state.
- *Respond.* Respond is to react quickly to an adversary's IO attack or intrusion.

*Note: The preceding effects terms can have different interpretations. The above list is accepted in joint doctrine for information operations. They may not align with Marine Corps terms for the effects of fires (lethal). It is always best to define how the term is being applied with respect to IO tasks.*

This Page Intentionally Left Blank

# CHAPTER 2
# INTEGRATION AND PLANNING

The primary focus of MAGTF IO activities will be at the operational and tactical levels of war. The Marine Corps organizes, trains, equips, and fights as a total force. Effective IO integration requires that the total capability of the Marine Corps be used to support the warfighting MAGTF. Information operations are conducted across the range of military operations. Information operations can make significant contributions to all levels of warfare. Information operations should not be relegated to just one type of military operation. Information operations are conducted during all phases of military operations. Information operations are planned, prepared, executed, and assessed during all phases of an operation in support of the MAGTF's mission.

Since MAGTFs may fight as a part of a larger joint force, their IO efforts will support and be coordinated with the campaign plans of the combatant commander, joint force, and adjacent commands. The joint force commander may have standing IO procedures and perhaps a standing IO plan based on the combatant commander's guidance for the theater of operations and the nature of the conflict. The joint force and component commanders will develop their own IO plans in support of their respective objectives. These IO plans are typically at the operational level. The MAGTF will develop an IO plan that will support MAGTF mission requirements while integrating the joint force commander's IO plan. The major subordinate commands must develop supporting IO plans that are appropriate for their level of command.

## Staff Responsibilities

Although information operations are not limited to the IRCs, they do encompass all actions taken to affect the decisionmaking within the information environment; therefore, IO planning requires a whole-of-staff approach in order to be effective. Those staff sections involved in IO planning include, but are not limited to, the operations section, intelligence section, communications sections, special staff, and IO cell.

While the commander has overall responsibility to decide and design how and who he wants to influence, his IO cell chief—residing within the G-3—has responsibility to plan, prepare, execute, and assess information operations in support of operations. All staff sections have a role to play in information operations. To relegate information operations to just one subsection of the G-3 severely limits the command's IO program and its effectiveness. Information operations that are not integrated with other staff actions often lead to instances where actions interfere with each other and are counterproductive to achieving the commander's desired effects. At best, nonintegrated information operations reduce the effectiveness of the action and, at worst, confuse the target audience leading to undesired effects.

### Operations Section

The commander is responsible for implementing plans that incorporate information operations into operations, but the operations section (G-3/S-3) is responsible for executing the plans. The future operations (FOps) section is responsible for overseeing the planning and coordination of the IO effort. The MAGTF IO officer, within G-3/S-3 FOps, is responsible for the following:

- Integrating and coordinating IO efforts.
- Responding directly to the commander via the G-3/S-3 for MAGTF information operations.
- Ensuring that the IO cell is incorporated into and provides input to the operational planning

team (OPT) during planning to ensure coordinated operations.
- Preparing the IO appendix to the operation order (OPORD).
- Directing personnel within the MAGTF IO cell as well as augmentees from external agencies who are assigned to the IO cell.
- Ensuring that all information operations are coordinated within the MAGTF staff, higher headquarters, and external agencies.
- Coordinating and collaborating with the intelligence staff section (G-2/S-2).

The electronic warfare officer (EWO) will integrate EW operations through the EW coordination center or the IO cell when it is established.

The fire support coordinator, supporting arms coordinator, target information officer, and target intelligence officer will oversee the formation of the target list and the engagement of those targets, to include accepted targets nominated by the IO cell.

Public affairs officers (PAOs) will identify key public or target audiences with interest and impact in the area of operations, to include foreign and domestic audiences and local, regional, and international media. Public affairs and IO planners must plan, coordinate and deconflict activities, release of public information, and media analysis/assessment to achieve maximum effect, consistent with the Department of Defense (DOD) principles of information, policies, and public affairs (PA) guidance.

The COMCAM planner ensures that priorities are established for the provision of visual documentation for operational and combat support.

The civil affairs (CA) officer identifies key civil-military operations (CMO) targets and coordinates with the targeting cell. He provides the local populace news and information about CMO activities and support, which aids in neutralizing misinformation and hostile propaganda directed against civil authorities.

The current operations officer will assist the IO officer in the supervision and coordination of IO activities that support or are integrated into ongoing operations. The current operations officer supervises battle captains/watch officers and communicates with subordinate commanders to identify and monitor IO events within the MAGTF's area of operations. Additionally, the current operations officer must be prepared to execute IO battle drills if required.

The FOps officer will work closely with the IO officer to monitor current operations and ensure that planned MAGTF operations are conducted in order to achieve objectives across the operational environment. The FOps officer must be particularly mindful to ensure that operations in the physical dimension support the commander's objectives in the informational and cognitive dimensions.

### Intelligence Section

Intelligence is critical to the planning, execution, and assessment of information operations and must provide support across a range of military operations at all levels of war. The G-2/S-2 is the central point of contact for all intelligence support to information operations for the MAGTF staff. Coordination and interaction between the G-2/S-2 and the G-3/S-3 may be enhanced through liaison representatives embedded within the IO cell. See appendix A.

### Communications Section

The communications section (G-6/S-6) oversees the communications security (COMSEC) program, supports the installation and maintenance of information systems, assists the EWO in deconflicting EW jamming operations in order to avoid electronic fratricide, and coordinates active OPSEC measures and facilitation of specialized communications in support of IRCs and information operations.

### Special Staff

In support of the MAGTF mission, public affairs assists the MAGTF IO officer in keeping local populations informed by putting MAGTF actions into context, countering propaganda and misinformation, and by communicating proposed MAGTF actions in order to deter the adversary's actions. These efforts build support for military operations, help the local population develop informed perceptions about MAGTF activities, undermine adversarial propaganda, and shape the adversary's planning.

Chaplains, though not a traditional IRC, have a very important role to play in information operations. Recent operations in both Iraq and Afghanistan have seen the adversary use religion to bolster and justify recruiting and terrorist activities. Chaplains participating in key leader engagements can assist in co-opting religious leaders and degrading the adversary's use of religion.

The civil affairs officers from the G-9/S-9 section assist the MAGTF IO officer in integrating planned CMO into the information operations to ensure that information operations and CA are creating the most favorable effects for the MAGTF commander and are not at odds with the effects created in specific areas of the operational environment.

The SJA supports the MAGTF IO officer by ensuring all phases of the operation, to include any branches and sequels, are conducted in compliance with the applicable laws. In so doing, the SJA plays a critical role in the development and refinement of a proposed course of action (COA). The SJA should be involved early in IO planning in order to avoid delays in the execution of IO-related actions.

### Information Operations Cell

The IO cell is a task-organized group that will be established within a MAGTF and/or higher headquarters to integrate a variety of separate disciplines and functions pertaining to information operations for the command. A fully functioning IO cell integrates a broad range of potential IO actions and related activities that contribute to accomplishing the mission. Information operations integration requires extensive planning and coordination among all the elements of the staff. The IO cell, when established, is a mechanism for achieving that coordination.

The IO cell is composed of intelligence personnel, augmentees supporting IO activities, and representatives from staff elements and subject matter experts (SMEs) from appropriate warfighting functions. The size and structure of the cell are tailored to meet the mission and the commander's intent.

During planning, the IO cell should facilitate coordination between various staffs, organizations, and the MAGTF staff elements responsible for planning specific elements of information operations. During execution, the cell should remain available to assist in coordination, providing support or adjusting IO efforts as necessary. The IO cell should have the required communications connectivity, either through the combat operations center or separately, in order to effectively coordinate changing IO requirements.

## Integrated Information Operations Planning and the Marine Corps Planning Process

The commander and his planners must ensure that information operations planning begins at the earliest stage of operational planning, is consistent with the IO plans of the higher headquarters, and is fully integrated into the MAGTF's concept of operations. Military deception, MISO, and cyberspace operations require more time to plan due to the authorities that are required to execute these activities and the time required to establish and prepare observables for these activities.

Marines use the MCPP and the targeting process (D3A [decide, detect, deliver, assess]) in the development of the IO concept of support and IO plans. Two notable requirements in IO planning are as follows:

- A longer lead time is required to plan certain information operations (i.e., MILDEC, MISO, and cyberspace operations).
- The impact and threat of hostile information from outside the operational area due to the ease of information flow through information networks and the media, which creates operating boundaries in the information environment that are larger than the area of operations and are porous to outside influences.

During the planning process, the IO officer must be prepared to quickly articulate IO objectives and provide detailed information on how the integration of discrete IRCs will support the commander's desired end state.

The MCPP establishes procedures for analyzing a mission, developing and wargaming COAs against the adversary, comparing friendly COAs against the commander's criteria and each other, selecting a COA, and preparing an OPORD execution. Information operations planning is aligned with the MCPP steps and ensures that IO actions are coordinated with all six warfighting functions and the operations of higher, adjacent, and subordinate commands. See Marine Corps Warfighting Publication (MCWP) 5-1, *Marine Corps Planning Process*, for detailed information.

## Problem Framing

The purpose of problem framing is to gain an enhanced understanding of the environment and the nature of the problem. This understanding allows a commander to visualize the operation and describe his conceptual approach, providing context for the examination of what the command must accomplish, when and where it must be done, and most importantly, why the operation is being conducted. Since no amount of subsequent planning can solve a problem insufficiently understood, problem framing is critical.

The higher headquarters order is analyzed to extract IO planning guidance, such as limitations and planning factors. This guidance establishes the boundaries for IO planning, identifies target limitations based on policy and rules of engagement, and helps reduce the uncertainty associated with IO planning. This process also ensures that the MAGTF will nest its IO plan with that of the higher headquarters.

During problem framing, intelligence preparation of the battlespace (IPB) planning supports the commander as he develops his battlespace area evaluation. Assisted by the intelligence section, the MAGTF IO cell reviews known facts about the adversary and the information environment. Key actors must be identified early in the planning process. A key actor is a person or persons whose decisions will have an impact, either positively or negatively, on the commander's end state. As the planning process matures, these key actors may become the command's target audience, at which time, effort and resources are applied in order to effect their decisions. Intelligence preparation of the battlespace products relevant to further IO planning are developed or requested. Adversary centers of gravity (COGs) are determined, while potential risks and friendly vulnerabilities are also identified. Information gaps must be determined and requests submitted to resolve the uncertainties necessary for further planning. During the planning process, IO planners conduct an analysis that links national, combatant command, or joint strategic objectives to the MAGTF's operational and tactical tasks. By linking operational level objectives and tasks to strategic objectives, the IO planner will ensure that MAGTF activities are in concert with higher headquarters' desired end state.

An initial IO concept for support can be developed during problem framing. Friendly IO assets and capabilities, either organic or supporting the MAGTF, as well as additional IO force structure requirements, are identified. As problem framing is conducted, resource or capability shortfalls are noted. The IO cell identifies critical shortfalls and requests support from higher headquarters or external agencies to achieve projected, desired results. The IO concept of support must be focused by and in accordance with the commander's initial guidance. A staff estimate for IO is the most formal form of this IO concept of support and should be developed.

The IO cell must fully participate in MAGTF planning activities and coordinate its planning efforts with those of the MAGTF FOps section. An ad hoc organization known as the OPT (the IO cell should have a representative in the OPT) is usually formed by the FOps section. The OPT will be conducting problem framing. The results of each group's OPT and IO cell analyses should be combined. Friendly vulnerabilities can be incorporated into force protection planning, while the adversary's critical vulnerabilities determined through the OPT's COG analysis could include potential IO targets. Emerging themes and messages that can influence the battlespace to the advantage of the MAGTF can become the basis for an overall perception management operations.

During problem framing, IO planning results should be incorporated into the commander's planning guidance, IPB products, commander's critical information requirements (CCIRs), COG analysis, and other staff estimates.

At the end of problem framing, IO personnel should have developed the following:

- Staff estimate for information operations.
- A combined information overlay and a template of adversary operations in the information environment.
- An understanding of which decisionmakers should be targeted.
- IO essential tasks.
- Shortfalls in IRCs.
- IO limitations.
- IO critical information requirements.

Appendix B provides several examples of IO planning products.

#### *Essential Tasks for Information Operations*

Rarely will the MAGTF conduct information operations by itself. There will always be higher headquarters guidance and tasks. While some tasks may have been specifically assigned by the higher headquarters, others may be implied, meaning they are necessary to accomplish specified tasks or the overall mission. Implied tasks require resources and may not be administrative in nature. From the specified and implied tasks, IO personnel identify tasks that the command must accomplish to successfully affect adversary and friendly use of information. These become the unit's essential tasks for information operations. Essential tasks for information operations should be limited to no more than five; any more than that will overburden the subordinate element with developing tasks in support of essential IO tasks or may create an information operation that is too complex to execute.

A rule of thumb for validating an essential task is to ask: If the MAGTF accomplishes all other tasks marginally and does this one well, will it accomplish the mission? If the answer is no, then the task is not essential. If more than five essential tasks are identified, then IO personnel should question the validity of each essential task or the nature of the requirements levied on the MAGTF by higher headquarters.

#### *Shortfalls in Information Operations Capabilities*

Information operations personnel should determine if the MAGTF has the assets to perform the assigned tasks. This is done by identifying any and all organic and supporting IO-capable assets. Organic assets are resident in assigned or attached forces. Supporting assets are available to the MAGTF from a higher headquarters or US Government agency. Available assets are then compared with the IO mission requirements (specified and implied tasks) in order to identify capability shortfalls and any additional assets that are required. To ensure use of these assets, IO personnel must start coordination early.

Information operations planners face a challenge in expressing IO capabilities to the commander and staff. A simple list of IO-capable assets or units—such as, three ground-based jammers, three tactical MISO teams, or two COMCAM teams—does not help the commander visualize the command's capabilities in the information environment. In developing its product, IO personnel should consider three basic questions:

- What IO effects can be created or produced using the command's organic assets?
- What IO effects can be created or produced using supporting assets from the higher headquarters?
- What IO effects cannot be created or produced with available assets?

#### *Restraints and Constraints for Information Operations*

Restraints are the things that you cannot do and constraints are the things that you must do that do not qualify as specified tasks, but need to be identified and carried forward into COA development and subsequent planning as they can affect how operations will be conducted.

Like most other operations, information operations are restrained by rules of engagement; US national policy; international politics; and other legal, moral, cultural, and operational factors. Additionally, IO personnel should consider that IRCs have restraints of their own; in particular, MILDEC, MISO, cyberspace operations, and electronic warfare. Common restraints include approval authorities for deception operations, MISO products, MISO themes to avoid, allied forces' national policies and capabilities, restricted targets and frequencies, and PA guidance. To enhance understanding, limitations for information operations can be organized in terms of information content and flow.

Information content is the substance, value, or meaning of the information, normally comprised within the words and images; includes the intended action or inaction the information was designed to elicit. Examples include the following:

- Avoid themes that favor any ethnic group.
- Receive MISO product approval from the combatant commander.
- Receive deception approval from joint task force (JTF) commander.
- Stress themes that highlight the importance of reconciliation.

Information flow describes how information is transferred or exchanged between a transmitter/source and a receiver and includes the means, mediums, and paths utilized in the exchange. Examples include the following:

- No cross-boundary electronic attack.
- US MISO products cannot be disseminated by allied forces.
- PA posture for the operation is passive.
- Religious structures are identified on the restricted target list.
- COMCAM priorities.

#### *Critical Information Requirements for Information Operations*

Only the commander decides what information is critical, but the staff may propose CCIRs to the commander. The CCIRs are continually reviewed and updated or deleted as required. Initially, CCIRs may reflect the nature of planning and identify intelligence or information requirements to assist with the planning and decision process. As the planning moves forward and execution looms, CCIRs will normally change to reflect key information/intelligence requirements tied to decision points or needed for execution.

### Course of Action Development

During COA development, planners use the mission statement, commander's intent, and commander's planning guidance to develop COAs.

Course of action development provides options for how the mission and commander's intent might be accomplished while continuing to refine the understanding of the problem. The IO planner's goal is to develop a concept of support that will generate effects that create information superiority over the adversary at the proper time and place. An IO concept of support should be examined to ensure that it is suitable, feasible, acceptable, distinguishable, and complete with respect to the current and anticipated situation, mission, and commander's intent.

Planning that is started during problem framing will continue during COA development. The IPB products that are requested and developed will be reviewed for applicability with the commander's planning guidance. As necessary, IO-related IPB products will be modified and updated. As new information is received, CCIRs may be revised and additional requirements submitted.

Information operations cell planning efforts will continue to be closely linked with those of the OPT. The IO planner can assist the OPT by graphically displaying the significant characteristics of the information environment, allowing the OPT to see the capabilities of both friendly and adversary forces. See JP 2-01.3, *Joint Intelligence Preparation of the Operational Environment*, for a detailed discussion on the combined information overlay. In coordination with the red cell and the G-2, the IO cell will conduct nodal analysis to assess relative IRCs and provide the OPT with an understanding of the strengths and weaknesses of both friendly and adversary forces. The IO cell will conduct an assessment of friendly vulnerabilities to adversary information actions. The IO cell will also continue to refine its analysis of the adversary COG to determine the critical adversary vulnerabilities most susceptible to information operations. The refined COG and critical vulnerabilities are used in the development of the initial COAs.

The IO cell will closely follow the development of the OPT's COAs to ensure that the IO concept of support adequately supports these COAs. The IO cell may formulate an IO concept of support that will identify IO actions to be implemented regardless of the eventual COA that is adopted. In addition, the IO cell may create a concept of support for every COA developed by the OPT. Just as every COA will have to meet the OPT's criteria for suitability, feasibility, acceptability, distinguishability, and completeness, the IO cell must ensure that the IO concept of support can pass similar review. Each IO concept of support must address the following:

- What IO tasks will be accomplished?
- Who will execute the IO tasks (IO assets capabilities)?
- When will IO tasks be executed?
- Where will the IO tasks occur?
- Why is each IO task required (intended effect)?
- How will the MAGTF employ IRCs and other organic capabilities to accomplish the tasks?
- How is the IO concept nested with the higher headquarter's IO plan and scheme of manuever?

At the conclusion of COA development, the OPT or IO cell should have developed the following:

- An overall IO concept.
- An IO concept of support for each COA to include objectives and purposes for essential IO tasks, target nominations, and an assessment plan to measure the effectivness of the tasks.
- Recommendations for the commander's wargaming guidance and evaluation criteria.
- Updated IO-associated IPB products.
- Input to the COA graphic and narrative.
- An initial staff estimate for information operations with additional asset requirements or required support from higher headquarters.

## Course of Action War Game

The COA war game examines and refines the broad option(s) in light of adversary capabilities and potential actions/reactions as well as the characteristics peculiar to the operational environment. Each friendly COA is wargamed against selected adversary COAs. Course of action wargaming assists the planners in identifying strengths and weaknesses, associated risks, and asset shortfalls for each friendly COA. The IO cell's objective in the war game is to refine and validate both the overall IO concept of support as well as the specific IO concepts of support for each COA, while also fully participating in the COA war game. The IO actions are integrated into the COA war game in an interactive process to determine the impact on both friendly and adversary capabilities. The IO cell should observe and record the advantages and disadvantages of each COA and the capability of information operations to support each COA. For future planning, it should also identify possible branches and potential sequels based on the IO concept.

At the conclusion of the COA war game, the IO cell reviews its planning products and refines them to support the next step in the MCPP. These planning products include the following:

- Updated input to IPB products.
- Refined staff estimate for information operations.
- Refined input to CCIRs.
- Task organization and asset shortfalls for IO resources.
- Information operations input to COA synchronization matrix.

### Course of Action Comparison and Decision

In COA comparison and decision, the commander evaluates all friendly COAs against his established criteria, against each other, and then selects the COA that will best accomplish the mission. As appropriate, the IO cell will provide additional comparison criteria directly relevant to information operations that may assist the commander in his decision. The IO results from the COA war game may be briefed as a separate, supporting concept by the IO cell or presented by the OPT as an element of the overall plan.

In any event, the IO cell is responsible for ensuring that the commander is apprised of the effects that have been created by operations in the information environment. The IO cell is also responsible for ensuring that the impact and anticipated effect of IO actions upon the adversary targets for each COA and the relative merit of each COA from an IO perspective are provided to the commander.

### Orders Development

During orders development, the staff takes the commander's COA decision, mission statement, intent, and guidance and develops orders to direct the actions of the unit. Orders serve as the principal means by which the commander expresses his decision, commander's intent, and guidance.

The information operations cell is responsible for taking the overall IO concept of support and the concept of support specific to the COA selected by the commander and turning them into appropriate sections of the OPORD under the direction of the MAGTF IO officer. Specifically, Appendix 3 (Information Operations) to Annex C (Operations) describes the information operation as a whole and how information operations will gain information superiority in support of the scheme of maneuver. See appendix C for a sample format of an OPORD. The IO cell must be careful to not let the requirement to develop and explain IRCs and contributions to the operation overwhelm the primary purposes of the IO appendix, which are to—

- Provide operational details on information operations.
- Focus element and unit tasks on creating specific effects in the information environment.
- Provide the information needed to assess information operations.

Because information operations are multidisciplined, it is found in various portions of the MAGTF OPORD. The disciplines of IO are included as tabs to Appendix 3 (Information Operations), Annex C (Operations) to the

OPORD and in the OPORD annexes for communication systems, public affairs, CMO, information management, and special technical operations (STO).

During orders reconciliation and crosswalk, the information operations cell may be called upon to review the IO sections of the orders, identify gaps in planning or discrepancies, provide corrective action, and finalize IPB products. If fragmentary orders are issued, then the IO cell will ensure that appropriate instructions are given to IO-capable units.

### Transition

Transition is the orderly handover of a plan or order as it is passed to those tasked with execution of the operation. It provides those who will execute the plan or order with the situational awareness and rationale for key decisions necessary to ensure that there is a coherent shift from planning to execution and may involve a wide range of briefs, drills or rehearsals (subject to the variables of echelon of command), mission complexity, and, most importantly, time.

The IO cell monitors the transition from planning to execution and continues to support both current and future operations. The IO cell assists in the transition briefings for the remainder of the staff and subordinate commands to ensure that the IO portions of the order are known and understood. If drills are held, then the IO cell will assist as necessary. During the confirmation brief, the IO cell will ensure that the IO-capable units address their tasked IO actions as part of their overall plan to identify any remaining discrepancies or gaps in planning.

Successful information operations give subordinates maximum latitude for initiative, and postures the unit for follow-on missions. Likewise, with a little foresight, IO personnel can use one information operation to jump start another. Occasionally, a tactical level information operation may be the perfect jump start for an operational level information operations and so on.

## Transitioning From Planning to Battle Rhythm

Having completed the MCPP steps and arrived at an executable COA, the MAGTF will be challenged to monitor the execution of the IO plan and make changes that are consistent with evolving operations. The MAGTF IO cell is useful in providing IO support to the steps of the MCPP and can help the MAGTF develop the following essential building blocks:

- Stated objectives (based on desired operational effect).
- IO synchronization matrix that links mutually supporting IO actions.
- Integrated target list.

These building blocks help sustain ongoing information operations. Sustained information operations are supported by the MAGTF intelligence cycle, battle damage assesment (BDA) cycle, targeting cycle, and the MAGTF operations battle rhythm. These processes allow the MAGTF to analyze the information intelligence cycle, assess the functional capability (or destruction) of the adversary BDA cycle, re-engage as necessary to maintain constant pressure on the adversary's targeting cycle, and modify and issue changes to ongoing plans. It is the integration of these cycles that determines the daily IO battle rhythm.

This Page Intentionally Left Blank

# CHAPTER 3
# KEY INFORMATION-RELATED CAPABILITIES

Information operations are multidisciplined and include a variety of elements that must be employed together within an integrated strategy. Some of these elements are more offensive, defensive, or informational in nature, but it is their integration into the concept of operations that ensures successful employment of information operations in support of the MAGTF. Integration of information operations is an essential part of MAGTF operations in expeditionary and joint environments. Information operations can mitigate the effects of a crisis and can help prevent or resolve conflict.

When deterrence fails, information operations help Marines win in war by providing essential protection and enhancing the effective use of force. Information operations enhance the operational capability of the MAGTF through employment of a wide range of organic and external capabilities.

## Military Deception

The purpose of MILDEC is to cause adversaries to form inaccurate impressions about friendly force capabilities or intentions by feeding information through their intelligence collection or information assets. Military deception targets the adversary decisionmaker's intelligence collection, analysis, and dissemination systems and requires a thorough knowledge of adversaries and their decisionmaking processes.

Military deception operations are actions executed to deliberately mislead the adversary's military decisionmakers as to friendly military capabilities, intentions, and operations; thereby, causing the adversary to take specific actions that will contribute to the accomplishment of the friendly mission.

Military deception operations depend on an integrated effort by all warfighting functions to create a credible story. Intelligence operations identify appropriate deception targets, assist in developing a credible story, identify and focus on appropriate targets, and assess the effectiveness of the MILDEC plan. Military deception operations are a powerful tool, but are not without cost. Forces and resources must be committed to the deception effort to make it believable, possibly to the short-term detriment of some other aspects of the operations. Feasible COAs rejected during planning can be particularly effective as the basis for MILDEC operations. For more information on MILDEC, see JP 3-13.4, *Military Deception*, or the classified MCRP 3-40.4A, *Multi-Service Tactics, Techniques, and Procedures for Military Deception (MILDEC) Operations.*

### Types of Deception Operations

A deception operation may contain one or more of the following: feint, demonstration, ruse, and/or display.

A feint is a limited objective attack that involves contact with the adversary. A feint is conducted for the purpose of deceiving the adversary as to the location and/or time of the actual main offensive action. Feints may vary in size from a raid to a supporting attack. A feint may occur before, during, or after the main attack and may be independent of the main effort. Feints may be employed to cause the adversary to react in one of three predicable ways: employ his reserves improperly, shift his supporting fires, or reveal his defensive fires.

A demonstration is an attack or show of force on a front where a decision is not sought and made with the aim of deceiving the adversary. A demonstration differs from a feint in that no contact with the adversary is intended.

A ruse is a trick of war that places false information in the adversary's hand. Ruses are generally single, deliberate actions. It may be necessary to group several ruses together to ensure credibility of a deception story. Ruses are extremely susceptible to detection because of inconsistencies and may present the adversary with a windfall of information that he is inclined to reject.

A display is a static portrayal of an activity force or equipment intended to deceive the adversary's visual observation. Displays are simulations, disguises, or portrayals that project to the adversary the appearance of objects that do not exist or appear to be something else. Displays include simulations, disguises, decoys, and dummies. They may include the use of heat, smoke, electronic emissions, false tracks, and fake command posts.

## Deception in Support of the Offense

The adversary commander is the target for MILDEC in support of the offense. Goals may include the following:

- Achieve surprise.
- Preserve friendly forces, equipment, and installations from destruction.
- Minimize a physical advantage the adversary may have.
- Gain time.
- Cause the adversary to employ forces, including intelligence, in ways that are advantageous to the MAGTF.
- Cause the adversary to reveal strengths, dispositions, and future intentions.
- Influence the adversary's intelligence collection and analytical capability.
- Condition the adversary to particular patterns of friendly behavior that can be exploited at a time chosen by the MAGTF.
- Cause the adversary to waste combat power with inappropriate or delayed actions.

## Deception in Support of the Defense

Military deception can help protect the MAGTF from the adversary's offensive IO efforts. Deception that misleads an adversary about friendly C2 capabilities or limitations contributes to friendly protection. An adversary commander who is deceived about friendly C2 capabilities and limitations may be more likely to misallocate resources in his effort to attack or exploit friendly C2 systems.

## Operations Security and Deception

Operations security and deception have much in common. Both require the management of indicators. Operations security is used to deny information or to hide what is real and seeks to limit an adversary's ability to detect or derive useful information from his observations of friendly activities. Deception is used to feed information or to show what is not real and seeks to create or increase the likely detection of certain indicators that the adversary can observe and that will cause an adversary to derive an incorrect conclusion.

## Special Considerations for Deception Planning

When planning for deception operations, the staff must consider classification requirements as well as any possible unintended effects that may be a result of the operation:

- *Classification Requirements.* Due to the sensitive nature of deception operations, deception planning is restricted to those personnel who have a need to know. Deception operations depend on the knowledge and utilization of adversary intelligence collection systems to deliver a deception story to an adversary. Compromise of friendly knowledge of adversary intelligence systems would be harmful and could have far-reaching strategic and operational effects.

- *Unintended Effects*. Third parties, such as neutral or friendly forces not aware of the deception, may receive and act upon deception information that is intended for the adversary. Deception planners should minimize the risk to other parties.

### Staff Responsibilities

The G-3/S-3 has primary responsibility for deception. Normally, a deception officer is appointed and is responsible to the G-3/S-3 for deception planning and oversight.

### Deception and the Operation Order

Tab A to Appendix 3 (Information Operations) of Annex C (Operations) of the OPORD is the deception tab. This tab implements the recommended COA for deception. The deception tab details the specific tasks to be performed and specifies coordinating instructions for the control and management of deception missions.

## Electronic Warfare

Electronic warfare is military action involving the use of electromagnetic and directed energy to control the electromagnetic spectrum or to attack the adversary. (JP 1-02) Electronic warfare consists of three divisions: electronic attack, electronic protection, and electronic warfare support. Electronic warfare denies the opponent an advantage in the electromagnetic spectrum and ensures friendly unimpeded access to the electromagnetic spectrum portion of the information environment. Electronic warfare can be applied from air, sea, land, and space by manned and unmanned systems, and it is employed to support military operations involving various levels of detection, denial, deception, disruption, degradation, protection, and destruction. Contributing to the success of information operations, electronic warfare uses offensive and defensive tactics and techniques in a variety of combinations to shape, disrupt, and exploit adversarial use of the electromagnetic spectrum while protecting friendly freedom of action in that spectrum. For more information on electronic warfare see JP 3-13.1, *Electronic Warfare*, or MCWP 3-40.5, *Electronic Warfare*.

### Electronic Attack

Electronic attack is a division of electronic warfare involving the use of electromagnetic energy, directed energy, or antiradiation weapons to attack personnel, facilities, or equipment with the intent of degrading, neutralizing, or destroying enemy combat capability and is considered a form of fires. (JP 1-02) Electronic attack includes the following:

- Actions taken to prevent or reduce an adversary's effective use of the electromagnetic spectrum, such as jamming and the use of antiradiation weapons.
- Employment of weapons that use either electromagnetic or directed energy as their primary destructive mechanism such as lasers, radio frequency weapons, and particle beams.

### Electronic Protection

Electronic protection is a division of electronic warfare involving actions taken to protect personnel, facilities, and equipment from any effects of friendly or enemy use of the electromagnetic spectrum that degrade, neutralize, or destroy friendly combat capability. (JP 1-02)

### Electronic Warfare Support

Electronic warfare support is a division of electronic warfare involving actions tasked by, or under the direct control of, an operational commander, to search for, intercept, identify, and locate or localize sources of intentional and unintentional radiated electromagnetic energy for the purpose of immediate threat recognition, targeting, planning and conduct of future operations. (JP 1-02)

Electronic warfare support provides information required for decisions involving EW operations and other tactical actions such as threat avoidance, targeting, and homing. Electronic warfare support data can be used to produce signals intelligence, provide targeting for electronic or destructive attack, and produce measurement and signature intelligence.

## Marine Corps Electronic Warfare Organizations

The Marine Corps has two types of EW units: the radio battalion (RadBn) and the Marine tactical electronic warfare squadron (VMAQ).

The RadBn provides COMSEC monitoring, tactical signals intelligence (SIGINT), electronic warfare, and special intelligence communications support to the MAGTF. The role and structure of the RadBn continue to evolve with the evolution of communications technology.

A VMAQ provides EW support to the MAGTF and other designated forces. The VMAQ conducts tactical jamming to prevent, delay, or disrupt the adversary's ability to use early warning, acquisition, fire or missile control, counterbattery, and battlefield surveillance radars. Tactical jamming also denies and/or degrades enemy communication capabilities. In addition, the VMAQ conducts electronic reconnaissance and electronic intelligence operations. There are four VMAQs (designated VMAQ-1 through VMAQ-4) assigned to MAG-14 [Marine Aircraft Group-14], 2d MAW [2d Marine Aircraft Wing]. Each squadron has five EA-6B Prowler aircraft.

## Staff Responsibilities

Electronic warfare is the responsibility of the G-3/S-3. An EWO is normally appointed to be responsible for planning, coordinating, and tasking EW operations and activities. The EWO coordinates with the G-2/S-2 to establish priorities between EW and SIGINT missions. The EWO also coordinates with the G-6/S-6 to facilitate maximum use of the electromagnetic spectrum through electronic protection and to minimize electromagnetic interference.

## Electronic Warfare Coordination Cell

The electronic warfare coordination cell (EWCC) is a dedicated EW planning cell that may be established to coordinate EW activities. The MAGTF commander will normally plan, synchronize, coordinate, and deconflict EW operations through the EWCC, which facilitates coordination of EW operations with other fires, communications systems, and information systems. This center coordinates efforts by the G-2/S-2, G-3/S-3, and G-6/S-6 to eliminate conflicts between battlespace functions. The EWCC is under staff cognizance of the G-3/S-3. Assigned personnel identify and resolve potential conflicts in planned operations. The EWCC includes an EWO, a communications system and information systems representative, and other liaison officers such as RadBn or VMAQ SMEs, Marine air control group radar officer, or representatives from other Services as needed.

MAGTF staffs will provide personnel to incorporate an EWCC with the Marine expeditionary force G-3/S-3. Personnel will also be provided for liaison teams to higher headquarters EW coordination organizations when required.

## Electronic Warfare Addendums to the Operation Order

Tab B (Electronic Warfare) to Appendix 3 (Information Operations) of Annex C (Operations) of the OPORD is the EW tab. Tab B details specific EW tasks to be performed and specifies coordinating instructions for the control and management of EW missions.

Appendix 2 (Signals Intelligence) to Annex B (Intelligence) of the OPORD contains specific instructions for SIGINT operations.

## Operations Security

Operations security is the key to information denial. It gives the commander the capability to identify indicators that can be observed by the adversary's intelligence systems. These indicators could be interpreted or pieced together to derive critical information regarding friendly force dispositions, intent, and/or COAs that must be protected. The goal of OPSEC is to identify, select, and execute measures that eliminate or reduce indications and other sources of information, which may be exploited by an adversary, to an acceptable level.

Operations security is a process of identifying critical information and subsequently analyzing friendly actions attendant to military operations and other activities to—

- Identify those actions that can be observed by the adversary's intelligence systems.
- Determine indicators that the adversary's intelligence systems might obtain that could be interpreted or pieced together to derive critical information in time to be useful to the adversary.
- Select and execute measures that eliminate or reduce to an acceptable level the vulnerabilities of friendly actions to adversary exploitation. For more information on operations security see JP 3-13.3, *Operations Security,* or MCWP 3-40.9, *Operations Security (OPSEC).*

### Operations Security in Support of the Offense

Although primarily associated with defensive measures, OPSEC contributes to the offense by depriving the adversary of information that slows the adversary's decision cycle, thereby providing opportunity for attainment of friendly objectives.

### Operations Security in Support of the Defense

The overall goal of OPSEC is denial and the establishment of essential secrecy. The key element that OPSEC protects is the commander's concept of operation. A good OPSEC plan denies information to the adversary intelligence system, reducing its ability to orient combat power against friendly operations.

### Operations Security Process

Operations security planning is accomplished through the OPSEC process. The OPSEC process has five distinctive steps that provide a framework for the systematic identification, analysis, and protection of information necessary to maintain essential secrecy (see JP 3-13.3):

- Identification of critical information.
- Analysis of threats.
- Analysis of vulnerabilities.
- Assessment of risk.
- Application of appropriate OPSEC measures.

### Staff Responsibilities

The G-3/S-3 has primary responsibility for OPSEC. Normally, an OPSEC officer is appointed and is responsible to the G-3/S-3 for OPSEC planning and oversight. In joint operations, an OPSEC working group may be established to recommend OPSEC measures, coordinate or conduct OPSEC surveys, and write the OPSEC portion of the OPORD.

### Support Agencies

The counterintelligence (CI)/human intelligence (HUMINT) teams perform a wide range of duties such as security briefings, countersabotage, counterespionage, and countersurveillance inspections. Counterintelligence measures enhance security, aid in reducing risks to a command, and are essential in achieving operational surprise during military operations. Counterintelligence can provide a significant contribution to a unit's OPSEC program. Counterintelligence personnel can support a command's OPSEC program by conducting the following:

- Counterintelligence surveys.
- Physical security evaluations.
- Security inspections.
- Vacated command post inspections.
- Penetration inspections.
- Security education.

Normally, there is a CI/HUMINT company located within the intelligence battalion. Additional information on CI/HUMINT is provided in MCWP 2-6, *Counterintelligence.*

The Naval Criminal Investigative Service (NCIS) operates a worldwide organization to fulfill the investigative and counterintelligence responsibilities of the Department of the Navy. Within its charter, the NCIS has exclusive jurisdiction in matters involving actual, potential, or suspected espionage, sabotage, and subversion including defection. In a combat environment, this CI jurisdiction is assigned to Marine counterintelligence, assuming that NCIS assets are not locally available.

### Operations Security and the Operation Order

Tab C (Operations Security) to Appendix 3 (Information Operations) of Annex C (Operations) of the OPORD is the OPSEC tab. This tab implements the recommended COA for OPSEC. It details specific OPSEC tasks to be performed and specifies coordinating instructions for the control and management of OPSEC tasks.

## Military Information Support Operations

Military information support operations are planned operations to convey selected information and indicators to foreign audiences to influence their emotions, motives, objective reasoning, and ultimately the behavior of foreign governments, organizations, groups, and individuals in a manner favorable to the originator's objectives. (JP 1-02)

At the strategic level, MISO may take the form of political or diplomatic positions, announcements, or communiques. At the operational level, MISO can include the distribution of leaflets, radio and television broadcasts, and other means of transmitting information that provide information intended to influence a selected group. It may be used to encourage adversary forces to defect, desert, flee, surrender, or take any other action beneficial to friendly forces. At the tactical level, MISO enables the tactical commander to directly communicate and empathize with target audiences. Tactical level MISO includes face-to-face contact and the use of loudspeakers or other means to deliver MISO messages.

Military information support operations shape attitudes and influence a foreign audience's behavior. The mere presence of Marine Corps forces may be a MISO activity in itself, bringing influence on a situation through a display of purpose. Military information support operations may also support military deception operations.

### Integration

Military information support operations is only one of the means available to influence adversary attitudes and behaviors. When MISO is used concurrently with other information-related activities, it must be closely integrated with those capabilities in order to convey selected information in a synchronized way. Information operations personnel will coordinate public affairs (the delivery of the truth), OPSEC (the protection of friendly critical information), MILDEC (the concealment of friendly intentions and creation of misleading perceptions), and CMO (the delivery of friendly civil actions) with MISO operations.

### Employment

During peacetime, MISO activities that support combatant commanders take the form of overt peacetime MISO programs. These programs are proposed by combatant commanders through the Chairman of the Joint Chiefs of Staff (CJCS) who, in turn, refers them to the Assistant Secretary of Defense for Special Operations and Low-Intensity Conflict for review and approval. During contingencies, a MISO concept plan that is broad in scope is forwarded from the combatant commander to the joint staff for approval of overarching themes, objectives, and guidance, but not products. Once the concept plan is approved, a more detailed theater MISO plan is developed. Once a campaign plan is approved, the combatant commander or joint force commander is delegated MISO approval authority. This does not mean that the supported combatant commander has also been delegated approval for MISO product dissemination. In some cases, MISO products may be politically or religiously sensitive and may require separate approval for dissemination. The CJCS execute order, which is authorized by the Secretary of Defense, should designate who has authority for MISO product approval and who has authority for MISO product dissemination. The MAGTF's MISO actions must complement and support ongoing theater and joint force MISO activities.

The MAGTF will not normally identify, plan, or execute complex MISO activities; such as those requiring detailed theme development, intricate target analysis, or the use of sophisticated media. These missions will typically be conducted by external MISO units such as, a US Army military information support group (MISG), or US Air Force 193d Special Operations Wing. However, the MAGTF commander is responsible for providing MISO support and conducting tactical MISO (primarily through words and actions) in support of the MAGTF's mission. The presence and actions of Marines on the battlefield has an inherent psychological impact on the adversary. Marines execute observable actions that support psychological objectives.

The adversary is likely to employ MISO to influence the local populace, attempt to weaken the political and military will of US forces, and degrade the US and world community support for military action. The MAGTF's counteractions should be tailored to limit the adversary's opportunities to exploit the presence of Marines and their actions for MISO purposes. Behavior may generate either negative or positive support from the local population. Detailed knowledge of the host nation's culture and individual self-discipline is required.

Military information support operations may be integrated as a nonlethal fire support asset and are planned by the G-3/S-3 and coordinated with public affairs and CMO.

### Staff Responsibilities

Overall responsibility for the conduct of MISO falls under the cognizance of the G-3/S-3. The MISO officer is responsible to the G-3/S-3 for MISO planning and oversight. The MISO officer will write the MISO portion of the OPORD and coordinate and conduct approved MISO activities in support of tactical operations. If a designated MISO officer is not on hand, a MISO officer may be appointed to provide control and management of the MISO effort and to meet liaison requirements.

### Additional Support

Contingency operations that require the activation of a JTF normally require the formation of a joint military information support task force (JMISTF). When established, the JMISTF is responsible for planning and supervising the joint MISO effort. The JMISTF is subordinate to the combatant commander or the JTF J-3. Liaison between Marine Corps units serving as the Marine Corps force component of the JTF and the JMISTF is required.

The Marine Corps has a limited-capability MISO section that is dedicated to conducting tactical MISO. The MISO section is located within the Marine Corps Information Operations Center. If required, additional MISO support may be provided by one of the US Army's MISGs.

The Army has the preponderance of MISO assets within DOD. There is one Active Component MISG with a worldwide capability under the US Special Operations Command (SOCOM) and three Reserve Component MISGs under the US Army Civil Affairs and Psychological Operations Command. A MAGTF serving as a JTF could potentially be augmented or supported by any number of US Army MISO elements from either the Active or Reserve Component.

*Note: On 15 August 2011, the US Army directed the provisional establishment of the Military Information Support Operations Command (MISOC) with an initial operational capability to provide military information support forces to combatant commanders, US ambassadors, and other agencies in order to synchronize plans and to execute, inform, and influence activities across the range of military operations. The provisional status is expected to be rescinded in Fiscal Year 2014, when the Force Design Update is fully funded and implemented by the US Army.*

The Air Force's 193d Special Operations Wing of the Pennsylvania Air National Guard flies the EC-130E Commando Solo. This provides an airborne radio and television broadcast capability that can be used for MISO purposes. The Active Air Force Component maintains additional dissemination capability for airborne leaflet drops.

### Military Information Support Operations and the Operation Order

Tab D (Military Information Support Operations) of Appendix 3 (Information Operations) to Annex C (Operations) of the OPORD implements the recommended COA for MISO. Tab D details specific MISO tasks to be performed and specifies coordinating instructions for the control and management of MISO missions.

## Cyberspace Operations

Cyberspace operations are one of the latest capabilities developed in support of military operations, which stems from the increasing use of networked computers and supporting information technology infrastructure systems by military and civilian organizations. In order to attack, deceive, degrade, disrupt, deny, exploit, and defend electronic information and infrastructure, cyberspace operations are used along with electronic warfare. For the purpose of military operations, cyberspace operations are divided into offensive cyberspace operations (OCO) and defensive cyberspace operations (DCO):

- Offensive cyberspace operations are intended to project power by the application of force in or through cyberspace. (JP 1-02)
- Defensive cyberspace operations are passive and active cyberspace operations intended to preserve the ability to utilize friendly cyberspace capabilities and protect data, networks, net-centric capabilities, and other designated systems. (JP 1-02)
- Cyberspace ISR is an intelligence action conducted by the joint force commander authorized by an executive order or conducted by attached signals intelligence units under temporary delegated signals intelligence operational tasking authority [SOTA] (see JP 3-12 for more information).
- Cyberspace operational preparation of the environment (OPE) consists of the non-intelligence enabling activities conducted to plan and prepare for potential follow-on military operations (see JP 3-12 for more information).
- Department of Defense information network operations are operations to design, build, configure, secure, operate, maintain, and sustain Department of Defense networks to create and preserve information assurance on the Department of Defense information networks. (JP 1-02)

Due to the continued expansion of wireless networking and the integration of computers and radio frequency communications, there will be operations and capabilities that blur the line between cyberspace operations and EW and may require case-by-case determination when electronic warfare and cyberspace operations are assigned separate release authorities.

### Staff Responsibilities

Cyberspace operations encompass a broad range of mutually supporting staff functions. Key staff elements include the MAGTF G-2/S-2, G-6/S-6, and G-3/S-3. Additionally, the MAGTF information management officer, information security manager, special security officer, and information systems security officer perform important supporting functions.

### Cyberspace Operations Addendums to the Operation Order

Several appendices of the OPORD relate to cyberspace operations: Appendix 1 (Information Systems Security) to Annex K (Combat Information Systems) and Appendix 2 (Communications Security) to Annex K. Annex B (Intelligence) of the OPORD is the basic intelligence annex and contains elements related to cyberspace ISR and OPE; for example, Tab A (Communications Intelligence Collection Requirements) to Appendix 2 (Signals Intelligence).

## Physical Attack

Physical attack is the application of combat power to destroy or neutralize adversary forces and installations. It includes direct and indirect fires from ground, sea, and air platforms and also direct actions by special operations forces.

Physical attack applies friendly combat power against the adversary. It reduces adversary combat power by destroying adversary forces, equipment, installations, and networks. Within information operations, physical destruction is the tailored application of combat power to create desired operational effects.

Rules of engagement play a major role in determining if destruction is a viable option during a particular phase of the operation. Target planners may use physical destruction against command and control elements of the adversary's C2 system. However, the adversary may be able to recover from physical destruction given sufficient time, resources, and redundancy. Planners should have some preplanned measure of effectiveness (MOE) to judge the results of physical destruction and be prepared to monitor targets after attack to determine their operational status. Critical adversary C2 nodes identified as effectively reconstituted should be considered for reattack if analysis determines that they are still operationally effective. Information operations integration with the BDA cycle is essential.

As an integrated part of information operations, physical attack is the systematic degradation or destruction of selected adversary C2 systems that allows the MAGTF to gain an informational advantage. Command and control nodes must be functionally destroyed. If an adversary C2 node receives only cosmetic structural damage, it may remain operational despite its structural damage. The adversary may be able to reconstitute C2 nodes and re-establish effective command and control via alternate means. Therefore, C2 targets may need to be attacked in depth to create desired effects. Restrike may be required to maintain suppression of adversary command and control.

However, the total destruction of the hostile C2 system may not be attainable or desirable. Friendly forces may need to use adversary C2 systems during the post-conflict phase of military operations. The careful selection and prioritization of C2 physical destruction targets build the strongest case when competing against other type missions for weapons and delivery platforms. See also MCWP 3-16, *Fire Support Coordination in the Ground Combat Element.*

Tab E (Physical Attack) of Appendix 3 (Information Operations) to Annex C (Operations) of the OPORD is the physical attack/destruction tab. This tab implements the recommended COA for attack. Tab E details specific IO-related attack tasks to be performed and specifies coordinating instructions for the control and management of IO-related attack missions if required.

## Information Assurance

Marines depend on information to plan operations, deploy forces, and execute missions. While information and information systems enable and enhance warfighting capabilities, they are also vulnerable to attack and exploitation and must be protected. The security of friendly information and information systems is critical to gaining and maintaining information superiority. For more information on information assurance (IA), see JP 3-13, *Information Operations.*

Information assurance is actions that protect and defend information systems by ensuring availability, integrity, authentication, confidentiality, and nonrepudiation. This includes providing for restoration of information systems by incorporating protection, detection, and reaction capabilities. (JP 1-02) Information assurance capabilities include information security (INFOSEC), computer security, and COMSEC:

- Information security includes those measures necessary to detect, document, and counter such threats. Information security is composed of computer security and COMSEC.
- Computer security is the protection resulting from all measures to deny unauthorized access and exploitation of friendly computer systems. (JP 1-02)
- Communications security is the protection resulting from all measures designed to deny unauthorized persons information of value that might be derived from the possession and study of telecommunications, or to mislead unauthorized persons in their interpretation of the results of such possession and study. (JP 1-02) Communications security includes cryptosecurity, transmission security, emission security, and the physical security of COMSEC materials and information.

### Defense in Depth

The primary method for protecting information and information systems is through defense in depth. In order to prevent potential breakdown of barriers and invasion of the innermost or most valuable part of the system, defenses must be constructed in successive layers and safeguards positioned at different locations. These different locations may include local computing networks, enclave boundaries, networks, and supporting infrastructures. Use of a deliberate risk analysis process can ensure that the most effective defense in depth strategy is employed given the resources available.

### Education, Training, and Awareness

A key component for success in information protection is education and training of information and information systems users, administrators, managers, engineers, designers, and requirements developers. Awareness heightens threat appreciation and the importance of adhering to protective measures. Education provides the concepts and knowledge to develop appropriate technologies, policies, procedures, and operations to protect systems. Training develops the skills and abilities within the system administrator and user communities to mitigate system vulnerabilities, implement and maintain protected systems, and detect any attempts at exploitation.

### Training and Certification

Headquarters, Marine Corps, Command, Control, Communications, and Comptuers oversees the Marine Corps Certification and Accreditation Program. The program is based on the Computer Security Act of 1987 (Public Law 100-235) requiring "Each Federal agency shall provide for the mandatory periodic training in computer security awareness and accepted computer security practice of all employees who are involved with the management, use, or operation of each Federal computer system within or under the supervision of that agency."

All Marines, Marine Corps civilian employees, and contractor personnel who perform Marine Corps duties as system administrators will be certified as a level 1, 2, or 3 system administrator. Once all requirements have been met by the system administrator for certification at a specific level, a System Administrator Information Assurance Certificate can be awarded.

### System Certification and Accreditation

All DOD information systems and networks will be certified and accredited in accordance with DODI [Department of Defense Instruction] 8510.01, *DOD Information Assurance Certification and Accreditation Process (DIACAP).* Certification and accreditation of information systems that process Top Secret sensitive compartmented information will comply with the requirements of DCID [Director of Central Intelligence Directive] 6/3, *Protecting Sensitive Compartmented Information Within Information Systems.*

Additionally, all Marines, Marine Corps civilian employees, and contractor personnel who perform Marine Corps duties in the administration of DOD computer systems in the Marine Corps enclave will be identified as either an information assurance manager (IAM) or information assurance technician (IAT), level 1, 2, or 3 in accordance with Department of Defense Directive 8570.01, *Information Assurance Training, Certification, and Workforce Management.* All personnel designated as an IAM or IAT are required to complete the appropriate certification level commensurate with their IAM or IAT classification in accordance with the guidelines set forth in Department of Defense Directive 8570.01.

### Risk Management

Risk management decisions determine limits for applying countermeasures. Risk management includes consideration of information needs, the value of the information at risk, system vulnerabilities, threats posed by adversaries and natural phenomena, and resources available for protection and defense. These risks, once identified, must be categorized by severity and probability. Another important part of risk management is the development of means to mitigate those risks that may have severe impacts on the commander's desired end state.

### Staff Responsibilities

Overall responsibility for the conduct of information assurance falls under the cognizance of the G-6/S-6. Defense of the network includes other discrete supporting functions, such as OPSEC, which are the responsibility of the G-3/S-3.

### Support Agencies

The Marine Corps Network Operations and Security Center (MCNOSC) is located in Quantico, VA. The MCNOSC provides continuous, secure, global communications and operational sustainment and defense of the Marine Corps Enterprise Network (MCEN) for Marine Corps forces worldwide in order to facilitate the exchange of information across the defense information infrastructure. The MCNOSC exists to supply customer support to the MCEN and maintains a 24/7 helpdesk.

The responsibility of all Marines to report a virus hit or a threatening attempt to access a system is crucial. Because an attempt on a Marine Corps system could be part of a larger, overall attempt to disrupt or exploit Marine Corps information systems, the attempted breach can only be discovered and defended against if all attempts are reported. When a virus or attempted compromise occurs, the local IAM is contacted to obtain immediate assistance. Initial reports are initiated according to the local/regional base or station's guidance. At minimum, the MCNOSC help desk is contacted to report the incident.

The Service computer emergency response team for the Marine Corps is the Marine Corps Computer Emergency Response Team (MARCERT), which is an element of the MCNOSC located in Quantico, VA. The MARCERT provides real-time, 24-hour observation of the MCEN for network and host-based intrusion incidents based upon specified criteria. Valid incidents are analyzed from strategic and operational perspectives for impact upon the MCEN. This data is also warehoused to provide Marine Corps force DCO with usable information to perform incident profiling, trend analysis, and predictive analysis. The MARCERT provides guidance and support to Marine Corps organizations' vulnerability testing and malicious code incident response teams.

Joint Task Force–Global Network Operations (JTF-GNO) serves as the focal point within DOD to organize a united effort to defend computer networks and systems. It monitors incidents and potential threats to DOD systems and establishes links to other Federal agencies through the National Infrastructure Protection Center. When attacks are detected, JTF-GNO is responsible for DOD-wide recovery operations to stop or contain damage and restore network functions to DOD operations. The JTF-GNO is collocated with, and supported by, the Defense Information Systems Agency (DISA) in order to take advantage of the existing operational computer network capabilities of DISA's Global Operations and Security Center.

Defense Information Systems Agency operates a program known as the DISA Vulnerability Analysis and Assistance Program, which specifically focuses on automated information system vulnerability. Upon customer request, this program collects, identifies, analyzes, assesses, and resolves INFOSEC vulnerabilities.

The National Security Agency has a COMSEC monitoring program that focuses on telecommunications systems using wire and electronic communications.

The INFOSEC program management office is a joint DISA and National Security Agency organization charged with the execution of the defense INFOSEC program. The primary responsibility of the joint program office is to assure the effective and coherent application of INFOSEC measures to the overall defense information system and its individual component parts: the defense information system network, the defense integrated secure network, the defense data network, the defense message system, the interoperable tactical/strategic data network, and the defense data centers.

Marine Corps Intelligence Activity is the first line of defense with relation to the certification and accreditation of information systems that process Top Secret sensitive compartmented information within the Marine Corps operating structure. Marine Corps Intelligence Activity is also the first point of contact for issues dealing with DCO in the sensitive compartmented information computing environment.

### Information Assurance Addendums to the Operation Order

Appendix 1 (Information Systems Security) to Annex K (Combat Information Systems) of the OPORD is the IA appendix. This appendix implements the recommended COA for information assurance. It details specific tasks to be performed and specifies coordinating instructions for the control and management of information assurance.

## Physical Security

Physical security is that part of security concerned with physical measures designed to safeguard personnel; to prevent unauthorized access to equipment, installations, material, and documents; and to safeguard them against espionage, sabotage, damage, and theft. (JP 1-02)

Physical security contributes directly to information protection. Information, information-based processes, and information systems—such as C2 systems, weapon systems, and information infrastructures—are protected relative to the value of the information they contain and the risks associated with the compromise or loss of information. For more information on physical security see JP 6-0, *Joint Communications System.*

### Staff Responsibilities

In general, physical security is an operations function and is the responsibility of the G-3/S-3. However, specific measures related to the protection of information and information systems are developed and implemented by the G-6/S-6.

### Physical Security Addendums to the Operation Order

Tab B (Physical Security) to Appendix 15 (Force Protection) of Annex C (Operations) of the OPORD is the physical security tab. However, physical security activities related to the protection of information may also be included in Appendix 1 (Information Systems Security) or Appendix 2 (Communications Security) to Annex K (Combat Information Systems) of the OPORD.

## Counterintelligence

Counterintelligence is information gathered and activities conducted to identify, deceive, exploit, disrupt, or protect against espionage, other intelligence activities, sabotage, or assassinations conducted for or on behalf of foreign powers, organizations or persons or their agents, or international terrorist organizations or activities. (JP 1-02)

Counterintelligence is the intelligence function concerned with identifying and counteracting the threat posed by hostile intelligence capabilities and by organizations or individuals engaged in espionage, sabotage, subversion, or terrorism. The principal objective of counterintelligence is to assist with protecting friendly forces. Counterintelligence enhances command security by denying adversaries information that might be used against friendly forces and to provide protection by identifying and neutralizing espionage, sabotage, subversion, or terrorism organization or efforts.

Counterintelligence provides critical intelligence support to command force protection efforts by helping identify potential threats, adversary capabilities, and planned intentions to friendly operations while helping deceive the adversary as to friendly capabilities, vulnerabilities, and intentions. Combating terrorism makes us a less lucrative target. Counterintelligence increases uncertainty for the adversary, thereby making a significant contribution to the success of friendly operations. Counterintelligence also identifies friendly vulnerabilities, evaluates security measures, and assists with implementing appropriate security plans. Physical security reduces vulnerability. Operations security reduces exposure. The integration of intelligence, counterintelligence, and operations culminates in a cohesive unit force protection program. See MCWP 2-6.

### Staff Responsibilities

The unit intelligence officer plans, implements, and supervises the CI effort for the commander. The G-2/S-2 may have access to or request support from MAGTF CI units and specialists to assist in developing CI estimates and plans. Members of the command are involved in executing the CI plan and implementing appropriate CI measures. Key participants in this process and their responsibilities include the following:

- Unit security manager: overall integration and effectiveness of unit security practices.
- G-3/S-3: force protection, OPSEC, counterreconnaissance, and deception.
- G-6/S-6: communications system security.
- G-1/S-1: information and personnel security.
- Headquarters commandant: physical security.

### Counterintelligence Addendums to the Operation Order

Appendix 3 (Counterintelligence) to Annex B (Intelligence) of the OPORD is the CI appendix.

## Public Affairs

Public affairs are those public information, command information, and community engagement activities directed toward both the external and internal publics with interest in the Department of Defense. (JP 1-02) The Marine Corps PA mission is to communicate and engage; building an understanding, credibility, trust, and mutually beneficial relationships with domestic and foreign publics on whom the Marine Corps' mission success or failure depends.

Public affairs methods range from direct communication with key publics, such as face-to-face engagement or social media outreach, to indirect communication through traditional media channels or other third parties. Additionally, public affairs provides the MAGTF commander a means by which to communicate with all publics since public affairs can legally engage American, international, and host-nation audiences, as well as friendly, neutral, or adversary audiences.

In its operational role, MAGTF PA efforts have impacts within the battlespace that may often have a strategic effect on the mission. As such, public affairs and information operations are considered related activities that contribute significantly to the commander's communication strategy. While PA and IO are separate functional areas for authoritative and organizational purposes, each directly supports military objectives, counters adversary propaganda and misinformation, and deters adversary actions. Effective employment of both requires planning, message development, and media analysis; but, each effort may differ with respect to audience, scope, and intent. For maximum effectiveness, PA and IO planners will coordinate their efforts and deconflict activities consistent with DOD principles of information, organizational policy, statutory limitations, and OPSEC. Commanders, therefore, must ensure continual collaboration between PA and IO activities as part of operational planning. (For more information, see MCWP 3-33.3, *Marine Corps Public Affairs*.)

Enlisted PA Marines, called combat correspondents, are trained still photographers, videographers, and writers who can support the MAGTF across the range of military operations and can aid the IO officer by creating truthful content and communication products for dissemination. Public affairs Marines also possess dissemination capabilities that can help the MAGTF transmit first truth accounts from the battefield or operating environment to key publics.

### Public Affairs, Military Information Support Operations, and Civil-Military Operations

In an expeditionary setting, public affairs, MISO, and CMO all may disseminate information to local populations. Public affairs elements have primary responsibility for dealing with news media outlets and will assist the other functions in passing information to the public through appropriate news outlets. However, MISO and CMO are not otherwise restricted from using other available message channels to disseminate their message, to include electronic media. Public affairs efforts that may affect MISO and CMO missions include electronic information activities, imagery release, and news media engagement. Accordingly, MISO, CMO, and PA planners must actively coordinate within the IO working group or cell or coordinate directly when there is no IO coordination capability established.

### Public Affairs and Military Deception

Public affairs should plan, coordinate, and deconflict with MILDEC operations consistent with policy, statutory limitations, and operations security. The primary purpose of this coordination is to safeguard essential elements of friendly information and preserve the effectiveness of deception efforts. The public affairs officer is responsible to ensure that PA actions related to MILDEC maintain the integrity, reputation, and credibility of public affairs as a source for truthful information.

### Public Affairs, Cyberspace Operations, and Electronic Warfare

Various PA activities, such as facilitating embedded news media access, are often impacted by cyberspace operations and EW capabilities. Public affairs officers are responsible for coordinating with cyberspace operations and/or EW activities within the IO working group or cell in order to ensure PA operations are not inadvertently affected.

### Staff Responsibilities

Public affairs is a command responsibility and a function of command and control and is considered a special staff function executed by the MAGTF PAO.

### Public Affairs Addendums to the Operation Order

The PAO participates in the MCPP to ensure PA considerations are included in problem framing, COA development and selection, and are integrated into the OPORD. Throughout the planning process, the PA planner contributes to the development of the combined information overlay, and he also develops, uses, and updates the PA estimate, the PA guidance (if developed already), and Annex F (Public Affairs) of the OPORD. Annex F defines the PA mission, articulates communication goals, details specific PA tasks, identifies communication assumptions, and specifies coordinating instructions for the control and management of PA efforts.

## Civil-Military Operations

Civil-military operations are the activities of a commander that establish, maintain, influence, or exploit relations between military forces, governmental and nongovernmental civilian organizations and authorities, and the civilian populace in a friendly, neutral, or hostile operational area in order to facilitate military operations, to consolidate and achieve operational US objectives. Civil-military operations may include performance by military forces of activities and functions normally the responsibility of the local, regional, or national government. These activities may occur prior to, during, or subsequent to other military actions. They may also occur, if directed, in the absence of other military operations. Civil-military operations may be performed by designated civil affairs, by other military forces, or by a combination of civil affairs and other forces. (JP 1-02) Civil affairs is the designated Active and Reserve component forces and units organized, trained, and equipped specifically to conduct civil affairs operations and to support civil-military operations. (JP 1-02)

Each military operation has a civil dimension. The civil dimension requires commanders to consider how their actions affect, and are affected by, the presence of noncombatants. Accordingly, CMO have become an integral element of military operations. Through careful planning, coordination, and execution, CMO can help the MAGTF win by shaping the battlespace, enhancing freedom of action, isolating the adversary, meeting legal and moral obligations to civilians, and providing access to additional capabilities.

Civil-military operations are applicable at the strategic, operational, and tactical levels. Marines are deployed across the globe to support regional engagement strategies. Marines further national goals through the forward presence of expeditionary units and are involved in multinational training activities and exercises that contribute to international cooperation and stability. The Marines respond to complex emergencies, such as natural disasters, that overwhelm civil authorities and they contribute to peacekeeping and peace enforcement missions and are prepared to use force and/or the threat of force to deter conflict. If efforts to preserve peace fail, Marines employ carefully focused military capability to accomplish national objectives swiftly and with as little loss of life as possible. Once hostilities are concluded, MAGTFs contribute to stabilization, recovery, and peaceful transition of control back to civil authorities.

In most cases, Marines will operate in close contact with civilians and their governments. They carefully develop, nurture, and maintain positive relations between the people, governments, and nongovernmental organizations in the area of operations. The activities that the commander undertakes to create and foster positive relations between military forces and civilians are included in CMO. Effective CMO further national goals, help military commanders meet their international obligations to civilians, and enhance the effective use of combat power. Effective CMO maximize civilian support for, and minimize civilian interference with, the mission.

There is a CMO component to each and every military operation, even though the MAGTF resources devoted to CMO will vary during each operation and throughout the various phases of each operation. Civil-military operations are not limited to operations in which the MAGTF provides support or services to civilians or their governments, such as humanitarian and civic assistance or disaster relief efforts. Civil-military operations are conducted to facilitate military operations, achieve military operational objectives, and satisfy US policy goals. For more detailed information on CMO see JP 3-57, *Civil-Military Operations*, and MCWP 3-33.1, *Marine Air-Ground Task Force Civil-Military Operations*.

Civil affairs describes designated personnel and distinct units. It is neither a mission nor an objective, but the name of a particular force that assists the MAGTF commander in planning, facilitating coordination, and conducting CMO. Expertise is available to CA forces that is not normally available to the MAGTF, they are organized and equipped specifically to support CMO. Civil-military operations build and use relationships with civilians and other groups to facilitate operational tasks across the full range of military operations. Any element of the MAGTF may participate in the planning and execution of CMO. Whether a Marine is an operational planner dealing with a member of a foreign government, a member of a team working with an international relief organization, or a rifleman at a checkpoint talking with a local farmer, that Marine is conducting CMO. Civil-military operations occur throughout the planning and execution of military operations and are not merely an adjunct specialty that occurs before or after hostilities. Civil affairs operations (CAO), however, are distinguishable from CMO to the extent that CAO are characterized by the application of functional specialties in areas that are normally the responsibility of the local government or civil authority. Civil affairs operations are accomplished by functional specialists with the requisite MOS [military occupational specialty], and they reside in the Army Reserve Component only. The Marine Corps only has two legal and public health functional specialists within the Reserve Component. Although the Marine Corps does limited CAO and can certainly leverage support from the whole of government to do it when required, the Marine Corps is not manned, trained, or equipped to specifically conduct CAO.

Civil-miliary operations, executed by all members of the MAGTF, may include performance by military forces of activities and functions normally the responsibility of local government.

Civil-military operations can assist to support friendly or host-nation civilian welfare, security, and developmental programs, and CAO can publicize the existence or success of these activities to generate target population confidence in and positive perception of US and host-nation actions. See MCWP 3-33.1.

### Tasks

Civil-military operations focus on the relationship between military forces, governmental and nongovernmental civilian organizations and authorities, and the civilian populace in areas where military forces are present. While executing CMO, the MAGTF is responsible for five core tasks:

- Facilitating populace and resources control.
- Facilitating foreign humanitarian assistance.
- Facilitating nation assistance.
- Managing civil information.
- Facilitating support to civil administration responsibilities.

### Staff Responsibilities

Civil-military operations are a function of operations. The CA officer normally operates under the staff cognizance of the G-3/S-3. However, if civil-military considerations are a priority, the MAGTF commander may choose to designate the CA officer as a member of the general/executive staff. When trained CA personnel are not immediately available, the commander may designate a staff member to undertake the function.

### Civil Information Management

Civil information management is the process that includes the planning, collection, analysis, and production of civil information that is consolidated in a central database and shared with the supported elements, higher headquarters, other US Government and DOD agencies, international organizations, and nongovernmental organizations. Civil affairs teams and all Marines within the MAGTF will conduct civil reconnaissance and push/pull civil information such as ASCOPE [areas, structures, capabilities, organizations, people, and events] and PMESII [political, military, economic, social, information, and infrastructure] to higher headquarters. Information operations, as well as all other warfighting functions, can use this information and analysis in their planning process and make better informed recommendations to the commander.

### Civil-Military Operations Addendums to the Operation Order

Annex G (Civil-Military Operations) of the OPORD is the CMO annex. This annex implements the recommended COA for CMO. This annex details specific CMO tasks to be performed and specifies coordinating instructions for the control and management of CMO missions, if required.

## Combat Camera

Combat camera is the acquisition and utilization of still and motion imagery in support of operational and planning requirements across the range of military operations and during exercises. (MCRP 5-12C) Official visual documentation is used for operational and combat support as well as public information purposes. It is an essential visual record of Marine Corps commands throughout significant and often historical events. Complete access to areas of operations and timely exploitation of collected imagery are key to COMCAM success. For more information on COMCAM, see MCWP 3-33.7, *MAGTF Combat Camera.*

The mission of COMCAM is to provided the President, Secretary of Defense, CJCS, Military Departments, combatant commanders, and on scene commander with a directed image capability in support of operational and planning requirements during world crisis, contingencies, exercises, and wartime operations. (Marine Corps

Order 3104.1_, *Marine Corps Combat Camera Program*) Combat camera is a fundamental tool of commanders and decisionmakers and—

- Provides commanders with combat trained documentation teams that are primarily suppliers of operational imagery.
- Supports combat, information, humanitarian, special force intelligence, surveillance, and reconnaissance (ISR); engineering; legal; and PA missions.
- Provides valuable imagery, simultaneously, at the strategic, operational, and tactical levels of war.
- Speeds decisionmaking and facilitates the execution of missions at lower levels through vertical and horizontal information flow.

Marine Corps COMCAM teams are organized, trained, and equipped to provide rapid deployment of COMCAM assets in support of exercises, operations, and contingencies that support the operating forces and are available for tasking by—

- The Secretary of Defense, the CJCS, and Federal agencies as directed.
- Unified and subunified combatant commanders.
- Joint and combined task force commanders and their staffs.
- Marine Corps component commanders and their staffs.

Challenges faced by commanders on today's battlefields make COMCAM operations more critical and difficult to execute. Commanders will exploit imagery at various times and various sources such as ISR, public affairs, coalition forces, or civilian media. Therefore, MAGTF COMCAM Marines must be prepared to incorporate COMCAM assets into missions across the full range of military operations and be flexible to task-organize COMCAM for any size MAGTF and operation.

The COMCAM Marines support a commander's situational awareness, IO, PA, and CA objectives to include ISR, BDA, MILDEC, legal, and history functions. Combat camera supports the commander's imagery requirements and produces timely products supporting the commander's intent and mission objectives.

The MAGTF COMCAM officer serves as a battlestaff officer who advises the MAGTF commander on issues, capabilities, and requirements pertaining to COMCAM operations. Normally assigned to the assistant chief of staff, G-3, or the IO cell, the COMCAM officer manages all the MAGTF commander's COMCAM assets to include table of organization, table of equipment, and augmentation tasks from higher command; task-organizes COMCAM personnel for any operational commitments; and develops Marine expeditionary force/Marine expeditionary brigade operational annexes and OPORDs pertaining to COMCAM.

Combat camera personnel are assigned to the Marine expeditionary unit command element. Additional assets within ground combat element, aviation combat element, and logistics combat element support these personnel based on requirements. Regardless of size, COMCAM units maintain the capability to acquire, edit, disseminate, archive, manage, and transmit imagery. All COMCAM units are equipped to acquire imagery in darkness and inclement weather.

## Defense Support to Public Diplomacy

Defense support to public diplomacy consists of activities and measures taken by DOD components, not solely in the area of information operations, to support and facilitate the public diplomacy efforts of the US Government.

Department of Defense contributes to public diplomacy, which includes those overt international information activities of the US Government designed to promote US foreign policy objectives by seeking to understand, inform, and influence foreign audiences and opinion makers and by broadening the dialogue between American citizens and institutions and their counterparts abroad. When approved, MISO assets may be employed in support of defense support to public diplomacy as part of security cooperation initiatives or in support of US embassy public diplomacy programs. Much of the operational level IO activity conducted in any theater will be directly linked to public diplomacy objectives. Defense support to public diplomacy requires coordination across US Government departments and agencies, and amongst all DOD components.

This Page Intentionally Left Blank

# CHAPTER 4
# INFORMATION OPERATIONS INTELLIGENCE INTEGRATION

Critical to the planning, execution, and assessment of information operations is information operations intelligence integration (IOII). Information operations require accurate, timely, and detailed intelligence if it is to be successful. Early integration between Marine IO staffs involved in planning and executing IO actions and IOII staffs is imperative. The complex nature of the information environment levies requirements on the intelligence cycle not normally associated with normal operational planning. Information operations planners must understand that limited intelligence resources, legal constraints, long lead times, and the dynamic nature of the information environment have an affect on IOII. The IO requirements are almost limitless, while collection resources are limited. The information environment changes over time according to different factors. The intelligence needed to affect adversary or other target audience decisions often requires specific sources and methods to be positioned and employed over a long period of time to collect and analyze the needed information.

In order to effectively engage the intelligence system, the IO staff should clearly articulate intelligence requirements so that the G-2/S-2 staff can effectively work on behalf of the IO staff. The IO staff should establish relationships with the G-2/S-2 staff that will facilitate successful IO planning and execution initiatives.

Information operations intelligence integration is conducted as part of the IPB process. The same four-step IPB process that is used for traditional operations is also used for information operations:

- Define the battlespace environment.
- Describe the battlespace effects.
- Evaluate the adversary.
- Determine adversary COA.

The primary difference between IPB for traditional operations and IO is the focus and the degree of detail required. Intelligence preparation of the battlespace is critical for the conduct of information operations in support of stability operations, civil support operations, and counterinsurgency operations.

The function of intelligence for information operations in support of counterinsurgency is to understand the operational environment/battlespace environment, with emphasis on the local population, host nation, and insurgents. Commanders and planners require insight into cultures, perceptions, values, beliefs, interests, and decisionmaking processes of individuals and groups. An early analysis of a key target audience's information environment must be conducted prior to the execution of any detailed planning efforts. This analysis continues throughout the planning and execution in order to achieve a better visibility and understanding of that information environment. These requirements are the basis of collection and analytical efforts.

Information operations intelligence integration in support of stability operations or defense support of civil authorities operations utilizes IPB that integrates adversary doctrine and operational patterns with terrain, weather, and civil considerations such as cultural, religious, ethnographic, political, social, economic, legal, criminal, and demographic information. Intelligence preparation of the battlespace relates these factors to the specific mission and situation. See MCRP 2-3A, *Intelligence Preparation of the Battlefield/*

*Battlespace*, for further information on IPB in support of these operations.

## Intelligence Support to Assessments

Intelligence support to information operations presents new and unique challenges to intelligence professionals throughout the PDE&A [planning, decision, execution, and assessment] cycle because information operations must be worked in ways that do not fit neatly into the patterns applied in other forms of intelligence support. This is true in the combat assessment phase and its subsequent impact on the collection phase. Early in planning, operations and intelligence personnel must develop MOEs and tailor an intelligence collection plan that adequately assesses those MOEs. Measures of effectiveness are continually refined throughout the process so that the impact of operations on the information environment can be evaluated. Analysts must have a major role in defining suitable MOEs for specific IO actions in order to properly resource collection assets.

Intelligence analysts help assess task accomplishment by supporting MOE, measure of performance, and reattack recommendations. At the strategic and operational levels, IPB products provide much of the substantive baseline analysis and characterization of systems and functional capabilities required for target system analysis and task assessment. At the operational level, the IPB process supports target development by determining the anticipated times and locations where adversary targets are expected to appear. At the tactical level, IOII support may also include analysis of specific target composition and vulnerability. This data enables target systems analysts to develop the specific battle damage indicators and measures of performance to assess task accomplishment. Intelligence professionals must work with operators to establish IO MOEs, and must seek to develop and apply intelligence efforts in the fields of signals and HUMINT earlier in the planning process. Collection must be tailored to evaluate MOEs to aid the commander making operational decisions.

## Intelligence Support to Operations Security

An adversary will seek to collect critical information in order to achieve an operational advantage. Critical information consists of the significant information and indicators that can be used by the adversary to gain real advantage, decisively assure success, or preclude failure. Operations security, an operations function, seeks to reduce or deny the adversary's ability to collect information concerning friendly dispositions, capabilities, vulnerabilities, and intentions regarding both training and operations.

Intelligence support to OPSEC will focus on analysis of the adversary's ability to collect against friendly forces. Intelligence efforts involve the research and analysis of intelligence, counterintelligence, and open source information to identify the likely adversaries within the planned operation. Once identified, intelligence personnel will analyze and interpret collected information to identify indications of how an adversary could collect critical information and will seek to understand the adversary's decision cycle and any bias towards certain friendly information/intelligence collectors or disciplines.

Intelligence personnel also will assist operations in assessing friendly vulnerabilities and an adversary's ability to exploit those vulnerabilities in order to counter command implemented OPSEC measures. In addition, they will recommend physical and virtual offensive and defensive methods that will degrade an adversary's communications systems and ISR capabilities.

## Intelligence Support to Military Information Support Operations

Military information support operations are an operations function that aims to influence adversary attitudes and behavior, thereby affecting the achievement of military objectives. Effective MISO can degrade adversary command and control. The MISO staff works closely with the intelligence staff to plan MISO and effectively integrate these with the other IO elements. Operations security may be essential to the MISO plan. Equally, it may be desirable in support of MISO to reveal certain aspects of friendly dispositions, capabilities, and intentions for MILDEC purposes.

Intelligence support to MISO includes identifying target audiences and other groups, their locations, conditions, strengths, vulnerabilities, susceptibilities, political environment, cultural environment, cultural norms, values, perceptions, attitudes, public opinion, tribal connections, alliances, beliefs, ideology, and behaviors. Several organizations (including Marine Corps Intelligence Activity, the Defense Intelligence Agency, and the Joint Information Operations Warfare Command) can provide the basic psychological intelligence on the cultural, religious, social, and economic aspects of the target country/population and its government/leadership, communications, and media. Sometimes referred to as human factors analysis, this data is often compiled during peacetime. During operations, this data is supplemented by intelligence provided by the G-2/S-2.

The intelligence assessment contributes to the development of psychological assessments. The conditions and attitudes of target groups are likely to change as the situation develops. Current all-source intelligence, in particular HUMINT and SIGINT, is vital in the planning phase and throughout the execution of MISO. Intelligence will help assess the effectiveness of current MISO activites, reinforce success and assist the commander in the allocation of limited resources. The intelligence staff also monitors the effect of the adversary's MISO on the MAGTF force in order to support defensive operations. Counterintelligence provides intelligence on subversion (and can be tasked to counteract subversion), which forms part of the adversary's MISO campaign.

## Intelligence Support to Deception

Deception is an operations function that aims to present a deliberately false picture to the adversary to cause him to act contrary to his interests and in favor of the commander's objectives. Deception is highly complex, in particular those aspects that seek to exploit adversary command and control, and it demands security at the highest level. Operations security is essential to deception, because it conceals those aspects and indicators that would allow the adversary to determine the reality behind the deception.

Deception uses selected conduits, identified by intelligence, to feed information to the targeted adversary decisionmaker. Electronic warfare, cyberspace operations, counterintelligence, and physical attack support deception by shaping the conduits that feed information to the targeted adversary. While the selected conduits are not targeted, other conduits with information that may degrade the deception's effectiveness and success are targeted for electronic attack or physical attack. Intelligence must monitor and support the identification of deception conduits as well as conduits targeted with electronic attack, cyberspace operations, or physical attack.

Intelligence supports deception by identifying the capabilities and limitations of the adversary's intelligence-gathering systems as well as the adversary's biases and perceptions. This requires the identification of the adversary's decisionmaking processes and patterns. The analysis of the capabilities and limitations of the adversary's CI and security services is also required.

During the execution of deception operations, the adversary's response must be monitored to determine whether the deception operation is achieving its aim. In analyzing this intelligence, attention must also be paid to possible adversary deception operations.

## Intelligence Support to Electronic Warfare

The interception, identification, analysis, and, where possible, the understanding of the adversary's electromagnetic spectrum can provide early warning of adversary action and support force protection. It is especially important for IO planners to locate the adversary's C2 means in order to identify his communications architecture, including his offensive EW capability, and to highlight critical/vulnerable C2 systems.

Intelligence support to EW establishes target acquisition priorities based on the CCIR and concept for future operations. The decision to target adversary command and control must be based on an assessment of the balance between destruction, neutralization, and exploitation, and between hard-kill and soft-kill methods. For example, in order to support the electronic deception plan, it may be necessary to ensure that certain adversary EW support systems are protected from attack. Such key decisions must be made at the highest level and included in the commander's guidance. Decisions on targeting will also have to be coordinated with allies.

## Intelligence Support to Physical Attack

Information operations intelligence integration should not be considered as supporting only nonlethal actions. Information operations has an extremely important function in supporting attacks that cause physical destruction, but can only be effective if strongly supported by intelligence resources. Careful intelligence integration can determine what targets to select for physical destruction and whether such an attack will support, or hinder, the effect a commander wants to create on a target audience. The target audience may be a decisionmaker whose decisions can impact a commander's end state or others who are influenced by that decisionmaker. A target can be a system that supports the flow of information to a decisionmaker, a person who provides advice and counsel to that decisionmaker, or a mechanism that allows a decisionmaker to project information.

Intelligence support can help determine the proper target and how its removal or degradation will impact the decisionmaker by—

- Assessing if a physical attack will create or alter perceptions, interrupt the flow of information forcing a decisionmaker to make decisions based on incomplete information.
- Driving an adversary to use certain exploitable information systems.
- Preventing the projection of an adversary's propaganda.
- Removing decisionmakers resulting in a disruption in an adversary's chain of command.

Likewise, it can assess the second and third order effects the attack may produce on different target audiences. Information operations intelligence integration support to physical attacks must work in conjunction with IO planners and be fully integrated into the targeting cycle.

## Targeting and Enabling Support to Cyberspace Operations

Cyberspace operations consist of OCO, DCO, cyberspace ISR, cyberspace OPE, and Department of Defense information network operations. Cyberspace ISR and OPE are conducted pursuant to military authorities and must be coordinated and deconflicted with other US

Government departments and in accordance with the Department of Defense, the Department of Justice, and the intelligence community agreements and Executive Order 12333, *United States Intelligence Activities*. Cyberspace ISR includes ISR activities in cyberspace conducted to gather intelligence from target and adversary systems that may be required to support future operations, including OCO or DCO. These activities synchronize and integrate the planning and enable operation of cyberspace sensors; assets; and processing, exploitation, and dissemination systems in direct support of current and future operations. Cyberspace ISR focuses on tactical and operational intelligence and on mapping the adversary's cyberspace to support military planning. Cyberspace ISR requires appropriate deconfliction and cyberspace forces that are trained and certified to a common standard with the intelligence community.

Cyberspace OPE seeks to gain and maintain access to systems and processes and to position capabilities to facilitate follow-on actions. This includes identifying data, software, system/network configurations and identifiers, or physical structures connected to (or associated with) the network for the purposes of determining system vulnerabilities, actions taken to assure future access and/or control of the system, network, or data during anticipated hostilities (e.g., tagging malware for recognition by network defenses, delivering dormant payloads for future activation). Cyberspace OPE requires cyberspace forces trained to a standard that prevents compromise of related intelligence community operations.

Cyberspace ISR and OPE are critical enabling activities supporting OCO and DCO. The RadBn and Marine cryptologic support battalion are organic, major contributors of intelligence information supporting cyberspace operations. The Marine Corps Service component in US Cyber Command provides additional support to cyberspace operations. All cyberspace ISR efforts conducted by tactical units must be coordinated and deconflicted with other US Government departments and appropriate national agencies and the IO cell of the supported and/or higher unit.

Intelligence support to cyberspace operations requires an assessment of adversary information capabilities including friendly systems likely to be targeted by the adversary; the adversary's ability to exploit friendly systems; the adversary's ability to detect, attribute, and mitigate operations against their network and likely COAs.

## Intelligence Support to Information Assurance

A coordinated IA plan to protect friendly C2 systems from adversary attack will make an adversary's information operations more difficult. Information operations activities must also protect the intelligence and information conduits that feed the C2 system and friendly commanders. Intelligence provides the assessment of adversary IO capability and intentions.

This Page Intentionally Left Blank

# APPENDIX A
# INFORMATION OPERATIONS CELL RESPONSIBILITIES

The IO cell is composed of intelligence personnel, augmentees supporting IO activities, representatives from staff elements, and SMEs from appropriate warfighting functions. The size and structure of the cell is tailored to the mission and the commander's intent. The IO cell is responsible for the following:

- Planning the overall IO effort including preparing Appendix 3 (Information Operations) to Annex C (Operations), to the MAGTF OPORD.
- Coordinating to ensure synchronization with Annex F (Public Affairs), Annex G (Civil-Military Operations), Annex K (Combat Information Systems), Annex S (Special Technical Operations), and Annex U (Information Management).
- Developing IO concepts of support.
- Recommending IO priorities.
- Coordinating subordinate IO plans.
- Coordinating the planning and execution of IO activities between organizations responsible for each IO element.
- Coordinating nodal analysis and compiling IO target list.
- Submitting IO targets for inclusion in MAGTF targeting plans.
- Ensuring the OPSEC plan provides necessary command and control and communications protection and is coordinated with the deception plan and operations.
- Ensuring that other IO elements support the deception effort.
- Ensuring MISO themes support, and are supported by, the other IO elements.
- Coordinating IO intelligence integration.
- Coordinating and deconflicting IO with STO.
- Recommending additions, deletions, and modifications to rules of engagement.
- Coordinating EW and cyberspace operations actions with the appropriate staff planner.

## Information Operations Officer

The IO officer is responsible to the commander via the G-3/S-3 for synchronizing IRCs that support IO tasks. He also has the following responsibilities:

- Establishes the IO working group (IOWG) to coordinate, synchronize, and integrate IO efforts and develops measurements of effectiveness and performance in order to assess the effectiveness of IO actions.
- Owns no assets and must work with the staff in order to integrate information operations into planning functions.
- Ensures IO representation and input are provided to MAGTF OPT.
- Ensures the staff understands the IRCs and limitations.
- Identifies the commander's end state in conjunction with the command's planning efforts and formulates an IO plan and/or IO concept of support to achieve end state.
- Is responsible for preparing the IO annex to the OPORD.
- Assists in the integration and synchronization of the execution of IO actions.
- Determines the effectiveness of the IO concept of support and makes recommendations to the G-3/S-3 to adjust accordingly.
- Oversees personnel within the IO cell and calls plenary IO cell meetings to include external support augmentees as appropriate.

- Coordinates all IO matters with higher, adjacent, and subordinate units.
- Requests external support from and coordinates IO activities with IO organizations such as Joint Information Operations Warfare Center, Joint Warfare Analysis Center, National Security Agency, and Defense Intelligence Agency, as required.

## Intelligence (G-2/S-2) Member

The G-2/S-2 member provides timely and directed IO intelligence integration and has the following responsibilities:

- Coordinates the development and prioritization of IO intelligence requirements.
- Satisfies IO intelligence requirements through the fusion of all-source intelligence to include open source.
- Provides an information environment assessment of the area of operations and continually refines that assessment.
- Identifies target audiences/potential actors whose decisions may impact a commander's end state.
- Recommends methods that will impact an adversary's ability to collect, protect, or project information.
- Provides intelligence gain/loss analysis and reconciles restricted C2 targets on the restricted frequency list.
- Assists in the development of measures of effectiveness and coordinates mechanisms needed to collect the required data to determine the level of success of the IO concept of support.
- Coordinates with intelligence analysts to identify collection requirements based on specific needs identified by the IO cell.
- Coordinates development of targeting products to support IO planning.
- Assists with the preparation of IO portions of MAGTF operation plans.
- Informs MAGTF G-2s/S-2s of IO planning or execution activity to engage appropriate ISR capabilities for targeting and impact assessment.
- Provides assistance (through the IO cell) in assessing the operational impact and recommends appropriate recovery/response actions for computer intrusions affecting MAGTF computer infrastructures in support of the G-6/S-6 mission supporting information assurance.
- Coordinates COMSEC monitoring support in concert with G-3/S-3 and G-6/S-6 from the Joint Communications Security Monitoring Activity (JCMA), including JCMA's force protection communications support and the RadBns, during operations and exercises.
- Identifies areas of OPSEC concern for JCMA and the RadBn focus.
- Integrates COMSEC monitoring activities with trusted agents for other IO activities; such as, MISO, deception, OPSEC, and CI functions to enhance IO efforts.
- Identifies, in coordination with headquarters staff representatives, critical MAGTF information resources outside the MAGTF area of operations.
- Prepares notification messages for supporting commands or agencies to highlight the need to monitor and protect critical nodes.
- Participates in the IOWG, as required.

## Communications System (G-6/S-6) Member

The G-6/S-6 member provides information on signal security and COMSEC efforts and recommends adjustments. The G-6/S-6 also has the following responsibilities:

- Identifies critical command and control and communication system nodes for protection.
- Provides protected and restricted frequencies to the restricted frequency list.
- Coordinates and reports on JCMA monitoring of MAGTF communications architecture.
- Participates in the IOWG, as required.

### Operations Security Officer

The OPSEC officer oversees overall OPSEC efforts and is responsible for the following:

- Develops and updates the OPSEC plan.
- Initiates an OPSEC feedback program to monitor OPSEC effectiveness.
- Coordinates all OPSEC activities with external agencies and organizations.
- Participates in the IOWG, as required.

### Military Information Support Operations Officer

The MISO officer maintains a thorough knowledge of all MISO plans and actions. He also is responsible for the following:

- Provides expert advice on MISO matters.
- Coordinates MISO plans, actions, and support with other IO elements, especially OPSEC and deception.
- Participates in the IOWG, as required.

### Deception Officer

The deception officer heads the deception cell and has the following responsibilities:

- Coordinates development and update of deception plan, including obtaining higher-level authority if required.
- Monitors and controls dissemination of deception-related information; ensures security of material is maintained.
- Coordinates deception plans with other IO elements.
- Coordinates with the G-2/S-2 for feedback on deception success.
- Monitors and controls execution of the deception event schedule.
- Participates in the IOWG, as required.

### Electronic Warfare Officer

The EWO oversees the EWCC under the direction of the G-3/S-3 and has the following additional responsibilities:

- Prepares EW plans.
- Coordinates EW operations with internal units and external agencies.
- Coordinates EW operations with other IO elements.
- Establishes and maintains the restricted frequency list with the G-6/S-6.
- Participates in the IOWG, as required.

### Cyberspace Operations Officer

The cyberspace operations officer plans and coordinates offensive cyberspace, defensive cyberspace, cyberspace ISR, cyberspace OPE, and Department of Defense information network operations with internal units and external agencies. He also coordinates cyberspace operations with other IO elements and US Government departments and agencies, and participates in the IOWG, as required.

### Special Technical Operations Officer

The STO officer plans, coordinates, and deconflicts STO activities. He also has the following responsibilities:

- Ensures the IO cell is aware of STO activities as required.
- Conducts liaison with higher STO representatives to facilitate coordination and release and execution authority for STO.
- Participates in the IOWG, as required

### Public Affairs Officer

The PAO provides advice to the IO cell on all PA matters and ensures PA considerations and themes support and are supported by the IO plan. The PAO also coordinates PA plans, actions, and programs with IO efforts with particular emphasis on MISO, OPSEC, EW, and MILDEC activities.

### Targeting Representative

The targeting representative provides entry for IO targets into the targeting cycle and is responsible for the following:

- Ensures IO targets are given proper consideration in the targeting process.
- Provides IO cell recommendations to the restricted target list.
- Participates in the IOWG, as required.

### Counterintelligence Officer

The CI officer assesses defensive IO posture from a CI perspective and recommends corrective actions. The CI officer also participates in the IOWG, as required.

### Other Representatives

Other IO cell members have the following responsibilities:

- Attends IO cell sessions as invited by IO officer.
- Provides expert advice and opinions.
- Coordinates with parent organizations in support of MAGTF IO.
- Participates in the IOWG, as required.
- Conduct legal analysis of proposed operations within the context of applicable laws and authorities.

# APPENDIX B
# INFORMATION OPERATIONS PLANNING PRODUCTS

## Information Operations

The staff estimate for information operations is an estimate focused on the information environment and the use of information by adversary and friendly forces. It assesses the situation in the information environment and analyzes the best way to achieve information superiority for the assigned mission. See figure B-1 on page B-2.

## Combined Information Overlay

The impact of the information environment should be analyzed to consider how significant characteristics affect friendly, neutral, and adversary capabilities and broad COAs. Significant characteristics, further analyzed within the physical, informational, and cognitive dimensions, can be graphically represented on a combined information overlay (see fig. B-2 on page B-3). The analyst can use this overlay to identify strengths and/or vulnerabilities within the information environment that can be exploited by friendly or adversary forces. The intelligence analyst works closely with the IO officer to ensure the combined information overlay is continually updated throughout the planning process.

## Information Operations Concept of Support

The information operations concept of support shown in figure B-3, on page B-4, describes how available forces will achieve information superiority. It states when and where information superiority needs to be achieved and describes how information operations will support the operation and how information operations capabilities will be employed. Information operations personnel develop an IO concept of support for each assigned mission or COA based on what the command's assets and resources can do to achieve the IO objectives.

**Sub-IE: North**
Populace: Supports adversary, multiple rural TAs
Info Flow: Cell phone, internet, TV, radio
Info Infrastructure: Well-developed and multiple conduits, supports adversary C2
COA Considerations: Adversary propaganda flow
Conditions: Inner LOCs favor adversary

**Sub-IE: Central**
Populace: Supports government, urban hubs
Info Flow: Multimedia, cell phone, broadcasts affected by CF versus border state
Info Infrastructure: Unreliable, frequent power outages, follows main LOCs
COA Considerations: Adversary focus, intimidation main effort
Conditions: Favor friendly forces

**Sub-IE: South**
Populace: Supports government, rural strong tribal/clan links
Info Flow: Slow, F2F, TV, radio
Info Infrastructure: Dilapidated, unreliable, frequent power outages, follows main LOCs
COA Considerations: Area is an information vacuum, requires multiengagements
Conditions: Favor friendly forces

**Adversary**

**Collect:**
Capabilities: HUMINT, SIGINT
Vulnerabilities: Loyalty of followers, cell paranoia
Recent Activity: Penetration of local police

**Protect:**
Capabilities: Intimidation of populace
Vulnerabilities: Couriers, internet, cell phones
Recent Activity: Unsecure communications

**Project:**
Capabilities: F2F, radio, internet
Vulnerabilities: C2
Recent Activity: Anti-US themes

**Likely COA:** Incite civil unrest in center of AOR, discredit CF actions; build legitimacy/recruit with local militia

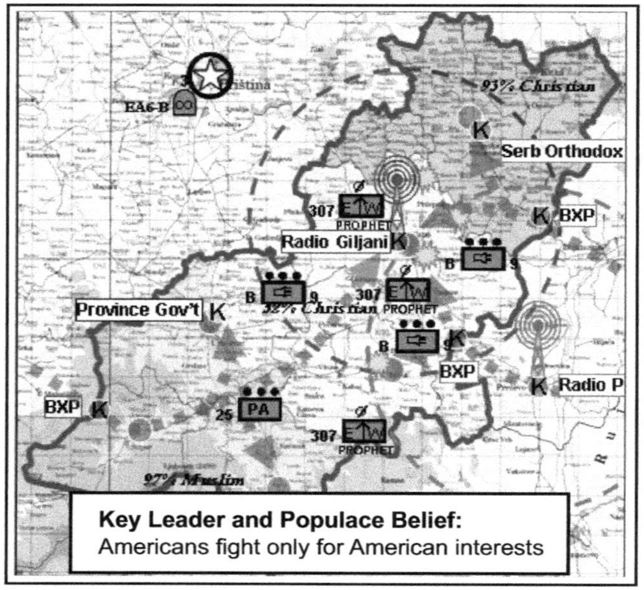

EA6-B
93% Christian
Serb Orthodox
307
PROPHET
Radio Giljani
BXP
Province Gov't
32% Christian
PA
25
Radio P
97% Muslim
Key Leader and Populace Belief:
Americans fight only for American interests

**Friendly**

**Organic:**

EA:
307
EA
Prophet
PA:
25
PA
MISO:
1
3
Supporting:
3
EA:
EA6-B

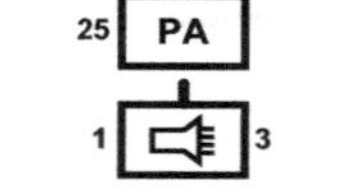

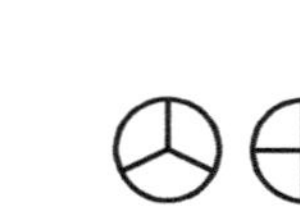

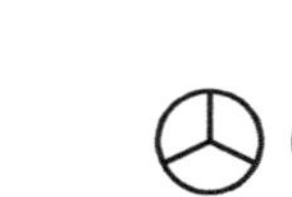

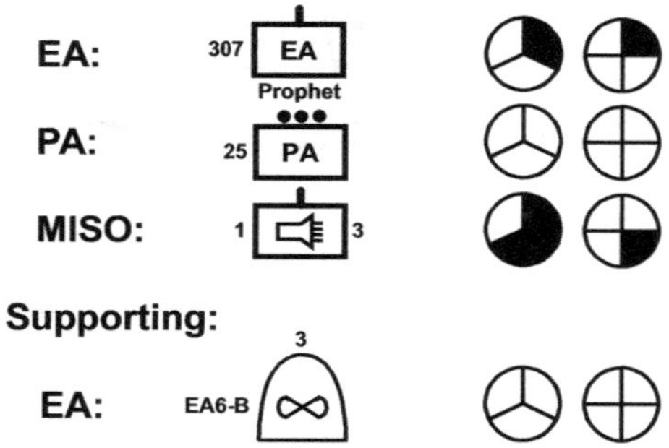

**Vulnerabilities:**
- Non-secure handheld radios

**COA Considerations:**
- Intel loss versus gain with EA
- Interdict border state info flow

LEGEND

| | | | | | |
|---|---|---|---|---|---|
| **AOR** | area of responsibility | **F2F** | face to face | **Intel** | intelligence |
| **BXP** | border crossing point | **Govt** | government | **LOC** | line of communications |
| **CF** | coalition force | **IE** | information environment | **MISO** | military information support operations |
| **EA** | electronic attack | **Info** | information | **TV** | television |

**Figure B-1. Example of a Staff Estimate for Information Operations: Graphical Display.**

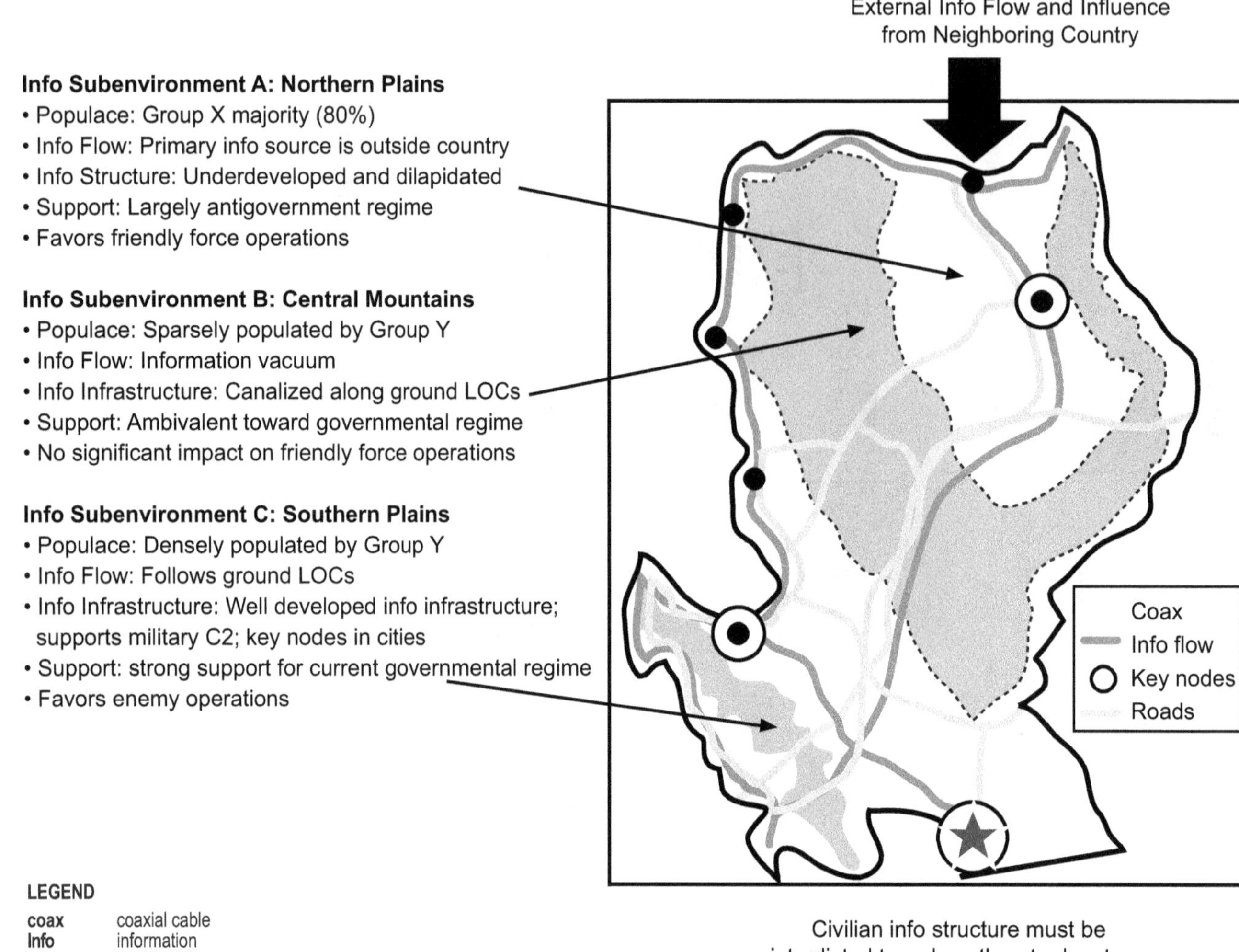
External Info Flow and Influence from Neighboring Country
Info Subenvironment A: Northern Plains
• Populace: Group X majority (80%)
• Info Flow: Primary info source is outside country
• Info Structure: Underdeveloped and dilapidated
• Support: Largely antigovernment regime
• Favors friendly force operations
Info Subenvironment B: Central Mountains
• Populace: Sparsely populated by Group Y
• Info Flow: Information vacuum
• Info Infrastructure: Canalized along ground LOCs
• Support: Ambivalent toward governmental regime
• No significant impact on friendly force operations
Info Subenvironment C: Southern Plains
• Populace: Densely populated by Group Y
• Info Flow: Follows ground LOCs
• Info Infrastructure: Well developed info infrastructure; supports military C2; key nodes in cities
• Support: strong support for current governmental regime
• Favors enemy operations
Coax
Info flow
Key nodes
Roads
LEGEND
coax coaxial cable
Info information
LOCs lines of communications
Civilian info structure must be interdicted to reduce threat advantage

**Figure B-2. Example of Combined Information Overlay.**

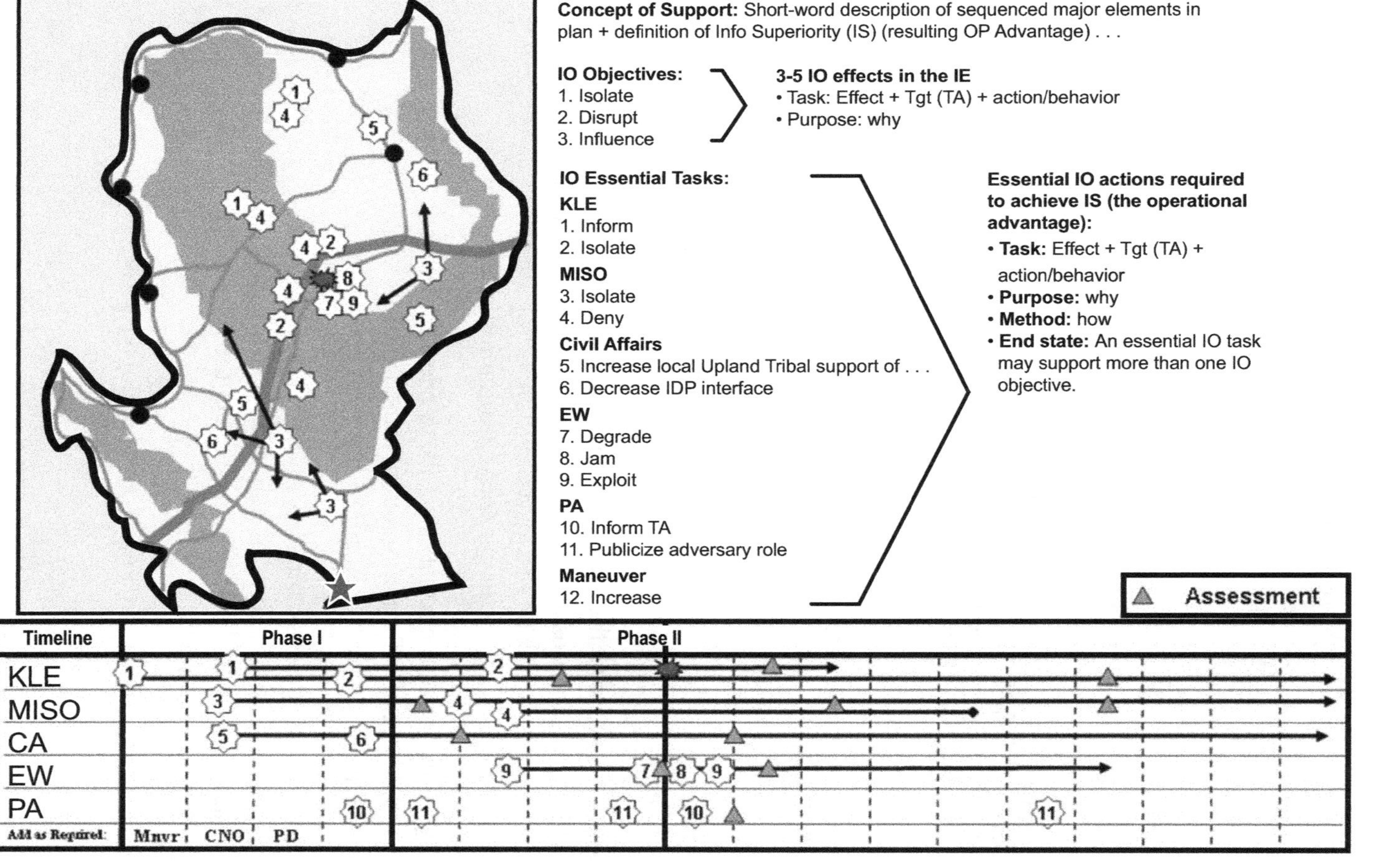

Concept of Support: Short-word description of sequenced major elements in plan + definition of Info Superiority (IS) (resulting OP Advantage) . . .
IO Objectives:
1. Isolate
2. Disrupt
3. Influence
3-5 IO effects in the IE
• Task: Effect + Tgt (TA) + action/behavior
• Purpose: why
IO Essential Tasks:
KLE
1. Inform
2. Isolate
MISO
3. Isolate
4. Deny
Civil Affairs
5. Increase local Upland Tribal support of . . .
6. Decrease IDP interface
EW
7. Degrade
8. Jam
9. Exploit
PA
10. Inform TA
11. Publicize adversary role
Maneuver
12. Increase
Essential IO actions required to achieve IS (the operational advantage):
• Task: Effect + Tgt (TA) + action/behavior
• Purpose: why
• Method: how
• End state: An essential IO task may support more than one IO objective.
Assessment
Timeline
Phase I
Phase II
KLE
MISO
CA
EW
PA
Add as Required:
Mnvr
CNO
PD


LEGEND

| | | | |
|---|---|---|---|
| IE | information environment | OP | operational |
| IDP | internal displaced persons | PD | public diplomacy |
| IO | information operations | TA | target audience |
| IS | information superiority | Tgt | target |

**Figure B-3. Example of an Information Operations Concept of Support Sketch.**

# APPENDIX C
# SAMPLE OF APPENDIX 3 TO ANNEX C INFORMATION OPERATIONS

CLASSIFICATION

Copy no. ____ of ____ copies
OFFICIAL DESIGNATION OF COMMAND
PLACE OF ISSUE
Date/time group
Message reference number

APPENDIX 3 (Information Operations) TO ANNEX C (Operations) TO OPERATION ORDER OR PLAN (Number) (Operation CODEWORD) (U)
INFORMATION OPERATIONS (U)

(U) REFERENCES:

(a) Any relevant plans or orders.
(b) Required maps and charts.
(c) Other relevant documents.

1. (U) Situation. Summarize the overall operational situation as it relates to information operations.

a. (U) Adversary. Summarize the adversary situation, force disposition, intelligence capabilities, and possible courses of action. If applicable, reference intelligence estimates or summaries. Address any specific information that bears directly on the planned information operations.

b. (U) Friendly. Summarize the situation of those friendly forces that may directly affect attainment of information operations objectives. Address any critical limitations and any other planned information operations.

c. (U) Assumptions. List any assumptions made of friendly, adversary, or third party capabilities, limitations, or courses of action. Describe the conditions that the commander believes will exist at the time the plan becomes an order. Omit in orders.

2. (U) Mission. Provide the command's mission from the base order.

Page number

CLASSIFICATION

CLASSIFICATION

3. (U) Execution

a. (U) Concept of Support. Summarize how the commander visualizes the execution of information operations from its beginning to its termination. Describe how information operations will support the command's mission. Summarize the concepts for supervision and termination of information operations.

(1) (U) The concept of support may be a single paragraph or divided into two or more paragraphs depending upon the complexity of the operation.

(2) (U) When an operation involves various phases, such as peace or prehostilities or crisis, war, or post-hostilities, the concept of support should include subparagraphs describing the role of information operations in each phase.

b. (U) Information Operations Tasks. Identify the major tasks for each of the five elements of information operations. The five elements of information operations listed below are covered in tabs A through E.

(1) (U) Military deception.

(2) (U) Electronic warfare.

(3) (U) Operations security.

(4) (U) Military information support operations.

(5) (U) Physical attack.

c. (U) Coordinating Instructions. Address any mutual support issues relating to the elements of IO.

4. (U) Administration and Logistics. Address any IO administrative or logistic requirements.

5. (U) Command and Control. List any IO command and control instructions. State the command structure for information operations. Identify any special IO communications and reporting requirements.

Page number

CLASSIFICATION

CLASSIFICATION

ACKNOWLEDGE RECEIPT

Name
Rank and Service
Title

TABS:

A – Military Deception
B – Electronic Warfare
C – Operations Security
D – Military Information Support Operations
E – Physical Attack

OFFICIAL:
s/
Name
Rank and Service
Title

Page number

CLASSIFICATION

This Page Intentionally Left Blank

# Glossary

## Section I. Acronyms and Abbreviations

BDA . . . . . . . . . . . . . . battle damage assessment

C2 . . . . . . . . . . . . . . . . . . . .command and control
CA. . . . . . . . . . . . . . . . . . . . . . . . . . . .civil affairs
CAO . . . . . . . . . . . . . . . . . civil affairs operations
CCIR. . . . . . . . . . . . . . . . . . . . . . . . commander's critical information requirement
CI . . . . . . . . . . . . . . . . . . . . . .counterintelligence
CJCS . . . . . Chairman of the Joint Chiefs of Staff
CMO . . . . . . . . . . . . . . . .civil-military operations
COA . . . . . . . . . . . . . . . . . . . . . . course of action
COG . . . . . . . . . . . . . . . . . . . . . .center of gravity
COMCAM . . . . . . . . . . . . . . . . . .combat camera
COMSEC . . . . . . . . . . . communications security

DCO . . . . . . . . . defensive cyberspace operations
DISA . . . . .Defense Information Systems Agency
DOD . . . . . . . . . . . . . . . . Department of Defense

EW . . . . . . . . . . . . . . . . . . . . . .electronic warfare
EWCC. . . . . .electronic warfare coordination cell
EWO . . . . . . . . . . . . . . .electronic warfare officer

FOps . . . . . . . . . . . . . . . . . . . . . future operations

G-1 . . . . . . . . . . . . . . . . . . personnel staff section
G-2 . . . . . . . . . . . . . . . . intelligence staff section
G-3 . . . . . . . . . . . . . . . . . operations staff section
G-6 . . . . . . .communications system staff section
G-9 . . . . . . . . . . . . . . . . .civil affairs staff section

HUMINT . . . . . . . . . . . . . . . .human intelligence

IA . . . . . . . . . . . . . . . . . . . information assurance
IAM. . . . . . . . . . . information assurance manager
IAT . . . . . . . . . .information assurance technician
INFOSEC . . . . . . . . . . . . . . . information security
IO . . . . . . . . . . . . . . . . . . .information operations
IOII . . . . . . . . . . . . . . . . . .information operations intelligence integration
IOWG . . . . . . . . . . . . . . . .information operations working group
IPB . . . . . . . . . . . . . . . . . intelligence preparation of the battlespace
IRC . . . . . . . . . . . . information-related capability
ISR . . . . . . . . . . . . . . . .intelligence, surveillance, and reconnaissance

J-3 . . . . . . . . operations directorate of a joint staff
JCMA . . . . . . . . . Joint Communications Security Monitoring Activity
JMISTF . . . . . . . . . . . . .joint military information support task force
JP. . . . . . . . . . . . . . . . . . . . . . . . . .joint publication
JTF . . . . . . . . . . . . . . . . . . . . . . . . joint task force
JTF-GNO . . . . . . . . . . .Joint Task Force - Global Network Operations

MAGTF . . . . . . . . . Marine air-ground task force
MARCERT. . . . . . . . . . Marine Corps Computer Emergency Response Team
MCEN. . . . . . . .Marine Corps enterprise network
MCNOSC . . . . . . . . . . . . Marine Corps Network Operations and Security Center
MCPP . . . . . . . . . Marine Corps Planning Process
MCRP . . . . . .Marine Corps reference publication
MCWP . . . . . . . . . . . . . . . . . . . . . Marine Corps warfighting publication
MILDEC. . . . . . . . . . . . . . . . . military deception
MISG . . . . . . military information support group
MISO . . . . . . . . . . . . . . . . . .military information support operations
MOE . . . . . . . . . . . . . . . measure of effectiveness

NCIS . . . . . . . . . . . . . . . . . . . . . . .Naval Criminal Investigative Service

OCO . . . . . . . . . offensive cyberspace operations
OPORD. . . . . . . . . . . . . . . . . . . . .operation order
OPSEC . . . . . . . . . . . . . . . . . . .operations security
OPT. . . . . . . . . . . . . . . operational planning team
OPE. . . . . . . . . . . . . . . . . operational preparation of the environment

PA . . . . . . . . . . . . . . . . . . . . . . . . . . public affairs
PAO . . . . . . . . . . . . . . . . . . .public affairs officer

RadBn . . . . . . . . . . . . . . . . . . . . . radio battalion

S-1 . . . . . . . . . . . . . . . . . . . . . . . personnel officer
S-2 . . . . . . . . . . . . . . . . . . . . . . intelligence officer
S-3 . . . . . . . . . . . . . . . . . . . . . . . operations officer
S-6 . . . . . . . . . . . . communications system officer
S-9 . . . . . . . . . . . . . . . . . . . . . . . civil affairs officer
SIGINT . . . . . . . . . . . . . . . . . . signals intelligence
SJA . . . . . . . . . . . . . . . . . . . . staff judge advocate
SME . . . . . . . . . . . . . . . . . . subject matter expert
STO . . . . . . . . . . . . . . special technical operations

US . . . . . . . . . . . . . . . . . . . . . . . . . . United States

VMAQ . . . . . . Marine tactical electronic warfare squadron

## SECTION II. DEFINITIONS

**area of operations**—An operational area defined by the joint force commander for land and maritime forces that should be large enough to accomplish their missions and protect their forces. Also called **AO**. (JP 1-02)

**branch**—4. The contingency options built into the base plan used for changing the mission, orientation, or direction of movement of a force to aid success of the operation based on anticipated events, opportunities, or disruptions caused by enemy actions and reactions. See also **sequel**. (JP 1-02, part 4 of a 4 part definition)

**center of gravity**—The source of power that provides moral or physical strength, freedom of action, or will to act. Also called **COG**. See also **decisive point**. (JP 1-02)

**civil affairs**—Designated Active and Reserve Component forces and units organized, trained, and equipped specifically to conduct civil affairs operations and to support civil-military operations. Also called **CA**. See also **civil-military operations**. (JP 1-02)

**civil affairs operations**—Those military operations conducted by civil affairs forces that (1) enhance the relationship between military forces and civil authorities in localities where military forces are present; (2) require coordination with other interagency organizations, intergovernmental organizations, nongovernmental organizations, indigenous populations and institutions, and the private sector; and (3) involve application of functional specialty skills that normally are the responsibility of civil government to enhance the conduct of civil-military operations. Also called **CAO**. See also **civil affairs; civil-military operations**. (JP 1-02)

**civil information management**—The process whereby civil information is collected, consolidated in a central database, and shared with the supported elements, higher headquarters, other US Government and Department of Defense agencies, international organizations, and nongovernmental organizations. (This term and its definition are proposed for inclusion in the next edition of MCRP 5-12C.)

**civil-military operations**—The activities of a commander that establish, maintain, influence, or exploit relations between military forces, governmental and nongovernmental civilian organizations and authorities, and the civilian populace in a friendly, neutral, or hostile operational area in order to facilitate military operations, to consolidate and achieve operational US objectives. Civil-military operations may include performance by military forces of activities and functions normally the responsibility of the local, regional, or national government. These activities may occur prior to, during, or subsequent to other military actions. They may also occur, if directed, in the absence of other military operations. Civil-military operations may be performed by designated civil affairs, by other military forces, or by a combination of civil affairs and other forces. Also called **CMO**. (JP 1-02)

**combat camera**—The acquisition and utilization of still and motion imagery in support of operational and planning requirements across the range of military operations and during exercises. Also called **COMCAM**. (MCRP 5-12C)

**communications security**—The protection resulting from all measures designed to deny unauthorized persons information of value that might be derived from the possession and study of telecommunications, or to mislead unauthorized persons in their interpretation of the results of such possession and study. (JP 1-02)

**computer security**—The protection resulting from all measures to deny unauthorized access and exploitation of friendly computer systems. (JP 1-02)

**counterintelligence**—Information gathered and activities conducted to identify, deceive, exploit, disrupt, or protect against espionage, other intelligence activities, sabotage, or assassinations conducted for or on behalf of foreign powers, organizations or persons or their agents, or international terrorist organizations or activities. Also called **CI**. (JP 1-02)

**cyberspace intelligence, surveillance, and reconnaissance**—An intelligence action conducted by the joint force commander authorized by an executive order or conducted by attached signals intelligence units under temporary delegated signals intelligence operational tasking authority.

**cyberspace operational preparation of the environment**—Consists of the non-intelligence enabling activities conducted to plan and prepare for potential follow-on military operations.

**cyberspace operations**—The employment of cyberspace capabilities where the primary purpose is to achieve objectives in or through cyberspace. (JP 1-02)

**decisive point**—A geographic place, specific key event, critical factor, or function that, when acted upon, allows commanders to gain a marked advantage over an adversary or contribute materially to achieving success. See also **center of gravity**. (JP 1-02)

**defensive cyberspace operations**—Passive and active cyberspace operations intended to preserve the ability to utilize friendly cyberspace capabilities and protect data, networks, net-centric capabilities, and other designated systems. Also called **DCO.** (JP 1-02)

**demonstration**—2. In military deception, a show of force in an area where a decision is not sought that is made to deceive an adversary. It is similar to a feint but no actual contact with the adversary is intended. (JP 1-02 part 2 of a 2 part definition)

**Department of Defense information network operations**—Operations to design, build, configure, secure, operate, maintain, and sustain Department of Defense networks to create and preserve information assurance on the Department of Defense information networks. (JP 1-02)

**display**—In military deception, a static portrayal of an activity, force, or equipment intended to deceive the adversary's visual observation. (JP 1-02)

**electronic attack**—Division of electronic warfare involving the use of electromagnetic energy, directed energy, or antiradiation weapons to attack personnel, facilities, or equipment with the intent of degrading, neutralizing, or destroying enemy combat capability and is considered a form of fires. Also called **EA**. See also **electronic protection; electronic warfare; electronic warfare support**. (JP 1-02)

**electronic protection**—Division of electronic warfare involving actions taken to protect personnel, facilities, and equipment from any effects of friendly or enemy use of the electromagnetic spectrum that degrade, neutralize, or destroy friendly combat capability. Also called **EP**. See also **electronic attack, electronic warfare; electronic warfare support**. (JP 1-02)

**electronic warfare**—Military action involving the use of electromagnetic and directed energy to control the electromagnetic spectrum or to attack the enemy. Also called **EW**. (JP 1-02)

**electronic warfare support**—Division of electronic warfare involving actions tasked by, or under direct control of, an operational commander to search for, intercept, identify, and locate or localize sources of intentional and unintentional radiated electromagnetic energy for the purpose of immediate threat recognition, targeting, planning and conduct of future operations.

Also called **ES**. See also **electronic attack; electronic protection; electronic warfare**. (JP 1-02)

**feint**—In military deception, an offensive action involving contact with the adversary conducted for the purpose of deceiving the adversary as to the location and/or time of the actual main offensive action. (JP 1-02)

**information assurance**—Measures that protect and defend information and information systems by ensuring their availability, integrity, authentication, confidentiality, and nonrepudiation. This includes providing for restoration of information systems by incorporating protection, detection, and reaction capabilities. Also called **IA**. (JP 1-02)

**information environment**—The aggregate of individuals, organizations, and systems that collect, process, disseminate, or act on information. (JP 1-02)

**information operations**—The integration, coordination, and synchronization of all actions taken in the information environment to affect a target audience's behavior in order to create an operational advantage for the commander. Also called **IO** (This term and its definition are proposed for inclusion in the next edition of MCRP 5-12C)

**information operations intelligence integration**—The integration of intelligence disciplines and analytic methods to characterize and forecast, identify vulnerabilities, determine effects, and assess the information environment. Also called **IOII**. (JP 1-02)

**information-related capability**—A capability, function, or activity that uses data, information, or electromagnetic spectrum to produce lethal or nonlethal effects in the physical or informational dimensions with an expressed intent to cause deliberate effects within the cognitive dimension of the information environment. Also called **IRC**. (Proposed for inclusion in the next edition of MCRP 5-12C)

**information superiority**—The operational advantage derived from the ability to collect, process, and disseminate an uninterrupted flow of information while exploiting or denying an adversary's ability to do the same. See also **information operations**. (JP 1-02)

**measure of effectiveness**—A criterion used to assess changes in system behavior, capability, or operational environment that is tied to measuring the attainment of an end state, achievement of an objective, or creation of an effect. Also called **MOE**. (JP 1-02)

**measure of performance**—A criterion used to assess friendly actions that is tied to measuring task accomplishment. Also called **MOP**. (JP 1-02)

**military deception**—Actions executed to deliberately mislead adversary, paramilitary, or violent extremist organization military decision makers, thereby causing the adversary to take specific actions (or inactions) that will contribute to the accomplishment of the friendly mission. Also called **MILDEC**. (JP 1-02)

**military information support operations**—Planned operations to convey selected information and indicators to foreign audiences to influence their emotions, motives, objective reasoning, and ultimately the behavior of foreign governments, organizations, groups, and individuals in a manner favorable to the originator's objectives. Also called **MISO**. (JP 1-02)

**offensive cyberspace operations**—Cyberspace operations intended to project power by the application of force in or through cyberspace. Also called **OCO**. (JP 1-02)

**operations security**—A process of identifying critical information and subsequently analyzing friendly actions attendant to military operations and other activities. Also called **OPSEC**. (JP 1-02)

**physical attack**—The application of combat power to destroy or neutralize enemy forces and installations. It includes direct and indirect fires from ground, sea, and air platforms. It also includes direct actions by special operations forces. (This term and its definition are proposed for inclusion in the next edition of MCRP 5-12C)

**physical security**—1. That part of security concerned with physical measures designed to safeguard personnel; to prevent unauthorized access to equipment, installations, material, and documents; and to safeguard them against espionage, sabotage, damage, and theft. (JP 1-02, part 1 of a 2 part definition)

**public affairs**—Those public information, command information, and community engagement activities directed toward both the external and internal publics with interest in the Department of Defense. Also called **PA**. (JP 1-02)

**public affairs guidance**—Constraints and restraints established by proper authority regarding public information, command information, and community relations activities. It may also address the method(s), timing, location, and other details governing the release of information to the public. Also called **PAG**. See also **public affairs**. (JP 1-02)

**public diplomacy**—1. Those overt international public information activities of the United States Government designed to promote United States foreign policy objectives by seeking to understand, inform, and influence foreign audiences and opinion makers, and by broadening the dialogue between American citizens and institutions and their counterparts abroad. 2. In peace building, civilian agency efforts to promote an understanding of the reconstruction efforts, rule of law, and civic responsibility through public affairs and international public diplomacy operations. (JP 1-02)

**ruse**—In military deception, a trick of war designed to deceive the adversary, usually involving the deliberate exposure of false information to the adversary's intelligence collection system. (JP 1-02)

**security cooperation**—All Department of Defense interactions with foreign defense establishments to build defense relationships that promote specific US security interests, develop allied and friendly military capabilities for self-defense and multinational operations, and provide US forces with peacetime and contingency access to a host nation. Also called **SC**. (JP 1-02)

**sequel**—The subsequent major operation or phase based on the possible outcomes (success, stalemate, or defeat) of the current major operation or phase. See also **branch**. (JP 1-02)

**staff judge advocate**—A judge advocate so designated in the Army, Air Force, or Marine Corps, and the principal legal advisor of a Navy, Coast Guard, or joint force command who is a judge advocate. Also called **SJA**. (JP 1-02)

**target**—1. An entity or object considered for possible engagement or other action. 2. In intelligence usage, a country, area, installation, agency, or person against which intelligence operations are directed. 3. An area designated and numbered for future firing. 4. In gunfire support usage, an impact burst that hits the target. (JP 1-02)

**target audience**—An individual or group selected for influence. Also called **TA**. (JP 1-02)

# REFERENCES AND RELATED PUBLICATIONS

## Federal Publications

Executive Order

| | |
|---|---|
| 12333 | United States Intelligence Activities |

United States Code

| | |
|---|---|
| Title 10 | Armed Forces |

## Department of Defense Issuances

Department of Defense Directives (DODDs)

| | |
|---|---|
| S-3600.1 | Information Operations |
| 8570.01 | Information Assurance (IA) Training, Certification, and Workforce Management |

Department of Defense Instruction (DODI)

| | |
|---|---|
| 8510.01 | DOD Information Assurance Certification and Accreditation Process (DIACAP) |

## Joint Publications (JPs)

| | |
|---|---|
| 1-02 | Department of Defense Dictionary of Military and Associated Terms |
| 2-01.3 | Joint Intelligence Preparation of the Operational Environment |
| 3-13 | Information Operations |
| 3-13.1 | Electronic Warfare |
| 3-13.2 | Military Information Support Operations |
| 3-13.3 | Operations Security |
| 3-13.4 | Military Deception |
| 3-57 | Civil-Military Operations |
| 3-61 | Public Affairs |
| 6-0 | Joint Communications System |

## Marine Corps Publications

Marine Corps Warfighting Publications (MCWPs)

| | |
|---|---|
| 2-1 | Intelligence Operations |
| 2-6 | Counterintelligence |
| 3-16 | Fire Support Coordination in the Ground Combat Element |
| 3-33.1 | Marine Air-Ground Task Force Civil-Military Operations |
| 3-33.3 | Marine Corps Public Affairs |
| 3-33.7 | MAGTF Combat Camera |
| 3-40.2 | Information Management |
| 3-40.3 | MAGTF Communications System |
| 3-40.5 | Electronic Warfare |
| 3-40.6 | Psychological Operations |

3-40.9 Operations Security (OPSEC)
5-1 Marine Corps Planning Process

Marine Corps Reference Publications (MCRPs)
2-3A Intelligence Preparation of the Battlefield/Battlespace
3-33.7A Multi-Service Tactics, Techniques, and Procedures for Combat Camera Operations
3-40.4A Multi-Service Tactics, Techniques, and Procedures for Military Deception (MILDEC) Operations (classified)
5-12C Marine Corps Supplement to the Department of Defense Dictionary of Military and Associated Terms

Marine Corps Orders (MCOs)
3070.2 The Marine Corps Operations Security (OPSEC) Program
3104.1_ Marine Corps Combat Camera Program
3120.10 Marine Corps Information Operations Program

Miscellaneous
*Marine Corps Operating Concept for Information Operations*

## Miscellaneous

Director of Central Intelligence Directive (DCID) 6/3, *Protecting Sensitive Compartmented Information Within Information Systems*

# Information Operations

**27 November 2012**
**Incorporating Change 1**
**20 November 2014**

# PREFACE

## 1. Scope

This publication provides joint doctrine for the planning, preparation, execution, and assessment of information operations across the range of military operations.

## 2. Purpose

This publication has been prepared under the direction of the Chairman of the Joint Chiefs of Staff. It sets forth joint doctrine to govern the activities and performance of the Armed Forces of the United States in joint operations and provides the doctrinal basis for US military coordination with other US Government departments and agencies during operations and for US military involvement in multinational operations. It provides military guidance for the exercise of authority by combatant commanders and other joint force commanders (JFCs) and prescribes joint doctrine for operations, education, and training. It provides military guidance for use by the Armed Forces in preparing their appropriate plans. It is not the intent of this publication to restrict the authority of the JFC from organizing the force and executing the mission in a manner the JFC deems most appropriate to ensure unity of effort in the accomplishment of the overall objective.

## 3. Application

a. Joint doctrine established in this publication applies to the Joint Staff, commanders of combatant commands, subunified commands, joint task forces, subordinate components of these commands, and the Services.

b. The guidance in this publication is authoritative; as such, this doctrine will be followed except when, in the judgment of the commander, exceptional circumstances dictate otherwise. If conflicts arise between the contents of this publication and the contents of Service publications, this publication will take precedence unless the Chairman of the Joint Chiefs of Staff, normally in coordination with the other members of the Joint Chiefs of Staff, has provided more current and specific guidance. Commanders of forces operating as part of a multinational (alliance or coalition) military command should follow multinational doctrine and procedures ratified by the United States. For doctrine and procedures not ratified by the United States, commanders should evaluate and follow the multinational command's doctrine and procedures, where applicable and consistent with United States law, regulations, and doctrine.

For the Chairman of the Joint Chiefs of Staff:

CURTIS M. SCAPARROTTI
Lieutenant General, U.S. Army
Director, Joint Staff

Intentionally Blank

## SUMMARY OF CHANGES
## CHANGE 1 TO JOINT PUBLICATION 3-13
## DATED 27 NOVEMBER 2012

- **Describes techniques for assessing information related capabilities (IRC) and techniques for assessing the integration of the IRCs in support of the joint force commander's objectives.**

- **Expands guidance for the 8-step assessment process.**

- **Provides additional information about private sector assessment techniques, including the theory of change.**

- **Expands discussion of sound assessment with a focused, organized approach that is being developed in conjunction with the initial operation plan.**

- **Emphasizes the need for assessments to be periodically adjusted to avoid becoming obsolete.**

Intentionally Blank

# TABLE OF CONTENTS

PAGE

Intentionally Blank

EXECUTIVE SUMMARY
## COMMANDER'S OVERVIEW

- **Provides an Overview of Information Operations (IO) and the Information Environment**
- **Describes IO and Its Relationships and Integration**
- **Addresses IO Authorities, Responsibilities, and Legal Considerations**
- **Explains Integrating Information-Related Capabilities into the Joint Operation Planning Process**
- **Covers Multinational Information Operations**

---

### Overview

***The ability to share information in near real time, anonymously and/or securely, is a capability that is both an asset and a potential vulnerability to us, our allies, and our adversaries.***

The instruments of national power (diplomatic, informational, military, and economic) provide leaders in the US with the means and ways of dealing with crises around the world. Employing these means in the information environment requires the ability to securely transmit, receive, store, and process information in near real time. The nation's state and non-state adversaries are equally aware of the significance of this new technology, and will use information-related capabilities (IRCs) to gain advantages in the information environment, just as they would use more traditional military technologies to gain advantages in other operational environments. As the strategic environment continues to change, so does information operations (IO). Based on these changes, **the Secretary of Defense now characterizes IO as the integrated employment, during military operations, of IRCs in concert with other lines of operation to influence, disrupt, corrupt, or usurp the decision making of adversaries and potential adversaries while protecting our own.**

***The Information Environment***

The information environment is the aggregate of individuals, organizations, and systems that collect, process, disseminate, or act on information. This environment consists of three

***The joint force commander's operational environment is the composite of the conditions, circumstances, and influences that affect employment of capabilities and bear on the decisions of the commander (encompassing physical areas and factors of the air, land, maritime, and space domains) as well as the information environment (which includes cyberspace).***

interrelated dimensions, which continuously interact with individuals, organizations, and systems. These dimensions are known as physical, informational, and cognitive. The physical dimension is composed of command and control systems, key decision makers, and supporting infrastructure that enable individuals and organizations to create effects. The informational dimension specifies where and how information is collected, processed, stored, disseminated, and protected. The cognitive dimension encompasses the minds of those who transmit, receive, and respond to or act on information.

***The Information and Influence Relational Framework and the Application of Information-Related Capabilities***

IRCs are the tools, techniques, or activities that affect any of the three dimensions of the information environment. The joint force (means) employs IRCs (ways) to affect the information provided to or disseminated from the target audience (TA) in the physical and informational dimensions of the information environment to affect decision making.

**Information Operations**

***Information Operations and the Information-Influence Relational Framework***

The relational framework describes the application, integration, and synchronization of IRCs to influence, disrupt, corrupt, or usurp the decision making of TAs to create a desired effect to support achievement of an objective.

***The Information Operations Staff and Information Operations Cell***

Joint force commanders (JFCs) may establish an IO staff to provide command-level oversight and collaborate with all staff directorates and supporting organizations on all aspects of IO. Most combatant commands (CCMDs) include an IO staff to serve as the focal point for IO. Faced with an ongoing or emerging crisis within a geographic combatant commander's (GCC's) area of responsibility, a JFC can establish an IO cell to provide additional expertise and coordination across the staff and interagency.

*Relationships and Integration*

IO is not about ownership of individual capabilities but rather the use of those capabilities as force multipliers to create a desired effect. There are many military capabilities that contribute to IO and should be taken into consideration during the planning process. These include: strategic communication, joint interagency coordination group, public affairs, civil-military operations, cyberspace operations (CO), information assurance, space operations, military information support operations (MISO), intelligence, military deception, operations security, special technical operations, joint electromagnetic spectrum operations, and key leader engagement.

## Authorities, Responsibilities, and Legal Considerations

*Authorities*

*The authority to employ information-related capabilities is rooted foremost in Title 10, United States Code.*

Department of Defense (DOD) and Chairman of the Joint Chiefs of Staff (CJCS) directives delegate authorities to DOD components. Among these directives, Department of Defense Directive 3600.01, *Information Operations*, is the principal IO policy document. Its joint counterpart, Chairman of the Joint Chiefs of Staff Instruction 3210.01, *Joint Information Operations Policy,* provides joint policy regarding the use of IRCs, professional qualifications for the joint IO force, as well as joint IO education and training requirements. Based upon the contents of these two documents, authority to conduct joint IO is vested in the combatant commander (CCDR), who in turn can delegate operational authority to a subordinate JFC, as appropriate.

*Responsibilities*

**Under Secretary of Defense for Policy** oversees and manages DOD-level IO programs and activities.

**Under Secretary of Defense for Intelligence** develops, coordinates, and oversees the implementation of DOD intelligence policy, programs, and guidance for intelligence activities supporting IO.

**Joint Staff.** As the Joint IO Proponent, the Deputy Director for Global Operations (J-39 DDGO) serves as the CJCS's focal point for IO and coordinates with the Joint Staff, CCMDs, and other organizations that have direct or supporting IO responsibilities.

**Joint Information Operations Warfare Center (JIOWC)** is a CJCS controlled activity reporting to the operations directorate of a joint staff via J-39 DDGO. The JIOWC supports the Joint Staff by ensuring operational integration of IRCs in support of IO, improving DOD's ability to meet CCMD IRC requirements, as well as developing and refining IRCs for use in support of IO across DOD.

**Combatant Commands.** The Unified Command Plan provides guidance to CCDRs, assigning them missions and force structure, as well as geographic or functional areas of responsibility. In addition to these responsibilities, the Commander, United States Special Operations Command, is also responsible for integrating and coordinating MISO. This responsibility is focused on enhancing interoperability and providing other CCDRs with MISO planning and execution capabilities. In similar fashion, the Commander, United States Strategic Command is responsible for advocating on behalf of the IRCs of electronic warfare and CO.

**Service component command** responsibilities include recommending to the JFC the proper employment of the Service component IRCs in support of joint IO.

Like Service component commands, **functional component commands** have authority over forces or in the case of IO, IRCs, as delegated by the establishing authority (normally a CCDR or JFC).

***Legal Considerations***

IO planners deal with legal considerations of an extremely diverse and complex nature. For this reason, joint IO planners should consult their staff judge advocate or legal advisor for expert advice.

## Integrating Information-Related Capabilities into the Joint Operation Planning Process

*Information Operations Planning*

The IO cell chief is responsible to the JFC for integrating IRCs into the joint operation planning process (JOPP). Thus, the IO staff is responsible for coordinating and synchronizing IRCs to accomplish the JFC's objectives. The IO cell chief ensures joint IO planners adequately represent the IO cell within the joint planning group and other JFC planning processes. Doing so will help ensure that IRCs are integrated with all planning efforts. As part of JOPP, designation of release and execution authorities for IRCs is required. Normally, the JFC is designated in the execution order as the execution authority. Given the fact that IRC effects are often required across multiple operational phases, each capability requires separate and distinct authorities.

*Information Operations Phasing and Synchronization*

Through its contributions to the GCC's theater campaign plan, it is clear that joint IO is expected to play a major role in all phases of joint operations. This means that the GCC's IO staff and IO cell must account for logical transitions from phase to phase, as joint IO moves from the main effort to a supporting effort.

## Multinational Information Operations

*Other Nations and Information Operations*

Multinational partners recognize a variety of information concepts and possess sophisticated doctrine, procedures, and capabilities. Given these potentially diverse perspectives regarding IO, it is essential for the multinational force commander (MNFC) to resolve potential conflicts as soon as possible. It is vital to integrate multinational partners into IO planning as early as possible to gain agreement on an integrated and achievable IO strategy.

*Multinational Organization for Information Operations Planning*

When the JFC is also the MNFC, the joint force staff should be augmented by planners and subject matter experts from the multinational force (MNF). MNF IO planners and IRC specialists should be trained on US and MNF doctrine, requirements, resources, and how the MNF is structured to integrate IRCs. IO planners should seek to accommodate the requirements of each multinational partner, within given constraints, with the goal of using all the available expertise and capabilities of the MNF.

***Multinational Policy Coordination***

**The Joint Staff coordinates US positions on IO matters** delegated to them as a matter of law or policy, and discusses them bilaterally, or in multinational organizations, to achieve interoperability and compatibility in fulfilling common requirements. Direct discussions regarding multinational IO planning in specific theaters are the responsibility of the GCC.

## Information Operations Assessment

***Information Operations assessment is iterative, continuously repeating rounds of analysis within the operations cycle in order to measure the progress of information related capabilities toward achieving objectives.***

Assessment of IO is a key component of the commander's decision cycle, helping to determine the results of tactical actions in the context of overall mission objectives and providing potential recommendations for refinement of future plans. Assessments also provide opportunities to identify IRC shortfalls, changes in parameters and/or conditions in the information environment, which may cause unintended effects in the employment of IRCs, and resource issues that may be impeding joint IO effectiveness.

***The Information Operations Assessment Process***

A solution to these assessment requirements is the eight-step assessment process.

- Focused characterization of the information environment
- Integrate information operations assessment into plans and develop the assessment plan
- Develop information operations assessment information requirements and collection plans
- Build/modify information operations assessment baseline
- Coordinate and execute information operations and collection activities

- Monitor and collect focused information environment data for information operations assessment
- Analyze information operations assessment data
- Report information operations assessment results and recommendations

*Measures and Indicators*

Measures of performance (MOPs) and measures of effectiveness (MOEs) help accomplish the assessment process by qualifying or quantifying the intangible attributes of the information environment. The MOP for any one action should be whether or not the TA was exposed to the IO action or activity. MOEs should be observable, to aid with collection; quantifiable, to increase objectivity; precise, to ensure accuracy; and correlated with the progress of the operation, to attain timeliness. Indicators are crucial because they aid the joint IO planner in informing MOEs and should be identifiable across the center of gravity critical factors.

*Considerations*

Assessment teams may not have direct access to a TA for a variety of reasons. The goal of measurement is not to achieve perfect accuracy or precision—given the ever present biases of theory and the limitations of tools that exist—but rather, to reduce uncertainty about the value being measured.

## CONCLUSION

This publication provides joint doctrine for the planning, preparation, execution, and assessment of information operations across the range of military operations.

Intentionally Blank

# CHAPTER I
# OVERVIEW

> *"The most hateful human misfortune is for a wise man to have no influence."*
>
> **Greek Historian Herodotus, 484-425 BC**

## 1. Introduction

a. The growth of communication networks has decreased the number of isolated populations in the world. The emergence of advanced wired and wireless information technology facilitates global communication by corporations, violent extremist organizations, and individuals. The ability to share information in near real time, anonymously and/or securely, is a capability that is both an asset and a potential vulnerability to us, our allies, and our adversaries. Information is a powerful tool to influence, disrupt, corrupt, or usurp an adversary's ability to make and share decisions.

b. The instruments of national power (diplomatic, informational, military, and economic) provide leaders in the United States with the means and ways of dealing with crises around the world. Employing these means in the information environment requires the ability to securely transmit, receive, store, and process information in near real time. The nation's state and non-state adversaries are equally aware of the significance of this new technology, and will use information-related capabilities (IRCs) to gain advantages in the information environment, just as they would use more traditional military technologies to gain advantages in other operational environments. These realities have transformed the information environment into a battlefield, which poses both a threat to the Department of Defense (DOD), combatant commands (CCMDs), and Service components and serves as a force multiplier when leveraged effectively.

c. As the strategic environment continues to change, so does IO. Based on these changes, the Secretary of Defense now characterizes IO as the integrated employment, during military operations, of IRCs in concert with other lines of operation to influence, disrupt, corrupt, or usurp the decision making of adversaries and potential adversaries while protecting our own. This revised characterization has led to a reassessment of how essential the information environment can be and how IRCs can be effectively integrated into joint operations to create effects and operationally exploitable conditions necessary for achieving the joint force commander's (JFC's) objectives.

## 2. The Information Environment

The information environment is the aggregate of individuals, organizations, and systems that collect, process, disseminate, or act on information. This environment consists of three interrelated dimensions which continuously interact with individuals, organizations, and systems. These dimensions are the physical, informational, and cognitive (see Figure I-1). The JFC's operational environment is the composite of the conditions, circumstances, and influences that affect employment of capabilities and bear on the decisions of the commander

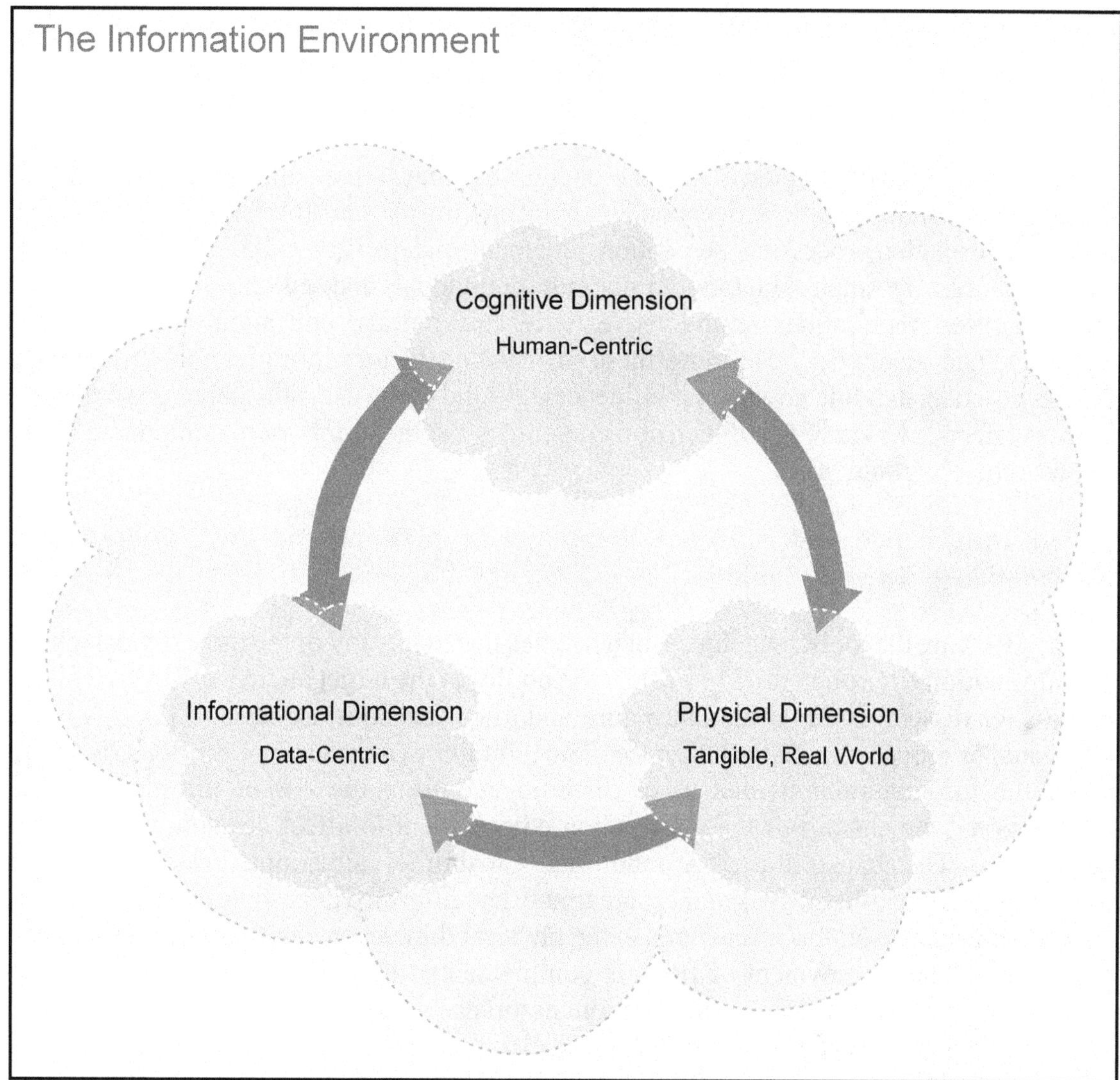


**Figure I-1. The Information Environment**

(encompassing physical areas and factors of the air, land, maritime, and space domains) as well as the information environment (which includes cyberspace).

a. **The Physical Dimension.** The physical dimension is composed of command and control (C2) systems, key decision makers, and supporting infrastructure that enable individuals and organizations to create effects. It is the dimension where physical platforms and the communications networks that connect them reside. The physical dimension includes, but is not limited to, human beings, C2 facilities, newspapers, books, microwave towers, computer processing units, laptops, smart phones, tablet computers, or any other objects that are subject to empirical measurement. The physical dimension is not confined solely to military or even nation-based systems and processes; it is a defused network connected across national, economic, and geographical boundaries.

b. **The Informational Dimension.** The informational dimension encompasses where and how information is collected, processed, stored, disseminated, and protected. It is the dimension where the C2 of military forces is exercised and where the commander's intent is conveyed. Actions in this dimension affect the content and flow of information.

c. **The Cognitive Dimension.** The cognitive dimension encompasses the minds of those who transmit, receive, and respond to or act on information. It refers to individuals' or groups' information processing, perception, judgment, and decision making. These elements are influenced by many factors, to include individual and cultural beliefs, norms, vulnerabilities, motivations, emotions, experiences, morals, education, mental health, identities, and ideologies. Defining these influencing factors in a given environment is critical for understanding how to best influence the mind of the decision maker and create the desired effects. As such, this dimension constitutes the most important component of the information environment.

## 3. The Information and Influence Relational Framework and the Application of Information-Related Capabilities

a. IRCs are the tools, techniques, or activities that affect any of the three dimensions of the information environment. They affect the ability of the target audience (TA) to collect, process, or disseminate information before and after decisions are made. The TA is the individual or group selected for influence. The joint force (means) employs IRCs (ways) to affect the information provided to or disseminated from the TA in the physical and informational dimensions of the information environment to affect decision making (see Figure I-2). The change in the TA conditions, capabilities, situational awareness, and in some cases, the inability to make and share timely and informed decisions, contributes to the desired end state. Actions or inactions in the physical dimension can be assessed for future operations. The employment of IRCs is complemented by a set of capabilities such as operations security (OPSEC), information assurance (IA), counterdeception, physical security, electronic warfare (EW) support, and electronic protection. These capabilities are critical to enabling and protecting the JFC's C2 of forces. Key components in this process are:

(1) **Information.** Data in context to inform or provide meaning for action.

(2) **Data.** Interpreted signals that can reduce uncertainty or equivocality.

(3) **Knowledge.** Information in context to enable direct action. Knowledge can be further broken down into the following:

(a) **Explicit Knowledge.** Knowledge that has been articulated through words, diagrams, formulas, computer programs, and like means.

(b) **Tacit Knowledge.** Knowledge that cannot be or has not been articulated through words, diagrams, formulas, computer programs, and like means.

(4) **Influence.** The act or power to produce a desired outcome or end on a TA.

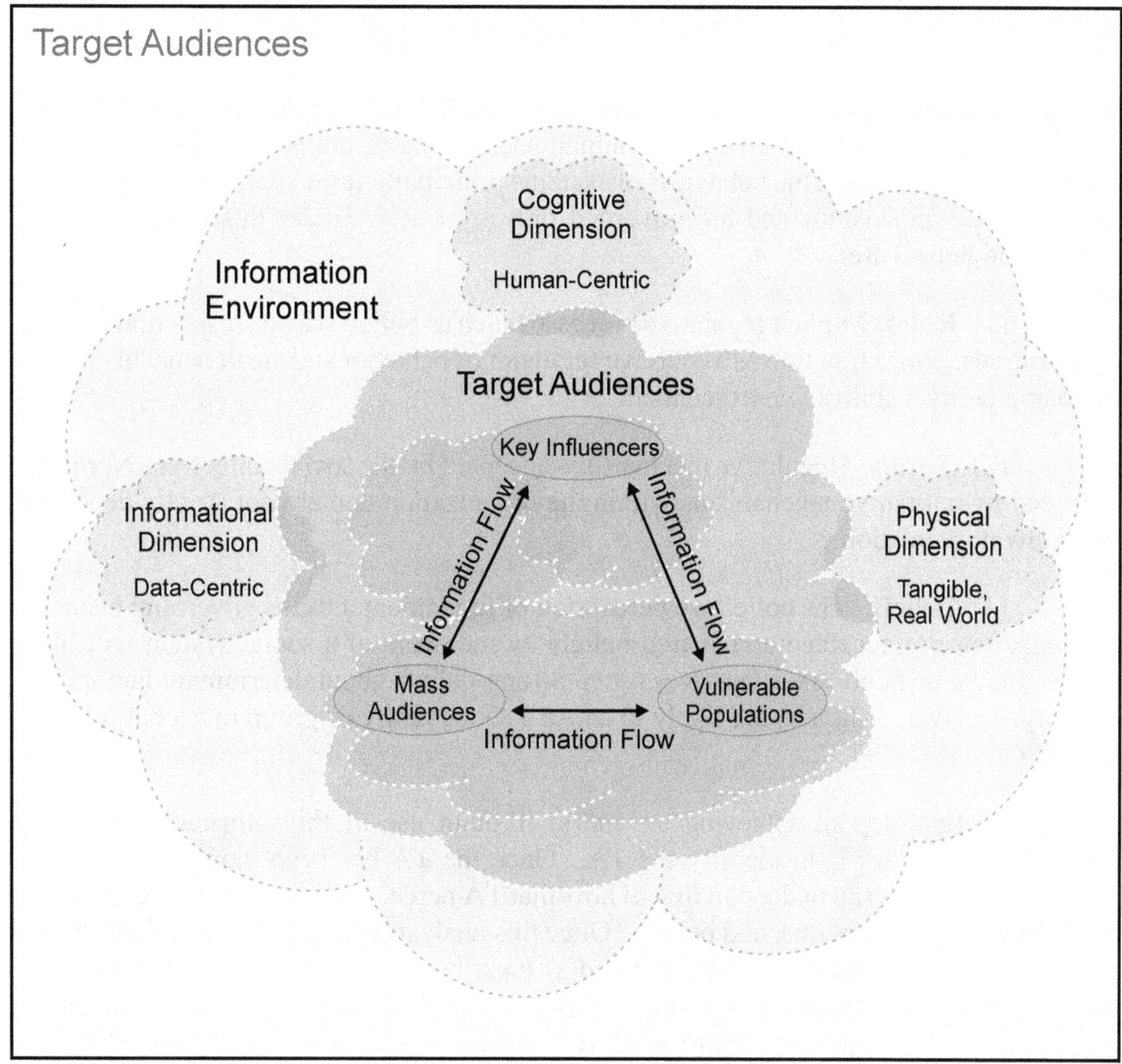


**Figure I-2. Target Audiences**

(5) **Means.** The resources available to a national government, non-nation actor, or adversary in pursuit of its end(s). These resources include, but are not limited to, public- and private-sector enterprise assets or entities.

(6) **Ways.** How means can be applied, in order to achieve a desired end(s). They can be characterized as persuasive or coercive.

(7) **Information-Related Capabilities.** Tools, techniques, or activities using data, information, or knowledge to create effects and operationally desirable conditions within the physical, informational, and cognitive dimensions of the information environment.

(8) **Target Audience.** An individual or group selected for influence.

(9) **Ends.** A consequence of the way of applying IRCs.

(10) Using the framework, the physical, informational, and cognitive dimensions of the information environment provide access points for influencing TAs (see Figure I-2).

b. The purpose of integrating the employment of IRCs is to influence a TA. While the behavior of individuals and groups, as human social entities, are principally governed by rules, norms, and beliefs, the behaviors of systems principally reside within the physical and informational dimensions and are governed only by rules. Under this construct, rules, norms, and beliefs are:

(1) **Rules.** Explicit regulative processes such as policies, laws, inspection routines, or incentives. Rules function as a coercive regulator of behavior and are dependent upon the imposing entity's ability to enforce them.

(2) **Norms.** Regulative mechanisms accepted by the social collective. Norms are enforced by normative mechanisms within the organization and are not strictly dependent upon law or regulation.

(3) **Beliefs.** The collective perception of fundamental truths governing behavior. The adherence to accepted and shared beliefs by members of a social system will likely persist and be difficult to change over time. Strong beliefs about determinant factors (i.e., security, survival, or honor) are likely to cause a social entity or group to accept rules and norms.

c. The first step in achieving an end(s) through use of the information-influence relational framework is to identify the TA. Once the TA has been identified, it will be necessary to develop an understanding of how that TA perceives its environment, to include analysis of TA rules, norms, and beliefs. Once this analysis is complete, the application of means available to achieve the desired end(s) must be evaluated (see Figure I-3). Such means may include (but are not limited to) diplomatic, informational, military, or economic actions, as well as academic, commercial, religious, or ethnic pronouncements. When the specific means or combinations of means are determined, the next step is to identify the specific ways to create a desired effect.

d. Influencing the behavior of TAs requires producing effects in ways that modify rules, norms, or beliefs. Effects can be created by means (e.g., governmental, academic, cultural, and private enterprise) using specific ways (i.e., IRCs) to affect how the TAs collect, process, perceive, disseminate, and act (or do not act) on information (see Figure I-4).

e. Upon deciding to persuade or coerce a TA, the commander must then determine what IRCs it can apply to individuals, organizations, or systems in order to produce a desired effect(s) (see Figure I-5). As stated, IRCs can be capabilities, techniques, or activities, but they do not necessarily have to be technology-based. Additionally, it is important to focus on the fact that IRCs may come from a wide variety of sources. **Therefore, in IO, it is not the ownership of the capabilities and techniques that is important, but rather their integrated application in order to achieve a JFC's end state.**

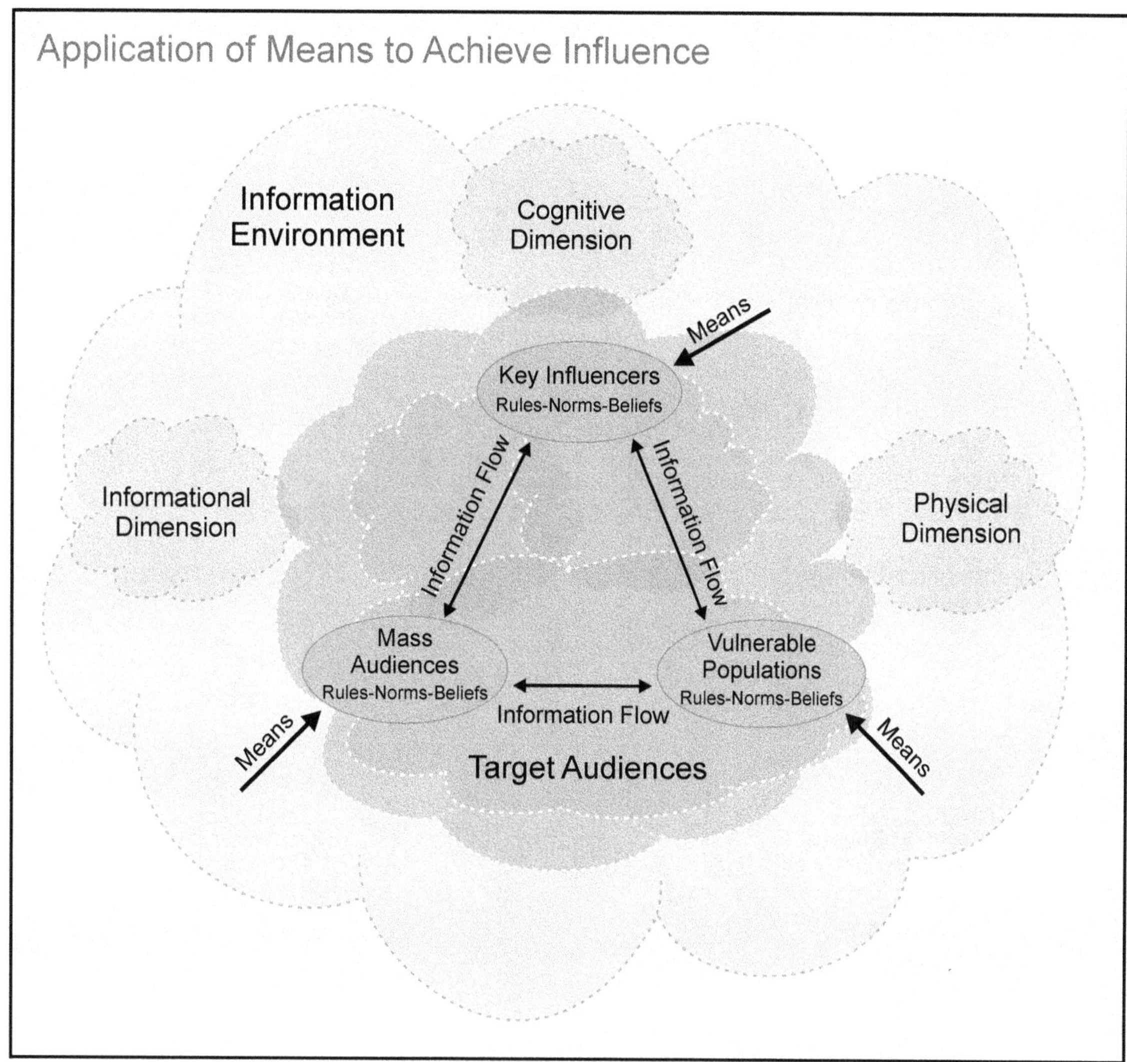


**Figure I-3. Application of Means to Achieve Influence**

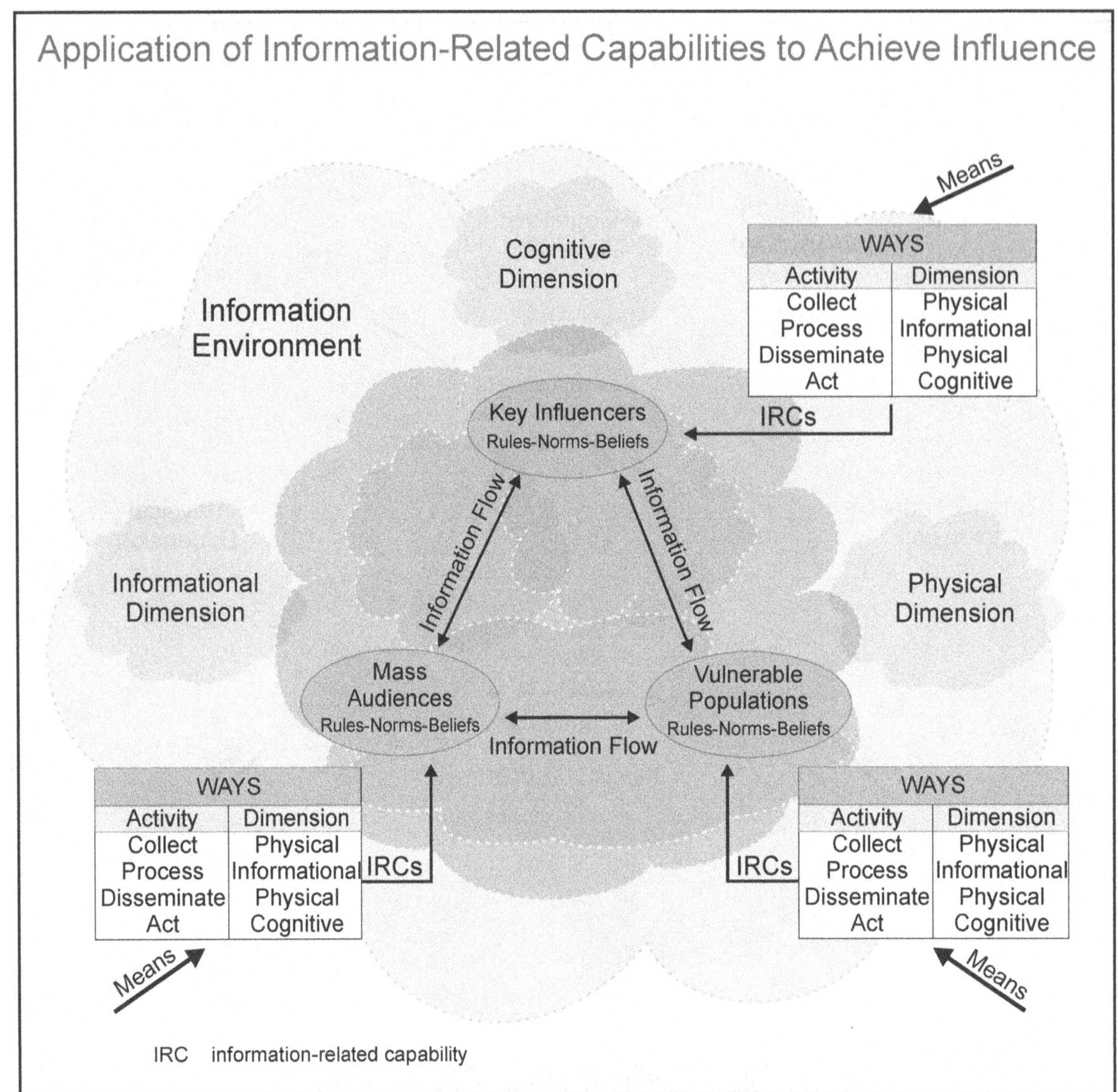


**Figure I-4. Application of Information-Related Capabilities to Achieve Influence**

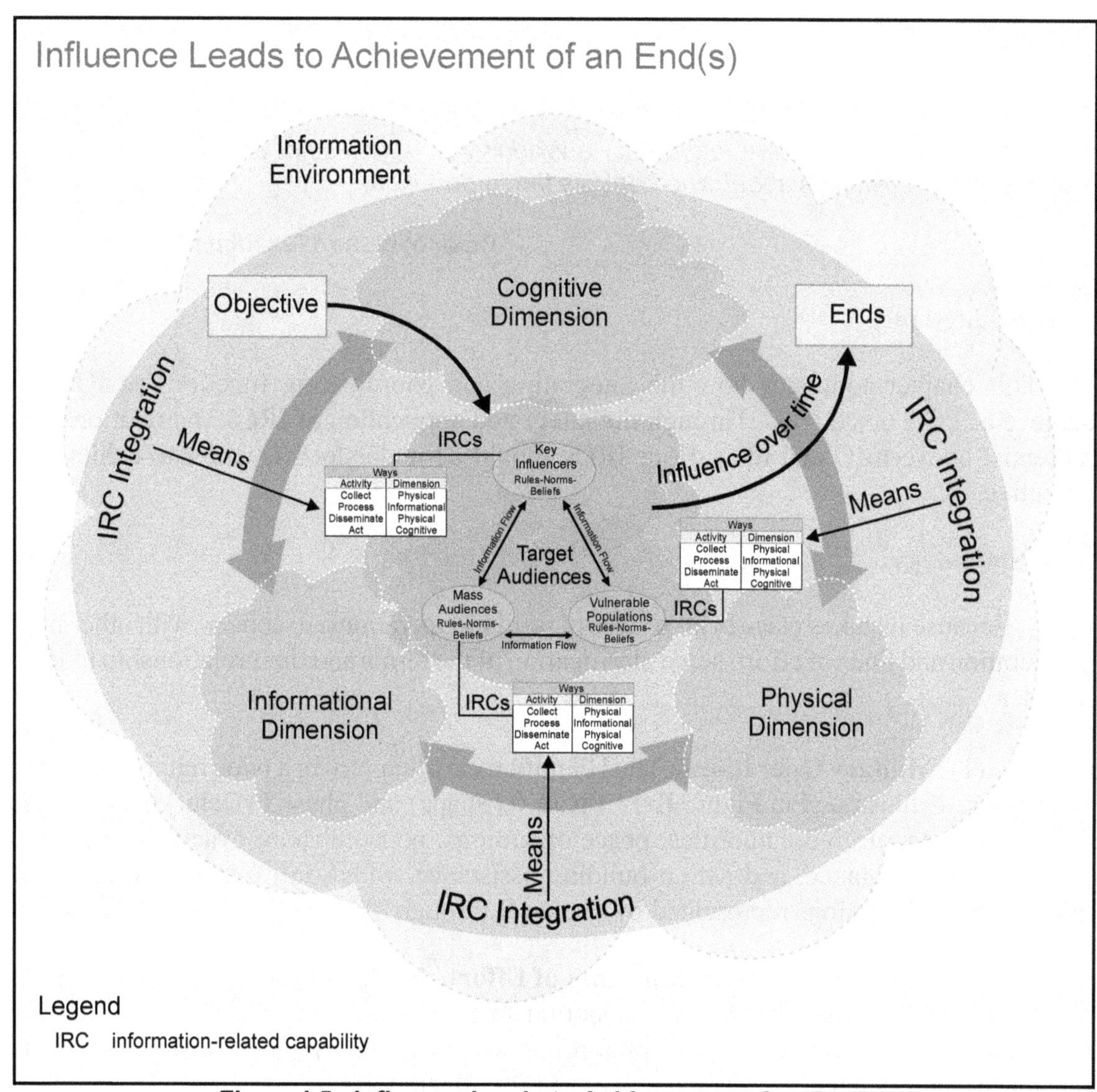


**Figure I-5. Influence Leads to Achievement of an End(s)**

# CHAPTER II
## INFORMATION OPERATIONS

*"There is a war out there, old friend- a World War. And it's not about whose got the most bullets; it's about who controls the information."*

**Cosmo, in the 1992 Film "Sneakers"**

### 1. Introduction

This chapter addresses how the integrating and coordinating functions of IO help achieve a JFC's objectives. Through the integrated application of IRCs, the relationships that exist between IO and the various IRCs should be understood in order to achieve an objective.

### 2. Terminology

a. Because IO takes place in all phases of military operations, in concert with other lines of operation and lines of effort, some clarification of the terms and their relationship to IO is in order.

(1) **Military Operations.** The US military participates in a wide range of military operations, as illustrated in Figure II-1. Phase 0 (Shape) and phase I (Deter) may include defense support of civil authorities, peace operations, noncombatant evacuation, foreign humanitarian assistance, and nation-building assistance, which fall outside the realm of major combat operations represented by phases II through V.

(2) **Lines of Operation and Lines of Effort.** IO should support multiple lines of operation and at times may be the supported line of operation. IO may also support numerous lines of effort when positional references to an enemy or adversary have little relevance, such as in counterinsurgency or stability operations.

b. IO integrates IRCs (ways) with other lines of operation and lines of effort (means) to create a desired effect on an adversary or potential adversary to achieve an objective (ends).

### 3. Information Operations and the Information-Influence Relational Framework

Influence is at the heart of diplomacy and military operations, with integration of IRCs providing a powerful means for influence. The relational framework describes the application, integration, and synchronization of IRCs to influence, disrupt, corrupt, or usurp the decision making of TAs to create a desired effect to support achievement of an objective. Using this description, the following example illustrates how IRCs can be employed to create a specific effect against an adversary or potential adversary.

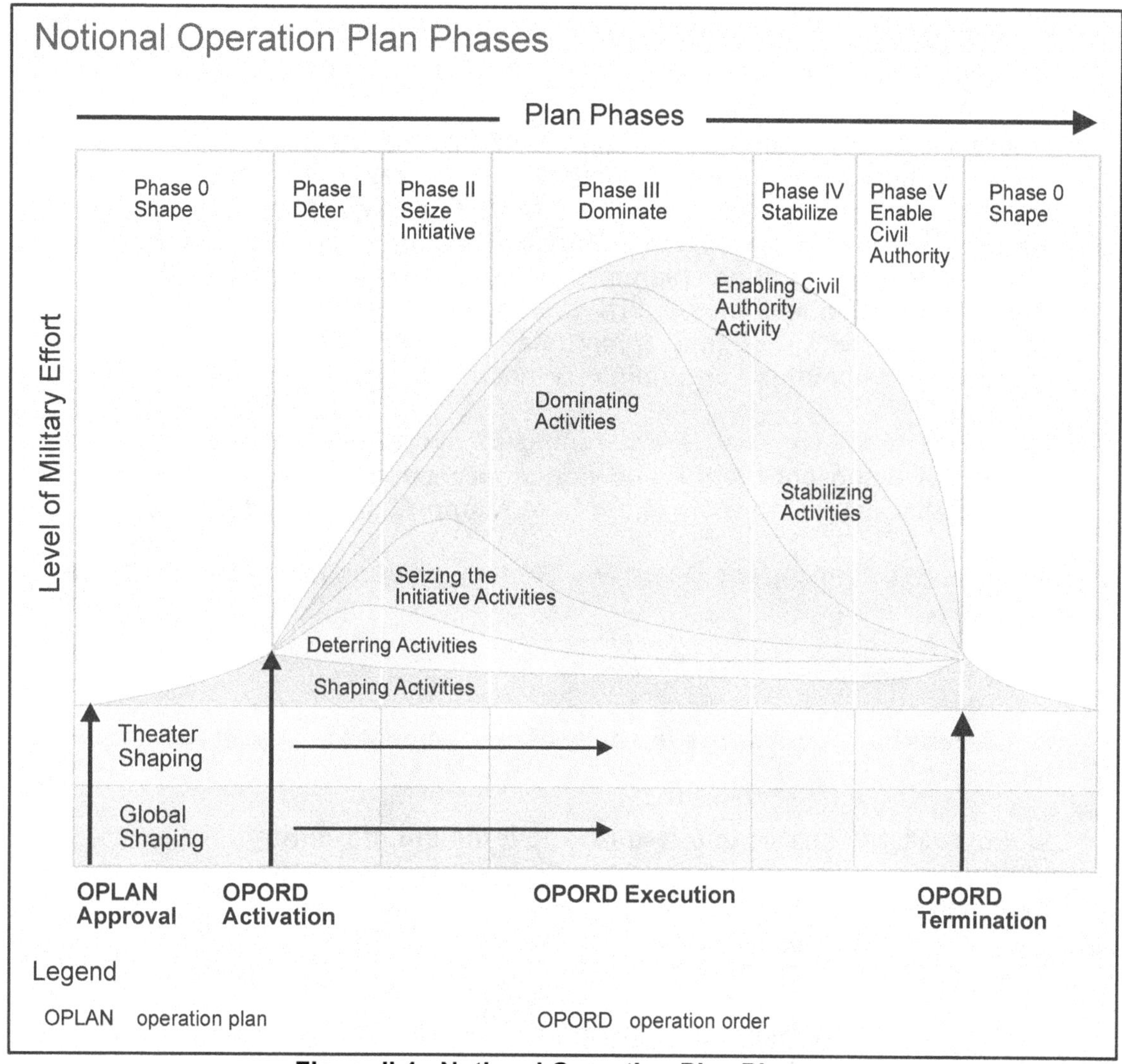


**Figure II-1. Notional Operation Plan Phases**

## 4. The Information Operations Staff and Information Operations Cell

Within the joint community, the integration of IRCs to achieve the commander's objectives is managed through an IO staff or IO cell. JFCs may establish an IO staff to provide command-level oversight and collaborate with all staff directorates and supporting organizations on all aspects of IO. Most CCMDs include an IO staff to serve as the focal point for IO. Faced with an ongoing or emerging crisis within a geographic combatant commander's (GCC's) area of responsibility (AOR), a JFC can establish an IO cell to provide additional expertise and coordination across the staff and interagency.

**APPLICATION OF INFORMATION-RELATED CAPABILITIES TO THE INFORMATION AND INFLUENCE RELATIONAL FRAMEWORK**

**This example provides insight as to how information-related capabilities (IRCs) can be used to create lethal and nonlethal effects to support achievement of the objectives to reach the desired end state. The integration and synchronization of these IRCs require participation from not just information operations planners, but also organizations across multiple lines of operation and lines of effort. They may also include input from or coordination with national ministries, provincial governments, local authorities, and cultural and religious leaders to create the desired effect.**

**Situation: An adversary is attempting to overthrow the government of Country X using both lethal and nonlethal means to demonstrate to the citizens that the government is not fit to support and protect its people.**

**Joint Force Commander's Objective: Protect government of Country X from being overthrown.**

**Desired Effects:**

**1. Citizens have confidence in ability of government to support and protect its people.**

**2. Adversary is unable to overthrow government of Country X.**

**Potential Target Audience(s):**

**1. Adversary leadership (adversary).**

**2. Country X indigenous population (friendly, neutral, and potential adversary).**

**Potential <u>Means</u> available to achieve the commander's objective:**

- **Diplomatic action (e.g., demarche, public diplomacy)**
- **Informational assets (e.g., strategic communication, media)**
- **Military forces (e.g., security force assistance, combat operations, military information support operations, public affairs, military deception)**
- **Economic resources (e.g., sanctions against the adversary, infusion of capital to Country X for nation building)**
- **Commercial, cultural, or other private enterprise assets**

**Potential <u>Ways</u> (persuasive communications or coercive force):**

- **Targeted radio and television broadcasts**
- **Blockaded adversary ports**
- **Government/commercially operated Web sites**
- **Key leadership engagement**

**Regardless of the means and ways employed by the players within the information environment, the reality is that the strategic advantage rests with whoever applies their means and ways most efficiently.**

a. **IO Staff**

(1) In order to provide planning support, the IO staff includes IO planners and a complement of IRCs specialists to facilitate seamless integration of IRCs to support the JFC's concept of operations (CONOPS).

(2) IRC specialists can include, but are not limited to, personnel from the EW, cyberspace operations (CO), military information support operations (MISO), civil-military operations (CMO), military deception (MILDEC), intelligence, and public affairs (PA) communities. They provide valuable linkage between the planners within an IO staff and those communities that provide IRCs to facilitate seamless integration with the JFC's objectives.

b. **IO Cell**

(1) The IO cell integrates and synchronizes IRCs, to achieve national or combatant commander (CCDR) level objectives. Normally, the chief of the CCMD's IO staff will serve as the IO cell chief; however, at the joint task force level, someone else may serve as the IO cell chief. Some of the functions of the IO cell chief are listed in Figure II-2.

(2) The IO cell comprises representatives from a wide variety of organizations to coordinate and integrate additional activities in support of a JFC. When considering the notional example in Figure II-3, note that the specific makeup of an IO cell depends on the situation. It may include representatives from organizations outside DOD, even allied or multinational partners.

**Information Operations Cell Chief Functions**

- Coordinate the overall information operations (IO) portion of the plan for the joint force commander (JFC).
- Coordinate IO issues within the joint force staff and with counterpart IO planners on the component staffs and supporting organizations.
- Coordinate employment of information-related capabilities and activities to support the JFC concept of operations.
- Recommend IO priorities to accomplish planned objectives.
- Determine the availability of information-related capability resources to carry out IO plans.
- Request planning support from organizations that plan and execute information-related capabilities.
- Serve as the primary "advocate" throughout the target nomination and review process for targets that, if engaged, will create a desired effect within the information environment.
- Coordinate the planning and execution of information-related capabilities among joint organizations (including components) and agencies that support IO objectives.
- Identify and coordinate intelligence and assessment requirements that support IO planning and associated activities.
- Coordinate support with the Joint Information Operations Warfare Center, Joint Warfare Analysis Center, and other joint centers and agencies.

**Figure II-2. Information Operations Cell Chief Functions**

## 5. Relationships and Integration

a. IO is not about ownership of individual capabilities but rather the use of those capabilities as force multipliers to create a desired effect. There are many military capabilities that contribute to IO and should be taken into consideration during the planning process.

(1) **Strategic Communication (SC)**

(a) The SC process consists of focused United States Government (USG) efforts to create, strengthen, or preserve conditions favorable for the advancement of national interests, policies, and objectives by understanding and engaging key audiences through the use of coordinated programs, plans, themes, messages, and products synchronized with the actions of all instruments of national power. SC is a whole-of-government approach, driven by interagency processes and integration that are focused upon effectively communicating national strategy.

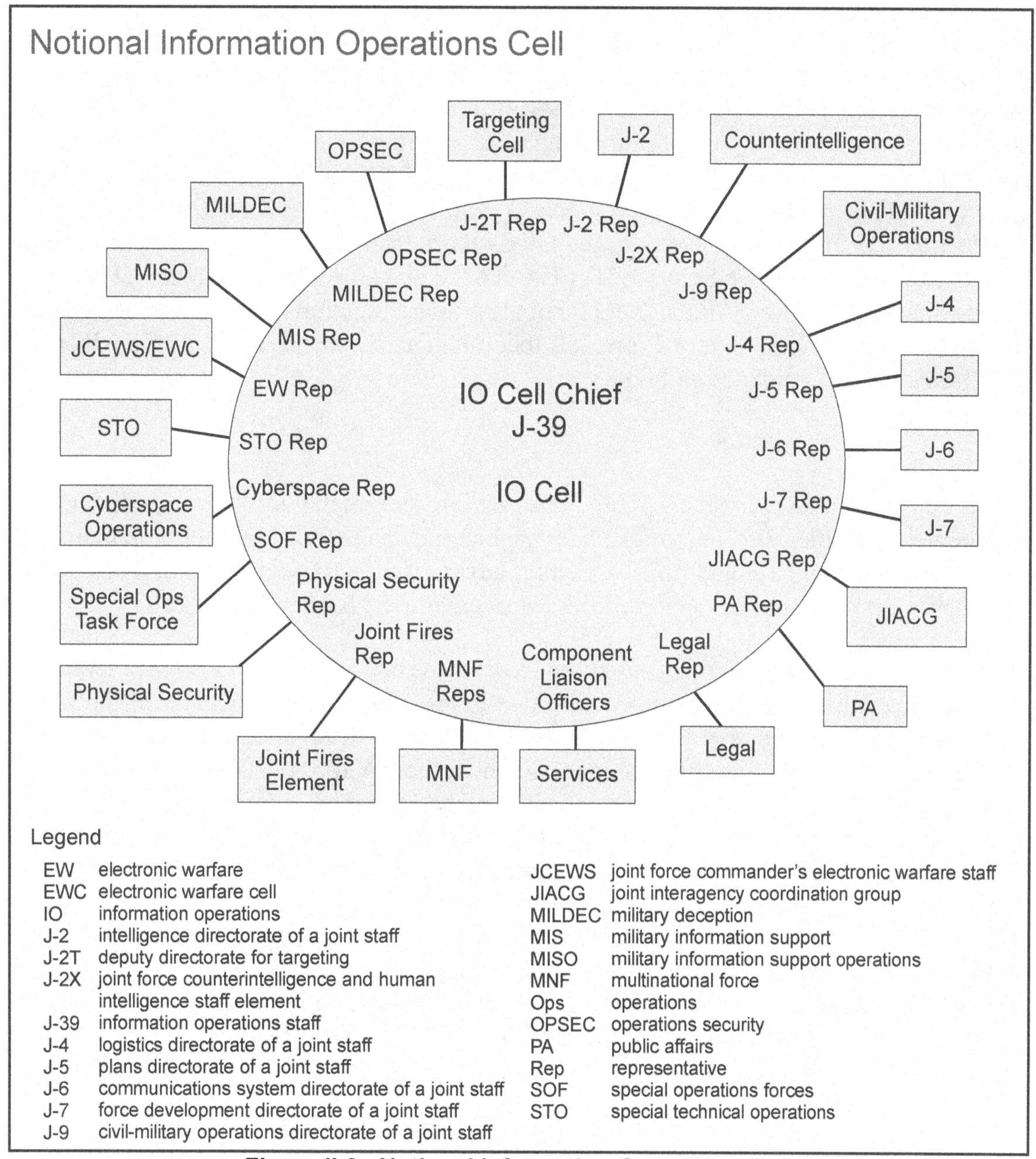


**Figure II-3. Notional Information Operations Cell**

(b) The elements and organizations that implement strategic guidance, both internal and external to the joint force, must not only understand and be aware of the joint force's IO objectives; they must also work closely with members of the interagency community, in order to ensure full coordination and synchronization of USG efforts. Hence, the JFC's IO objectives should complement the overall objectives in accordance with strategic guidance. The joint interagency coordination group (JIACG) representative within the IO cell facilitates coordination to comply with strategic guidance and facilitate SC.

(2) **Joint Interagency Coordination Group.** Interagency coordination occurs between DOD and other USG departments and agencies, as well as with private-sector entities, nongovernmental organizations, and critical infrastructure activities, for the purpose of accomplishing national objectives. Many of these objectives require the combined and coordinated use of the diplomatic, informational, military, and economic instruments of national power. Due to their forward presence, the CCMDs are well situated to coordinate activities with elements of the USG, regional organizations, foreign forces, and host nations. In order to accomplish this function, the GCCs have established JIACGs as part of their normal staff structures (see Figure II-4). The JIACG is well suited to help the IO cell with interagency coordination. Although IO is not the primary function of the JIACG, the group's linkage to the IO cell and the rest of the interagency is an important enabler for synchronization of guidance and IO.

(3) **Public Affairs**

(a) PA comprises public information, command information, and public engagement activities directed toward both the internal and external publics with interest in DOD. External publics include allies, neutrals, adversaries, and potential adversaries. When addressing external publics, opportunities for overlap exist between PA and IO.

(b) By maintaining situational awareness between IO and PA the potential for information conflict can be minimized. The IO cell provides an excellent place to coordinate IO and PA activities that may affect the adversary or potential adversary. Because there will be situations, such as counterpropaganda, in which the TA for both IO and PA converge, close cooperation and deconfliction are extremely important. Such coordination and deconfliction efforts can begin in the IO cell. However, since it involves more than just IO equities, final coordination should occur within the joint planning group (JPG).

(c) While the IO cell can help synchronize and deconflict specific IO-related and PA objectives, when implementing strategic guidance that affects the adversary, care must be taken to carefully follow all legal and policy constraints in conducting the different activities. For example, see Department of Defense Directive (DODD) S-3321.1, *Overt Psychological Operations Conducted by the Military Services in Peacetime and in Contingencies Short of Declared War.*

(4) **Civil-Military Operations**

(a) CMO is another area that can directly affect and be affected by IO. CMO activities establish, maintain, influence, or exploit relations between military forces, governmental and nongovernmental civilian organizations and authorities, and the civilian populace in a friendly, neutral, or hostile operational area in order to achieve US objectives. These activities may occur prior to, during, or subsequent to other military operations. In CMO, personnel perform functions normally provided by the local, regional, or national government, placing them into direct contact with civilian populations. This level of interaction results in CMO having a significant effect on the perceptions of the local populace. Since this populace may include potential adversaries, their perceptions are of great interest to the IO community. For this reason, CMO representation in the IO cell can

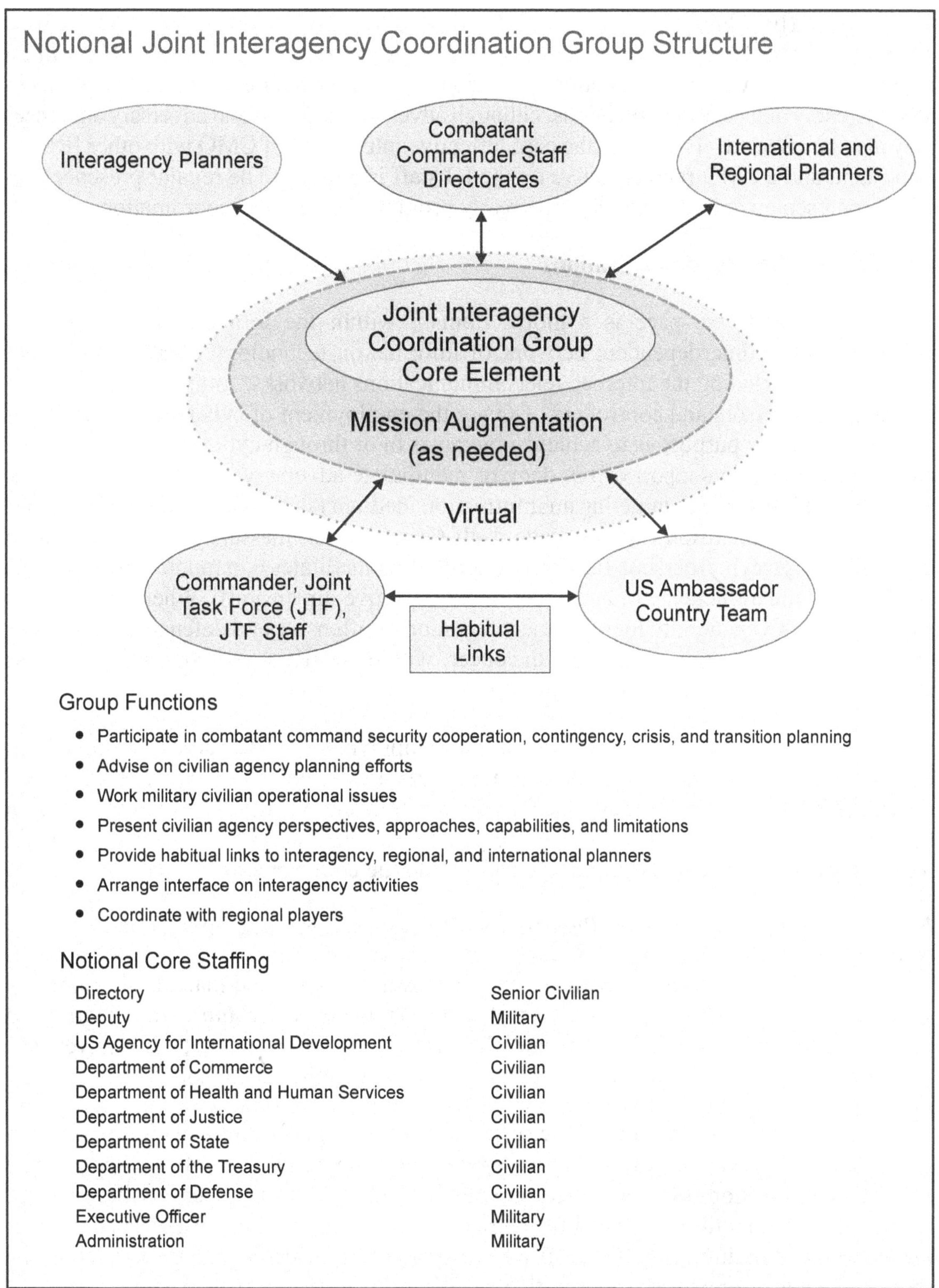


**Figure II-4. Notional Joint Interagency Coordination Group Structure**

assist in identifying TAs; synchronizing communications media, assets, and messages; and providing news and information to the local population.

(b) Although CMO and IO have much in common, they are distinct disciplines. The TA for much of IO is the adversary; however, the effects of IRCs often reach supporting friendly and neutral populations as well. In a similar vein, CMO seeks to affect friendly and neutral populations, although adversary and potential adversary audiences may also be affected. This being the case, effective integration of CMO with other IRCs is important, and a CMO representative on the IO staff is critical. The regular presence of a CMO representative in the IO cell will greatly promote this level of coordination.

(5) **Cyberspace Operations**

(a) Cyberspace is a global domain within the information environment consisting of the interdependent network of information technology infrastructures and resident data, including the Internet, telecommunications networks, computer systems, and embedded processors and controllers. CO are the employment of cyberspace capabilities where the primary purpose is to achieve objectives in or through cyberspace. Cyberspace capabilities, when in support of IO, deny or manipulate adversary or potential adversary decision making, through targeting an information medium (such as a wireless access point in the physical dimension), the message itself (an encrypted message in the information dimension), or a cyber-persona (an online identity that facilitates communication, decision making, and the influencing of audiences in the cognitive dimension). When employed in support of IO, CO generally focus on the integration of offensive and defensive capabilities exercised in and through cyberspace, in concert with other IRCs, and coordination across multiple lines of operation and lines of effort.

(b) As a process that integrates the employment of IRCs across multiple lines of effort and lines of operation to affect an adversary or potential adversary decision maker, IO can target either the medium (a component within the physical dimension such as a microwave tower) or the message itself (e.g., an encrypted message in the informational dimension). CO is one of several IRCs available to the commander.

*For more information, see Joint Publication (JP) 3-12,* Cyberspace Operations.

(6) **Information Assurance.** IA is necessary to gain and maintain information superiority. The JFC relies on IA to protect infrastructure to ensure its availability, to position information for influence, and for delivery of information to the adversary. Furthermore, IA and CO are interrelated and rely on each other to support IO.

(7) **Space Operations.** Space capabilities are a significant force multiplier when integrated with joint operations. Space operations support IO through the space force enhancement functions of intelligence, surveillance, and reconnaissance; missile warning; environmental monitoring; satellite communications; and space-based positioning, navigation, and timing. The IO cell is a key place for coordinating and deconflicting the space force enhancement functions with other IRCs.

(8) **Military Information Support Operations.** MISO are planned operations to convey selected information and indicators to foreign audiences to influence their emotions, motives, objective reasoning, and ultimately the behavior of foreign governments,

organizations, groups, and individuals. MISO focuses on the cognitive dimension of the information environment where its TA includes not just potential and actual adversaries, but also friendly and neutral populations. MISO are applicable to a wide range of military operations such as stability operations, security cooperation, maritime interdiction, noncombatant evacuation, foreign humanitarian operations, counterdrug, force protection, and counter-trafficking. Given the wide range of activities in which MISO are employed, the military information support representative within the IO cell should consistently interact with the PA, CMO, JIACG, and IO planners.

(9) **Intelligence**

(a) Intelligence is a vital military capability that supports IO. The utilization of information operations intelligence integration (IOII) greatly facilitates understanding the interrelationship between the physical, informational, and cognitive dimensions of the information environment.

(b) By providing population-centric socio-cultural intelligence and physical network lay downs, including the information transmitted via those networks, intelligence can greatly assist IRC planners and IO integrators in determining the proper effect to elicit the specific response desired. Intelligence is an integrated process, fusing collection, analysis, and dissemination to provide products that will expose a TA's potential capabilities or vulnerabilities. Intelligence uses a variety of technical and nontechnical tools to assess the information environment, thereby providing insight into a TA.

(c) A joint intelligence support element (JISE) may establish an IO support office (see Figure II-5) to provide IOII. This is due to the long lead time needed to establish information baseline characterizations, provide timely intelligence during IO planning and execution efforts, and to properly assess effects in the information environment. In addition to generating intelligence products to support the IO cell, the JISE IO support office can also work with the JISE collection management office to facilitate development of collection requirements in support of IO assessment efforts.

(10) **Military Deception**

(a) One of the oldest IRCs used to influence an adversary's perceptions is MILDEC. MILDEC can be characterized as actions executed to deliberately mislead adversary decision makers, creating conditions that will contribute to the accomplishment of the friendly mission. While MILDEC requires a thorough knowledge of an adversary or potential adversary's decision-making processes, it is important to remember that it is focused on desired behavior. It is not enough to simply mislead the adversary or potential adversary; MILDEC is designed to cause them to behave in a manner advantageous to the friendly mission, such as misallocation of resources, attacking at a time and place advantageous to friendly forces, or avoid taking action at all.

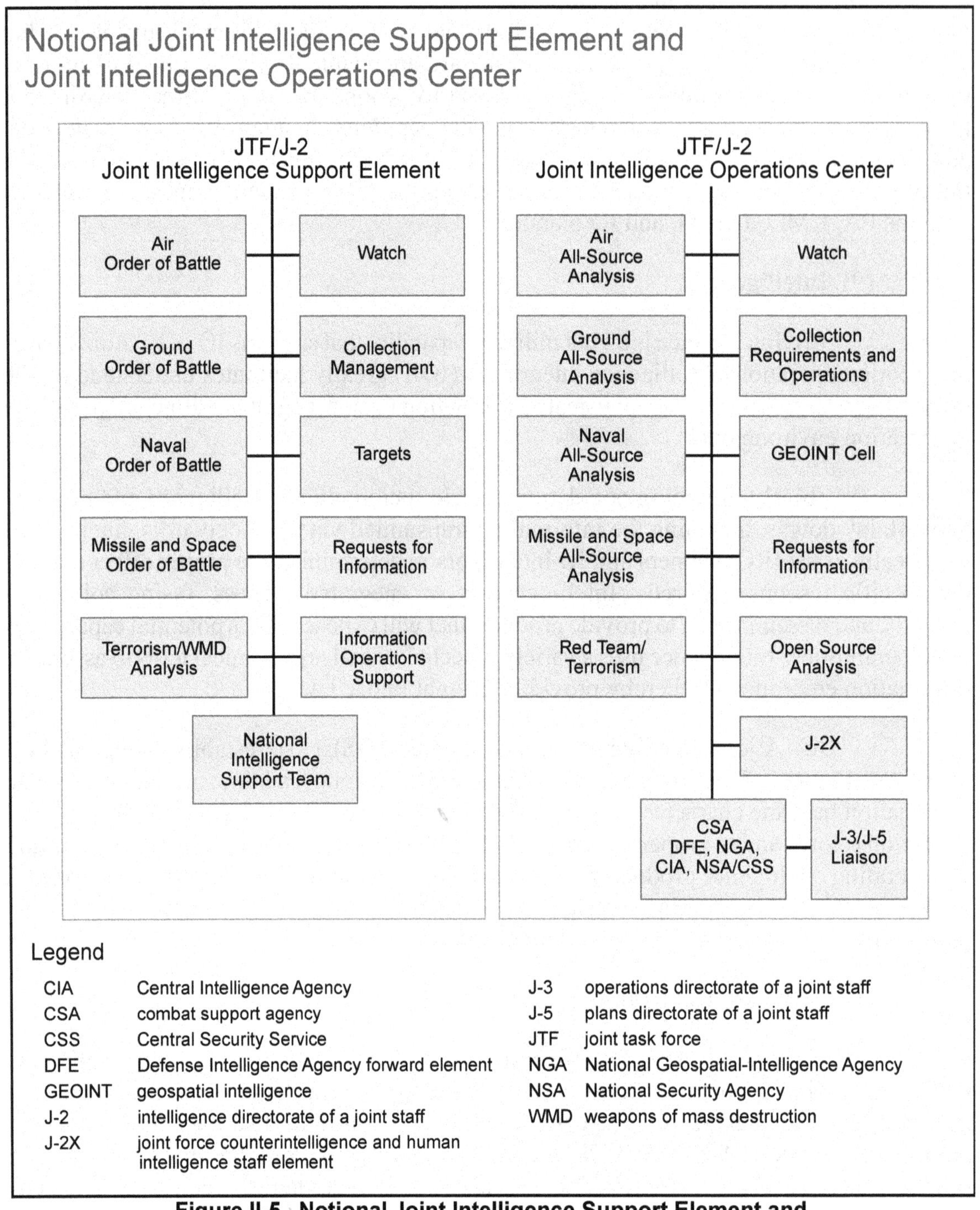


**Figure II-5. Notional Joint Intelligence Support Element and Joint Intelligence Operations Center**

(b) When integrated with other IRCs, MILDEC can be a particularly powerful way to affect the decision-making processes of an adversary or potential adversary. The IO cell provides a coordinating mechanism for enabling or integrating MILDEC with other IRCs.

(c) MILDEC differs from other IRCs in several ways. Due to the sensitive nature of MILDEC plans, goals, and objectives, a strict need-to-know should be enforced.

(11) **Operations Security**

(a) OPSEC is a standardized process designed to meet operational needs by mitigating risks associated with specific vulnerabilities in order to deny adversaries critical information and observable indicators. OPSEC identifies critical information and actions attendant to friendly military operations to deny observables to adversary intelligence systems. Once vulnerabilities are identified, other IRCs (e.g., MILDEC, CO) can be used to satisfy OPSEC requirements. OPSEC practices must balance the responsibility to account to the American public with the need to protect critical information. The need to practice OPSEC should not be used as an excuse to deny noncritical information to the public.

(b) The effective application, coordination, and synchronization of other IRCs are critical components in the execution of OPSEC. Because a specified IO task is "to protect our own" decision makers, OPSEC planners require complete situational awareness, regarding friendly activities to facilitate the safeguarding of critical information. This kind of situational awareness exists within the IO cell, where a wide range of planners work in concert to integrate and synchronize their actions to achieve a common IO objective.

(12) **Special Technical Operations (STO).** IO need to be deconflicted and synchronized with STO. Detailed information related to STO and its contribution to IO can be obtained from the STO planners at CCMD or Service component headquarters. IO and STO are separate, but have potential crossover, and for this reason an STO planner is a valuable member of the IO cell.

(13) **Joint Electromagnetic Spectrum Operations (JEMSO)**

(a) All information-related mission areas increasingly depend on the electromagnetic spectrum (EMS). JEMSO, consisting of EW and joint EMS management operations, enable EMS-dependent systems to function in their intended operational environment. EW is the mission area ultimately responsible for securing and maintaining freedom of action in the EMS for friendly forces while exploiting or denying it to adversaries. JEMSO therefore supports IO by enabling successful mission area operations.

(b) EW activities are normally planned and managed by personnel dedicated to JEMSO and members of either the joint force commander's electronic warfare staff (JCEWS) or joint electronic warfare cell (EWC). The JCEWS or EWC integrates their efforts into the JFC's targeting cycle and coordinates with, the JFC's IO cell to align objective priorities and help synchronize EW employment with other IRCs.

*For more information on EW, see JP 3-13.1,* Electronic Warfare. *For more information on JEMSO, see JP 6-01,* Joint Electromagnetic Spectrum Management Operations.

(14) **Key Leader Engagement (KLE)**

(a) KLEs are deliberate, planned engagements between US military leaders and the leaders of foreign audiences that have defined objectives, such as a change in policy or supporting the JFC's objectives. These engagements can be used to shape and influence foreign leaders at the strategic, operational, and tactical levels, and may also be directed toward specific groups such as religious leaders, academic leaders, and tribal leaders; e.g., to solidify trust and confidence in US forces.

(b) KLEs may be applicable to a wide range of operations such as stability operations, counterinsurgency operations, noncombatant evacuation operations, security cooperation activities, and humanitarian operations. When fully integrated with other IRCs into operations, KLEs can effectively shape and influence the leaders of foreign audiences.

b. The capabilities discussed above do not constitute a comprehensive list of all possible capabilities that can contribute to IO. This means that individual capability ownership will be highly diversified. The ability to access these capabilities will be directly related to how well commanders understand and appreciate the importance of IO.

Intentionally Blank

# CHAPTER III
## AUTHORITIES, RESPONSIBILITIES, AND LEGAL CONSIDERATIONS

> *"Well may the boldest fear and the wisest tremble when incurring responsibilities on which may depend our country's peace and prosperity."*
>
> **President James K. Polk, 1845 Inaugural Address**

### 1. Introduction

This chapter describes the JFC's authority for the conduct of IO; delineates various roles and responsibilities established in DODD 3600.01, *Information Operations;* and addresses legal considerations in the planning and execution of IO.

### 2. Authorities

a. The authority to employ IRCs is rooted foremost in Title 10, United States Code (USC). While Title 10, USC, does not specify IO separately, it does provide the legal basis for the roles, missions, and organization of DOD and the Services. Title 10, USC, Section 164, gives command authority over assigned forces to the CCDR, which provides that individual with the authority to organize and employ commands and forces, assign tasks, designate objectives, and provide authoritative direction over all aspects of military operations.

b. DOD and Chairman of the Joint Chiefs of Staff (CJCS) directives delegate authorities to DOD components. Among these directives, DODD 3600.01, *Information Operations*, is the principal IO policy document. Its joint counterpart, Chairman of the Joint Chiefs of Staff Instruction (CJCSI) 3210.01, *Joint Information Operations Policy,* provides joint policy regarding the use of IRCs, professional qualifications for the joint IO force, as well as joint IO education and training requirements. Based upon the contents of these two documents, authority to conduct joint IO is vested in the CCDR, who in turn can delegate operational authority to a subordinate JFC, as appropriate.

c. The nature of IO is such that the exercise of operational authority inherently requires a detailed and rigorous legal interpretation of authority and/or legality of specific actions. Legal considerations are addressed in more detail later in this chapter.

### 3. Responsibilities

a. **Under Secretary of Defense for Policy (USD[P]).** The USD(P) oversees and manages DOD-level IO programs and activities. In this capacity, USD(P) manages guidance publications (e.g., DODD 3600.01) and all IO policy on behalf of the Secretary of Defense. The office of the USD(P) coordinates IO for all DOD components in the interagency process.

b. **Under Secretary of Defense for Intelligence (USD[I]).** USD(I) develops, coordinates, and oversees the implementation of DOD intelligence policy, programs, and guidance for intelligence activities supporting IO.

c. **Joint Staff.** In accordance with the Secretary of Defense memorandum on *Strategic Communication and Information Operations in the DOD*, dated 25 January 2011, the Joint Staff is assigned the responsibility for joint IO proponency. CJCS responsibilities for IO are both general (such as establishing doctrine, as well as providing advice, and recommendations to the President and Secretary of Defense) and specific (e.g., joint IO policy). As the Joint IO Proponent, the Deputy Director for Global Operations (J-39 DDGO) serves as the CJCS's focal point for IO and coordinates with the Joint Staff, CCMDs, and other organizations that have direct or supporting IO responsibilities. Joint Staff J-39 DDGO also provides IO-related advice and advocacy on behalf of the CCMDs to the CJCS and across DOD. As designated in the Secretary of Defense memorandum on SC and IO, the Joint Staff also serves as the proponent for the IRCs of MILDEC and OPSEC.

d. **Joint Information Operations Warfare Center (JIOWC).** The JIOWC is a CJCS-controlled activity reporting to the operations directorate of a joint staff (J-3) via J-39 DDGO. The JIOWC supports the Joint Staff by ensuring operational integration of IRCs in support of IO, improving DOD's ability to meet CCMD IRC requirements, as well as developing and refining IRCs for use in support of IO across DOD. JIOWC's specific organizational responsibilities include:

(1) Provide IO subject matter experts and advice to the Joint Staff and the CCMDs.

(2) Develop and maintain a joint IO assessment framework.

(3) Assist the Joint IO Proponent in advocating for and integrating CCMD IO requirements.

(4) Upon the direction of the Joint IO Proponent, provide support in coordination and integration of DOD IRCs for JFCs, Service component commanders, and DOD agencies.

e. **Combatant Commands.** The Unified Command Plan provides guidance to CCDRs, assigning them missions and force structure, as well as geographic or functional areas of responsibility. In addition to these responsibilities, the Commander, United States Special Operations Command, is also responsible for integrating and coordinating MISO. This responsibility is focused on enhancing interoperability and providing other CCDRs with MISO planning and execution capabilities. In similar fashion, the Commander, United States Strategic Command (USSTRATCOM) is responsible for advocating on behalf of the IRCs of EW and CO. The Commander, USSTRATCOM, is also focused on enhancing interoperability and providing other CCDRs with contingency EW expertise in support of their missions. For CO, the Commander, USSTRATCOM, synchronizes CO planning. CCDRs integrate, plan, execute, and assess IO when conducting operations or campaigns.

f. **Service Component Commands.** Service component command responsibilities are derived from their parent Service. These responsibilities include recommending to the JFC the proper employment of the Service component IRCs in support of joint IO. The JFC will execute IO using component capabilities.

g. **Functional Component Commands.** Like Service component commands, functional component commands have authority over forces or in the case of IO, IRCs, as delegated by the establishing authority (normally a CCDR or JFC). Functional component commands may be tasked to plan and execute IO as an integrated part of joint operations.

## 4. Legal Considerations

a. **Introduction.** US military activities in the information environment, as with all military operations, are conducted as a matter of law and policy. Joint IO will always involve legal and policy questions, requiring not just local review, but often national-level coordination and approval. The US Constitution, laws, regulations, and policy, and international law set boundaries for all military activity, to include IO. Whether physically operating from locations outside the US or virtually from any location in the information environment, US forces are required by law and policy to act in accordance with US law and the law of war.

b. **Legal Considerations.** IO planners deal with legal considerations of an extremely diverse and complex nature. Legal interpretations can occasionally differ, given the complexity of technologies involved, the significance of legal interests potentially affected, and the challenges inherent for law and policy to keep pace with the technological changes and implementation of IRCs. Additionally, policies are regularly added, amended, and rescinded in an effort to provide clarity. As a result, IO remains a dynamic arena, which can be further complicated by multinational operations, as each nation has its own laws, policies, and processes for approving plans. The brief discussion in this publication is not a substitute for sound legal advice regarding specific IRC- and IO-related activities. For this reason, joint IO planners should consult their staff judge advocate or legal advisor for expert advice.

c. **Implications Beyond the JFC.** Bilateral agreements to which the US is a signatory may have provisions concerning the conduct of IO as well as IRCs when they are used in support of IO. IO planners at all levels should consider the following broad areas within each planning iteration in consultation with the appropriate legal advisor:

(1) Could the execution of a particular IRC be considered a hostile act by an adversary or potential adversary?

(2) Do any non-US laws concerning national security, privacy, or information exchange, criminal and/or civil issues apply?

(3) What are the international treaties, agreements, or customary laws recognized by an adversary or potential adversary that apply to IRCs?

(4) How is the joint force interacting with or being supported by US intelligence organizations and other interagency entities?

Intentionally Blank

# CHAPTER IV
# INTEGRATING INFORMATION-RELATED CAPABILITIES INTO THE JOINT OPERATION PLANNING PROCESS

> *"Support planning is conducted in parallel with other planning and encompasses such essential factors as IO [information operations], SC [strategic communication]..."*
>
> **Joint Publication 5-0, *Joint Operation Planning*, 11 August 2011**

## 1. Introduction

The IO cell chief is responsible to the JFC for integrating IRCs into the joint operation planning process (JOPP). Thus, the IO staff is responsible for coordinating and synchronizing IRCs to accomplish the JFC's objectives. Coordinated IO are essential in employing the elements of operational design. Conversely, uncoordinated IO efforts can compromise, complicate, negate, and pose risks to the successful accomplishment of the JFC and USG objectives. Additionally, when uncoordinated, other USG and/or multinational information activities, may complicate, defeat, or render DOD IO ineffective. For this reason, the JFC's objectives require early detailed IO staff planning, coordination, and deconfliction between the USG and partner nations' efforts within the AOR, in order to effectively synchronize and integrate IRCs.

## 2. Information Operations Planning

a. **The IO cell and the JPG.** The IO cell chief ensures joint IO planners adequately represent the IO cell within the JPG and other JFC planning processes. Doing so will help ensure that IRCs are integrated with all planning efforts. Joint IO planners should be integrated with the joint force planning, directing, monitoring, and assessing process.

b. **IO Planning Considerations**

(1) IO planners seek to create an operational advantage that results in coordinated effects that directly support the JFC's objectives. IRCs can be executed throughout the operational environment, but often directly impact the content and flow of information.

(2) IO planning begins at the **earliest stage** of JOPP and must be an integral part of, not an addition to, the overall planning effort. IRCs can be used in all phases of a campaign or operation, but their effective employment during the shape and deter phases can have a significant impact on remaining phases.

(3) The use of IO to achieve the JFC's objectives requires the ability to integrate IRCs and interagency support into a comprehensive and coherent strategy that supports the JFC's overall mission objectives. The GCC's theater security cooperation guidance contained in the theater campaign plan (TCP) serves as an excellent platform to embed specific long-term information objectives during phase 0 operations. For this reason, the IO

staff and IO cell should work closely with their plans directorate staff as well as the JIACG in the development of the security cooperation portion of the TCP.

(4) Many IRCs require long lead time for development of the joint intelligence preparation of the operational environment (JIPOE) and release authority. The intelligence directorate of a joint staff (J-2) identifies intelligence and information gaps, shortfalls, and priorities as part of the JIPOE process in the early stages of the JOPP. Concurrently, the IO cell must identify similar intelligence gaps in its understanding of the information environment to determine if it has sufficient information to successfully plan IO. Where identified shortfalls exist, the IO cell may need to work with J-2 to submit requests for information (RFIs) to the J-2 to fill gaps that cannot be filled internally.

(5) There may be times where the JFC may lack sufficient detailed intelligence data and intelligence staff personnel to provide IOII. Similarly, a JFC's staff may lack dedicated resources to provide support. For this reason, it is imperative the IO cell take a proactive approach to intelligence support. The IO cell must also review and provide input to the commander's critical information requirements (CCIRs), especially priority intelligence requirements (PIRs) and information requirements. The joint intelligence staff, using PIRs as a basis, develops information requirements that are most critical. These are also known as essential elements of information (EEIs). In the course of mission analysis, the intelligence analyst identifies the intelligence required to CCIRs. Intelligence staffs develop more specific questions known as information requirements. EEIs pertinent to the IO staff may include target information specifics, such as messages and counter-messages, adversary propaganda, and responses of individuals, groups, and organizations to adversary propaganda.

(6) As part of JOPP, designation of release and execution authorities for IRCs is required. For example, release authority provides approval for the employment of specific IRCs in support of a commander's objectives and normally specifies the allocation of specific offensive means and IRCs. For its part, the execution authority constitutes the authority to employ IRCs. Normally, the JFC is designated in the execution order as the execution authority. Given the fact that IRC effects are often required across multiple operational phases, each capability requires separate and distinct authorities.

c. **IO and the Joint Operation Planning Process**

Throughout JOPP, IRCs are integrated with the JFC's overall CONOPS (see Figure IV-1). An overview of the seven steps of JOPP follow; however, a more detailed discussion of the planning process can be found in JP 5-0, *Joint Operation Planning.*

(1) **Planning Initiation.** Integration of IRCs into joint operations should begin at step 1, planning initiation. Key IO staff actions during this step include the following:

(a) Review key strategic documents.

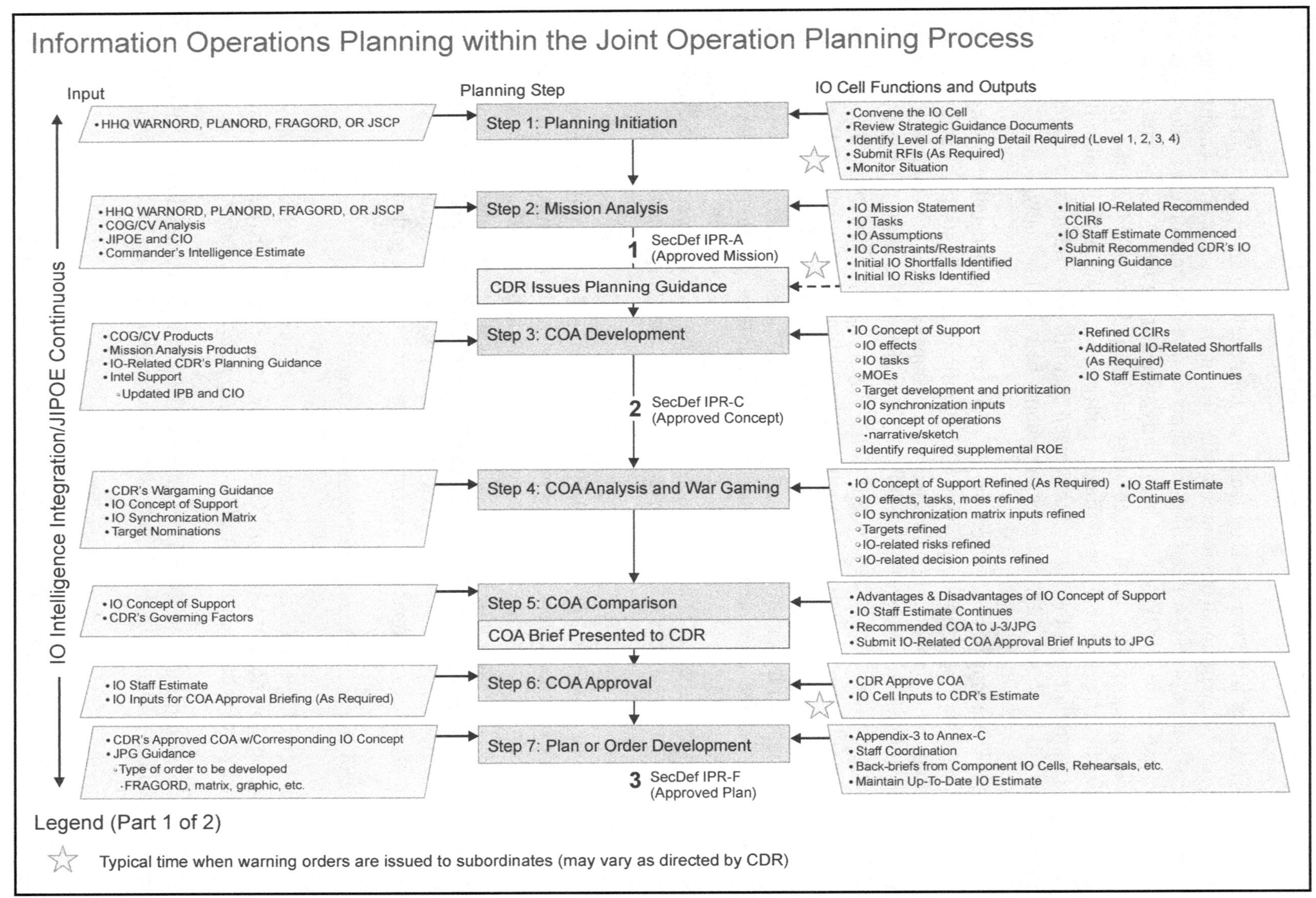


**Figure IV-1. Information Operations Planning within the Joint Operation Planning Process**

## Information Operations Planning within the Joint Operation Planning Process (continued)

Legend (Part 2 of 2)

| | | | |
|---|---|---|---|
| CCIR | commander's critical information requirement | J-3 | operations directorate of a joint staff |
| CDR | commander | JIPOE | joint intelligence preparation of the operational environment |
| CIO | combined information overlay | JPG | joint planning group |
| COA | course of action | JSCP | Joint Strategic Capabilities Plan |
| COG | center of gravity | MOE | measure of effectiveness |
| CV | critical vulnerability | PLANORD | planning order |
| FRAGORD | fragmentary order | RFI | request for information |
| HHQ | higher headquarters | ROE | rules of engagement |
| IPB | intelligence preparation of the battlespace | SecDef | Secretary of Defense |
| IPR | in-progress review | WARNORD | warning order |
| IO | information operations | | |

**Figure IV-1. Information Operations Planning within the Joint Operation Planning Process (cont'd)**

(b) Monitor the situation, receive initial planning guidance, and review staff estimates from applicable operation plans (OPLANs) and concept plans (CONPLANs).

(c) Alert subordinate and supporting commanders of potential tasking with regard to IO planning support.

(d) Gauge initial scope of IO required for the operation.

(e) Identify location, standard operating procedures, and battle rhythm of other staff organizations that require integration and divide coordination responsibilities among the IO staff.

(f) Identify and request appropriate authorities.

(g) Begin identifying information required for mission analysis and course of action (COA) development.

(h) Identify IO planning support requirements (including staff augmentation, support products, and services) and issue requests for support according to procedures established locally and by various supporting organizations.

(i) Validate, initiate, and revise PIRs and RFIs, keeping in mind the long lead times associated with satisfying IO requirements.

(j) Provide IO input and recommendations to COAs, and provide resolutions to conflicts that exist with other plans or lines of operation.

(k) In coordination with the targeting cell, submit potential candidate targets to JFC or component joint targeting coordination board (JTCB). For vetting, validation, and deconfliction follow local targeting cell procedures because these three separate processes do not always occur at the JTCB.

(l) Ensure IO staff and IO cell members participate in all JFC or component planning and targeting sessions and JTCBs.

(2) **Mission Analysis.** The purpose of step 2, mission analysis, is to understand the problem and purpose of an operation and issue the appropriate guidance to drive the remaining steps of the planning process. The end state of mission analysis is a clearly defined mission and thorough staff assessment of the joint operation. Mission analysis orients the JFC and staff on the problem and develops a common understanding, before moving forward in the planning process. During mission analysis, all staff sections, including the IO cell, will examine the mission from their own functional perspective and contribute the results of that analysis to the JPG. As IO impacts each element of the operational environment, it is important for the IO staff and IO cell during mission analysis to remain focused on the information environment. Key IO staff actions during mission analysis are:

(a) Assist the J-3 and J-2 in the identification of friendly and adversary center(s) of gravity and critical factors (e.g., critical capabilities, critical requirements, and critical vulnerabilities).

(b) Identify relevant aspects of the physical, informational, and cognitive dimensions (whether friendly, neutral, adversary, or potential adversary) of the information environment.

(c) Identify specified, implied, and essential tasks.

(d) Identify facts, assumptions, constraints, and restraints affecting IO planning.

(e) Analyze IRCs available to support IO and authorities required for their employment.

(f) Develop and refine proposed PIRs, RFIs, and CCIRs.

(g) Conduct initial IO-related risk assessment.

(h) Develop IO mission statement.

(i) Begin developing the initial IO staff estimate. This estimate forms the basis for the IO cell chief's recommendation to the JFC, regarding which COA it can best support.

(j) Conduct initial force allocation review.

(k) Identify and develop potential targets and coordinate with the targeting cell no later than the end of target development. Compile and maintain target folders in the Modernized Integrated Database. Coordinate with the J-2 and targeting cell for participation and representation in vetting, validation, and targeting boards (e.g., JTCB, joint targeting working group).

(l) Develop mission success criteria.

(3) **COA Development.** Output from mission analysis, such as initial staff estimates, mission and tasks, and JFC planning guidance are used in step 3, COA development. Key IO staff actions during this step include the following:

(a) Identify desired and undesired effects that support or degrade JFC's information objectives.

(b) Develop measures of effectiveness (MOEs) and measures of effectiveness indicators (MOEIs).

(c) Develop tasks for recommendation to the J-3.

(d) Recommend IRCs that may be used to accomplish supporting information tasks for each COA.

(e) Analyze required supplemental rules of engagement (ROE).

(f) Identify additional operational risks and controls/mitigation.

(g) Develop the IO CONOPS narrative/sketch.

(h) Synchronize IRCs in time, space, and purpose.

(i) Continue update/development of the IO staff estimate.

(j) Prepare inputs to the COA brief.

(k) Provide inputs to the target folder.

(4) **COA Analysis and War Gaming.** Based upon time available, the JFC staff should war game each tentative COA against adversary COAs identified through the JIPOE process. Key IO staff and IO cell actions during this step include the following:

(a) Analyze each COA from an IO functional perspective.

(b) Reveal key decision points.

(c) Recommend task adjustments to IRCs as appropriate.

(d) Provide IO-focused data for use in a synchronization matrix or other decision-making tool.

(e) Identify IO portions of branches and sequels.

(f) Identify possible high-value targets related to IO.

(g) Submit PIRs and recommend CCIRs for IO.

(h) Revise staff estimate.

(i) Assess risk.

(5) **COA Comparison.** Step 5, COA comparison, starts with all staff elements analyzing and evaluating the advantages and disadvantages of each COA from their respective viewpoints. Key IO staff and IO cell actions during this step include the following:

(a) Compare each COA based on mission and tasks.

(b) Compare each COA in relation to IO requirements versus available IRCs.

(c) Prioritize COAs from an IO perspective.

(d) Revise the IO staff estimate. During execution, the IO cell should maintain an estimate and update as required.

(6) **COA Approval.** Just like other elements of the JFC's staff, during step 6, COA approval, the IO staff provides the JFC with a clear recommendation of how IO can best contribute to mission accomplishment in the COA(s) being briefed. It is vital this recommendation is presented in a clear, concise manner that is not only able to be quickly grasped by the JFC, but can also be easily understood by peer, subordinate, and higher-headquarters command and staff elements. Failure to foster such an understanding of IO contribution to the approved COA can lead to poor execution and/or coordination of IRCs in subsequent operations.

(7) **Plan or Order Development.** Once a COA is selected and approved, the IO staff develops appendix 3 (Information Operations) to annex C (Operations) of the operation order (OPORD) or OPLAN. Because IRC integration is documented elsewhere in the OPORD or OPLAN, it is imperative that the IO staff conduct effective staff coordination within the JPG during step 7, plan or order development. Key staff actions during this step include the following:

(a) Refine tasks from the approved COA.

(b) Identify shortfalls of IRCs and recommend solutions.

(c) Facilitate development of supporting plans by keeping the responsible organizations informed of relevant details (as access restrictions allow) throughout the planning process.

(d) Advise the supported commander on IO issues and concerns during the supporting plan review and approval process.

(e) Participate in time-phased force and deployment data refinement to ensure IO supports the OPLAN or CONPLAN.

(f) Assist in the development of OPLAN or CONPLAN appendix 6 (IO Intelligence Integration) to annex B (Intelligence).

d. **Plan Refinement.** The information environment is continuously changing and it is critical for IO planners to remain in constant interaction with the JPG to provide updates to OPLANs or CONPLANs.

e. **Assessment of IO.** Assessment is integrated into all phases of the planning and execution cycle, and consists of assessment activities associated with tasks, events, or programs in support of joint military operations. Assessment seeks to analyze and inform on the performance and effectiveness of activities. The intent is to provide relevant feedback to decision makers in order to modify activities that achieve desired results. Assessment can also provide the programmatic community with relevant information that informs on return on investment and operational effectiveness of DOD IRCs. It is important to note that integration of assessment into planning is the first step of the assessment process. Planning for assessment is part of broader operational planning, rather than an afterthought. Iterative in nature, assessment supports the Adaptive Planning and Execution process, and provides feedback to operations and ultimately, IO enterprise programmatics.

*For more on assessments, see JP 5-0,* Joint Operation Planning.

f. **Relationship Between Measures of Performance (MOPs) and MOEs.** Effectiveness assessment is one of the greatest challenges facing a staff. Despite the continuing evolution of joint and Service doctrine and the refinement of supporting tactics, techniques, and procedures, assessing the effectiveness of IRCs continues to be challenging. MOEs attempt to accomplish this assessment by quantifying the intangible attributes within the information environment, in order to assess the effectiveness of IRCs against an adversary or potential adversary. Figures IV-2 and IV-3 are tangible examples of MOP and MOE sources that an IO planner would have to rely on for feedback.

(1) MOPs are criteria used to assess friendly accomplishment of tasks and mission execution.

Examples of Measures of Performance Feedback

- Numbers of populace listening to military information support operations (MISO) broadcasts
- Percentage of adversary command and control facilities attacked
- Number of civil-military operations projects initiated/number of projects completed
- Human intelligence reports number of MISO broadcasts during Commando Solo missions

**Figure IV-2. Examples of Measures of Performance Feedback**

Possible Sources of Measures of Effectiveness Feedback

- Intelligence assessments (human intelligence, etc.)
- Open source intelligence
- Internet (newsgroups, etc.)
- Military information support operations, and civil-military operations teams (face to face activities)
- Contact with the public
- Press inquiries and comments
- Department of State polls, reports and surveys (reports)
- Open Source Center
- Nongovernmental organizations, intergovernmental organizations, international organizations, and host nation organizations
- Foreign policy advisor meetings
- Commercial polls
- Operational analysis cells

**Figure IV-3. Possible Sources of Measures of Effectiveness Feedback**

(2) In contrast to MOPs, MOEs are criteria used to assess changes in system behavior, capability, or operational environment that are tied to measuring the attainment of an end state, achievement of an objective, or creation of an effect. Ultimately, MOEs determine whether actions being executed are creating desired effects, thereby accomplishing the JFC's information objectives and end state.

(3) MOEs and MOPs are both crafted and refined throughout JOPP. In developing MOEs and/or MOPs, the following general criteria should be considered:

(a) **Ends Related.** MOEs and/or MOPs should directly relate to the objectives and desired tasks required to accomplish effects and/or performance.

(b) **Measurable.** MOEs should be *specific, measurable,* and *observable.* Effectiveness or performance is measured either quantitatively (e.g., counting the number of attacks) or qualitatively (e.g., subjectively evaluating the level of confidence in the security forces). In the case of MOEs, **a baseline measurement must be established prior to the execution, against which to measure system changes.**

(c) **Timely.** A time for required feedback should be clearly stated for each MOE and/or MOP and a plan made to report within that specified time period.

(d) **Properly Resourced.** The collection, analysis, and reporting of MOE or MOP data requires personnel, financial, and materiel resources. The IO staff or IO cell should ensure that these resource requirements are built into IO planning during COA development and closely coordinated with the J-2 collection manager to ensure the means to assess these measures are in place.

(4) **Measure of Effectiveness Indicators.** An MOEI is a unit, location, or event observed or measured, that can be used to assess an MOE. These are often used to add quantitative data points to qualitative MOEs and can assist an IO staff or IO cell in answering a question related to a qualitative MOE. The identification of MOEIs aids the IO staff or IO cell in determining an MOE and can be identified from across the information environment. MOEIs can be independently weighted for their contribution to an MOE and should be based on separate criteria. Hundreds of MOEIs may be needed for a large scale contingency. Examples of how effects can be translated into MOEIs include the following:

(a) **Effect:** Increase in the city populace's participation in civil governance.

1. **MOE:** (Qualitative) Metropolitan citizens display increased support for the democratic leadership elected on 1 July. (What activity trends show progress toward or away from the desired behavior?)

2. **MOEI:**

a. A decrease in the number of anti-government rallies/demonstrations in a city since 1 July (this indicator might be weighted heavily at 60 percent of this MOE's total assessment based on rallies/demonstrations observed.)

b. An increase in the percentage of positive new government media stories since 1 July (this indicator might be weighted less heavily at 20 percent of this MOE's total assessment based on media monitoring.)

c. An increase in the number of citizens participating in democratic functions since 1 July (this indicator might be weighted at 20 percent of this MOE's total assessment based on government data/criteria like voter registration, city council meeting attendance, and business license registration.)

(b) **Effect:** Insurgent leadership does not orchestrate terrorist acts in the western region.

1. **MOE:** (Qualitative) Decrease in popular support toward extremists and insurgents.

2. **MOEI:**

a. An increase in the number of insurgents turned in/identified since 1 October.

b. An increase in the amount of money disbursed to citizens from the "rewards program" since 1 October.

c. The percentage of blogs supportive of the local officials.

**3. Information Operations Phasing and Synchronization**

Through its contributions to the GCC's TCP, it is clear that joint IO is expected to play a major role in all phases of joint operations. This means that the GCC's IO staff and IO cell must account for logical transitions from phase to phase, as joint IO moves from the main effort to a supporting effort. Regardless of what operational phase may be underway, it is always important for the IO staff and IO cell to determine what legal authorities the JFC requires to execute IRCs during the subsequent operations phase.

a. **Phase 0–Shape.** Joint IO planning should focus on supporting the TCP to deter adversaries and potential adversaries from posing significant threats to US objectives. Joint IO planners should access the JIACG through the IO cell or staff. Joint IO planning during this phase will need to prioritize and integrate efforts and resources to support activities throughout the interagency. Due to competing resources and the potential lack of available IRCs, executing joint IO during phase 0 can be challenging. For this reason, the IO staff and IO cell will need to consider how their IO activities fit in as part of a whole-of-government approach to effectively shape the information environment to achieve the CCDR's information objectives.

b. **Phase I–Deter.** During this phase, joint IO is often the main effort for the CCMD. Planning will likely emphasize the JFC's flexible deterrent options (FDOs), complementing US public diplomacy efforts, in order to influence a potential foreign adversary decision maker to make decisions favorable to US goals and objectives. Joint IO planning for this phase is especially complicated because the FDO typically must have a chance to work, while still allowing for a smooth transition to phase II and more intense levels of conflict, if it does not. Because the transition from phase I to phase II may not allow enough time for application of IRCs to create the desired effects on an adversary or potential adversary, the phase change may be abrupt.

c. **Phase II-Seize Initiative.** In phase II, joint IO is supporting multiple lines of operation. Joint IO planning during phase II should focus on maximizing synchronized IRC effects to support the JFC's objectives and the component missions while preparing the transition to the next phase.

d. **Phase III–Dominate.** Joint IO can be a supporting and/or a supported line of operation during phase III. Joint IO planning during phase III will involve developing an information advantage across multiple lines of operation to execute the mission.

e. **Phase IV–Stabilize.** CMO, or even IO, is likely the supported line of operation during phase IV. Joint IO planning during this phase will need to be flexible enough to simultaneously support CMO and combat operations. As the US military and interagency information activity capacity matures and eventually slows, the JFC should assist the host-nation security forces and government information capacity to resume and expand, as necessary. As host nation information capacity improves, the JFC should be able to refocus joint IO efforts to other mission areas. Expanding host-nation capacity through military and interagency efforts will help foster success in the next phase.

f. **Phase V-Enable Civil Authority.** During phase V, joint IO planning focuses on supporting the redeployment of US forces, as well as providing continued support to stability operations. IO planning during phase V should account for interagency and country team efforts to resume the lead mission for information within the host nation territory. The IO staff and cell can anticipate the possibility of long term US commercial and government support to the former adversary's economic and political interests to continue through the completion of this phase.

# CHAPTER V
## MULTINATIONAL INFORMATION OPERATIONS

> *"In order more effectively to achieve the objectives of this Treaty, the Parties, separately and jointly, by means of continuous and effective self-help and mutual aid, will maintain and develop their individual and collective capacity to resist armed attack."*
>
> **Article 3, The North Atlantic Treaty, April 4, 1949**

### 1. Introduction

Joint doctrine for multinational operations, including command and operations in a multinational environment, is described in JP 3-16, *Multinational Operations*. The purpose of this chapter is to highlight specific doctrinal components of IO in a multinational environment (see Figure V-1). In doing so, this chapter will build upon those aspects of IO addressed in JP 3-16. Additional data regarding IO in a multinational environment can be found in Allied Joint Publication (AJP)-3.10, *Allied Joint Doctrine for Information Operations*. This chapter includes IO coordination processes, staff requirements, planning formats, and matrices for staff and commanders involved in a multinational operation.

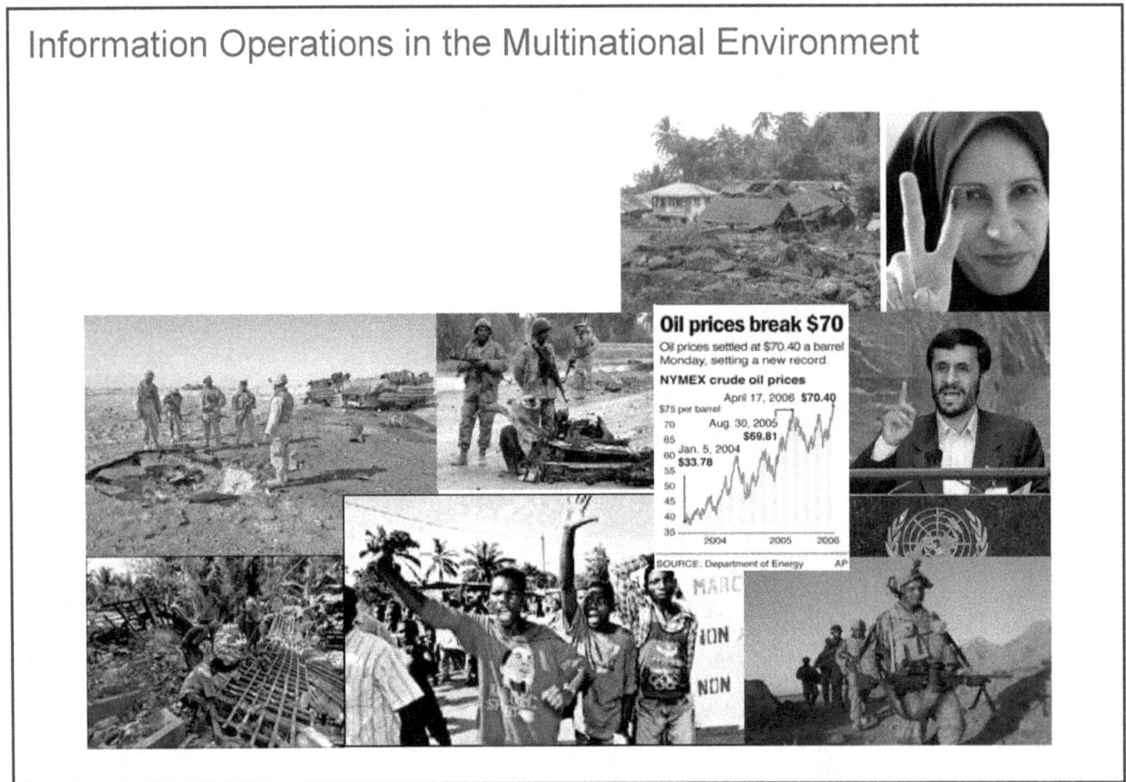


**Figure V-1. Information Operations in the Multinational Environment**

## 2. Other Nations and Information Operations

a. Multinational partners recognize a variety of information concepts and possess sophisticated doctrine, procedures, and capabilities. Given these potentially diverse perspectives regarding IO, it is essential for the multinational force commander (MNFC) to resolve potential conflicts as soon as possible. It is vital to integrate multinational partners into IO planning as early as possible to gain agreement on an integrated and achievable IO strategy. Initial requirements for coordinating, synchronizing, and when required integrating other nations into the US IO plan include:

(1) Clarifying all multinational partner information objectives.

(2) Understanding all multinational partner employment of IRCs.

(3) Establishing IO deconfliction procedures to avoid conflicting messages.

(4) Identifying multinational force (MNF) vulnerabilities as soon as possible.

(5) Developing a strategy to mitigate MNF IO vulnerabilities.

(6) Identifying MNF IRCs.

b. Regardless of the maturity of each partner's IO strategy, doctrine, capabilities, tactics, techniques, or procedures, every multinational partner can contribute to MNF IO by providing regional expertise to assist in planning and conducting IO. Multinational partners have developed unique approaches to IO that are tailored for specific targets in ways that may not be employed by the US. Such contributions complement US IO expertise and IRCs, potentially enhancing the quality of both the planning and execution of multinational IO.

## 3. Multinational Information Operations Considerations

a. Military operation planning processes, particularly for IO, whether JOPP based or based on established or agreed to multinational planning processes, include an understanding of multinational partner(s):

(1) Cultural values and institutions.

(2) Interests and concerns.

(3) Moral and ethical values.

(4) ROE and legal constraints.

(5) Challenges in multilingual planning for the employment of IRCs.

(6) IO doctrine, techniques, and procedures.

b. Sharing of information with multinational partners.

(1) Each nation has various IRCs to provide, in support of multinational objectives. These nations are obliged to protect information that they cannot share across the MNF. However, to plan thoroughly, all nations must be willing to share appropriate information to accomplish the assigned mission.

(2) Information sharing arrangements in formal alliances, to include US participation in United Nations missions, are worked out as part of alliance protocols. Information sharing arrangements in ad hoc multinational operations where coalitions are working together on a short-notice mission must be created during the establishment of the coalition.

(3) Using National Disclosure Policy (NDP) 1, *National Policy and Procedures for the Disclosure of Classified Military Information to Foreign Governments and International Organizations*, and Department of Defense Instruction (DODI) O-3600.02, *Information Operations (IO) Security Classification Guidance (U)*, as guidance, the senior US commander in a multinational operation must provide guidelines to the US-designated disclosure representative on information sharing and the release of classified information or capabilities to the MNF. NDP 1 provides policy and procedures in the form of specific disclosure criteria and limitations, definition of terms, release arrangements, and other guidance. The disclosure of classified information is never automatic. It is not necessary for MNFs to be made aware of all US intelligence, capabilities, or procedures that are required for planning and execution of IO. The JFC should request approval from higher command authorities to release information that has not been previously cleared for multinational partners.

(4) Information concerning US persons may only be collected, retained, or disseminated in accordance with law and regulation. Applicable provisions include: the Privacy Act, Title 5, USC, Section 552a; DODD 5200.27, *Acquisition of Information Concerning Persons and Organizations not Affiliated with the Department of Defense*; Executive Order 12333, *United States Intelligence Activities*; and DOD 5240.1-R, *Procedures Governing the Activities of DOD Intelligence Components that Affect United States Persons.*

## 4. Planning, Integration, and Command and Control of Information Operations in Multinational Operations

a. The role of IO in multinational operations is the prerogative of the MNFC. The mission of the MNF determines the role of IO in each specific operation.

b. Representation of key multinational partners in the MNF IO cell allows their expertise and capabilities to be utilized, and the IO portion of the plan to be better coordinated and more timely.

c. While some multinational partners may not have developed an IO concept or fielded IRCs, it is important that they fully appreciate the importance of the information in achieving the MNFC's objectives. For this reason, every effort should be made to provide basic-level IO training to multinational partners serving on the MNF IO staff. In cases where this is not possible, it may be necessary for the MNF headquarters staff to assist the subordinate MNFCs in planning and conducting IO.

d. MNF headquarters staff could be organized differently; however, as a general rule, an information operations coordination board (IOCB) or similar organization may exist (see Figure V-2). The IOCB is normally responsible for preparing inputs to relevant MNF headquarters internal and external processes such as joint targeting and provides a forum to outline current and future application of IRCs designed to achieve MNFC's objectives. A wide range of MNF headquarters staff organizations should participate in IOCB deliberations to ensure their input and subject matter expertise can be applied to satisfy a requirement in order to achieve MNFC's objectives.

e. Besides the coordination activities highlighted above, the IOCB should also participate in appropriate joint operations planning groups (JOPGs) and should take part in early discussions, including mission analysis. An IO presence on the JOPG is essential, as it is the IOCB which provides input to the overall estimate process in close coordination with other members of the MNF headquarters staff.

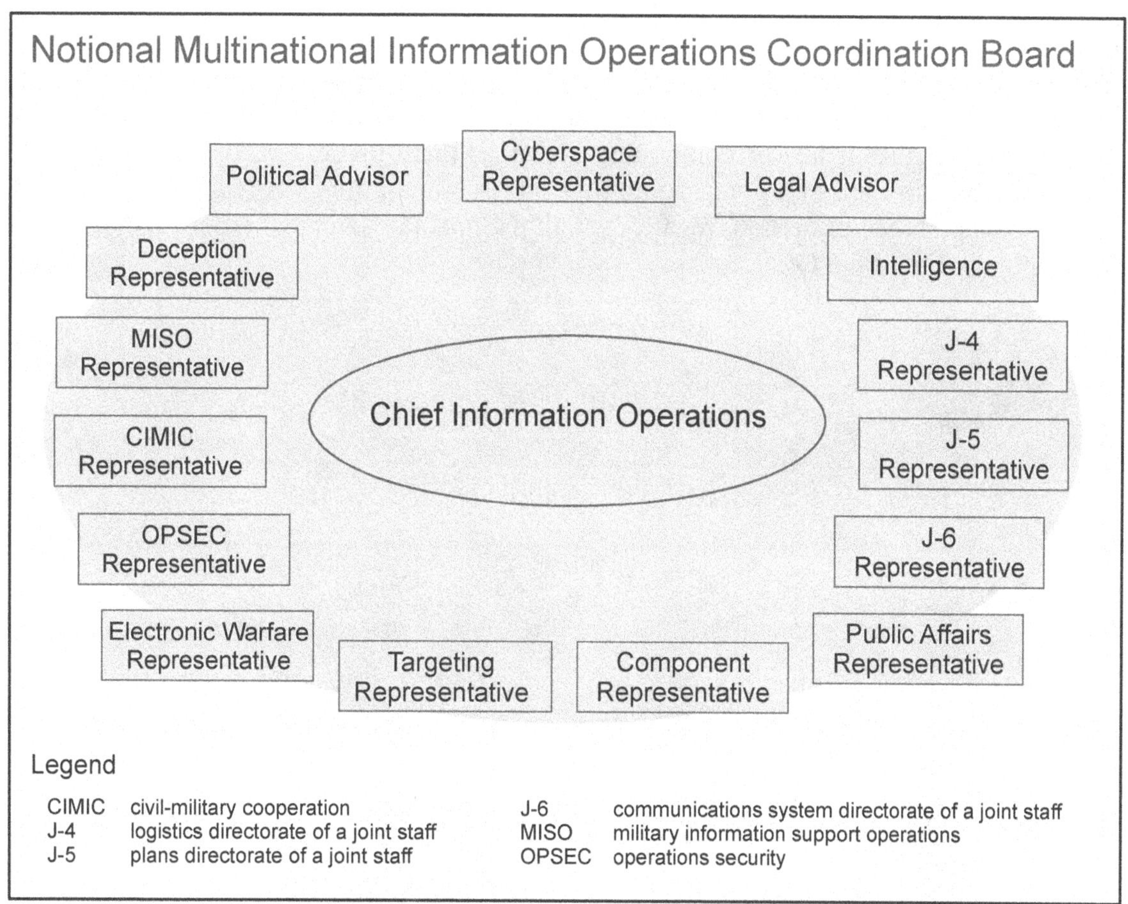


**Figure V-2. Notional Multinational Information Operations Coordination Board**

## 5. Multinational Organization for Information Operations Planning

a. When the JFC is also the MNFC, the joint force staff should be augmented by planners and subject matter experts from the MNF. MNF IO planners and IRC specialists should be trained on US and MNF doctrine, requirements, resources, and how the MNF is structured to integrate IRCs. IO planners should seek to accommodate the requirements of each multinational partner, within given constraints, with the goal of using all the available expertise and capabilities of the MNF.

b. In the case where the JFC is not the MNFC, it may be necessary for **the J-3 to brief the MNFC and staff on the advantages of integrating US IO processes and procedures to achieve MNF objectives.** The JFC should propose organizing a multinational IO staff using organizational criteria discussed earlier. If this is not acceptable to the MNFC, the JFC should assume responsibility for implementing IO within the joint force as a part of multinational operations to support multinational mission objectives.

## 6. Multinational Policy Coordination

The development of capabilities, tactics, techniques, procedures, plans, intelligence, and communications support applicable to IO requires coordination with the responsible DOD components and multinational partners. Coordination with partner nations above the JFC/MNFC level is normally effected within existing defense arrangements, including bilateral arrangements. **The Joint Staff coordinates US positions on IO matters** delegated to them as a matter of law or policy, and discusses them bilaterally, or in multinational organizations, to achieve interoperability and compatibility in fulfilling common requirements. Direct discussions regarding multinational IO planning in specific theaters are the responsibility of the GCC.

Intentionally Blank

# CHAPTER VI
## INFORMATION OPERATIONS ASSESSMENT

> *"Not everything that can be counted, counts, and not everything that counts can be counted."*
>
> **Dr. William Cameron, *Informal Sociology: A Casual Introduction to Sociological Thinking,* 1963**

### 1. Introduction

a. This chapter provides a framework to organize, develop, and execute assessment of IO, as conducted within the information environment. The term "assessment" has been used to describe everything from analysis (e.g., assessment of the enemy) to an estimate of the situation (pre-engagement assessment of blue and red forces). Within the context of this chapter, assessment is the determination of the progress toward achieving commander's objectives or attaining an end state, and focuses on the tactical and operational levels of assessment that assist and inform the JFC's decision making. Assessment considerations should be thoroughly integrated into IO planning.

b. Assessment of IO is a key component of the commander's decision cycle, helping to determine the results of tactical actions in the context of overall mission objectives and providing potential recommendations for refinement of future plans. The decision to adapt plans or shift resources is based upon the integration of intelligence in the operational environment and other staff estimates, as well as input from other mission partners, in pursuit of the desired end state.

c. Assessments also provide opportunities to identify IRC shortfalls, changes in parameters and/or conditions in the information environment, which may cause unintended effects in the employment of IRCs, and resource issues that may be impeding joint IO effectiveness.

### 2. Understanding Information Operations Assessment

a. Assessment consists of activities associated with tasks, events, or programs in support of the commander's desired end state. IO assessment is iterative, continuously repeating rounds of analysis within the operations cycle in order to measure the progress of IRCs toward achieving objectives. The assessment process begins with the earliest stages of the planning process and continues throughout the operation or campaign and may extend beyond the end of the operation to capture long-term effects of the IO effort. Integrating assessment from the start, to ensure future assessment requirements, enables the IO planner to ensure that desirable effects that support the commander's objectives are well-defined and measurable and provide feedback to commanders, operators, and planners as operations evolve.

b. Analysis of the information environment should begin before operations start, in order to establish baselines from which to measure change. During operations, data is continuously collected, recharacterizing our understanding of the information environment and providing the ability to measure changes and determine whether desired effects are being created.

## 3. Purpose of Assessment in Information Operations

Assessments help commanders better understand current conditions. The commander uses assessments to determine how the operation is progressing and whether the operation is creating the desired effects. Assessing the effectiveness of IO activities challenges both the staff and commander. There are numerous venues for informing and receiving information from the commander; they provide opportunities to identify IRC shortfalls and resource issues that may be impeding joint IO effectiveness.

## 4. Impact of the Information Environment on Assessment

a. Operation assessments in IO differ from assessments of other operations because the success of the operation mainly relies on nonlethal capabilities, often including reliance on measuring the cognitive dimension, or on nonmilitary factors outside the direct control of the JFC. This situation requires an assessment with a focused, organized approach that is developed in conjunction with the initial planning effort. It also requires a clear vision of the end state, an understanding of the commander's objectives, and an articulated statement of the ways in which the planned activities achieve objectives.

*For more discussion of objective and effects, see JP 5-0,* Joint Operation Planning.

b. The information environment is a complex entity, an "open system" affected by variables that are not constrained by geography. The mingling of people, information, capabilities, organizations, religions, and cultures that exist inside and outside a commander's operational area are examples of these variables. These variables can give commanders and their staffs the appreciation that the information environment is turbulent—constantly in motion and changing—which may make analysis seem like a daunting task, and make identifying an IRC (or IRCs) most likely to create a desired effect, feel nearly impossible. In a complex environment, seemingly minor events can produce enormous outcomes, far greater in effect than the initiating event, including secondary and tertiary effects that are difficult to anticipate and understand. This complexity is why assessment is required and why there may be specific capabilities required to conduct assessment and subsequent analysis.

c. A detailed study and analysis of the information environment affords the planner the ability to identify which forces impact the information environment and find order in the apparent chaos. Often the complexity of the information environment relative to a specific operational area requires assets and capabilities that exceed the organic capability of the command, making the required exhaustive study an impossible task. The gaps in capability and information are identified by planners and are transformed into information requirements and requests, request for forces and/or augmentation, and requests for support from external agencies. Examples of capabilities, forces, augmentation, and external support include specialized software, behavioral scientists, polling, social-science studies, operational research specialists, statisticians, demographic data held by commercial industry, reachback support to other mission partners, military information support personnel, access to external DOD databases, and support from academia. But the presence of sensitive variables can be a catalyst for exponential changes in outcomes, as in the aforementioned secondary and tertiary effects. Joint IO planners should be cautious about making direct causal statements, since many nonlinear feedback loops can render direct causal statements inaccurate. Incorrect assumptions about causality in a complex system can have disastrous effects on the planning of future operations and open the assessment to potential discredit, because counterexamples may exist.

## 5. The Information Operations Assessment Process

a. Integrating the employment of IRCs with other lines of operation is a unique requirement for joint staffs and is a discipline that is comparatively new. The variety of IRCs is broad, with specific capabilities having unique purposes and focus. For example, an EW asset may be able to focus on disrupting a very specific piece of adversary hardware while a team from the Army's military information support groups may sit down with the former president of a country to convince him to communicate a radio message to the people. The broad range of information-related activities occurring across the three dimensions of the information environment (physical, informational, and cognitive) demand a specific, validated, and formal assessment process to determine whether these actions are contributing towards the fulfillment of an objective. With the additional factor that some actions result in immediate effect (e.g., jamming a radio frequency or entire band [frequency modulation]) and others may take years or generations to fully create (e.g., eliminating police extortion of tourists), the assessment process must be able to report incremental effects in each dimension. In particular, when assessing the effect of an action or series of actions on behavior, the effects may need to be measured in terms such as cognitive, affective, and action or behavioral. Put another way, we may need to assess how a group thinks, feels, and acts, and whether those behaviors are a result of our deliberate actions intended to produce that effect, an unintended consequence of our actions, a result of another's action or activity, or a combination of all of these. A solution to these assessment requirements is the eight-step assessment process identified in Figure VI-1.

| **Information Operations Assessment Framework** | |
|---|---|
| Step 1 | Analyze the information environment |
| Step 2 | Integrate information operations assessment into plans and develop the assessment plan |
| Step 3 | Develop information operations assessment information requirements and collection plans |
| Step 4 | Build/modify information operations assessment baseline |
| Step 5 | Coordinate and Execute Information Operations and Coordinate Intelligence Collection Activities |
| Step 6 | Monitor and collect focused information environment data for information operations assessment |
| Step 7 | Analyze information operations assessment data |
| Step 8 | Report assessment results and make recommendations |

**Figure VI-1. Information Operations Assessment Framework**

b. **Step 1—Analyze the Information Environment**

(1) As the entire staff conducts analysis of the operational environment, the IO staff focuses on the information environment. This analysis occurs when planning for an operation begins or, in some cases, prior to planning for an operation, e.g., during routine analysis in support of theater security cooperation plan activities. It is a required step for viable planning and provides necessary data for, among other things, development of MOEs, determining potential target audiences and targets, baseline data from which change can be measured. Analysis is conducted by interdisciplinary teams and staff sections. The primary product of this step is a description of the information environment. This description should include categorization or delineation of the physical, informational, and cognitive dimensions.

(2) Analysis of the information environment identifies key functions and systems within the operational environment. The analysis provides the initial information to identify decision makers (cognitive), factors that guide the decision-making process (informational), and infrastructure that supports and communicates decisions and decision making (physical).

(3) Gaps in the ability to analyze the information environment and gaps in required information are identified and transformed into information requirements and requests, requests for forces and/or augmentation, and requests for support from external agencies. The information environment is fluid. Technological, cultural, and infrastructure changes, regardless of their source or cause, can all impact each dimension of the information environment. Once the initial analysis is complete, periodic analyses must be conducted to capture changes and update the analysis for the commander, staff, other units, and unified action partners. As assessments are executed and the subsequent data retrieved and analyzed, the effects of our actions on the information are codified. This information is captured, and updates the analysis of the information environment, as well. Much like a running estimate, the analysis of the information environment becomes a living document, continuously updated to provide a current, accurate picture.

c. **Step 2—Integrate Information Operations Assessment into Plans and Develop the Assessment Plan**

(1) Early integration of assessments into plans is paramount, especially in the information environment. One of the first things that must happen during planning is to ensure that the objectives to be assessed are clear, understandable, and measureable. Equally important is to consider as part of the assessment baseline, a control set of conditions within the information environment from which to assess the performance of the tasks assigned to any given IRC, in order to determine their potential impact on IO. In order to assess progress on the objectives, they should portray a progression from the baseline toward the desired end state. The end state should be realistic and attainable. During this step, several tasks occur; after identifying the commander's objectives and end state that are supportable by integrating IRCs with other lines of effort, supporting objectives and tasks are developed. This is followed by developing an initial assessment plan, which includes MOEs and impact indicators. Planners should also be aware that while each staff section participates in the planning process, quite often portions of individual staff sections are simultaneously working

on the steps of the planning process in greater depth and detail, not quite keeping pace with the entire staff effort as they work on subordinate and supporting staff tasks. The intelligence staff's efforts to analyze the operational environment are an example of this, as is the operations staff function of integrating IRCs.

(2) In order to achieve the objectives, specific effects need to be identified. It is during COA development, Step 3 of JOPP, that specific tasks are determined that will create the desired effects, based on the commander's objectives. Effects should be clearly distinguishable from the objective they support as a condition for success or progress and not be misidentified as another objective. These effects ultimately support tasks to influence, disrupt, corrupt, or usurp the decision making of our adversaries, or to protect our own. Effects should provide a clear and common description of the desired change in the information environment.

**UNDERSTANDING TASK AND OBJECTIVE, CAUSE AND EFFECT INTERRELATIONSHIPS**

**Understanding the interrelationships of the tasks and objectives, and the desired cause and effect, can be challenging for the planner. Mapping the expected change (a theory of change) provides the clear, logical connections between activities and desired outcomes by defining intermediate steps between current situation and desired outcome and establishing points of measurement. It should include clearly stated assumptions that can be challenged for correctness as activities are executed. The ability to challenge assumptions in light of executed activities allows the joint information operations planner to identify flawed connections between activity and outcome, incorrect assumptions, or the presence of spoilers. For example:**

***Training and arming local security guards increases their ability and willingness to resist insurgents, which will increase security in the locale. Increased security will lead to increased perceptions of security, which will promote participation in local government, which will lead to better governance. Improved security and better governance will lead to increased stability.***

- **Logical connection between activities and outcomes**
  - **Activity: training and arming local security guards**
  - **Outcome: increased ability to resist insurgents**
- **Clearly stated assumptions**
  - **Increased ability and willingness to resist increases security in the locale**
  - **Increased security leads to increased perceptions of security**

- **Intermediate steps and points of measurement**
  - **Measures of performance regarding training activities**
  - **Measures of effectiveness (MOEs) regarding willingness to resist**
  - **MOEs regarding increased local security**

(3) This expected change shows a logical connection between activities (training and arming locals) and desired outcomes (increased stability). It makes some assumptions, but those assumptions are clearly stated, so they can be challenged if they are believed to be incorrect. Further, those activities and assumptions suggest obvious things to measure, such as performance of the activities (the training and arming) and the outcome (change in stability). They also suggest measurement of more subtle elements of all the intermediate logical nodes such as capability and willingness of local security forces, change in security, change in perception of security, change in participation in local government, change in governance, and so on. Better still, if one of those measurements does not yield the desired result, the joint IO planner will be able to ascertain where in the chain the logic is breaking down (which hypotheses are not substantiated). They can then modify the expected change and the activities supporting it, reconnecting the logical pathway and continuing to push toward the objectives.

(4) Such an expected change might have begun as something quite simple: training and arming local security guards will lead to increased stability. While this gets at the kernel of the idea, it is not particularly helpful for building assessments. Stopping there would suggest only the need to measure the activity and the outcome. However, it leaves a huge assumptive gap. If training and arming security guards goes well, but stability does not increase, there will be no apparent reason why. To begin to expand on a simple expected change, the joint IO planner should ask the question, "Why? How might A lead to B?" (In this case, how would training and arming security guards lead to stability?) A thoughtful answer to this question usually leads to recognition of another node to the expected change. If needed, the question can be asked again relative to this new node, until the expected change is sufficiently articulated.

(5) Circumstances on the ground might also require the assumptions in an expected change to be more explicitly defined. For example, using the expected change articulated in the above example, the joint IO planner might observe that in successfully training and arming local security guards, they are better able to resist insurgents, leading to an increased perception of security, as reported in local polls. However, participation in local government, as measured through voting in local elections and attendance at local council meetings, has not increased. The existing expected change and associated measurements illustrate where the chain of logic is breaking down (somewhere between perceptions of security and participation in local governance), but it does not (yet) tell why that break is occurring. Adjusting the expected change by identifying the incorrect assumption or spoiling factor preventing the successful connection between security and local governance will also help improve achievement of the objective.

d. **Step 3—Develop Information Operations Assessment Information Requirements and Collection Plans**

(1) Critical to this step is ensuring that attributes are chosen that are relevant and applicable during the planning processes, as these will drive the determination of measures that display behavioral characteristics, attitudes, perceptions, and motivations that can be examined externally. Measures are categorized as follows:

(a) Qualitative—a categorical measurement expressed by means of a natural language description rather than in terms of numbers. Methodologies consist of focus groups, in-depth interviews, ethnography, media content analysis, after-action reports, and anecdotes (individual responses sampled consistently over time).

(b) Quantitative—a numerical measurement expressed in terms of numbers rather than means of a natural language description. Methodologies consist of surveys, polls, observational data (intelligence, surveillance, and reconnaissance), media analytics, and official statistics.

(2) An integrated collection management plan ensures that assessment data gathered at the tactical level is incorporated into operational planning. This collection management plan needs to satisfy information requirements with the assigned tactical, theater, and national intelligence sources and other collection resources. Just as crucial is realizing that not every information requirement will be answered by the intelligence community and therefore planners must consider collaborating with other sources of information. Planners must discuss collection from other sources of information with the collection manager and unit legal personnel to ensure that the information is included in the overall assessment and the process is in accordance with intelligence oversight regulations and policy.

(3) Including considerations for assessment collection in the plan will facilitate the return of data needed to accomplish the assessment. Incorporating the assessment plan with the directions to conduct an activity will help ensure that resource requirements for assessment are acknowledged when the plan is approved. The assessment plan should, at a minimum, include timing and frequency of data collection, identify the party to conduct the collection, and provide reporting instructions.

(4) A well-designed assessment plan will:

(a) Develop the commander's assessment questions.

(b) Document the expected change.

(c) Document the development of information requirements needed specifically for IO.

(d) Define key terms embedded within the end state with regard to the actors or TAs, operational activities, effects, acceptable conditions, rates of change, thresholds of success/failure, and technical/tactical triggers.

(e) Verify tactical objectives—support operational objectives.

(f) Identify strategic and operational considerations—in addition to tactical considerations, linking assessments to lines of operation and the associated desired conditions.

(g) Identify key nodes and connections in the expected change to be measured.

(h) Document collection and analysis methods.

(i) Establish a method to evaluate triggers to the commander's decision points.

(j) Establish methods to determine progress towards the desired end state.

(k) Establish methods to estimate risk to the mission.

(l) Develop recommendations for plan adjustments.

(m) Establish the format for reporting assessment results.

e. **Step 4—Build/Modify Information Operations Assessment Baseline.** A subset of JIPOE, the baseline is part of the overall characterization of the information environment that was accomplished in Step 1. It serves as a reference point for comparison, enabling an assessment of the way in which activities create desired effects. The baseline allows the commander and staff to set goals for desired rates of change within the information environment and establish thresholds for success and failure. This focuses information and intelligence collection on answering specific questions relating to the desired outcomes of the plan.

f. **Step 5—Coordinate and Execute Information Operations and Coordinate Intelligence Collection Activities**

(1) With information gained in steps 1 and 4, the joint IO planner should be able to build an understanding of the TA. This awareness will yield a collection plan that enables the joint IO planner to determine whether or not the TA is "seeing" the activities/actions presented. The collection method must perceive the TA reaction. IO planners, assessors, and intelligence planners need to be able to communicate effectively to accurately capture the required intelligence needed to perform IO assessments.

(2) Information requirements and subsequent indicator collection must be tightly managed during employment of IRCs in order to validate execution and to monitor TA response. In the information environment, coordination and timing are crucial because some IRCs are time sensitive and require immediate indicator monitoring to develop valid assessment data.

g. **Step 6—Monitor and Collect Information Environment Data for Information Operations Assessment**

(1) Monitoring is the continuous process of observing conditions relevant to current operations. Assessment data are collected, aggregated, consolidated and validated. Gaps in the assessment data are identified and highlighted in order to determine actions needed to alleviate shortfalls or make adjustments to the plan. As information and intelligence are collected during execution, assessments are used to validate or negate assumptions that define cause (action) and effect (conclusion) relationships between operational activities, objectives, and end states.

(2) If anticipated progress toward an end state does not occur, then the staff may conclude that the intended action does not have the intended effect. The uncertainty in the information environment makes the use of critical assumptions particularly important, as operation planning may need to be adjusted for elements that may not have initially been well understood when the plan was developed.

h. **Step 7—Analyze Information Operations Assessment Data**

(1) If available, personnel trained or qualified in analysis techniques should conduct data analysis. Analysis can be done outside the operational area by leveraging reachback capabilities. One of the more important factors for analysis is that it is conducted in an unbiased manner. This is more easily accomplished if the personnel conducting analysis are not the same personnel who developed the execution plan. Assessment data are analyzed and the results are compared to the baseline measurements and updated continuously as the staff continues its analysis of the information environment. These comparisons help the staff determine whether the information environment has changed and if so, the degree and area of that change, or if it remains unchanged. These changes are indications of effects on or in the information environment and help determine whether progress is being made toward achieving objectives. Assessment remains an iterative process. When problems or errors are found in the data, feedback about what occurred and where adjustments are necessary must be reported, as appropriate.

(2) Deficiency analysis must also occur in this step. If no changes were observed in the information environment, then a breakdown may have occurred somewhere. The plan might be flawed, execution might not have been successful, collection may not have been accomplished as prescribed, or more time may be needed to observe any changes.

i. **Step 8—Report Assessment Results and Make Recommendations**

As expressed earlier in this chapter, assessment results enable staffs to ensure that tasks stay linked to objectives and objectives remain relevant and linked to desired end states. They provide opportunities to identify IRC shortfalls and resource issues that may be impeding joint IO effectiveness. These results may also provide information to agencies outside of the command or chain of command. The primary purpose of reporting the results is to inform the command and staff concerning the progress of objective achievement and the effects on the information environment, and to enable decision making. The published assessment plan, staff standard operating procedures, battle rhythm, and orders are documents in which commanders can dictate how often assessment results are provided and the format in which they are reported. In designated venues and in the required format, the

IO staff reports progress and makes recommendations. They record the decision made and implement those decisions continuing the iterative assessment process.

## 6. Barriers to Information Operations Assessment

a. The preceding IO assessment methodology can support all operations, and most barriers to assessment can be overcome simply by considering assessment requirements as the plan is developed. But whatever the phase type of operation, the biggest barriers to assessment are generally self-generated.

b. Some of the self-generated barriers to assessment include the failure to establish objectives that are actually measurable, the failure to collect baseline data against which "post-test" data can be compared, and the failure to plan adequately for the collection of assessment data, including the use of intelligence assets.

c. There are other factors that complicate IO assessment. Foremost, it may be difficult or impossible to directly relate behavior change to an individual act or group of actions. Also, the logistics of data capture are not simple. Contingencies and operations in uncertain or hostile environments present unique challenges in terms of operational tempo and access to conduct assessments. Depending on the phase of the conflict, the operational tempo might present unique challenges to access or assessment. Rapidly changing conditions might also affect the accuracy and volume of data able to be collected. The cognitive biases of the analyst may also act as a barrier to influence accuracy.

## 7. Organizing for Operation Assessments

a. Integrating assessment into the planning effort is normally the responsibility of the lead planner, with assistance across the staff. The lead planner understands the complexity of the plan and decision points established as the plan develops. The lead planner also understands potential indicators of success or failure. For IO-specific assessments planning regarding collecting and analyzing the success of the IO message, the organization responsible for IO should build the IO assessment framework into the plan. This framework must include collection and reporting responsibilities.

b. As a plan becomes operationalized, the overall assessment responsibility typically transitions from the lead planner to the J-3. The IO lead provides the necessary IO-related information and analysis to guide the assessment and recommendations for implementing specific changes to better accomplish the mission.

c. When appropriate, the commander can establish an assessments cell or team to manage assessments activities. When utilized, this cell or team must have appropriate access to operational information, appropriate access to the planning process, and the representation of other staff elements, to include IRCs.

## 8. Measures and Indicators

a. As emphasized in Chapter IV, "Integrating Information-Related Capabilities into the Joint Operation Planning Process," paragraph 2.f., "Relationship Between Measures of

Performance (MOPs) and Measures of Effectiveness (MOEs)," MOPs and MOEs help accomplish the assessment process by qualifying or quantifying the intangible attributes of the information environment. This is done to assess the effectiveness of activities conducted in the information environment and to establish a direct cause between the activity and the effect desired.

b. MOPs should be developed during the operation planning process, should be tied directly to operation planning, and at a minimum, assess completion of the various phases of an activity or program. Further, MOPs should assess any action, activity, or operation at which IO actions or activities interact with the TA. For certain tasks there are TA capabilities (voice, text, video, or face-to-face). For instance, during a leaflet-drop, the point of dissemination of the leaflets would be an action or activity. The MOP for any one action should be whether or not the TA was exposed to the IO action or activity.

(1) For each activity phase, task, or touch point, a set of MOPs based on the operational plan outlined in the program description should be developed. Task MOPs are measured via internal reporting within units and commands. Touch-point MOPs can be measured in one of several ways. Whether or not a TA is aware of, interested in, or responding to, an IRC product or activity, can be directly ascertained by conducting a survey or interview. This information can also be gathered by direct observational methods such as field reconnaissance, surveillance, or intelligence collection. Information can also be gathered via indirect observations such as media reports, online activity, or atmospherics.

(2) The end state of operation planning is a multi-phased plan or order, from which planners can directly derive a list of MOPs, assuming a higher echelon has not already designated the MOPs.

c. MOEs need to be specific, clear, and observable to provide the commander effective feedback. In addition, there needs to be a direct link between the objectives, effects, and the TA. Most of the IRCs have their own doctrine and discuss MOEs with slightly different language, but with ultimately the same functions and roles.

(1) In line with JP 5-0, *Joint Operation Planning*, development of MOEs and their associated impact indicators (derived from measurable supporting objectives) must be done during the planning process. By determining the measure in the planning process, planners ensure that organic assets and enablers, such as intelligence assets, are identified to assist in evaluating MOEs in the conduct of IO.

(2) In developing IO MOEs, the following general guidelines should be considered. First, they should be related to the end state; that is, they should directly relate to the desired effects. They should also be measurable quantitatively or qualitatively. In order to measure effectiveness, *a baseline measurement must exist or be established prior to execution, against which to measure system changes.* They should be within a defined periodical or conditional assessment framework (i.e., the required feedback time, cyclical period, or conditions should be clearly stated for each MOE and a deadline made to report within a specified assessment period, which clearly delineates the beginning, progression, and termination of a cycle in which the effectiveness of the operations is to be assessed). Finally,

they need to be properly resourced. The collection, collation, analysis and reporting of MOE data requires personnel, budgetary, and materiel resources. IO staffs, along with their counterparts at the component level, should ensure that these resource requirements are built into the plan during its development.

(3) The more specific the MOE, the more readily the intelligence collection manager can determine how best to collect against the requirements and provide valuable feedback pertaining to them. The ability to establish MOEs and conduct combat assessment for IO requires observation and collection of information from diverse, nebulous and often untimely sources. These sources may include: human intelligence; signals intelligence; air and ground-based intelligence; surveillance and reconnaissance; open-source intelligence, including the Internet; contact with the public; press inquiries and comments; Department of State polls; reports and surveys; nongovernmental organizations; international organizations; and commercial polls.

(4) One of the biggest challenges with MOE development is the difficulty of defining variables and establishing causality. Therefore, it is more advisable to approach this from a correlational, versus a causality perspective, where unrealistic "zero-defect" predictability gives way to more attainable correlational analysis, which provides insights to the likelihood of particular events and effects given a certain criteria in terms of conditions and actors in the information environment. While the *Joint Munitions Effectiveness Manual* provides a certain level of predictability, which supports causality in the employment of certain munitions with desired effects, such methodology is not analogous to assessments within the information environment, as evidence seems to point out that correlation of indicators and events have proven more accurate than the evidence to support cause and effects relationships, particularly when it comes to behavior and intangible parameters of the cognitive elements of the information environment. IRCs, however, are directed at TAs and decision makers, and the systems that support them, making it much more difficult to establish concrete causal relationships, especially when assessing foreign public opinion or human behavior. Unforeseen factors can lead to erroneous interpretations, for example, a traffic accident in a foreign country involving a US service member or a local civilian's bias against US policies can cause a decline in public support, irrespective of otherwise successful IO.

(5) If IO effects and supporting IO tasks are not linked to the commander's objectives, or are not clearly written, measuring their effectiveness is difficult. Clearly written IO tasks must be linked to the commander's objectives to justify resources to measure their contributing effects. If MOEs are difficult to write for a specific IO effect, the effect should be reevaluated and a rewrite considered. When attempting to describe desired effects, it is important to keep the effect impact in mind, as a guide to what must be observed, collected, and measured. In order to effectively identify the assessment methodology and to be able to recreate the process as part of the scientific method, MOE development must be written with a documented pathway for effect creation. This path should consist of indicators leading to the projected creation of the desired effect. MOEs should be observable, to aid with collection; quantifiable, to increase objectivity; precise, to ensure accuracy; and correlated with the progress of the operation, to attain timeliness.

d. Indicators are crucial because they aid the joint IO planner in informing MOEs and should be identifiable across the center of gravity critical factors. They can be independently weighted for their contribution to a MOE and should be based on separate criteria. A single indicator can inform multiple MOEs. Dozens of indicators will be required for a large-scale operation.

## 9. Considerations

a. In the information environment, it is unlikely that universal measures and indicators will exist because of varying perspectives. In addition, any data collected is likely to be incomplete. Assessments need to be periodically adjusted to the changing situation in order to avoid becoming obsolete. In addition, assessments will usually need to be supplemented by subjective constructs that are a reflection of the joint IO planner's scope and perspective (e.g., intuition, anecdotal evidence, or limited set of evidence).

b. Assessment teams may not have direct access to a TA for a variety of reasons. The goal of measurement is not to achieve perfect accuracy or precision—given the ever present biases of theory and the limitations of tools that exist—but rather, to reduce uncertainty about the value being measured. Measurements of IO effects on TA can be accomplished in two ways: direct observation and indirect observation. Direct observation measures the attitudes or behaviors of the TA either by questioning the TA or observing behavior firsthand. Indirect observation measures otherwise inaccessible attitudes and behaviors by the effects that they have on more easily measurable phenomena. Direct observations are preferable for establishing baselines and measuring effectiveness, while indirect observations reduce uncertainty in measurements, to a lesser degree.

## 10. Categories of Assessment

a. Operation assessment of IO is an evaluation of the effectiveness of operational activities conducted in the information environment. Operation assessments primarily document mission success or failure for the commander and staff. However, operation assessments inform other types of assessment, such as programmatic and budgetary assessment. Programmatic assessment evaluates readiness and training, while budgetary assessment evaluates return on investment.

b. When categorized by the levels of warfare, there exists tactical, operational and strategic-level assessment. Tactical-level assessment evaluates the effectiveness of a specific, localized activity. Operational-level assessment evaluates progress towards accomplishment of a plan or campaign. Strategic level assessment evaluates progress towards accomplishment of a theater or national objective. The skilled IO planner will link tactical actions to operational and strategic objectives.

Intentionally Blank

# APPENDIX A
## REFERENCES

The development of JP 3-13 is based on the following primary references.

### 1. General

a. *National Security Strategy.*

b. *Unified Command Plan.*

c. Executive Order 12333, *United States Intelligence Activities.*

d. The Fourth Amendment to the US Constitution.

e. *The Privacy Act*, Title 5, USC, Section 552a.

f. *The Wiretap Act and the Pen/Trap Statute*, Title 18, USC, Sections 2510-2522 and 3121-3127.

g. *The Stored Communications Act*, Title 18, USC, Sections 2701-2712.

h. *The Foreign Intelligence Surveillance Act,* Title 50, USC.

### 2. Department of State Publications

Department of State Publication 9434, *Treaties In Force.*

### 3. Department of Defense Publications

a. Secretary of Defense Memorandum dated 25 January 2011, *Strategic Communication and Information Operations in the DOD.*

b. *National Military Strategy.*

c. DODD S-3321.1, *Overt Psychological Operations Conducted by the Military Services in Peacetime and in Contingencies Short of Declared War.*

d. DODD 3600.01, *Information Operations (IO).*

e. DODD 5200.27, *Acquisition of Information Concerning Persons and Organizations not Affiliated with the Department of Defense.*

f. DOD 5240.1-R, *Procedures Governing the Activities of DOD Intelligence Components that Affect United States Persons.*

g. DODI O-3600.02, *Information Operation (IO) Security Classification Guidance.*

**4. Chairman of the Joint Chiefs of Staff Publications**

a. CJCSI 1800.01D, *Officer Professional Military Education Policy (OPMEP).*

b. CJCSI 3141.01E, *Management and Review of Joint Strategic Capabilities Plan (JSCP)-Tasked Plans.*

c. CJCSI 3150.25E, *Joint Lessons Learned Program.*

d. CJCSI 3210.01B, *Joint Information Operations Policy.*

e. Chairman of the Joint Chiefs of Staff Manual (CJCSM) 3122.01A, *Joint Operation Planning and Execution System (JOPES) Volume I, Planning Policies and Procedures.*

f. CJCSM 3122.02D, *Joint Operation Planning and Execution System (JOPES) Volume III, Time-Phased Force and Deployment Data Development and Deployment Execution.*

g. CJCSM 3122.03C, *Joint Operation Planning and Execution System (JOPES) Volume II, Planning Formats.*

h. CJCSM 3500.03C, *Joint Training Manual for the Armed Forces of the United States.*

i. CJCSM 3500.04F, *Universal Joint Task Manual.*

j. JP 1, *Doctrine for the Armed Forces of the United States.*

k. JP 1-02, *Department of Defense Dictionary of Military and Associated Terms*.

l. JP 1-04, *Legal Support to Military Operations.*

m. JP 2-0, *Joint Intelligence.*

n. JP 2-01, *Joint and National Intelligence Support to Military Operations.*

o. JP 2-01.3, *Joint Intelligence Preparation of the Operational Environment.*

p. JP 2-03, *Geospatial Intelligence Support to Joint Operations.*

q. JP 3-0, *Joint Operations.*

r. JP 3-08, *Interorganizational Coordination During Joint Operations.*

s. JP 3-10, *Joint Security Operations in Theater.*

t. JP 3-12, *Cyberspace Operations.*

u. JP 3-13.1, *Electronic Warfare.*

v. JP 3-13.2, *Military Information Support Operations.*

w. JP 3-13.3, *Operations Security.*

x. JP 3-13.4, *Military Deception.*

y. JP 3-14, *Space Operations.*

z. JP 3-16, *Multinational Operations.*

aa. JP 3-57, *Civil-Military Operations.*

bb. JP 3-60, *Joint Targeting.*

cc. JP 3-61, *Public Affairs.*

dd. JP 5-0, *Joint Operation Planning.*

ee. JP 6-01, *Joint Electromagnetic Spectrum Management Operations.*

**5. Multinational Publication**

AJP 3-10, *Allied Joint Doctrine for Information Operations.*

Intentionally Blank

# APPENDIX B
## ADMINISTRATIVE INSTRUCTIONS

**1. User Comments**

Users in the field are highly encouraged to submit comments on this publication to: Joint Staff J-7, Deputy Director, Joint and Coalition Warfighting, Joint and Coalition Warfighting Center, ATTN: Joint Doctrine Support Division, 116 Lake View Parkway, Suffolk, VA 23435-2697. These comments should address content (accuracy, usefulness, consistency, and organization), writing, and appearance.

**2. Authorship**

The lead agent and the Joint Staff doctrine sponsor for this publication is the Director for Operations (J-3).

**3. Supersession**

This publication supersedes JP 3-13, 27 November 2012, *Information Operations*.

**4. Change Recommendations**

a. Recommendations for urgent changes to this publication should be submitted:

TO: JOINT STAFF WASHINGTON DC//J7-JEDD//

b. Routine changes should be submitted electronically to the Deputy Director, Joint and Coalition Warfighting, Joint Doctrine Support Division and info the lead agent and the Director for Joint Force Development, J-7/JEDD.

c. When a Joint Staff directorate submits a proposal to the CJCS that would change source document information reflected in this publication, that directorate will include a proposed change to this publication as an enclosure to its proposal. The Services and other organizations are requested to notify the Joint Staff J-7 when changes to source documents reflected in this publication are initiated.

**5. Distribution of Publications**

Local reproduction is authorized and access to unclassified publications is unrestricted. However, access to and reproduction authorization for classified JPs must be in accordance with DOD Manual 5200.1, *Information Security Program: Overview, Classification, and Declassification.*

**6. Distribution of Electronic Publications**

a. Joint Staff J-7 will not print copies of JPs for distribution. Electronic versions are available on JDEIS at https://jdeis.js.mil (NIPRNET) and http://jdeis.js.smil.mil (SIPRNET), and on the JEL at http://www.dtic.mil/doctrine (NIPRNET).

b. Only approved JPs and joint test publications are releasable outside the CCMDs, Services, and Joint Staff. Release of any classified JP to foreign governments or foreign nationals must be requested through the local embassy (Defense Attaché Office) to DIA, Defense Foreign Liaison/IE-3, 200 MacDill Blvd., Joint Base Anacostia-Bolling, Washington, DC 20340-5100.

c. JEL CD-ROM. Upon request of a joint doctrine development community member, the Joint Staff J-7 will produce and deliver one CD-ROM with current JPs. This JEL CD-ROM will be updated not less than semiannually and when received can be locally reproduced for use within the CCMDs and Services.

# GLOSSARY
## PART I—ABBREVIATIONS AND ACRONYMS

| | |
|---|---|
| AJP | allied joint publication |
| AOR | area of responsibility |
| | |
| C2 | command and control |
| CCDR | combatant commander |
| CCIR | commander's critical information requirement |
| CCMD | combatant command |
| CJCS | Chairman of the Joint Chiefs of Staff |
| CJCSI | Chairman of the Joint Chiefs of Staff instruction |
| CJCSM | Chairman of the Joint Chiefs of Staff manual |
| CMO | civil-military operations |
| CO | cyberspace operations |
| COA | course of action |
| CONOPS | concept of operations |
| CONPLAN | concept plan |
| | |
| DOD | Department of Defense |
| DODD | Department of Defense directive |
| DODI | Department of Defense instruction |
| | |
| EEI | essential element of information |
| EMS | electromagnetic spectrum |
| EW | electronic warfare |
| EWC | electronic warfare cell |
| | |
| FDO | flexible deterrent option |
| | |
| GCC | geographic combatant commander |
| | |
| IA | information assurance |
| IO | information operations |
| IOCB | information operations coordination board |
| IOII | information operations intelligence integration |
| IRC | information-related capability |
| | |
| J-2 | intelligence directorate of a joint staff |
| J-3 | operations directorate of a joint staff |
| J-39 DDGO | Joint Staff, Deputy Director for Global Operations |
| JCEWS | joint force commander's electronic warfare staff |
| JEMSO | joint electromagnetic spectrum operations |
| JFC | joint force commander |
| JIACG | joint interagency coordination group |
| JIOWC | Joint Information Operations Warfare Center |

| | |
|---|---|
| JIPOE | joint intelligence preparation of the operational environment |
| JISE | joint intelligence support element |
| JOPG | joint operations planning group |
| JOPP | joint operation planning process |
| JP | joint publication |
| JPG | joint planning group |
| JTCB | joint targeting coordination board |
| | |
| KLE | key leader engagement |
| | |
| MILDEC | military deception |
| MISO | military information support operations |
| MNF | multinational force |
| MNFC | multinational force commander |
| MOE | measure of effectiveness |
| MOEI | measure of effectiveness indicator |
| MOP | measure of performance |
| | |
| NDP | national disclosure policy |
| | |
| OPLAN | operation plan |
| OPORD | operation order |
| OPSEC | operations security |
| | |
| PA | public affairs |
| PIR | priority intelligence requirement |
| | |
| RFI | request for information |
| ROE | rules of engagement |
| | |
| SC | strategic communication |
| STO | special technical operations |
| | |
| TA | target audience |
| TCP | theater campaign plan |
| | |
| USC | United States Code |
| USD(I) | Under Secretary of Defense for Intelligence |
| USD(P) | Under Secretary of Defense for Policy |
| USG | United States Government |
| USSTRATCOM | United States Strategic Command |

## PART II—TERMS AND DEFINITIONS

**computer network attack.** None. (Approved for removal from JP 1-02.)

**computer network defense.** None. (Approved for removal from JP 1-02.)

**computer network exploitation.** None. (Approved for removal from JP 1-02.)

**computer network operations.** None. (Approved for removal from JP 1-02.)

**data.** None. (Approved for removal from JP 1-02.)

**data item.** None. (Approved for removal from JP 1-02.)

**defense information infrastructure.** None. (Approved for removal from JP 1-02.)

**defense support to public diplomacy.** None. (Approved for removal from JP 1-02.)

**global information infrastructure.** None. (Approved for removal from JP 1-02.)

**information-based processes.** None. (Approved for removal from JP 1-02.)

**information environment.** The aggregate of individuals, organizations, and systems that collect, process, disseminate, or act on information. (JP 1-02. SOURCE: JP 3-13)

**information operations.** The integrated employment, during military operations, of information-related capabilities in concert with other lines of operation to influence, disrupt, corrupt, or usurp the decision-making of adversaries and potential adversaries while protecting our own. Also called **IO.** (Approved for incorporation into JP 1-02 with JP 3-13 as the source JP.)

**information operations intelligence integration.** The integration of intelligence disciplines and analytic methods to characterize and forecast, identify vulnerabilities, determine effects, and assess the information environment. Also called **IOII.** (Approved for inclusion in JP 1-02.)

**information-related capability.** A tool, technique, or activity employed within a dimension of the information environment that can be used to create effects and operationally desirable conditions. Also called **IRC.** (Approved for inclusion in JP 1-02.)

**information security.** None. (Approved for removal from JP 1-02.)

**information superiority.** The operational advantage derived from the ability to collect, process, and disseminate an uninterrupted flow of information while exploiting or denying an adversary's ability to do the same. (JP 1-02. SOURCE: JP 3-13)

**information system.** None. (Approved for removal from JP 1-02.)

**national information infrastructure.** None. (Approved for removal from JP 1-02.)

**probe.** None. (Approved for removal from JP 1-02.)

**special information operations.** None. (Approved for removal from JP 1-02.)

**target audience.** An individual or group selected for influence. Also called **TA.** (JP 1-02. SOURCE: JP 3-13)

# JOINT DOCTRINE PUBLICATIONS HIERARCHY

JP 1
JOINT DOCTRINE
JP 1-0
PERSONNEL
JP 2-0
INTELLIGENCE
JP 3-0
OPERATIONS
JP 4-0
LOGISTICS
JP 5-0
PLANS
JP 6-0
COMMUNICATIONS SYSTEM

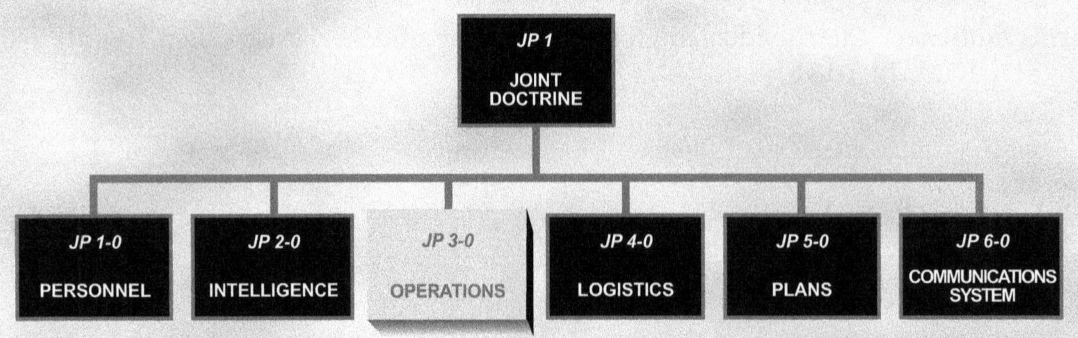

All joint publications are organized into a comprehensive hierarchy as shown in the chart above. **Joint Publication (JP) 3-13** is in the **Operations** series of joint doctrine publications. The diagram below illustrates an overview of the development process:

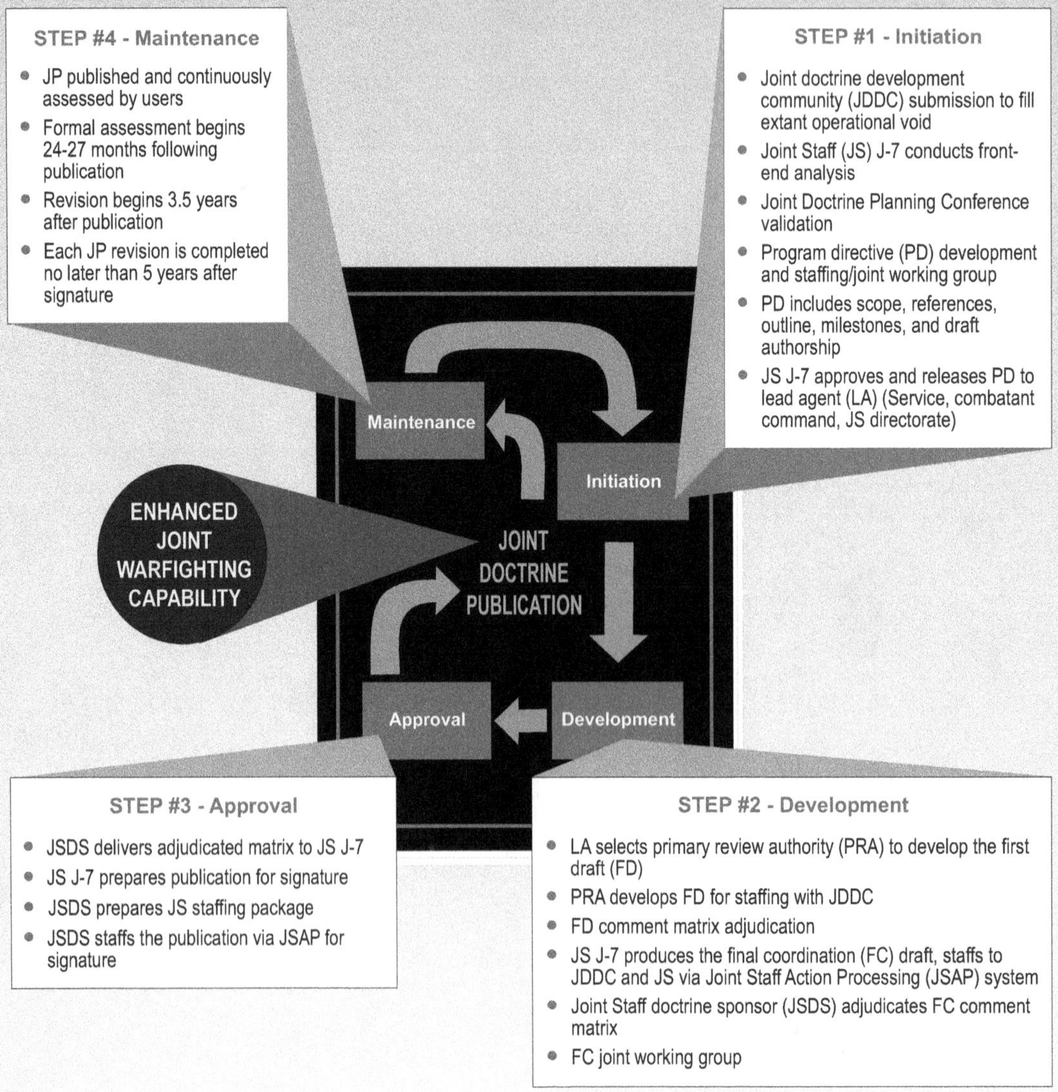

STEP #4 - Maintenance
• JP published and continuously assessed by users
• Formal assessment begins 24-27 months following publication
• Revision begins 3.5 years after publication
• Each JP revision is completed no later than 5 years after signature
STEP #1 - Initiation
• Joint doctrine development community (JDDC) submission to fill extant operational void
• Joint Staff (JS) J-7 conducts front-end analysis
• Joint Doctrine Planning Conference validation
• Program directive (PD) development and staffing/joint working group
• PD includes scope, references, outline, milestones, and draft authorship
• JS J-7 approves and releases PD to lead agent (LA) (Service, combatant command, JS directorate)
Maintenance
Initiation
ENHANCED JOINT WARFIGHTING CAPABILITY
JOINT DOCTRINE PUBLICATION
Approval
Development
STEP #3 - Approval
• JSDS delivers adjudicated matrix to JS J-7
• JS J-7 prepares publication for signature
• JSDS prepares JS staffing package
• JSDS staffs the publication via JSAP for signature
STEP #2 - Development
• LA selects primary review authority (PRA) to develop the first draft (FD)
• PRA develops FD for staffing with JDDC
• FD comment matrix adjudication
• JS J-7 produces the final coordination (FC) draft, staffs to JDDC and JS via Joint Staff Action Processing (JSAP) system
• Joint Staff doctrine sponsor (JSDS) adjudicates FC comment matrix
• FC joint working group

www.ingramcontent.com/pod-product-compliance
Lightning Source LLC
Chambersburg PA
CBHW062045050326
40690CB00016B/2988

* 9 7 8 1 7 1 7 2 2 1 7 6 6 *